PUBLIC POLICY
IN CANADA

Sixth Edition

PUBLIC POLICY IN CANADA

AN INTRODUCTION

Lydia Miljan

OXFORD

UNIVERSITY PRESS

OXFORD
UNIVERSITY PRESS

Oxford University Press is a department of the University of Oxford. It furthers the University's
objective of excellence in research, scholarship, and education by publishing worldwide. Oxford is
a registered trade mark of Oxford University Press in the UK and in certain other countries.

Published in Canada by
Oxford University Press
8 Sampson Mews, Suite 204,
Don Mills, Ontario M3C 0H5 Canada
www.oupcanada.com

Library and Archives Canada Cataloguing in Publication

Miljan, Lydia A. (Lydia Anita), 1963–
Public policy in Canada : an introduction / Lydia Miljan. — 6th ed.

Includes index.
ISBN 978-0-19-544277-9

1. Political planning—Canada—Textbooks.   2. Political planning—Canada—Statistics—
Textbooks.   I. Title.

JL75.B75 2012   320.60971   C2011-908057-5

Cover image: Barrett & MacKay/AllCanadaPhotos.com

This book is printed on permanent (acid-free) paper.

Printed and bound in the United States of America

3 4 5 — 15 14 13

Contents

Figures and Tables

List of Figures

List of Tables

Preface

The first edition of this book, by Stephen Brooks, was published in 1985. Since then it has undergone several revisions, updates, and additions. In 2002 Stephen asked me to update the fourth edition, and since the fifth edition I have taken full responsibility for the text. I would like to thank Stephen for his generosity not only in providing me with the opportunity but in giving me carte blanche to make the changes I wanted.

The speed of change in the major policy issues confronting Canadians over the past two decades has been amazing. Unease about inflation and unemployment in the 1980s was replaced in the 1990s by concern with pressing debt and deficit issues. A few years ago the most pressing public policy issue was what to do with the budgetary surpluses that the federal and many provincial governments had posted. Since the global recession started in 2008, governments moved back to posting deficits as a response to the financial crisis. At the same time, over the past five years Canada's currency has reached parity with the United States' greenback—something economists thought impossible only a few years earlier.

The political environment has also changed over the years. During the 1980s and 1990s Canadians enjoyed stable majority governments first under the Mulroney Conservatives and then under the Chrétien Liberals. The range of political parties has expanded and retracted with the creation of the Reform Party, its transformation into the Canadian Alliance, and finally the merger between the old Progressive Conservatives and the Alliance to create the Conservative Party of Canada. Meanwhile, the Bloc Québécois, formed in the early 1990s, became the official opposition, and its strength in Quebec gave rise to serious concerns over the possibility of separation. From 2004–10 we moved to minority parliaments, first with the Liberals and then with two back-to-back Conservative minority governments in 2006 and 2008. This pattern wasn't broken until 2011, when the Harper Conservatives achieved majority status, prompting *Maclean's* magazine to declare Canada was 'A nation turned upside down' (*Maclean's*, May 16, 2011). Not only is there a majority Conservative government, but the Bloc Québécois was reduced to four seats and the NDP, for the first time in its history, formed the official opposition.

The ebb and flow of the various parties' fortunes have had an impact on the policy choices and issues that confront Canadians. During the time when the Bloc held the majority of federal seats in Quebec the prospect of separation seemed very real. However, as the Conservative Party—to the shock of some and the dismay of others— has increased its support in the province, separation seems to have faded somewhat as a policy concern. Now that the NDP dominates the federal seats in Quebec we have, for the first time in nearly two decades, a federalist party representing Quebec interests in the House of Commons. As Chapter 1 points out, the symbolic recognition that the Québécois form a nation may have helped to mute nationalist aspirations, at least in the short term.

This book introduces the basic issues in the study of public policy in Canada. Six of its 11 chapters are devoted to the examination of particular policy fields. This approach reflects my belief that public policy is best introduced through the study of what governments actually do and the consequences of their actions. To this end, the text surveys a range of policy fields, from fiscal policy to the environment. The selection will not satisfy all tastes, but instructors can easily supplement this book with additional readings on any matters that they believe require a fuller treatment.

Professors in Canada have a number of choices when it comes to public policy textbooks. This book examines public policy from both a theoretical and practical standpoint. In addition to examining specific policy fields, each chapter attempts to bring real-world policy-making into consideration. Each chapter provides a break-out box that provides a specific policy issue or event that highlight's the message of the text. In some cases I present specific government policy or reports; in other cases, I use news stories to highlight the relevance of public policy to our daily lives. In addition to the information boxes, each chapter provides some questions for discussion or further reflection for students. Other features of the book include end-of-chapter definitions of the key terms used and a list of websites to aid in the examination of public policy issues.

Although the principal emphasis of this sixth edition is on policy fields, more general matters that must be a part of any introduction to public policy are addressed in Part I. Chapter 1 examines some of the fundamental concepts in the study of public policy. Chapter 2 is devoted to theoretical frameworks used to explain policy, in particular the pluralist, public choice, and class analysis models. Chapter 3 analyzes the context of policy-making, focusing on the ways in which core values, Canada's ties to the United States, regional divisions, and especially globalization affect policy-making. Policy implementation—the stage of the policy process that reminds us of Murphy's Law ('If anything can go wrong it will')—is the subject of Chapter 4. This edition sees the introduction of a new chapter on policy evaluation in Chapter 5; this chapter looks at how the government approaches evaluation and examines how this work is undertaken.

In Part II of this sixth edition, the chapters on macroeconomic policy, social policy, health care, family policy, Aboriginal policy, and environmental policy have all been updated.

It has again been a pleasure working with Oxford University Press. This edition has seen changes on the editorial as well as the authorial front. Caroline Starr got the sixth edition underway, Jodi Lewchuk moved the book from review through development, and Leanne Rancourt undertook the painstaking job of editing the text. In addition, I was aided in my research by three industrious graduate students: Ivan Jankovic, Greg Mancina, and Samantha Clarke. In particular I would like to single out Ivan, who was instrumental in helping me draft the new Chapter 5. I am honoured to have such care and attention paid to my work. Even so, all mistakes or errors remain mine.

Lydia Miljan
Kingsville, Ontario
March 2011

PART I

Understanding Public Policy

CHAPTER 1

Basic Concepts in the Study of Public Policy

Introduction

Canadians are used to thinking of their country as the world's best. Indeed, politicians— or at least those in power—regularly boast that this is so, and as evidence they point to the fact that Canada frequently ranks in the top five of the United Nations Human Development Index. More recently, Canadians swelled with pride after hosting the Winter Olympics in Vancouver, where Canadian athletes broke the record of the most gold medals won at home.

Of course, it is flattering to anyone's ego to hear that he or she is the best. Canadians can hardly be blamed if, after being told countless times that they are the envy of the world, many accept the claim at face value. But is complacent pride justified? It depends on whom you ask. A Quebec separatist would answer no. So too would many in Canada's Aboriginal community. Union leaders are likely to complain that working people have seen their rights diminished in many provinces and their incomes and job security eroded across the country. Many environmentalists worry that, after several years of declining commitment on the part of government, it will take a significant effort just to slow the pace of environmental degradation. Spokespersons for the feminist movement argue that complacency is far from justified when so much remains to be done to eliminate gender inequality. And anti-poverty activists insist that the extent of poverty in Canada is reason for shame, not pride.

Canada has so often been described as a society of whiners that many will dismiss criticisms such as these as the predictable bellyaching of special interest groups and professional malcontents. Moreover, it must be admitted that by any comparative standard rooted in the real world—as opposed to some idealized utopia—Canada is a pretty good place to live. In economic terms, Canada probably fared the best of any industrialized nation during the 2008–9 recession.[1] Not only was the recession short-lived in Canada (officially lasting only two quarters), it was less intense than in many other countries that faced enormous contractions in their housing sectors and sustained almost catastrophic losses in employment.

Canada is not perfect, however, and those who dare to question the 'best-country-in-the-world' boast should not be written off as ill-mannered party-poopers. Consider the following:

- As of 2008, Canadians earn on average about 83 per cent of what Americans do. Since the early 1980s Canada's productivity and real income growth have lagged behind the United States' by an average of 1 percentage point a year. This means that the income gap between Canada and the United States is double what it was in 1984. Real per capita incomes in Canada are still roughly $6400 below those in the United States.[2]
- Despite the cutbacks of the early 1990s and consistent surpluses from 1997 to 2008, the federal government is carrying a debt of more than $510 billion, much of which is owed to foreigners. The debts of provinces and municipalities add another $274 billion to this total. If the debt were to magically disappear tomorrow, federal taxes could be reduced by approximately 30 per cent without adding a drop of red ink to the budget. Or, if one prefers, Ottawa could increase its program spending by 30 per cent without running a deficit.
- Canadians requiring some form of elective surgery—hip replacement or cataract removal, for example—frequently have to wait several months. In some communities it can take a year or longer to see certain specialists. Although governments have begun to address this problem, much remains to be done if wait times are to be reduced to clinically acceptable levels.
- On a per capita basis, Canada is one of the world's top spenders on education. Some of that investment is paying off: In 2003, an international comparison of students' scores on math, science, and reading tests showed improvement over the 1999 scores. In 2009, Canada was ranked sixth in the areas of reading, mathematics, and science, well above many other Western nations.[3]

Like every other country, Canada has problems. That these problems are minor alongside those of Bangladesh or Afghanistan does not make them any less urgent for those whose lives they affect. Public policies are the actions taken by governments and their agents to that end, and they are the subject of this book.

What Is Public Policy?

One of the most frequently cited definitions of public policy is that given by American political scientist Thomas Dye. According to Dye, public policy is 'whatever governments choose to do or not to do'.[4] Policy, then, involves conscious choices that lead to deliberate action—the passage of a law, the spending of money, an official speech or gesture, or some other observable act—or inaction. No one would disagree that a concrete act like the passage of a law counts as policy. But can inaction reasonably be described as policy? The answer depends on the circumstances in which the failure to act takes place and whether the situation that action would have addressed is regarded as problematic. In some respects we must distinguish between a failure to act and a choice not to act.

Consider, for example, the case of toxic chemicals. For decades carcinogenic PCBs (polychlorinated biphenyls) were used, stored, and disposed of with little care for safety. There was no public policy on the handling of these deadly chemicals until it was realized that there was reason for concern. Clearly, this was an example of government failure to act as opposed to a choice not to act. When the public became aware of the cancer-causing properties of PCBs, their use, transportation, and elimination became policy issues. Government inaction before then obviously had health consequences for those who were exposed to PCBs and allowed for the accumulation of stockpiles of PCBs, which are regarded today as the most widely known and feared of toxic chemicals. But this was not deliberate inaction. There was no public policy on PCBs, just as there was no policy on the production and handling of many other industrial chemicals, because there was no significant public awareness that a problem existed. It makes no sense to speak of policy when an issue has not yet been formulated in problematic terms. Once it has, however, inaction by policy-makers becomes a deliberate policy choice.

In the case of PCBs, the risks to human health are not disputed, and once they became known to the public and policy-makers the question was not whether a problem requiring government action actually existed, but what measures were appropriate to deal with it. It often happens, however, that there is no agreement on the need for government action. Consider the case of income differences between male- and female-dominated occupations. Until a few decades ago it was considered quite normal that secretaries, receptionists, nurses, and child-care workers were generally paid less than men working in occupations demanding fewer skills, qualifications, and responsibilities. Such disparities were understood to be simply the product of voluntary occupational choices and the laws of supply and demand at work in labour markets. But as feminist theory developed during the 1960s and 1970s, inequalities in the workplace became contested terrain. Differences that previously had been either overlooked or explained away as normal and inevitable were interpreted by feminist critics as evidence of systemic discrimination and gender bias in labour markets. These critics proposed that governments step in and close the earnings gap by introducing pay equity policies that would require employers to pay employees in female-dominated occupations wages equal to those earned in male-dominated occupations characterized by similar skill requirements, qualifications, and responsibilities. Across North America, many governments have enacted such policies for their public-sector workforces; a few have extended these policies to cover private-sector employers.

In this case, unlike that of PCBs, no consensus exists that the problem is one that warrants government intervention. Nevertheless, the widespread awareness of gender-based pay differences and the controversy surrounding them marks a significant change from the situation a few decades ago. Today, when a government resists demands to adopt or extend pay equity policies, its resistance must be viewed as a deliberate choice. This was not the case in the days before the gender gap in remuneration was conceptualized as a problem.

Conscious choice, therefore, must be a part of any definition of public policy. But is policy necessarily what policy-makers say it is? In other words, if we want to determine what public policy is on some issue, should we direct our attention to official government pronouncements, or to the actual record of what has and has not been achieved?

In politics, as in life generally, no statement should be taken at face value. Vagueness and ambiguity are often deliberate and are always part of the recipe for political longevity in democratic political systems. To determine what actually constitutes public policy in some field we need to look carefully at both official claims and concrete actions, and we must remember that actions often speak louder than words.

At the same time it's important to keep in mind that even a government's more sincere efforts can misfire; sometimes policy fails to achieve the intended goal, and may even aggravate the situation it was intended to improve. Consider rent control policies. Critics have long argued that, in practice, such policies hurt the lower-income groups they are intended to benefit because they discourage developers and investors from building new rental accommodations for the low end of the market. With rent control, housing is kept affordable by government regulations limiting what a landlord can charge. Without the possibility of charging more, however, there is no incentive to invest in new housing. In addition, landlords soon find it too costly to maintain their buildings properly. As a consequence, the supply of housing units does not keep pace with demand, and low-income earners may not be able to find a place to live. In a market not limited by government regulations, the dwindling of supply would result in price increases, which in turn would lead property developers and investors to create more housing. As more housing became available, prices would be adjusted to suit both low- and high-income earners. In a rent-control situation, however, the dwindling supply does not lead to rent increases. As a consequence, buildings are not kept in good repair, and tenants must either make improvements on their own or live in rundown accommodation. Under these circumstances, are we justified in saying that government housing policy favours the less affluent?

Even more common than policy misfires are cases in which government action simply fails to accomplish its intended goals. In fact, a program, law, or regulation hardly ever 'solves' a problem in the sense of eliminating the conditions that inspired demands for action in the first place. When a problem does disappear, the reason often has less to do with government action than with changing societal conditions—including the emergence of new problems that push old ones below the surface of public consciousness. We have mentioned the case of official pronouncements that do not coincide with the observable actions of government, or that bear little resemblance to the facts of whatever situation they ostensibly address. When this happens (and it frequently does), we should not jump to the cynical conclusion that policy is just 'sound and fury signifying nothing'. Gestures, symbols, and words are important components of the political process. They are often valued in their own right, and their capacity both to reconcile and to divide should not be underestimated.

Since the ill-fated Meech Lake Accord (1987), which proposed the constitutional recognition of Quebec as a 'distinct society', the question of whether and how Quebec's distinctive character should be recognized has been a source of division in Canadian politics. This division resurfaced around the failed Charlottetown Accord (1992) and remained a subject of debate, prompting Ottawa and some of the provincial governments to continue searching for a constitutional formula that would satisfy French-speaking Quebecers' demands for recognition without offending the majority of Canadians who insisted on a single Canada and equal status for all provinces and citizens. The problem was not so much that non-Quebecers believed constitutional recognition of Quebec as a distinct society would have material consequences for which the rest of Canada would have to pay. Rather, they rejected the idea of distinct-society status for Quebec and the recognition of this special status in the Constitution. As in the material world, satisfying the aspirations of one group may mean denying those of another in the realm of what Raymond Breton calls the 'symbolic order'.

The question of Quebec's constitutional status became a subject of policy debate in the months leading up to the 2006 federal Liberal leadership contest. Michael Ignatieff, the front-runner, had thought that the party needed to decide on a policy to deal with the challenges coming from the separatist Bloc Québécois, and told the media that in his view 'Quebec is a nation.' The issue threatened to divide the Liberal party when the Bloc served notice that it would submit for debate a motion stating that 'Quebecers form a nation.'[5] Before that debate could take place, however, Conservative prime minister Stephen Harper amended the motion, proposing instead 'that this House recognize that the Québécois form a nation within a united Canada'.[6] This new motion passed, and Quebecers were given a form of symbolic recognition without any constitutional change. While the question of Quebec's nationhood is far from closed, this episode showed some desire on the part of parliamentarians to provide the symbolic recognition that had been lacking in the past.

The Agenda and Discourse of Public Policy

There is also a more general sense in which the symbols, gestures, and words manipulated by policy-makers are important. They constitute the **political agenda**, defining what is relevant in public life, how issues are understood, whose views should be taken seriously, and what sort of 'solutions' are tenable. A statement by a political leader, a law, or the media's coverage of a situation, event, or policy demand all serve to affirm the relevance of a problem and the values and conflicts associated with it. Political issues and policy problems are not inevitable and inherent; rather, they are constructed out of the conflicting values and terminologies that different groups put forward when they are competing for something that cannot be shared to satisfy all of them fully. These issues and problems are 'constructed' in the sense that they do not exist apart from the words and symbols used to describe them. Whether we even recognize them as political issues and policy problems, and what comes to mind when they are presented to our attention, depends on the particular forces that shape the political agenda in a given society. These forces change over time, and so, therefore, does the political agenda. As American political scientist Murray Edelman observes, 'conditions accepted as inevitable or unproblematic may come to be seen as problems; and damaging conditions may not be defined as political issues at all.'[7] Once we accept that the political agenda is not an inevitable product of social and economic conditions, we are confronted with the question of why some of these conditions come to be formulated as problems and others do not. To answer that question we need to look at the various agents of cultural learning—family, schools, mass media, the workplace—that together generate the ideological parameters of our society. To understand the practical importance of cultural learning, consider the following examples:

- In liberal democratic societies like Canada and the United States, we (most of us, anyway) are taught that achievement and opportunities are relatively open to those with ability and a willingness to work hard. Consequently, most of us are not seriously troubled by the fact that the bottom 20 per cent of Canada's population accounts for about half of 1 per cent of the country's wealth, while the richest 20 per cent controls some 70 per cent of the wealth.[8] In a different ideological setting, however, such inequality might be perceived as a problem.

- Similarly, until a couple of decades ago the existence of extensive and profound differences in the career opportunities, incomes, and social roles of men and women were not generally seen to be a problem. As cultural attitudes have changed, the unequal social conditions of males and females have become a prominent item on the political agendas of virtually all industrialized democracies. Gender politics and the policy debates that surround issues such as abortion, pay equity, affirmative action for women, pornography, publicly subsidized daycare, and sexual harassment are constructed out of the arguments, claims, and demands for action put forward by women's organizations and their spokespersons, and the counterarguments, claims, and demands of others who feel compelled to respond to their definition of the problem. The same can be said of any policy issue. What emerges from such exchanges is a **policy discourse**—an unfolding tapestry of words and symbols that structures thinking and action—constructed out of the multiple definitions (or denials) of the problem.

The capacity to influence this discourse is more than half the battle, as every group, organization, and individual with any political acumen knows. Hence the first line of attack is often through the mass media. Governments have a distinct advantage in the struggle to shape the contours of policy discourse. Not only do they have virtually guaranteed access to the public through mass media coverage of official statements, press conferences, and other orchestrated efforts to communicate a particular message (and influence public opinion), but they also are able to tell their story through paid advertisements (the federal government has for years been the largest advertiser in Canada) and through government information services directed at households and organizations. This advantage may be reduced in the future as the traditional blurring of the lines between the political party that forms the government and the government itself comes under increasing scrutiny. In January 2006, Ontario adopted new legislation that prevents the use of government advertising to promote the partisan interests of the political party in power (see Box 1.1). The Government Advertising Act, 2004, requires that all paid government advertising go through the auditor general's office to ensure that individual members of

BOX 1.1   Backgrounder: Ontario Government Advertising Act, 2004

The Government Advertising Act, 2004, requires the office of the auditor general to review paid government advertising in advance of its public release to ensure it is free of partisan content. Items for review consist of paid advertisements developed to appear on television, radio, billboards, in print, as well as print material the government pays to have distributed to households in Ontario by unaddressed bulk mail.

Effective June 29, 2006, the prohibition provisions of the Government Advertising Act, 2004, come into effect, meaning that ministries cannot use an item until the auditor general determines that it meets the standards of the Act. Any item the auditor general has determined does not meet the standards of the legislation cannot be used.

Government advertising must meet the following statutory standards:

1. It must be a reasonable means to
   - Inform the public of current or proposed government policies, programs or services available to them
   - Inform the public of their rights and responsibilities under the law
   - Encourage or discourage specific social behaviour in the public interest
   - Promote Ontario or any part of Ontario as a good place to live, work, invest, study or visit, or promote any economic activity or sector of Ontario's economy
2. It must include a statement that the item is paid for by the Government of Ontario.
3. It must not include the name, voice, or image of a member of the executive council (cabinet) or a member of the legislative assembly of Ontario unless the primary target audience is outside Ontario.
4. It must not be partisan.
5. A primary objective of the item must not be to foster a positive impression of the governing party or a negative impression of a person or entity who is critical of the government.

Advertisements or printed matter done on an urgent matter affecting public health or safety, public notices required by law, Government of Ontario tenders and job advertisements are exempt from the law.

Arm's-length provincial agencies, such as the Liquor Control Board of Ontario, the Workplace Safety and Insurance Board, and the Royal Ontario Museum, are also exempt from the legislation. The Act does not apply to MPPs or the legislative assembly.

Source: © Queen's Printer for Ontario, 2006. Reproduced with permission.

provincial parliament (MPPs) or cabinet ministers are not promoted in government ads and that those ads cannot be used to criticize other groups or political parties.

The messages that governments communicate, particularly when they touch on controversial issues, are often greeted with cynicism by the media and the public. But they receive a hearing all the same. One reason for this is the official authority of their source. Even if a governmental message is not considered credible, the government's capacity to influence the outcome of an issue means that the information it disseminates is not likely to be ignored. Cynicism, vocal opposition, and unsympathetic media coverage are not enough to close off the channels that the government can use to influence policy discourse. The 1989 introduction of the widely unpopular goods and services tax (GST) was followed by an extensive campaign of paid advertising and information, sent directly to businesses and households, intended to increase public acceptance of the GST. Only a couple of years earlier Ottawa had spent tens of millions of dollars on brochures and other information distributed to households 'explaining' the benefits that the Free Trade Agreement (FTA) with the United States would bring to Canada. The federal government spent $20 million to promote the economic action plan prior to the 2011 federal election campaign. It is never easy to determine exactly what impact these policy advocacy campaigns have on public opinion. But the very fact that such campaigns are conducted means that the information and arguments they convey automatically become part of the policy discourse on an issue.

Despite the formidable information and financial resources at their disposal, governments are a long way from being able to control either the policy agenda or the policy discourse that develops around a particular issue. Indeed, much of the time governments are on the defensive, reacting to the claims, demands, and interpretations put forward by opposition political parties, societal groups, and the media. Whose 'problems' reach the political agenda, and whose arguments, interpretations, and proposals are taken seriously in the policy-making process, is largely determined by the social power of those advancing them. In fact, the capacity to influence policy discourse would seem to be one barometer by which the power of different interests can be measured.

On the other hand, governments can also use the demands of societal groups to help them put forward policies and positions to the public. The emergence of the National Action Committee on the Status of Women (NAC), for instance, can be traced directly to government funding programs. In the 1970s, Pierre Trudeau's Liberal government wanted to pursue the agenda of a 'just society'. One policy plank of the just society was the equality of women. But Canadian women at the time had not organized into a cohesive lobby. Therefore Ottawa helped to create and fund the NAC, which used the resources provided by the federal government to lobby that same government for women's equality and eventually led the fight to ensure that women were specifically enumerated in the 1982 Charter of Rights and Freedoms. This is a classic example of how a government can establish and sustain a lobby group for the specific purpose of lending credibility to its own policy agenda by creating a favourable climate of public opinion.

This kind of manipulation notwithstanding, politics in the capitalist democracies is open-ended enough that ideas and reforms clearly not favoured by the powerful have often been woven into the fabric of policy discourse and institutionalized through public policies. One would be hard-pressed to explain the policy successes of the women's movement, and the acceptance of arguments associated with gender-based differences in such matters as employment and pay, from the standpoint of dominant class interests. Or consider the entry of Aboriginal rights, visible minorities, and the disabled into modern political discourse. Even though these groups operate far from the centres of social and economic power, they have been able to influence the political agenda and the actions of governments. Moreover, some policy issues can reach the public agenda without the backing of powerful social and economic interests. For example, therapies for treating the mentally ill or approaches for dealing with criminals and victims are policy domains in which scientific expertise may carry greater weight than usual because the issues involved do not capture the sustained attention of the public. We should not assume, therefore, an automatic and perfect correspondence between the pecking order of social and economic interests in society and the ideas that make it onto the political agenda and find expression in state actions.

Policy discourse is not, however, a free-for-all in which every voice has an equal opportunity to be heard. It has become popular to speak of **systemic bias**, a term intended to capture the selectiveness of the policy system. Some points of view, it is claimed, never get articulated, and some policy outcomes are virtually precluded by the biases inherent in the cultural and institutional fabric of society. At one level this is obviously true. For demographic, historical, and political reasons language has a prominence in Canadian politics that it does not have in the United States. Conversely, individual rights and freedoms occupy a more significant place in American political discourse than they do in Canada and most other capitalist democracies. Thus, in saying that any political system has particular biases we have not said much—or at least nothing very profound. The more interesting question is what these biases reveal about the sources and distribution of power and the capacity of different social and economic interests to influence the actions of government.

The Pattern of Public Policy

What governments do, how they do it, and what consequences arise are aspects of public policy that have changed dramatically over time. They reflect the scope, means, and distributional dimensions of public policy. Together, they provide the basis for comparing the pattern of public policy and the role of the state in different societies, and for charting and understanding the course of historical change within a society.

1. The Scope of Public Policy

We know that governments do more today than they did in the past. They pass more laws and regulations on a wider range of subjects than before, they spend a larger share of national income, they tax in more ways and at higher levels, and they employ more people to operate the machinery of government. The scope of their activities ranges from municipal bylaws requiring dog owners to 'stoop-and-scoop' when walking their pooch to laws affecting the more vital aspects of our lives.

Back in 1900, the Public Accounts of Canada listed only a couple of dozen separate departments and agencies of government. A century later, the federal public administration consists of 402 departments and agencies that are subject to the Financial Administration Act.[9] To appreciate the scale of government agencies and programs Figure 1.1 provides an overview of the various agencies and departments. At Confederation, total government expenditure in Canada accounted for a little more than 5 per cent of gross national expenditure (GNE). Today, government spending comes to about 45 per cent of GNE. The chief functions of Western governments in the nineteenth century were maintaining social order, ensuring defence, and facilitating economic development through measures ranging from railroad subsidies to tariffs. By comparison, governments today are involved in a bewildering range of functions that include all of the traditional ones plus education, health care, income support for various segments of the population, broadcasting, and much more. Until the early twentieth century, about three-quarters of government spending was on goods and services—what public finance economists call **exhaustive expenditures**. Today, however, more than half of total government spending involves **transfer payments** to individuals, families, and organizations.[10] This is money that the government handles, but does not itself spend on goods and services. The growth in transfer payments as a share of total government spending reflects the increasing importance of the government's redistributive role in society.

The redistributive function of the state is the battleground on which the ideological forces of the left and the right have slugged it out since the nineteenth century. Although it is popular today to argue that debates between the left and the right have lost their relevance, this is simply not true. If 'the left' is understood to prefer collectivist solutions to social and economic problems and to believe that individuals achieve dignity from the communal associations that give their lives meaning, while 'the right' is understood to prefer market solutions and to believe that personal dignity depends on one's own efforts, which tend to be undermined by collectivist policies, then the left-versus-right debate is still very much alive. In recent years, the concern shown by governments of virtually all partisan hues toward public-sector deficits and debt and the conversion of most governments to trade liberalism have contributed to the erroneous belief that collectivist (i.e., left-wing) ideology is in eclipse. But the facts—from hard measures of the government's presence in society, such as the share of national income it spends or the portion of personal income it takes in taxes, to softer measures of state intrusiveness, such as the range of activities that governments regulate—do not support the claim that the collectivist model of the state has gone down in defeat.

On the contrary, it is probably fair to say that the essential premise of the collectivist ethos is widely and uncritically accepted by both the elite and the general populations in Canada and other advanced industrial democracies. This premise is that communal goals, such as redistributing wealth, promoting economic growth, and protecting the weak, should be—in fact, can only be—pursued through the state. There are, quite naturally, differences over the precise character of these goals and how best to achieve them. But the belief that the clock can be turned back to the 'night watchman' state of capitalist democracy's youth has little more than a marginal following even in the United States, the most liberal (in the classical sense of emphasizing market and individual freedoms) of liberal democracies.

FIGURE 1.1 Public Sector Flow Chart

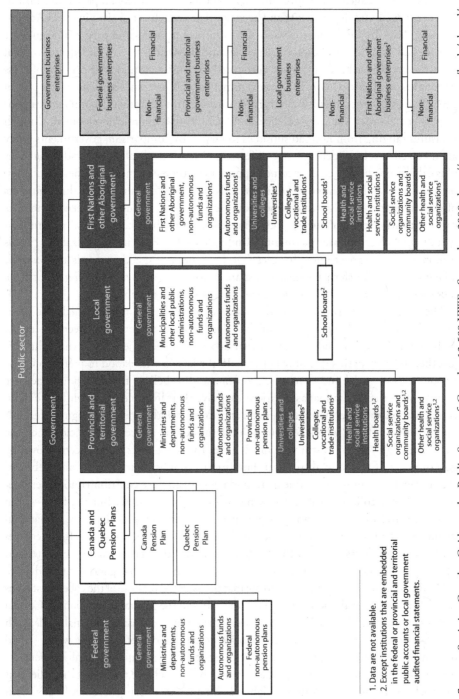

1. Data are not available.
2. Except institutions that are embedded in the federal or provincial and territorial public accounts or local government audited financial statements.

Source: Statistics Canada, Guide to the Public Sector of Canada, 12-589-XWE, September 2008; http://www.statcan.gc.ca/bsolc/olc-cel/olc-cel?lang=eng&catno=12-589-X

The appropriate scope of government activities is largely a matter of personal preference. Take something as mundane as the random stopping of automobiles by police to check for drunk drivers. Some people object to this practice on the grounds that it violates the individual's freedom—not the freedom to drive while intoxicated, but the freedom from arbitrary detention by the state. Others (probably most Canadians) are willing to tolerate the possibility that innocent people will be pulled over by the police, and perhaps even asked to take a breathalyzer test, as a reasonable infringement on individual freedom that contributes to public safety.

There is no one correct answer to the question of whether random spot checks of motorists are a good thing, just as there is no one correct answer to the question of whether a state that spends 45 per cent of national income is better or worse than one that spends 35 per cent. The answers to such questions depend on the context of the respondent. Someone who believes that the primary duty of government is the promotion of social justice will certainly have a different idea of the appropriate scope of government activities than someone who believes that government's primary duty is the protection of individual property rights. Where matters become really complicated is in cases where people agree on the goals but disagree on the means for achieving them. If the question of means is essentially a technical one, surely we might expect it to have a single objective answer. As it happens, however, our views on what means are best suited to achieve an agreed-upon goal are usually influenced by our premises and values.

2. The Choice of Policy Instrument

Ends and means are inseparable. To choose a particular goal requires that a plan of action, the means for achieving that goal, be developed and put into effect. The successful attainment of goals, including the policy objectives of governments, requires that the appropriate instruments be chosen to achieve them. This all sounds very rational and calculated. But in the real world of policy-making, as in other realms of life, the process by which these instruments are chosen is rarely rational. The selection of means is influenced by how things have been done in the past—by vested bureaucratic, political, and societal interests; by chance, including the particular individuals who happen to be involved in the decision; and by ideas and beliefs that may or may not be well founded. In addition, it appears that the means sometimes precede and determine the ends of policy.

Before World War II, for instance, taxes on personal and corporate incomes made up only a small portion of total government revenue: about 15 per cent in 1939.[11] Taxes on consumption and property were more important sources of government revenue. Today, income-based taxes, especially those on personal income, represent the single largest source of revenue for both Ottawa and the provinces. Payroll taxes like employment insurance premiums and Canada and Quebec Pension Plan contributions are also major sources of government revenue. These programs were not initiated until 1940 (unemployment insurance) and 1966 (CPP/QPP). The tax system has become one of the chief instruments for the pursuit of governments' economic, social, and even cultural policy objectives.

Regulation has also increased dramatically. Most federal and provincial regulatory laws have been enacted since 1950.[12] They affect activities from product labelling and the maximum allowable distance between the bars of a crib to Canadian content in television and radio programming and exports of energy. The post–World War II era has also seen an explosion in the number and diversity of government-owned corporations, most of which have been created since 1960.[13] These corporations are involved in activities as diverse as the production of electrical power, the provision of credit, the sale of wine and spirits, and the mining of potash. Although some of these corporations have been privatized since the 1980s, hundreds of enterprises are still owned by Ottawa or the provinces, including such important organizations as Hydro-Québec and the Canadian Broadcasting Corporation (CBC).

In recent years, controversy has surrounded all the most common tools of public policy. Sometimes the point at issue has been whether the goals associated with a particular policy instrument—Canadian culture and the CBC, Canadianization of the petroleum industry and Petro-Canada, telecommunications regulation and the Canadian Radio-television Telecommunications Commission (CRTC)—are worth pursuing. More often, however, debate has centred on whether there is a better, less costly way of achieving a given policy objective. Such debates have been fuelled by the arguments of economists, political journalists, and business organizations about the alleged inefficiencies of publicly owned businesses and the economic distortions produced by regulations. Taxation, subsidies, and spending programs have also come under heavy criticism for the same reasons—that they do not accomplish the goals they were ostensibly intended to promote. In other instances, they are argued to create new harms or exacerbate existing problems.

Evaluating how well a particular policy instrument achieves what is expected of it is not a simple task. To begin with, the government's goals may not be terribly clear, and may even be confused and contradictory. Even if the goals themselves can be identified with some precision, the only readily available standard for measuring how well they are being achieved is an economic one. It is fine to talk about 'justice', 'equity', 'national identity', 'the quality of life', and other such non-economic values. But these values do not carry price tags—indeed, it is often because the marketplace has no economic incentive to produce them that governments involve themselves in the promotion of these things—which makes it difficult to assess their worth.

The choice of means is not just about effectiveness; it is also about values. Some policy instruments, such as taxes and state-owned companies, are more intrusive than others, such as regulation or exhortation by government. Generally speaking, carrots (incentives) are less intrusive than sticks (commands and prohibitions) and are more likely to be preferred by those who are predisposed toward smaller governments and greater scope for individual choice.

3. Who Benefits and Who Pays?

Who benefits from public policy and who pays the bill is the subject of another ongoing debate. The very term 'welfare state' implies that wealth is to some degree transferred by the state from those who can afford to pay to those in need. And there is no doubt that the various taxation and spending policies of governments affect the distribution of wealth. To what degree these policies affect the distribution of wealth and to whose advantage are disputed issues.

Contrary to popular belief, the Canadian tax system does not redistribute income from society's more affluent classes to its most impoverished ones. The reason lies in the fact that several important taxes—notably sales and property taxes and capped payroll taxes—take a larger share out of the incomes of lower-income earners than they do from those with higher incomes. Although the personal income tax system is progressive (the rate at which one is taxed increases with one's income) and governments typically rebate part of the personal cost of regressive levies like the sales and property taxes to lower-income earners, the regressive impact of total taxation is far from eliminated. On the other hand, the total effect of the money transfers received through income security programs and public spending on education, housing, health care, transportation, and other programs does favour the poor. The bottom fifth of income earners in Canada accounted for 1 per cent of earned income but about 5 per cent when all sources of income were taken into account.[14] The difference can be traced to redistributive transfer payments such as social assistance, GST rebates, and the child tax benefit.

Governments in Canada also act in ways intended to affect the distribution of wealth between regions. These regional subsidies take three main forms:

1. Equalization payments from Ottawa to the less affluent provinces, intended to ensure 'that provincial governments have sufficient revenues to provide reasonably comparable levels of public service at reasonably comparable levels of taxation'[15]
2. Income transfers from Ottawa to individuals in the form of employment insurance (EI), which is a major source of income in communities where employment opportunities tend to be seasonal ·
3. Federal and provincial industrial assistance programs that subsidize businesses in economically depressed regions

As in the case of policies geared toward redistributing income between individuals, there is no agreement on the impact of these regionally targeted policies. The $14.1 billion a year that Ottawa transfers to the economically weaker provinces in the form of equalization payments certainly enable them to finance a level of services that would otherwise be beyond their fiscal means.[16] The fact that certain regions benefit more than others from the EI system reflects regional redistribution. But some have argued that these transfers impose a burden on the national economy without solving the problems responsible for the weak economies of the provinces that benefit from them. Others note that because of the dispersed reach of government, transfers and subsidies actually benefit middle- and high-income earners more than they do low-income earners. Art subsidies, higher education, and health care all benefit middle- and high-income earners disproportionately. Essentially, regional subsidies take money from poor people in rich provinces and give it to rich people in poor provinces. A study by the Atlantic Institute for Market Studies found that, on average, personal income tax is 33 per cent higher in the poorer provinces than in the so-called 'have' provinces. This increased tax burden also has the negative consequence of keeping economic activity down.[17]

Regional industrial assistance programs have come under the same criticism. But one should not jump to the conclusion that Ottawa's industrial assistance pipeline has flowed only one way, transferring money from the 'have' to the 'have-not' provinces. Any calculation of the regional impact of all forms of industrial support, from tariffs to government contracts to grants and loans to particular businesses, must certainly conclude that the big winners have been Ontario and Quebec—and that their gains have come at the expense of other regions.

Government's impact on the distribution of economic well-being does not stop at individuals and regions. In all industrial societies, Canada included, the state is in the business of protecting a vast range of producer and occupational groups from the unregulated workings of the market. The result is what Canadian economist Thomas Courchene calls the 'protected society'.[18] In such a society, any group with political clout can persuade the state to protect its narrow interests at the public's expense. Courchene's concept of the protected society recognizes that both the privileged and the disadvantaged elements in society may be 'welfare recipients'. Indeed, a federal government task force once described Canadian businesses as 'program junkies'[19] addicted to the billions of dollars worth of subsidies that successive governments have been willing to dole out to them. This addiction continues unabated, despite cuts to program spending in recent years. And it is not only business that slurps at the public trough. All manner of special interests are recipients of government largesse. The Public Accounts of Canada include hundreds of pages listing the organizations that have received government money, and their diversity is truly staggering. A recent annual list included such organizations as the International Fund for Ireland, the Canadian Association of Provincial Court Judges, the Association franco-yukonnaise, the Federation of Italian Canadians for Yesterday, Today and Tomorrow, Manufacturier de bas culotte d'Amour, and Canadian Manufacturers and Exporters. That these groups may be quite deserving of public support (although 'deserving' is in the eye of the beholder) is not the point. Rather, the point is that any accounting of the benefits and costs of public policy must include the multitude of subsidies and non-cash forms of support received by a universe of organized interests.

All the distributive effects of policy discussed to this point have involved material benefits and burdens. But as Raymond Breton observes, 'public institutions and their authorities are involved in the distribution of symbolic as well as material resources.'[20] We need only think of the outraged reaction of anglophone Canadians to the Quebec government's 1989 decision (in Bill 178) to invoke the notwithstanding clause of the Charter of Rights and Freedoms after the Supreme Court of Canada ruled that Quebec's restrictions on the language of signs violated the freedom of expression guaranteed in the Charter. Or recall the backlash generated among French-speaking Quebecers by the 1990 failure of the Meech Lake Accord proposals for constitutional reform, a failure they interpreted as proof of English Canada's rejection of equal status for French Canada. Support for separatism in Quebec reached levels never seen before or since the death of the Meech Lake Accord. When, during the 1997 election campaign, the

Reform Party brought attention to the fact that in recent decades Quebec seemed to have had a near hammerlock on the job of prime minister, regardless of whether the Liberal or Progressive Conservative party was in power, it was criticized for anti-Quebec, anti-French bigotry (although its statement of the simple truth appeared to score points with the electorate in English Canada).

All these examples have to do with the politics of recognition. It is normal for people to want to see themselves reflected in the institutions of their society, including its structures of power and its symbolic trappings. In some cases recognition is achieved through membership in a particular group with which one identifies closely (ethnic, linguistic, regional, gender, etc.); in others it consists in some form of official status for a group, as in the case of French and English language communities and Aboriginal Canadians; and for non-French, non-British Canadians it may also be achieved through official multiculturalism.

Like all politics, however, the politics of recognition is characterized by scarcity. Recognition for one community may require that the values and aspirations of others be denied or at least diluted. For example, consider the struggle over constitutional recognition of Quebec as a distinct society. Most francophone Quebecers believe such recognition to be a just expression of their two-nations understanding of Canada. Most anglophone Canadians have problems with such recognition precisely because they do not share this two-nations understanding of Canada. It simply is not possible to satisfy the symbolic desires of both English and French Canada on the issue of Quebec's constitutional status. Recognition and symbols are necessarily in limited supply. Although it might be tempting to believe that the solution to quarrels over recognition is to recognize all groups, the logical and practical absurdity of this soon becomes apparent. The social–symbolic value of recognition is diluted as it is extended to more and more groups, until it becomes worthless precisely because it is so common. Moreover, demands for recognition are often mutually exclusive. It would take some remarkable magician to reconcile distinct society status for Quebec with the notion of equality among all 10 provinces.

Government in Retreat?

In recent years it has become commonplace to argue that governments' ability to influence the societies and economies they preside over has declined. This argument has a number of variations, but the unifying thread that runs through all of them is the idea that the forces of globalization have increased all societies' exposure to the world around them while decreasing the ability of domestic policy-makers to control what happens in their backyard. As *The Economist* described the argument in 1995:

> The tasks that governments have traditionally regarded as their most important jobs, it is argued, have moved beyond their reach, and thus beyond the reach of voters. Global markets are in charge. No longer able to do big things that matter, governments busy themselves with small things, best done locally or not at all. Economic integration thus explains the political malaise affecting many of the world's big democracies.[21]

But globalization is not just about markets. It is also about information and culture in a world wired by computers and satellites. The instantaneous sharing of information and images through the Internet and satellite television has reduced the ability of both governments and domestic elites to control the flow of information reaching citizens. Cultural policies that rely on the ability of the state to restrict what its citizens see, hear, and read have become less tenable. Moreover, globalization is about transnational forums (like the United Nations Environment Programme, the annual G8 summits, and the UN Committee on Economic, Social and Cultural Rights), which define and debate policy issues, and about international institutions (like the UN Commission on Human Rights and the World Trade Organization), which establish rules that policy-makers may perceive as binding on them, or at least difficult to ignore. Many of these forums and institutions are market driven (e.g., the bodies that handle trading rules, financial transactions, and production standards). Others are generated by global—if mainly Western—social and political movements, such as environmentalism and feminism. International media and knowledge elites reinforce these forces of globalization.

Globalization is important in explaining the special challenges of governance in the early twenty-first century, but it is not the whole story. Another factor that complicates the job of policy-makers is what Neil Nevitte has called 'the decline of deference'.[22] Citizens in many democracies, including Canada, take a more cynical view of public authority than they did in the past and are more likely to perceive themselves as having rights that should take priority over the preferences of state authorities.

Evidence of these developments takes various forms. In Europe, the mass protests that took place in Belgium during 1996, in reaction to what most Belgians believed to be the indifference and lack of responsiveness of their country's judicial and political system to the disappearance and murder of young girls, became a symbol across Europe for popular rejection of old ways of conducting public business.[23] In Canada, the electorate's rejection of the 1992 Charlottetown Accord on the Constitution—an accord that was supported by most of the country's political and economic elites—was widely and rightly interpreted as a rejection of the elitist policy-making style that characterized Canadian politics until recent years (and has not disappeared entirely even today). More generally, the explosion—in Canada, the United States, and internationally—of what Mary Ann Glendon calls 'rights talk' is said to be a symptom of citizens' greater assertiveness in the face of the traditional authority of government. This new assertiveness may have roots in the cultural phenomenon known as post-materialism[24]—a shift away from material pre-occupations as matters of lifestyle, identity, and participation assume greater importance.

If modern governments seem less capable of steering the ship of state than their predecessors were, part of the explanation may involve simple hubris. *Hubris* is a Greek word that signifies arrogance arising from pride or passion. In retrospect, much of what came to be expected of governance in the twentieth century may have been a hubristic error. Keynesian economic policy is a major case in point. During the 1940s, governments in the Western industrialized democracies, including Canada, became converts to the belief that they could and should assume responsibility for the mainten-ance of steady economic growth and full employment. The buoyant economies of the 1950s and 1960s suggested that the policies proposed by the British economist John Maynard Keynes, which were spread throughout the Western world by a generation of economists and policy-makers trained in Keynesian macroeconomics, did what they were supposed to do. Governments quickly became accustomed to taking credit for what went right in the economy, while citizens came to expect policy-makers to promise economic growth, jobs, and rising incomes.

When the bubble burst in the 1970s, the optimistic interventionism on which Keynesian economics was premised came in for some hard scrutiny. And although Keynesian economics and policies still have their defenders, many argue that governments were given too much credit for prosperity that was actually fuelled by market factors. In retrospect, the brave assumptions of Keynesianism appear to be have been overly optimistic, and the image of the state as manager of the economy was flawed by hubris. In fact, far from improving the economy, governments' Keynesian public policy initiatives caused havoc, leading to double-digit unemployment, high inflation, and high interest rates during the 1970s and 1980s. This economic trio of despair contributed to the escalation of public debt and, many argue, put Canada's most-cherished social programs in jeopardy.

After the financial crisis emanating from the United States in 2008, many argued that the pendulum had swung too far toward markets and that the government was urgently needed to restore the economic system. The Organisation for Economic Co-operation and Development (OECD) responded to the crisis in two ways: first by emphasizing the need to 'align regulations and incentives in the financial sector to ensure tighter oversight', and second to 'urge governments to review and upgrade their national policies . . . to restore the conditions for economic growth'.[25] However, the renewed consensus on stimulus spending did not last long, and by the time the G8/G20 conferences were held in June 2010 governments had committed—albeit, in the case of the United States, reluctantly—to reduce deficits by 50 per cent by 2013.[26]

Inflated and probably unrealistic expectations for public policy were generated in other quarters as well. The intellectual movements known as **progressivism** in the United States and **Fabian socialism** in the United Kingdom both held high expectations for governments. They believed that the knowledge and insights of trained policy specialists could be used to improve the effectiveness of public policy and ultimately to solve social and economic problems. The **policy sciences movement** that emerged in the United States after World War II had as its goal the application of social scientific knowledge to public policy. Like progressivism and Fabian socialism, the policy sciences saw their own experts as the priesthood of a rational, knowledge-driven approach to resolving policy problems. And like these other intellectual movements, the policy sciences were inherently optimistic about the ability of government to act deliberately and effectively.

All these ideas percolated into Canada, reinforcing the optimistic expectations for state management of society that Keynesianism encouraged in the realm of economics. Pushed to their limit, they encouraged visions of a brave new world whose shape was described by Liberal prime minister Pierre Trudeau in the late 1960s: 'We . . . are aware that the many techniques of cybernetics, by transforming the control function and the manipulation of information, will transform our whole society. With this knowledge, we are wide awake, alert, capable of action; no longer are we blind, inert pawns of fate.'[27]

If the state seems to be in retreat today, one reason is surely the sheer breadth of the expectations held for public policy in the past. But if the scale of these expectations was unrealistic, the fact remains that governments in Canada and elsewhere continue to play an enormous role in society. The share of national wealth today that either is consumed directly by the public sector or passes through the state's hands in the form of transfers to individuals and organizations is about what it was two decades ago. Proportionately fewer workers are employed in the public sector today than in the past, and many programs have been scaled back or even eliminated at all levels of government. Nevertheless, the scope of the state's involvement in society remains vast and, in recent years, has actually increased in certain fields. Human rights is just one example of such expansion: As domestic and international forces have combined to raise the profile of such issues, rights considerations have been injected into entirely new domains.

It is quite simply wrong, therefore, to suggest that policy-makers have become the helpless pawns of forces over which they have little or no control. The truth is far less dramatic. Big new initiatives of the sort that were common in the 1960s and 1970s have become rare, but the shadow cast by the state is not much shorter today than it was in the past. The chief exception may be in economic policy, where globalization and international trade liberalization have pulled the rug out from under the possibility of an autonomously determined trade or monetary policy.

The Relevance of Studying Public Policy

As the scope of state intervention in Canada has increased and the forms of state action have grown more complex, it has become more difficult for laypersons to understand public policy. Yet the importance of such understanding has never been greater. Today the state really does accompany its citizens from the cradle (if not the womb) to the grave. But it is not always easy to make sense of what governments do and why. Confusion is a natural response to the enormous range of government programs, the Byzantine complications introduced by bureaucracy and multiple layers of government, and the information overload that seems to await anyone intent on sorting out what it all means. Retreat into apathy or uninformed cynicism (not the same as informed cynicism) is a common reaction, though not a helpful one.

Public policy is not, however, something that only specialists can grasp. Those motivated to understand what governments do, why they do it, and the consequences of their actions (or inaction) need not despair. This book is addressed to them. Its modest aim is to bring some meaning to the profusion of information about public policy that is daily conveyed by the mass media. Like a map, it seeks to identify important places that a traveller might wish to visit and to show the connecting routes between them. It does not presume to suggest what destination is most desirable.

Key Terms

exhaustive expenditures Government spending on goods and services.
Fabian socialism A British intellectual movement whose followers believed that gradual, incremental change, based on the insights of policy specialists, could improve public policy and ultimately lead to a fairer and more just society.

policy discourse An unfolding tapestry of words and symbols, constructed out of the multiple definitions (or denials) of a public problem, that structures thinking and action in that issue area.

policy sciences movement A public policy movement that emerged in the United States after World War II with the goal of integrating social scientific knowledge and its application to public policy.

political agenda Defining what is relevant in public life, how issues are defined, whose views should be taken seriously, and what sort of 'solutions' are tenable.

progressivism A movement based on the idea that the knowledge and insights of trained policy specialists could be used to improve the effectiveness of public policy and ultimately to solve social and economic problems.

systemic bias A term referring to the selective nature of the policy system—the idea that some points of view never get articulated and that some policy outcomes are virtually precluded by the biases inherent in the cultural and institutional fabric of society.

transfer payments Government spending directed to individuals, families, and organizations. This is money that the government handles but does not itself spend on goods and services.

Discussion Questions

1. Is the reduction of government funding for programs an example of governments choosing not to act?

2. The chapter suggests that it would be impossible for government to retreat from society. It also notes that there can be no single answer to the question of what the optimal level of government is, because such a concept is based on normative principles. Discuss what you believe to be the optimal level of government in Canada. Would that level be different for the United States or other industrialized nations? What might the optimal level be for an underdeveloped nation?

3. Box 1.1 focuses on Ontario's effort to prevent the use of government-funded advertising for partisan purposes. Do you think prohibiting government from using taxpayer money to promote its policies is a good or a bad development for democracy?

Websites

The following sites provide some interesting statistics and studies as well as information on the scope of government.

Government of Canada
http://canada.gc.ca
This central page offers links to and information on almost every aspect of the federal Canadian government.

Organisation for Economic Co-operation and Development (OECD)

www.oecd.org

The OECD brings together the governments of countries from around the world that are committed to democracy and the market economy. The website offers research reports and studies on the OECD nation.

Policy.ca

www.policy.ca

Operated through the Centre for Cyber Citizenship based at the University of Lethbridge, Policy.ca is a non-partisan public resource for issues in Canadian public policy. Its database includes public policy research publications, policy organizations and institutes, and researchers working in the field of public policy.

Public Policy Forum (PPF)

www.ppforum.ca

The Public Policy Forum brings together the public, private, and voluntary sectors and encourages open discussion amongst its leaders about governance and public policy.

Institute for Research on Public Policy (IRPP)

www.irpp.org

Seeking to improve public policy in Canada, this independent, national, and bilingual organization generates research on current and emerging policy issues of importance to Canadians and their governments.

Privy Council Office (PCO)

www.pco-bcp.gc.ca

The Privy Council Office provides advice and support to the prime minister and cabinet.

Statistics Canada

www.statcan.gc.ca

Statistics Canada is a federally legislated body required to provide statistics for the whole of Canada and each of the provinces and territories. The website provides statistics that help Canadians better understand their country—its population, resources, economy, society, and culture.

Treasury Board of Canada Secretariat

www.tbs-sct.gc.ca

The Treasury Board Secretariat provides advice and support to the ministers who make up the Treasury Board—the cabinet committee in charge of the government's spending. It also oversees the financial management functions in federal departments and agencies.

Theories of Public Policy

Introduction

This chapter explains the importance of theory to the study of public policy. The best place to start our discussion is with a definition. To put it in the simplest terms, a theory is an explanation of why things happen the way they do. The key word here is *why*. A theory is more than an empirical observation or formulation of what we know by experience. For example, to say that the sun appears to rise over the horizon every morning because, so far as we know, it has always done so, is only to state a repeated observation. To elevate this elementary observation to the status of theory it would be necessary to explain the sunrise in terms of the laws of motion that govern bodies moving through space. The theoretical explanation is characterized by *abstract* reasoning on the basis of *empirical* observation.

Theory is especially important to scientific research because it is not limited to explaining a single isolated phenomenon like a sunrise: It can also be generalized to explain events that have not actually been observed. So, for instance, our theory of why the sun appears to rise above the Earth's horizon each day should allow us to predict sunrises on other planets without ever having experienced them. The *predictive* nature of theory makes it particularly useful to the scientific understanding of any field of study.

To develop a theory about a phenomenon, it is necessary to describe that thing in symbolic terms. As we have noted above, the nature of theory is abstract. One way to describe the abstract nature of theories is as metaphors for reality.[1] In other words, theories often use the language of analogy, explaining unfamiliar things by drawing comparisons with things that we find easier to understand or relate to. Consider again our example: The sunrise is explained by the 'laws' of motion for celestial bodies. Of course there is no celestial parliament to pass such 'laws'—the language of 'law' is used as an analogy for the reality of why celestial bodies follow certain patterns of motion. At the same time, the 'law' metaphor suggests certain characteristics of the motion of celestial bodies, such as permanence, regularity, order, and so on. Because we easily relate to the characteristics of the metaphor of 'law' contained in the theory, it is easier to understand the phenomenon of sunrises. Similarly, theories can also be described as **models** of reality. Theories work as models the same way they work as metaphors—to simplify reality. Referring to theories as models simply invokes a certain visual imagery that helps us understand complex phenomena. For the purposes of our discussion, the terms 'theories', 'metaphors', and 'models' will be used interchangeably in this chapter.

Are all theories equally valid? How do we know whether one is better than another? Consider again our sunrise example. In order to explain the sunrise, one theory could argue that the Earth is a sphere that rotates on its axis as it orbits around the sun, thus causing the sun to appear to 'rise' every 24 hours, which is the length of time it takes the Earth to complete one rotation. Another theory could argue that the Earth is flat and the sun moves over the Earth from one end to the other until it appears again on the other side 24 hours later. Which theory is correct? How can we judge? Remember that theoretical explanation is characterized by abstract reasoning based on empirical observation. The key to judging any theory is to see how well it stands up to the facts of reality as we actually observe them. A good theory can either pass empirical testing or be deduced from the facts of reality, while a bad one cannot. In the case of our example, rational deduction had favoured the round-Earth theory for centuries before photographs of the Earth from space provided indisputable evidence refuting the flat-Earth theory.

Of course it is not always the case, even in the physical sciences, that a single theory is accepted as the only plausible one. Nevertheless, some theories are usually considered more plausible than others because they seem to make better sense of the facts. The best theory is always the one that explains the most about a phenomenon in the simplest way. That is, a good theory will tend to be not only consistent with the facts, but also easy to understand in itself. This characteristic of good theory is called 'parsimony'. A **parsimonious** theory 'explains a lot with a little'—the simplest, most accurate, and consistent explanation is always best. This is not to say that all theories must be rejected completely if they do not fit with more of the facts than another model. For instance, many researchers in the social sciences find it useful to consider a phenomenon from multiple theoretical perspectives because definitive empirical proofs for many theories simply do not exist. Still the point remains that the value of theoretical explanation lies in its ability to help make complex phenomena simple to understand, and a parsimonious model will be more helpful in this regard.

It is often difficult to remain objective when it comes to theory. Sometimes people will continue to support a theory even when it is not consistent with scientific facts because it serves their interests to do so. If someone or some group of people in society benefits from popular belief in a certain theory, they may strongly resist any effort to revise or move past it even when it is clearly not useful for understanding a phenomenon. In the seventeenth century, the religious establishment rejected Galileo's theories explaining celestial motion because they contradicted biblical teachings, and any challenge to the credibility of religious doctrine could undermine public confidence in religious leaders and their institutions. Thus, instead of revising the traditional theory that the Earth was the centre of the universe, religious leaders rejected Galileo.

It is also true that ideology can often be disguised as theory. For example, the Nazis in Germany used theories of racial superiority to justify the persecution and murder of millions of people because they were not of the 'superior' Aryan race. Similarly, Communist leaders in the former USSR and other countries around the world used totalitarian Marxist ideology to justify the persecution and murder of millions of people who opposed the imposition of socialist revolution or who were perceived to be of the wrong social class. Other instances in which 'theories' were used to justify political oppression include slavery, the subjugation of Aboriginal peoples, and the political disenfranchisement of women until the 1920s. These examples underline two essential points: that theory must not be taken lightly, especially when it is applied to politics, and that it is imperative to find some objective way to distinguish good theory from bad.

Objective assessment is particularly difficult when theory is married to the study of politics. One way to make it easier is to identify the nature of the theory in question. For instance, the types of political theories mentioned above should be distinguished from those applied to the study of public policy. The examples above are properly classified as **normative political theories**, since their intent is to justify some sort of action on the grounds of the moral imperatives implied within the theory. For example, Marxism is a normative theory because it analyzes politics as the struggle between classes, describes the exploitation of the working class as morally wrong, and prescribes a political solution through possibly violent revolution.

Normative theories can be contrasted with **positive theories**. Unlike normative theories of politics, positive theories of politics do not prescribe or imply moral imperatives—they simply attempt to explain politics *as it is*, not as it should be. In this sense, positive theories are more scientific in their approach to understanding politics. Positive theories do not have any *explicit* political interest, ideology, or agenda to promote—they are simply intended to help students of public policy better understand the ways politics works.[2]

Even so, positive theories may support or undermine *implicit* political interests, ideologies, and agendas. According to this argument, analyses of public policy that claim to be value-free simply do not acknowledge the value assumptions that underlie their interpretation of the policy process. The fact that we may be unaware of our value assumptions does not mean that we travel without normative baggage. Indeed, the claims to scientific objectivity and moral neutrality of such theories lend implicit support to the dominant ways of thinking about the public policy process that they accept so uncritically. This debate is a complicated and long-standing one, and interested readers will find no shortage of writing on the subject of how values intrude on social and political analysis. Careful students of public policy should be aware of the potential for 'normative' values to creep into 'positive' theories.

In conclusion, it is important to note that the nature and purpose of theory are the same across all scientific disciplines, whether the phenomenon to be explained is part of the physical world or the political process that produces public policy. As we shall see in the next section of this chapter, the field of public policy relies heavily on the use of theoretical concepts and models to understand the way things happen in politics and government. Stated simply, in the field of public policy the purposes of theory are

1. to simplify and clarify our thinking about government and politics;
2. to identify important political forces in society;
3. to communicate relevant knowledge about political life;
4. to direct inquiry into politics; and
5. to suggest explanations for political events and outcomes.[3]

The main theoretical frameworks associated with the contemporary study of public policy are introduced in this chapter. It is generally agreed that no single or even dominant theory of policy formation exists. There is no agreement, however, on what those main frameworks are. For instance, in an influential article published in 1976, Richard Simeon grouped explanations of public policy under five headings: 'policy as a consequence of the *environment*, of the distribution of *power*, of prevailing *ideas*, of *institutional* frameworks, and of the *process* of decision-making'.[4] Michael Atkinson and Marsha Chandler offer a leaner categorization of approaches, distinguishing between those that start from a *Marxist* view of the state (i.e., one focusing on class struggle) and those that see the state in the context of a competitive political marketplace in which class is only one of the lines of potential conflict. Proponents of this second approach describe it as *pluralist*.[5] Taking yet another approach, Bruce Doern and Richard Phidd identify four models of the policy process: *rational, incremental, public choice,* and *class analysis* (or Marxist). In addition, they offer their own approach, an eclectic framework that stresses the interaction of society's dominant ideas; the structure of government and the private sector, including the individuals who control them; and the processes that characterize the policy process. Their theoretical perspective is fairly described as *liberal-pluralist*.[6] Finally, in one of the major textbooks on Canadian politics, Robert Jackson and Doreen Jackson distinguish between theories of decision making (microlevel approaches) and theories of policy formation (macrolevel approaches). According to Jackson and Jackson, the second group of theories seeks to identify the broader determinants of state action and includes environmental determinism, pluralism, public choice theory, and neo-Marxist analysis.[7]

In view of the diversity of ways in which writers on public policy have categorized theoretical approaches to the field, one hesitates to develop yet another classification. Classification for its own sake is, after all, no virtue. The purpose should be to explain the different answers that theories give to the fundamental political questions of *why* the state behaves in particular ways and *who benefits*. In this chapter we suggest, for the sake of parsimony, that the theoretical perspectives found in the literature on public policy can be grouped into two very general categories. What the theories in the first category all share is the assumption that the outcome of public policy is largely (though not exclusively) determined by the nature or structure of politics, the bureaucracy, or society. This group can be labelled **structuralist theories**. The main theoretical models that fall under the structuralist label are Marxism, environmental determinism (including globalism, feminism, and culturalism), institutionalism, incrementalism, and systems theory. By contrast, the theories in the second category see the policy process as **dynamic**—that is, open to influence in a competitive environment. The three theories that see the public policy process as dynamic are pluralism, game theory, and public choice. This way of dividing up and labelling the world of theory has the virtue of identifying the outstanding characteristics of the main contemporary models for understanding public policy and allows distinctions to be drawn and similarities to be highlighted between these frameworks.

Structuralist Theories of the Public Policy Process

The Marxist Model: Class Structures of State and Society Determine Public Policy

The Marxist model of public policy is perhaps the most influential of the structuralist theoretical frameworks and offers the best example of a structuralist view on public policy. The **Marxist theory** of policy formation has four main elements: (1) the *division of society into classes*, with an individual's class position determined by his or her relationship to the means of production; (2) the *pre-eminence of class* as the basis for political and economic conflict; (3) the *inequality of classes*, with society divided into dominant and subordinate classes; and (4) the *bias of the state* in favour of the dominant class(es), which in a capitalist society will be the capitalists or bourgeoisie.

This much of Marxist theory has remained unchanged from the original writings of Karl Marx. Within contemporary Marxist theory (i.e., neo-Marxism), however, there are numerous divisions over some of these points, particularly the relationship of the state to dominant and subordinate classes. The complexities of these debates need not concern us here.[8] Our chief interest is in identifying how Marxist explanations of policy formation differ from other approaches.

In terms of world view, the Marxist perspective identifies antagonism between classes as the central fact of politics in all societies. This premise has often been disputed by non-Marxists, who in North America at least are able to point to the absence of electorally strong working-class parties and to the sense of 'middle-classness' that attitudinal surveys show to be widely shared in both Canadian and American society. While some students may quibble with the above statement, noting that the NDP became the official opposition in 2010, thus moving the progressive agenda forward, many believe that the NDP's success had more to do with the popularity of the late Jack Layton than with an embrace of the party's policy agenda. Moreover, critics of Marxist class analysis maintain that the declining size of the traditional blue-collar working class, the separation of ownership from effective control of the modern corporation (and therefore the declining importance of the individual capitalist), and the expansion of a middle class of relatively affluent professionals have actually weakened the political significance of class. These critics, therefore, dismiss the Marxist insistence on the primacy of class as an expression of ideological preference rather than a useful tool for understanding the public policy process.

Marxists acknowledge that the subjective sense of belonging to a social class is weak in many capitalist societies and that social divisions have become more complicated as a result of changes in the economies of these societies. But they are not prepared to jettison the concept of class. Instead, they argue that capitalism's proven capacity for coping with the challenges posed by periodic economic crises and by the political demands of subordinate classes can be traced to two main factors. One is the role played by a society's dominant ideology. According to Marxists, the subordinate classes in a society develop a *false consciousness* regarding their own best interests. Effectively, the dominance of liberal-capitalist ideology—beliefs about the importance of things like profits and private property, the possibility of upward socioeconomic mobility, and, most important, the effectiveness of the market as the basic organizing principle of the economy—is such that the working classes believe that what is best for a liberal-capitalist democracy must be best for them too. Marxists argue that this ideology, instilled and constantly reinforced by the media, schools, and other institutions of socialization, includes beliefs about the limits of state interference with the economy that have the effect of blunting fundamental criticism of the existing balance of economic and political power. A government that trespasses beyond the limits set by these widely shared beliefs risks a serious decline in popular support.

Even more important, such a government risks a damaging loss of *business confidence*. This constraint on state action, the second main factor used by Marxists to explain the staying power of capitalism, is virtually identical to what Charles Lindblom calls the 'automatic punishing recoil' of the market.[9] It reinforces the ideological limits on public policy by ensuring that actions that threaten business interests (as defined by those who make investment and other decisions affecting economic activity) are punished.

Why should a government—especially one whose main electoral base strength lies elsewhere, with numerically large subordinate classes—care about the business community's reaction? Marxists argue that a crisis of business confidence would undermine the government's ability to finance state activities through taxation and borrowing. Moreover, an economic downturn is likely to result in reduced popular support for the government and increased support for a rival party whose policies appear more likely to generate business confidence and growth in jobs and incomes. Theoretically, a government could always respond to the economic sanctions of the market by taking over businesses and placing restrictions on the transfer of capital out of the country. In practice, however, the economic ties that link capitalist societies mean that this sort of radical political agenda would be poorly received by foreign investors, currency traders, and creditors as well. Thus, international as well as domestic business confidence serves as a brake on reformist policy.

Marxists argue that there is a tension between the state's responsiveness to popular demands and its structural need and ideological disposition to support the general interests of capital. This tension (or 'contradiction', to use Marxist terminology) surfaces at the level of public policy in two functionally different types of policies: legitimation and accumulation policies.[10] **Legitimation policies** reduce interclass conflict by providing subordinate classes with benefits that reduce their dissatisfaction with the inequalities generated by the capitalist economy. Social welfare policies and labour legislation are examples of state actions that promote social harmony by legitimizing the existing capitalist system in the eyes of those classes who benefit least from its operation. These policies indirectly support the interests of capital because they maintain the social conditions necessary for profitable business activity. **Accumulation policies**, by contrast, directly support profit-oriented business activity. Examples include grants and tax subsidies to business, tariff and non-tariff protection for industries, state expenditure on public works needed for business activity, and laws that control the cost of labour or reduce the likelihood of work stoppages. Some Marxists have argued that there is an inherent contradiction in capitalist society because state support for social welfare policies has increasingly collided with what the state must do to support capital accumulation. Marxist analysis attributes this contradiction in the policies pursued by governments in capitalist societies to the ascendance of 'neo-conservatism' (often synonymous with 'neo-liberalism') and its ideological pressure to cut back on social spending.

Let us pause to take stock. The Marxist theory of policy formation argues that class divisions are the main sources of political conflict, even if many (perhaps most) people in the society do not think in terms of class. The fact that people don't think in class terms demonstrates the strength of the dominant liberal-capitalist ideology supplied by the media, schools, and other agents of socialization. As well, the weakness of a subjective sense of class reflects the fact that many of the demands of subordinate classes—for public education, health care, pensions, and income during unemployment— have been met, reducing the class friction that existed in the past. Failure to recognize the class struggle, however, does not mean that class is irrelevant to an understanding of state action.

When Marxists argue that the state in capitalist societies serves the interests of the dominant economic class, they do not mean that every state action reflects the interests of the business/investment community. Nor are they suggesting that those who control the means of production always agree on what the state should and should not do. The point is that the overall pattern of public policy supports the *general* interests of capital. The reason for this is that policy-makers usually believe such policies to be in the public interest. Also, failure to maintain some minimum level of business confidence leads to economic downturn, the consequences of which are reduced popular support for the government and losses in the state's ability to finance its activities. This second factor is an important structural constraint on policy-makers in capitalist societies.

Two features of the Marxist model need to be stressed. First, for the state to serve the general interests of capital, it is not necessary that policy-makers be drawn from the dominant class. In fact, some Marxists argue that the fewer the personal ties between the state and the dominant class, the more effective the state will be in maintaining the interests of this class, since the public will more readily accept capitalist domination if it can be persuaded that the government is not controlled by any one class.[11] Second, some Marxists believe—contrary to pure Marxist theory—that policy-makers are in fact receptive to the demands of subordinate classes. Their willingness to implement reforms that may be opposed by powerful business interests does not reflect any special vision on their part about what concessions must be made to save the capitalist system from what they believe is the short-sightedness of individual capitalists. Rather, it reflects the fact that governments are subject to popular pressures through elections, and that those who manage the state need to appeal to many different parts of the business community. For this reason they may often be willing to act in ways that offend certain parts of that community. This does not mean that state managers are more astute about what needs to be done to maintain the capitalist system than are the capitalists themselves. It does mean, however, that their concern for the overall level of economic activity—a factor that influences both the popular support of governments and the capacity of the state to finance its activities—frees policy-makers from the narrower interests of particular parts of the business community. Marxists will argue that rational self-interest looks somewhat different from the standpoint of state managers than it does from the standpoint of individual capitalists. As Fred Block writes, 'Unlike the individual capitalists, the state managers do not have to operate on the basis of a narrow profit-maximizing rationality; they are capable of intervening in the economy on the basis of a more general rationality.'[12]

Marxists argue that it would be a mistake to think that policy-makers consciously ask themselves, 'What must we do to preserve the capitalist system?' There is no need for them to pose this question consciously because their conception of the 'national interest' coincides with the general interest of capital. As Ralph Miliband explains, 'if the state acts in ways which are congruent with the interests and purposes of capital, it is not because it is driven out of dire compulsion to do so, but because it wants to do so.'[13] Ideology reinforces the structural mechanisms described earlier, thereby ensuring that business interests are treated with a respect that is not accorded to mere 'interest groups'. At the same time, the ideological dispositions of policy-makers help to explain differences between capitalist societies in the scope of state economic intervention and the extent of the social reforms undertaken by governments in these societies.

The openness of governments to the demands of subordinate classes—demands that may be vigorously opposed by spokespersons for the business community—was mentioned earlier. A couple of qualifications should be added. First, the limits of this openness are set by policy-makers' perceptions of how much reform the business community will tolerate before the combined responses of individual corporations and investors produce a crippling downturn in economic activity. Second, the concessions made to the demands of subordinate classes are likely to take forms that minimize the burden on the business community. There is strong evidence in support of this second point. As we will see in Chapter 7, on social policy, most of the costs of financing social services—programs that are usually pointed to as evidence of government's responsiveness to popular pressures—are borne by the middle classes. In a very real sense, the welfare state depends on the middle classes to pay for the services consumed by the middle and lower classes. Redistributive policies have not been pursued at the expense of capitalist interests.

Globalization: The Structure of Global Governance Determines Public Policy

One of the most influential contemporary theoretical models in public policy analysis in recent years has been the **globalization** framework.[14] According to this model, the liberalization of international trade and investment, the rapid advancement and spread of communications technology, and the explosion in global transportation have combined to make the state impotent in many areas of public policy. The globalization model is based on the belief that the policy options available to the governments of individual states are increasingly limited by (1) large multinational corporations in industries from natural resources (especially oil) to textiles (e.g., Nike) and (2) international institutions such as the United Nations (UN), the Group of Eight (G8) major industrialized countries, the World Trade Organization (WTO), and the International Monetary Fund (IMF).

Globalization theorists argue that the structure of governance institutions such as the UN, G8, and WTO favours the advancement of international capitalism by punishing countries that adopt policies contrary to liberal economics. For instance, opponents of globalization often point to the IMF's rules governing loans to governments. These rules punish governments that refuse to limit the size and scope of their activities and usually require recipient governments to reduce social spending, liberalize investment laws, and introduce tax cuts. Globalization theorists argue that desperately poor governments have no choice but to comply with such demands because of the penalties that international organizations like the IMF can impose on them. Thus, the globalization model assumes that the *structure* of international capitalism and the institutions that support it determine the public policy choices governments can make. This characteristic of the globalization model identifies it with structuralism as an explanatory framework for public policy because it is based on the belief that decisions of the state are determined by the structure of institutions of global governance.

Institutionalism and Incrementalism: The Structure of Institutions or the Nature of Bureaucracy Determines Public Policy

Institutionalism and incrementalism are separate theoretical models of public policy, but both are concerned with how government institutions influence public policy. **Institutionalism** is based on the belief that public policy outcomes are determined by the structural configuration of the state itself. That is, the types of policies that can be adopted by a government largely depend on how that society's political institutions are designed. As Michael Atkinson puts it, institutionalism

> involves an assessment of political institutions such as federalism, Parliament, cabinet, and the bureaucracy. These institutions are, of course, influenced by political ideas and economic relationships, but in Canada political institutions have also been treated as important in and of themselves. Federalism for example does not merely replicate the regional character of the country, it reinforces it. Parliament does not simply reflect power relationships in society, it legitimizes them. The courts do more than adjudicate, they define the limits of political action. In this view political institutions, regardless of their origins, make an independent contribution to both the conduct of politics in Canada and to policy outcomes.[15]

There are many policy implications that can arise from the structure of the state. To illustrate, consider that Canadian federalism is decentralized in practice. That is, the provincial governments have constitutional control over many areas of public policy, and the federal government is prohibited from involving itself in these areas.

For instance, the Constitution gives exclusive authority to the provinces over such policy areas as health care, social welfare, and education. While it is true that the federal government often intervenes in these areas, it does so only with the tacit permission of the provincial governments. Some institutionalist theories observe that the decentralized nature of Canadian federalism has created a competitive environment among provincial governments that has prevented further expansion of the welfare state.[16] To see how this competition between governments can develop, consider welfare policy. If one province, say Saskatchewan, were to increase its welfare benefits to a level higher than that in other provinces, it would simultaneously have to raise taxes and increase government spending. But if other provinces did not adopt the same policies, then welfare recipients in those other provinces would be tempted to move to Saskatchewan to obtain the higher benefits. This could create an overload of demand on public finances for the Saskatchewan government. Simultaneously, the higher tax levels required to maintain this level of spending in the province would drive out business, investment, and those wishing to escape the burden of high taxes. As a result, Saskatchewan would be faced with both increasing expenses and shrinking revenues. This is surely a recipe for bankruptcy. Therefore, institutionalists argue that if authority for welfare policy were centralized in the federal government, benefits would be the same across the entire country and welfare programs could safely be expanded because taxpayers would have nowhere to go to escape higher levels of taxation; nor would recipients have any incentive to move from one province to another. It is in this sense that the design or structure of political institutions is seen as determining the kinds of policies that can be implemented by governments.[17]

Incrementalism is also concerned with how the structure of institutions influences public policy outcomes. However, incremental models analyze the decision-making process of the people who produce public policy within institutions, as opposed to the design of institutions themselves. **Incrementalism** views the public policy process as a matter of slow and small adjustments to past decisions. That is, current policy decisions really represent only incremental changes from existing policies. Incremental theory claims that this is the case because of the uncertainty that surrounds many political decisions and the reluctance of policy-makers to make radical changes in the absence of complete information about the potential outcomes. These factors lead to minor, sometimes insignificant changes to public policy as a safer approach to change. Thus, the nature of bureaucratic decision making also structures the policy process.[18]

Other Structural Models of Public Policy

A number of other theoretical frameworks fall under the broad heading of structuralism. One of them is **environmental determinism**. Before we discuss this model, it is necessary to define what we mean by 'environmental' in this context. Environmental determinism is not to be confused with ecological issues like air and water pollution or the protection of natural habitats for wildlife. 'Environment' is used here to refer to the circumstances beyond government control that influence the kinds of public policies adopted by the state. These external circumstances can include the nature of the societal culture (**culturalism**) or the distribution of power by gender in society (a focus of concern for **feminism**). In other words, environmental determinism is based on the belief that the public policy decisions of government are largely *predetermined* or at least heavily influenced by factors that lie outside the control of policymakers. Environmental determinism sees dominant cultural values like liberalism as reinforcing public policies favourable to capitalism and democracy. It may also see the dependency of a region on trade for its economic growth as another factor reinforcing capitalist policies. Finally, it may see the public policy process as being structured to the advantage of one gender over another. In these senses, the cultural values, economic makeup, and gender distribution of power in a particular political environment predetermine the range of public policy options that a government will consider.

The Marxist model also qualifies as a theory of environmental determinism because it sees the societal environment as structured by class and ideology. The relatively more complex theoretical modelling of Marxism justifies its separate consideration from these other frameworks, which might be seen as branches of the Marxist theoretical approach to public policy. It is interesting to note the obvious similarities between the Marxist framework and the perspectives discussed under the 'structuralist' heading. All of them can be described as 'structuralist' because they all believe that the *structure* of the environment in which governments make their decisions determines the options available and, therefore, the outcomes of public policy.

Systems Theory: A Bridge between Structural and Dynamic Theories

A theoretical model that borrows from the more dynamic view of pluralism discussed below and yet shares some characteristics with structural theories of public policy is David Easton's **systems theory**. Systems theory is a pluralist analysis with a functionalist orientation. Functionalist methodologies seek to explain behaviour by identifying the purposes it serves in relation to a social (or economic, or political) system. The behaviour of individuals, groups, or classes is interpreted in light of what the social system requires to maintain itself. That is, behaviour serves to perpetuate the system, and the system reinforces this behaviour. According to Easton's theory, the public policy system is affected not only by 'inputs' in the form of political demands and support for policies, but also by 'outputs'—the decisions or policies it produces.[19] This model sees the state as passive in the public policy process and the policy process as potentially dynamic because of the interaction of inputs in the system. Yet, as Easton says,

> the behaviour of every political system is to some degree imposed upon it by the kind of system it is, that is, by its own structure and internal needs. But its behavior also reflects the strains occasioned by the specific setting within which the system operates. It may be argued that most of the significant changes within a political system have their origin in shifts among the external variables . . . [yet] if a structured system is to maintain itself, it must provide mechanisms

whereby its members are integrated or induced to cooperate in some minimal degree so that they can make authoritative decisions.[20]

A simplified version of Easton's model is portrayed in Figure 2.1. The metaphorical analogy to the way in which a computer or a machine works is obvious.

FIGURE 2.1 David Easton's Simplified Model of the Political System

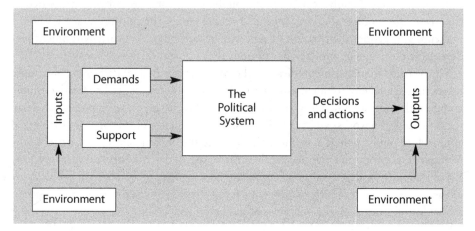

Source: David Easton, *A Systems Analysis of Political Life* (New York, NY: John Wiley and Sons, 1965), 32, Diagram 2.

The systems analysis approach to understanding public policy is both structural and dynamic, depending on which aspect of the model is emphasized. In this sense, Easton's systems theory provides a bridge between structural theories and more dynamic theories of public policy.

Dynamic Models of the Public Policy Process

The Pluralist Model: Group Competition in the Political Marketplace

Pluralism has been one of the most influential theoretical models of public policy. The **pluralist model** is based on the observation that interest groups influence the outcome of government decisions. This theory starts with the realization that society is actually a collection of individuals, each with his or her own specific interests. Yet these individuals, or at least the more perceptive ones, realize that they stand a better chance of achieving their goals if they join with others who have similar goals. Thus, groups form to influence the behaviour of governments. The key feature of the pluralist view of public policy is that it considers the competition between groups to be essentially open: Groups can enter and exit the competition without structural barriers, and influence within the policy process is largely dynamic.

This is a short, and obviously very simplified, explanation of a model of politics that heavily influenced North American political science for much of the twentieth century. Applied to policy formation, it sees state action as the outcome of competition between organized groups that seek to protect or promote the interests of their members. Although different versions of the pluralist model disagree on how 'open' this competition is, they share a world view that distinguishes them from Marxist theories of public policy. For Marxists, the foremost line of political conflict is the one that divides economic classes. All other lines of conflict—'cleavages', in the jargon of political sociology—are subordinate to and shaped by class struggle. Pluralists, on the other hand, concede that economic factors are important determinants of political conflict, but they view other lines of division, including ethnicity, language, religion, gender, region, and ideology, as having a significance that is not necessarily less than that of class. Moreover, these non-class divisions are not, in the pluralist model, merely class conflicts dressed up in ways that make them more difficult to recognize. As one textbook on Canadian politics puts it, 'From the [pluralist] perspective . . . ethnicity, culture, religion, language, occupation, economic sector, region, level of income, gender and ideology are all important determinants of political phenomena, independent of the class structure.'[21]

However, the pluralist model of politics does view policy-making in democratic societies as a competition between elites. One of the first to attempt to reconcile the fact that political decision making is concentrated in the hands of elites with the fundamental democratic premise that all just rule derives from the consent of the governed was Joseph Schumpeter. In *Capitalism, Socialism and Democracy*[22] he argued that the competition for political office is the key feature of democratic politics. Schumpeter likened this competition between elites for the votes of the general population to the operation of an economic market: Voters (like consumers) choose between the policies (products) offered by competing parties (sellers). This reconciliation of elitist decision making with democratic values proved to be enormously influential. It was reformulated by the American political scientist Robert Dahl in his definition of democracy as *polyarchy*, the rule of multiple minorities.[23] According to Dahl, minority rule takes place against the backdrop of a social consensus on democratic values that serves as a check on undemocratic behaviour by elites.

A number of implications for the theory of policy-making flowed from this work. First, the state was viewed as essentially democratic. Though controlled by elites, governments were compelled to be at least minimally responsive to popular demands because of the risk that they might be replaced by another elite coalition at the next election. Second, individuals and organized groups were the relevant units for policy analysis. Political conflict was seen in terms of shifting constellations of actors that varied from issue to issue, so that opponents on one policy question might find themselves allies on a different question. Third, ideas were viewed as a major determinant of policy. The perceptions and beliefs of individuals were considered crucial to understanding their behaviour and, ultimately, policy outcomes. Major policy trends, such as the emergence of the welfare state, and cross-national differences in policy were explained in terms of national values—if not those of the general population, then those of political elites.[24] In summary, classic models of pluralism view the public policy process as dynamic instead of structural in nature.

Some pluralist theorists, however, have noticed that certain groups possess greater resources than others and that some demands tend to receive a more sympathetic hearing from government than others. Moreover, it is difficult to ignore evidence that many individuals are effectively excluded from the competition because they are not organized into groups with representative spokespersons. Thus, some argue that even though the pluralist model holds organization and power to be theoretically open to all, in reality some parts of society, particularly the poor and less-educated, are less likely than others to mobilize in a concerted effort to influence state action. In other words, the policy process is characterized by group competition, but the competition is more structural and less dynamic than earlier models of pluralism admit.

Some pluralists have put forward various explanations to account for the dominant position of business in the political marketplace. Robert Heilbroner has suggested that, in America at least, the dominant ideology compels non-business interests to 'accommodate their proposals for social change to the limits of adaptability of the prevailing business order'.[25] In *Politics and Markets*, Charles Lindblom attributes the 'privileged position of business' to a combination of superior financial resources and lobbying organization, greater access than other groups to government officials, and, most importantly, propagandistic activities that reinforce the ideological dominance of business values, both directly through political advertising and indirectly through commercial advertising.[26] A somewhat different perspective is offered by Theodore Lowi. He argues that the policy process 'is biased not so much in favor of the rich as in favor of the established and organized'.[27] While Lowi views political power as something that derives from organization per se, he too acknowledges that business interests occupy a privileged position within the policy-making system. According to Lowi, both the state and private business have a fundamental interest in stability. From the government's side, this means sensitivity toward the conditions necessary to ensure business performance.

Another explanation of the unequal competition of interests to come out of the pluralist theoretical framework is that offered by Lindblom in an article entitled 'The Market as Prison'.[28] Lindblom argues that policy-making in capitalist societies is imprisoned by the fact that a market economy operates on the basis of inducements. Short of replacing the market system with a centrally directed command economy, businesses cannot be ordered to produce or to invest. They must be persuaded—incentives and disincentives must be used to get them to behave in ways desired by policy-makers. When state action, real or anticipated, is perceived by business people to be harmful to their interests, they react by cutting back on production, deferring or cancelling new investment, and perhaps shifting production to other countries. The reaction is automatic, triggered by a change in the environment in which business operates. And to the extent that it means unemployment and economic slowdown, the reaction is also punishing to the government. Lindblom writes, 'When a decline in prosperity and employment is brought about by decisions of corporate and other business executives, it is not they but government officials who consequently are retired from their offices.'[29] Hence the special sensitivity of public officials to business interests. Change is not impossible, but it is greatly constrained by the automatic punishment the market system imposes on governments that trespass beyond the line of business tolerance. None of this would be true were it not for the fact that in capitalist societies the market is a *chose donnée* in our thinking about policy. Interference with it might be desirable. But its elimination is unthinkable. The bars that imprison policy-makers are both structural (the reaction of businesspeople) and ideological.

This explanation of business power has long been familiar to Marxist theorists. What Lindblom calls the 'automatic punishing recoil' of the market to reforms perceived to threaten business interests has been called a 'capital strike' by others. But Lindblom's explanation is not a Marxist one. Though he assigns central importance to economic factors as determinants of policy, he continues to treat business as a societal interest, albeit the most powerful one. The world view that underpins Lindblom's theory does not see society in class terms or politics as class struggle. Though he arrives at conclusions quite similar to those of Marxist theorists, his reasoning is still within the pluralist world view. Nonetheless, Lindblom's approach leans toward a structural view of pluralist models of public policy.

William D. Coleman and Grace Skogstad offer another theoretical framework that can more accurately be classified as 'structural-pluralist'.[30] Like Lindblom and Lowi, these theorists noticed that some groups seem to have privileged access to the policy-making process. In fact, Coleman and Skogstad noticed that this privileged access persisted over time and the groups enjoying these political advantages were able to exclude other groups from the policy-making process in their interest area. Essentially, public policy became divided up into separate policy areas dominated by long-term participant groups with specific policy interests and agendas that were able to prevent new participants from influencing the policy area. These long-term groups formed what Coleman and Skogstad called 'policy communities'. In addition, this theoretical model identified the relationships that developed between group interests and policy-makers and other interests within the policy community as 'policy networks'. This term suggests the closed and privileged nature of influence within specific policy areas. It also implies that the network's interest in a particular policy can determine that policy's success or failure. Within the labour law policy community, for instance, one would typically expect to find politicians, bureaucrats, business, and labour. Groups with a minor interest in labour law (e.g., feminists seeking special provisions for maternity leave or religious minorities seeking exemption from the mandatory payment of union dues) would presumably be less active than those within the inner circle of the policy community. Policy networks need not always be formal, and they can be loosely structured. Recent research using network theory shows the links between different aspects of governance in modern society. The 'policy community' model of public policy thus represents an example of the structural side of the normally dynamic nature of pluralist political theory.

There are three assumptions that researchers work with when analyzing policy networks. First is the assumption that modern governance is non-hierarchical. This means that there are few policy solutions that are actually imposed from above. Governance requires give and take between public and private actors, as well as between different groups in society. The second assumption is that the relationships must be disentangled if they are to be understood. Finally, while networks do influence policy, in the end it is government that is responsible for governance.[31]

The Public Choice Model: *Homo Economicus* and *Homo Politicus*

In 1986, American economist James Buchanan was awarded the Nobel Prize in Economic Sciences. The selection jury for this prestigious award cited his application of economic theory to political and constitutional issues as the basis for their choice. Buchanan is one of the founders of a theoretical approach that in Canada is usually referred to as public choice theory, in the United States as political economy, and in Europe as political economics or the economic theory of politics. His Nobel Prize was a highly visible indication of the growing importance of a theoretical model that has acquired many converts in academe, especially in North America. The formal emergence of public choice as a theoretical framework for the study of public policy came about after World War II. The first works to use an economic analogy to describe the political process were Duncan Black (1948), James Buchanan (1949), and Kenneth Arrow (1950). Their early work inspired a large number of other works in the field, including classics by Anthony Downs (1957), James Buchanan and Gordon Tullock (1962), William Riker (1962), and Mancur Olson (1965).[32]

Public choice theory represents the colonization of traditional political science concerns by economics. Proponents of this approach attempt to explain the political behaviour of individuals and interest groups, as well as the policy decisions of governments, in terms of a theory of rational choice developed in microeconomics. The central figure of microeconomic theory is *homo economicus*, or 'economic man'. This term is used to describe the behaviour of utility-maximizing individuals—people who seek to maximize their self-interest or personal gain and minimize their losses in any economic situation. This is called 'rational' economic behaviour, or *rational choice*. Under the public choice model, *homo politicus*, 'political man', is also assumed to operate on the basis of rational self-interest, seeking to maximize satisfaction at the least cost within the limits imposed by the information at hand. This assumption is based on the common-sense observation that the average person does not have two personalities: The same person who makes economic decisions also has to make political decisions, so why have two different concepts of human behaviour? If the behaviour attributed to economic decision making is assumed to be empirically sound, then it should apply to political behaviour as well.

The public choice model has some similarities with the pluralist model. We have seen already that the pluralist model views the state as the forum for a multi-levelled competition between conflicting group interests. This competition may be *unequal*; no serious analysis would deny that state organizations sometimes defend and advance their own interests, as opposed to simply mediating the competing demands of societal groups. But the pluralist world view insists on the competitive nature of politics and on the 'group' or 'interest' as the basic unit of analysis for understanding the policy process. The public choice model shares the same competitive world view, as shown by its use of the terms 'log-rolling', 'bargaining', 'accommodation', and 'exchange'. In fact, public choice is a revised version of the pluralist model. This is evident in its characterization of the state. In the words of one of the main Canadian contributors to public choice theory, 'the role of the State in a modern representative democracy is centrally concerned with mediating interest group conflicts over distributive claims.'[33] Buchanan and Tullock acknowledge the similarity of pluralist and public choice approaches when they write that '[t]hroughout our analysis the word "group" could be substituted for the word "individual" without significantly affecting the results.'[34]

What is different about the public choice model is its strict insistence on the individual as the basic unit of analysis; Buchanan and Tullock refer to this characteristic as 'methodological individualism'.[35] The state is viewed in terms of the individual politicians and bureaucrats who occupy particular positions within it, and these people are understood to act on the basis of rational self-interest under conditions of imperfect knowledge. Politicians, bureaucrats, and interest group leaders are 'political entrepreneurs'. Politicians seek to be elected and, once elected, to maintain themselves in power (their motivations for seeking office are beside the point). Bureaucrats seek promotion or more control over the environment within which their organization is situated. Expansion, increased budgets, new policy tasks, and capturing chief responsibility for a policy field are all means toward these goals. Based on the assumption that the rational self-interest postulate is at least more plausible than any other explanation of individual behaviour, the public choice model explains policy as the outcome of strategic behaviour within a system of overlapping games that connect the state to society for the purpose of maximizing self-interest.

It is important to keep in mind that none of the sets of participants in the decision-making process acts in a single-minded way. For example, the bureaucracy is divided into 'spender' organizations with large budgets, for whom financial restraint means placing limits on the goals that individual bureaucrats pursue, and 'savers' who operate under a very different system of incentives for behaviour. The incentive system of individual bureaucrats also varies according to the societal interests that 'consume' the services they provide, their regional focus, and their function. These divisions lead to competition and bargaining *within* the bureaucratic game. This is also true of the political game. Behind the facade of unity that typically characterizes the usual single-party government in Canada (coalition governments introduce another level of complexity), the fact that the re-election prospects of individual members of the government are tied to different constituencies (regional, special interest, and ideological) and to the various parts of the state bureaucracy they oversee ensures that they too are involved in this process of bargaining within the state.

The behaviour of those who take part in the bureaucratic and political 'games' is influenced by the actual and anticipated behaviour of special interest groups, the media, and various segments of the electorate. Politics involves a continuous and multi-levelled process of bargaining in which power comes from control of resources that can be used as the basis for profitable exchange.

Thus, as in the economy, power is a *transactional* property pervading the political marketplace. It is expressed in a number of ways (see Figure 2.2 for a graphic illustration):

- the votes of electors;
- the perceived capacity of the media to influence the views held by voters on particular issues and in relation to particular political parties or interests;
- the ability of special interest groups to mobilize supporters and allies for collective action, and to offer inducements or deploy what politicians believe to be credible threats;
- the control that bureaucrats exercise over the flow of vital information and the delivery of programs; and
- the capacity of governments to manage the public agenda and to confer benefits on voters or special interest groups whose support is up for grabs and to impose costs on those whose support is lost anyway. Where there is no avoiding the imposition of costs on possible supporters, this will be done in ways that soften or hide their impact.

It may sound as though the public choice model portrays policy formation as a wide-open melee—a sort of analytical version of Thomas Hobbes's state of nature.[36]

FIGURE 2.2 The Policy Process Viewed from the Public Choice Perspective: Four Interrelated Games

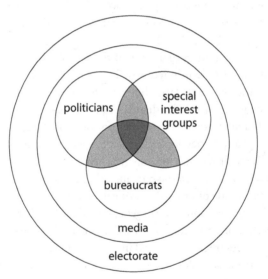

Notes:
1. The darkest area of this figure is the heart of the decision-making process.
2. The lighter shaded areas show the interplay between each pair of policy participants.
3. The media interact with each set of policy participants, as well as being the channel through which the electorate perceives these participants and, to some degree, the channel through which the individual players learn about what is happening in their own and other games.
4. Voters are treated as non-participants in the decision-making process. They are important primarily because they choose the players in the political game.

Source: M.J. Trebilcock et al., *The Choice of Governing Instrument* (Ottawa, ON: Economic Council of Canada, 1982), Figure 2-1, 6–7. Reprinted by permission of the author.

This would be an incorrect conclusion. What keeps competition in the political marketplace from degenerating into a no-holds-barred free-for-all is the existence of rules—that is, the Constitution and laws—that constrain an individual's choices. Furthermore, as in the economic marketplace, the 'wrong' rules will distort the behaviour of individuals, resulting in outcomes that are inefficient from the standpoint of society as a whole. Those who use this theoretical approach acknowledge that the Constitution operates as a constraint on the behaviour of participants in the policy-making process. Indeed, constitutional rules assume major importance in the public choice model. If one accepts that individuals act on the basis of rational self-interest and that it is unrealistic to assume otherwise, it follows that the way to change policy outcomes is to alter the incentives and constraints that influence individual decisions. To see how the rules of the game can create incentives for individuals, consider the argument that Trebilcock and his colleagues made in *The Choice of Governing Instrument*. They argued that Canada's federal division of powers has sometimes caused governments to select inefficient means for achieving their policy goals. These means have been more costly and have therefore imposed a greater burden on taxpayers than different means would have done, had the Constitution not made them unavailable to that level of government.[37]

At this point it is useful to draw attention to the game terminology used to describe the public choice models above. The use of the terminology of games is a distinctive element within the public choice framework. Known as **game theory**, this model uses the metaphor of competitive gaming to help us understand public policy and politics. Those familiar with the movie *A Beautiful Mind* will perhaps recognize the name of the character played by Russell Crowe: John Nash. Nash developed a Nobel Prize–winning theory of politics and bargaining based on game theory that was influential in the study of public policy. For the purposes of this chapter it is not necessary to get too far into a discussion of game theory's importance within the public choice framework. However, a brief description of the characteristics of this highly metaphorical approach to public policy is warranted. According to Tom Flanagan,

> Game theory is a branch of mathematics involving models of situations in which outcomes are interdependent. That is, no player can determine the result by himself, for the outcome arises from the interplay of the choices made by all the players. A game model requires the following elements: players, rules of the game, strategies, payoffs and a solution (or solutions).[38]

Game theory models, then, are representations of the realities of the process of politics and public policy, including the elements of competition, strategy, bargaining, and negotiation. Nonetheless, the game analogy seems to fit with the empirical evidence of political activity in many ways. Thus, the framework offered by game theory is a useful tool for public policy theorists within the public choice framework.

The apparent advantage of the public choice framework over other models of public policy is the capacity of the scientific (especially mathematical and quantitative) methods associated with it. Its logical rigour and formally stated assumptions give it an air of moral neutrality. However, some critics have questioned whether the public choice model is as scientific as its proponents claim. Is public choice strictly a positive theoretical model, or does it also have normative dimensions?

One assessment of the ideological disposition of public choice theory is provided by one of its Canadian scholars, Mark Sproule-Jones. He states that the 'public-choice approach is normative in cast, and is aimed at determining what kinds of institutional arrangements and constitutional arrangements work better for citizens.'[39] It is clear from the work that has been done within the economics of politics framework that many of its supporters define 'better' as that which interferes least with individual choice and which achieves a given policy outcome at the least cost. The first of these criteria, individual choice, is obviously a liberal value based on the belief that the rights and freedoms of the individual should be the foremost concern of government. The second criterion, economic efficiency, is probably one that people of all ideological stripes can agree on. A third criterion used by public choice theory is that of 'institutional fairness'. As Sproule-Jones puts it, 'If individuals perceive the institutional and constitutional arrangements as being fair to them as well as to others, then the policy outputs or policy changes can be evaluated as fair.'[40] This assumption is also grounded in liberal philosophy's belief in the primacy of the individual. Although the normative aspects of the public choice framework are not the focus of research on public policy under that model, structural approaches quite explicitly focus on linking their theories to specific normative goals.

Many of the conclusions put forward in early formulations of public choice theory also led to formal criticisms of the theoretical assumptions of the public choice approach. One of the most famous of these assumptions is the 'invisible hand' theorem. According to this fundamental tenet of economics, competitive markets lead to a distribution of resources that is 'Pareto optimal'—that is, equilibrium will be reached where everyone's individual utility is maximized and any government intervention will serve only to lead to a zero-sum outcome in which some are better off and equal numbers are worse off. But does 'Pareto optimality' apply to public policy? In particular, the conclusions drawn from two classic works by Kenneth Arrow and Mancur Olson questioned the assumptions behind a liberal-democratic view of politics in capitalist states. Arrow, for instance, used economic analysis to theorize that no democratic institution could possibly produce an outcome that was Pareto optimal because of the way choices cancel each other out when large groups of people are making decisions among multiple alternatives. Ultimately, Arrow believed that democratic ideals were impossible and that, in reality, all decisions are dictatorial in the sense that some small minority wins approval for what it wants over the preferences of a majority of others. One example of this phenomenon might be the results of our first-past-the-post electoral system. The division of political party choices into more than two options leads voters to elect governments that reflect the preferences of only a minority of voters (a minority of the popular vote) but nevertheless gain majority control of the seats in Parliament because the alternative choices cancel each other out (by splitting the vote). The same thing can occur in any vote taken in any organization where there are at least three voters and three options. Arrow's observation, known as the 'impossibility theorem', presents a pessimistic view of the potential for democratic institutions.[41]

Another pessimistic view of democracy came from the work of Mancur Olson.[42] He postulated that if individuals were truly motivated by reason they would not participate in interest group activity. For example, if people are rational, they calculate the costs and benefits (or utility) of an action for themselves. If the costs of a certain action exceed the benefits, rational people will forgo that action. If the benefits exceed the costs, then participation is expected. Sounds simple enough, doesn't it? Well, Olson reasoned that if rational individuals considered the extremely remote *possibility* that their single, individual, personal involvement in an interest group would affect the outcome of public policy, they would reason that the costs must outweigh the benefits. That is, they could obtain the same policy outcome if they didn't participate as if they did. So why would a rational person waste time, effort, or money (costs) to support interest group activities? Olson concluded that politically active people are not motivated by rational self-interest (in the economic sense), but by altruistic or idealistic goals.

Other authors, such as Green and Shapiro (1994), have applied the same reasoning about rationally consistent behaviour to the act of voting to show that rational people would not vote.[43] When they observed empirically that most people do vote, they assumed that the rational-actor model of political behaviour did not explain very much about politics. However, recent modifications to public choice and rational choice theories assume that some individual utility preferences include altruistic (as opposed to self-interested) behaviour. This makes activities such as political participation rational still—but only in a much broader sense. The literature on public choice continues to grow and develop in the contemporary study of public policy, and many revisions to the theory have formally answered some of these criticisms.

The Perspectives Compared

Each of the theoretical perspectives examined in this chapter represents a different lens through which policy may be viewed. They vary in terms of the assumptions they make about the basis of political conflict, the level at which they analyze the policy process, and the methods they tend to use to explain state actions. It would be a mistake, however, to see these perspectives as mutually exclusive. Rather, they may be usefully seen as emphasizing different aspects of the process through which policy is determined. Very different explanations of how an issue reaches the policy agenda and what the influences are that determine the response of policy-makers may appear equally reasonable when viewing isolated aspects of the policy process. Does this mean that the choice of theoretical perspective, like that in clothes, is a matter of taste? And if no single perspective holds a monopoly on insight, is not the best approach to understanding policy one that combines various separate theories?

The answer to both these questions is a qualified no. It *is* reasonable to see each of these theoretical perspectives as providing an incomplete explanation of policy formation. This does not require that they all be considered equally useful. Each perspective has particular strengths on its 'home turf'. For example, the Marxist perspective bases its analysis of public policy on the unequal competition between classes that is generated by the capitalist economy. Its home turf involves the limits that the economic system places on the behaviour of the state, and the relationship between the economy and political power. In contrast, the pluralist perspective emphasizes the competitive character of politics, focusing on group interests and the behaviour and motivations of individuals. These features of pluralism are confirmed by the reality of individuals differing over what the state should do—individuals who join forces with others who have similar views or interests to increase their political leverage. Similarly, the home turf of the public choice perspective is the realm of individual decision making. From the standpoint of actual behaviour, it is undeniable that the individual ultimately makes decisions and acts on them. Abstract collectivist concepts like 'groups', 'classes', and 'the state' cannot be said to have the capability to 'act' or 'decide' on public policy because they really are only collections of individuals. Thus, the strength of the public choice approach is its treatment of individual choice. The main points of similarity and difference between the perspectives are summarized in Table 2.1.

So how does one decide which theoretical perspective or combination of perspectives is *scientifically* the most valid? Ideally, the test should be their ability to provide a convincing explanation of the relationship of 'facts'. But the facts are themselves disputed by different theories. For example, a pluralist is likely to see class either as a subjective phenomenon—and therefore to measure it using attitudinal surveys—or as an objective condition that has roughly the same meaning as social status, in which case income or occupational prestige may be used to distinguish between various gradations of class (e.g., lower, middle, and upper). A Marxist will view the facts, in this case the reality of classes, very differently. Individuals' beliefs about whether classes exist and their self-perception of what class they belong to are considered irrelevant. Nor will classes be considered to be the same as status groups. Class is an objective condition determined by one's relationship to the mode of production. For Marxists, the facts are that classes exist and that the relationships between classes are the key to understanding politics. These are facts regardless of whether a society's dominant ideology acknowledges the significance of class. For a public choice theorist, the concept of class is not only artificial but totally misleading. Individuals act on the basis of their perception of personal self-interest, not on the basis of class membership.

Conclusion

Members of different theoretical 'camps' have difficulty communicating with one another, largely because they cannot even agree on the 'facts'. This communication gap reflects the differences in the world views that underlie competing theoretical perspectives. An appeal to the 'facts' is unlikely to settle a theoretical dispute when the basic information, let alone its interpretation, is contested. An appeal to 'common sense' runs up against the same problem. A theory is like a story—it gives an account of some part of reality. The story will strike each of us as more or less convincing, and

TABLE 2.1 Three Theoretical Perspectives on Policy Formation

1. Level of analysis

Pluralist	Individuals, organized groups
Public Choice	Individuals
Marxist	Societal forces, classes

2. Major features of the perspective's world view

Pluralist	a) Voluntaristic: policy outcomes are relatively 'open' due to the fact that individuals, alone and collectively, act on the basis of attitudes and perceptions that are changeable b) Politics is competitive, although the competition may not be an equal one
Public Choice	a) Voluntaristic; the individual is the basic unit of social action b) Politics is competitive; power in the political marketplace is determined by control over resources that can be used as the basis of profitable exchange
Marxist	a) Deterministic; the antagonistic relationship between classes determines the course of history b) Politics is not competitive; patterns of domination/subordination derive from a society's mode of production

3. Chief constraints on policy-makers

Pluralist	Dominant ideology, balance of power between societal interests
Public Choice	The possession by non-state actors of resources that can be used to reward or punish the behaviour of state actors; competition between political and bureaucratic actors within the state and between levels of government
Marxist	The capitalist economic system; this includes a major structural constraint, i.e., the refusal of the business community to invest and its capacity to move production to another jurisdiction, and reinforcing ideological constraint, i.e., the widespread acceptance of values supportive of capitalism

4. How the state is viewed

Pluralist	a) Reactive, but with a margin of independence from societal interests: the state itself and its component parts have and pursue their own interests in addition to mediating societal ones b) Essentially democratic
Public Choice	a) Active and reactive; in pursuing their own self-interest state actors are compelled to respond to non-state actors, including voters, special interest groups, and media, whom they perceive as having the capacity to influence the attainment of their own goals b) Democratic but also heavily bureaucratic
Marxist	a) Reactive, but with a margin of independence from the narrower interests of individual capitalists; this independence enables the state to respond, within limits, to the demands of subordinate classes and to act in the general interest of capital b) Capitalist

thus we can evaluate different theoretical 'stories' in terms of the plausibility of each one's interpretation of experience. This is not a solution to the communication gap, however. It simply shifts the problem from the storytellers to their listeners. If a story's truth, like beauty, is in the eye of the beholder, then we are left with personal taste as the final judge of the validity of a particular theoretical story. And we are back to the proposition, dismissed earlier in this chapter, that theory is like opinion: a matter of personal preference.

Some differences in interpretation and explanation simply cannot be resolved and must ultimately be ascribed to the personal and social characteristics of the beholders. If two people look at Canadian society, one may see evidence of significant opportunities for upward socioeconomic mobility while the other sees evidence of the barriers to mobility. These two people may even agree on the numbers, but interpret them in very different ways.

Or consider the case of two people trying to explain the growth in social spending by the state in capitalist societies. One person points to a combination of the popular pressures generated by the growth of an urban–industrial society and the extension of voting rights to all adults, along with changing elite and popular views on the appropriate role of the state. The growth in social spending is explained as the product of popular demand and changing social values. A second person agrees that there has been increasing popular demand for social services and that ideas regarding both the scope and areas of appropriate state activity have changed. But this second person explains the growth in social spending as the product of class conflict under capitalism. Social spending by the state responds to the demands of the enfranchised subordinate classes that are produced by the twin processes of industrialization and urbanization. But it also responds to capital's need to preserve its ability to exploit the labour of subordinate classes. This is done by making public some of the social costs generated by the capitalist economy. Thus, according to this view, social spending attenuates class frictions by meeting the demands of subordinate classes while making sure that the burden of paying for social spending is not borne entirely (or even mainly) by the business community. Whereas the first explanation identifies the power of groups and ideas as the main determinants of the increase in social spending by the state, the second points to class conflict. *The difference in their explanation of this policy trend is likely to reflect differences in the answer they give to the question of who benefits from state action.* Where the first person emphasizes the benefits experienced by those who are the immediate consumers of social services, the second emphasizes the indirect benefits that capital enjoys. This difference in explanation is not one that an appeal to either the 'facts' or 'common sense' is likely to resolve.

If all the differences in the way theoretical perspectives interpret and explain the reality of policy formation were of this sort, one would be justified in treating all theories as if they were of equal worth. But in practical terms, agreement on some facts and their meanings obviously is possible; otherwise, there would be no basis for communication whatsoever. It is in this area of shared perception that useful comparison of these theories' explanatory power can be made and reinforced by appeals to objective empirical measures that test their assumptions.

Key Terms

accumulation policies Policies that directly support profit-oriented business activity.

culturalism An approach to understanding public policy that focuses on the structural influence of culture.

dynamic theories Theories of public policy that see the policy process as open to competitive influences.

environmental determinism A theory that sees the public policy process as structured by broad societal factors like culture and gender.

feminism An approach to understanding public policy that focuses on the structural influence of gender.

game theory A theory that explains the policy process by analogy with the characteristics of gaming and strategy.

globalization A theory that explains the policy process in terms of the influence of the global advancement of trade, technology, transportation, and liberal ideology.

incrementalism A theory of public policy that explains current policy as the result of minor changes to previous policy decisions and predicts slow, insignificant developments.

institutionalism A theory of public policy that views policy outcomes as being structured by the design of political institutions.

legitimation policies Policies that reduce interclass conflict by providing subordinate classes with benefits that reduce their dissatisfaction with the inequalities generated by the capitalist economy.

Marxist theory A theory that views public policy as a product of class divisions in society.

models Theoretical tools that use analogy and abstract visual imagery to create a linguistic representation of reality.

normative political theories Theories that do not merely try to explain public policy but also make moral judgments about its outcomes.

parsimonious The least complex explanation for an observation.

pluralist model A theory of public policy that sees the policy process as an open competition among organized interest groups.

positive theories Theories that attempt to explain the policy process as it is without making moral judgments about it. Positive theories emphasize scientific inquiry and empirical testing.

public choice theory An approach to understanding public policy that uses analogies with economic understandings of human behaviour to explain politics.

structuralist theories A category of theories of public policy that holds the policy process and its outcomes to be determined by the broad characteristics of society, such as class, gender, culture, economics, etc.

systems theory An approach to the study of public policy that views the policy process as a self-perpetuating system that structures its outcomes in order to maintain itself.

BOX 2.1 Ottawa's BHP Betrayal

The Canadian government has damaged the reputation of Canada as an open economy committed to free flows of capital by rejecting BHP Billiton's proposed US$39 billion bid for PotashCorp. In the process, it has created a major headache for BHP Billiton's Marius Kloppers, who has massive financial firepower that politicians and regulators are preventing him from deploying.

While BHP Billiton's ambition of acquiring PotashCorp isn't quite dead—the Canadians have given it 30 days to make further representations and offer further undertakings—the decision announced by Industry Minister Tony Clement is going to be very difficult to reverse.

That's despite the fact that PotashCorp is majority foreign owned already, that BHP Billiton would have ultimately distributed more than US$40 billion to PotashCorp shareholders, would have spent $12 billion developing its own Jansen potash project, would have provided thousands of new jobs, and would have relocated the effective head office of PotashCorp from Chicago to Saskatchewan.

BHP Billiton had offered to deal with the one obvious near-term adverse impact of the acquisition—the effect on Saskatchewan's revenues as the costs of developing Jansen were set against PotashCorp's earnings—by ensuring there was no tax impact. In the longer term, the Jansen project would increase the province's tax and economic bases.

While Clement's statement said the Canadian government remains committed to an open climate for investment, its actions have betrayed its words. The rejection will be interpreted as a turning point in its attitude toward foreign capital and can only encourage the protectionists.

Saskatchewan's premier, Brad Wall, responded to the decision by saying that the province was open to investment and takeovers, but there might be 'strategic considerations' that would be taken into account. 'Maybe Canada has entered a new phase in terms of how we look at these deals,' he said.

Those comments from the key figure in the campaign against BHP Billiton will reinforce perceptions that Canada's attitude toward foreign investment, particularly in the resource sector, has been altered quite fundamentally. Wall had previously, like the Harper government, been regarded as pro-business and supportive of foreign investment.

There is also an element of moral hazard created by the decision, which if maintained at the end of the 30 days would signal that PotashCorp—or any other large Canadian resource company—is takeover proof.

PotashCorp has fought ferociously against the takeover, stirring up parochial sentiment and trying to drum up competing bids from Chinese state-owned competitors, sovereign wealth funds, pension funds, and even its Russian competitors.

Presumably today's decision means that none of those parties would be allowed to achieve a controlling interest in the company, which would mean that Potash-Corp shareholders may have just seen their control premium expropriated.

For BHP Billiton and Kloppers, a final rejection of the bid for PotashCorp, following the aborted bid for Rio Tinto and the regulatory rejections of the proposed iron ore production joint venture, would be a massive setback to its growth ambitions.

If he is unable to make any meaningful acquisitions, . . . Kloppers will come under extreme pressure to return a lot of capital to shareholders.

The only obvious opportunity to deploy capital on a scale that would make a difference to the group . . . would appear to be the oil and gas sector.

Expanding its exposure to oil and gas would probably improve the resilience of its cash flows, but wouldn't bring the same level of benefit that acquiring Potash-Corp and entering a completely new market through a sector-leading, long-life, tier-one resource would have provided.

Source: Stephen Bartholomeusz, "Ottawa's BHP Betrayal," November 4, 2010, *The Business Spectator*

Discussion Questions

1. Based on Box 2.1, which theory of the public policy process do you think best explains the Conservative government's decision to not allow a foreign takeover of a Canadian company?

2. Testing theories of public policy empirically allows us to judge their scientific value. Can the normative or moral value systems that underlie theories of public policy also be judged objectively? For example, can one say definitively that the normative values that inform a theory are good or bad? Are there ways of deducing the answer to this question?

Websites

The following sites represent a variety of approaches to the study of policy. No research institute devotes itself exclusively to one perspective. Rather, these sites provide examples of how different research institutes represent the pluralist, public choice, and Marxist perspectives.

Canadian Centre for Policy Alternatives (CCPA)

www.policyalternatives.ca

CCPA is an independent, politically non-partisan research institute concerned with issues of social, economic, and environmental justice. It is known as a progressive voice in public policy debate.

C.D. Howe Institute

www.cdhowe.org

The C.D. Howe Institute is a national, politically non-partisan organization that focuses its efforts on using economic and social policy to raise Canadians' standard of living. Like the Fraser Institute, its work emphasizes free-market principles for policy-making.

Fraser Institute

www.fraserinstitute.org

The Fraser Institute is an independent educational organization focused on economic and social research. Its objective is to redirect public attention to the role played by free markets in providing for the well-being of Canadians.

Institute on Governance

www.iog.ca

The Institute on Governance works with a variety of partners, including government agencies, international organizations, NGOs (non-governmental organizations), and the private sector, to promote good governance. The range of 'Knowledge Areas' listed on its website—Aboriginal Governance, Board and Organizational Governance, Building Strong Partnerships, Health and Innovation, International Programming, and Modernizing Government—suggests a pluralist approach.

Parkland Institute

www.parklandinstitute.ca

This research network, based at the University of Alberta, operates within the distinctive tradition of Canadian political economy. Although politically it is non-partisan, its perspectives tend to suggest a Marxist approach.

CHAPTER 3
The Context of Policy-Making in Canada

Introduction

The path leading from an idea to its embodiment in public policy is sometimes short and direct. More often, however, it is long and sinuous, marked by detours, roadblocks, and even dead ends. Sometimes the path is barely visible, obscured by the struggle of contending interests and ideas, by the inconsistencies or contradictions of government action (and inaction), or by fuzziness in how an issue is defined. Some students of public policy have argued that actions typically precede policies: that governments act first and only then develop the justifications for their actions that we call public policies. But whether the idea comes first or the other way around, the process of policy-making is usually too complex for any one-size-fits-all explanation.

Attempts to understand the process of policy-making usually distinguish between what happens inside the state system—the 'black box' of Easton's systems model of politics—and the societal factors that influence the behaviour of policy-makers. It also has been usual to draw a distinction between the domestic and foreign policy-making processes, which focus on different sets of actors and influences. As Bruce Doern and his colleagues put it, 'experts in international political economy and foreign policy [tend] to concentrate on international relations, integration, and conflict but to oversimplify domestic politics and policy institutions.'[1] Those who study domestic politics and policy-making 'tend to treat international conditions simply as contextual factors and to ignore the influence of international agreements, regimes, and agencies'.[2]

These distinctions often do not hold up well under closer scrutiny. What Léon Dion called the *governmentalization of society*, and Alan Cairns described as the *embedded state*, undermines the usefulness of an analytical framework premised on the distinction between state and societal influences on policy. The phenomena of globalization and internationalization have increased the exposure of domestic institutions and interests to forces outside national borders, requiring that these forces be integrated into our understanding of how domestic policy-making works. A framework is needed to enable the student of public policy to identify those factors that affect policy, while avoiding the straitjacket of a priori thinking about the relative importance of these factors and the relationships between them.

This is a tall order. It is not our intention here to try to develop such an integrated framework for the understanding of policy. Instead, we will examine several **contextual influences** on policy that constitute the background of policy-making. These influences may be distinguished from **proximate influences**, including the machinery of government, political parties, interest groups, and so on, whose impact on policy is more direct. These two sets of factors are listed in Table 3.1.

TABLE 3.1 Contextual and Proximate Influences on Policy-Making

Contextual	Proximate
political culture	the cabinet
the Constitution	the legislature
characteristics of the economy and society	courts
globalization	media system
	public opinion
	political parties
	interest groups
	social movements

Contextual Influences on Policy-Making

1. Political Culture

Political culture consists of the dominant and relatively durable beliefs and values concerning political life that characterize a society. These ideas involve the sorts of things that are generally taken for granted, such as the goodness of equality or the importance of respect for authority, and are shared by the vast majority of the population. A broad consensus on fundamental political values and beliefs is an important ingredient for political stability. Where this consensus is lacking or subject to stress, the peaceful resolution of political differences becomes more difficult and the job of governing becomes more problematic.

There is no agreement on the character of political culture in Canada. Indeed, disagreement begins with the question of whether Canada has one, two, or several distinct political cultures. Those who argue that there is a single Canadian political culture almost always describe that culture in comparison to the United States. In this vein, Canada's tradition is said to be counterrevolutionary, in contrast to the revolutionary tradition of the United States, and Canadians are perceived as being more deferential toward authority, more collectivist and less individualistic (this view is often reflected in claims that Canadians are more caring and compassionate than Americans), more tolerant of hierarchical social distinctions, and so on.[3]

Those who argue that Canada has two distinct political cultures associate these cultures with the two dominant language communities, French and English. One branch of this approach developed out of the **fragment theory** of Louis Hartz and has been applied to the Canadian case by Kenneth McRae and Gad Horowitz, among others.[4]

It characterizes English-speaking Canada as a liberal society with Tory 'touches'—the importance of these Tory elements has long been a matter of dispute—and French-speaking Canada as a pre-liberal feudal society whose democratization and liberalization were retarded by its feudal past.

A third approach to Canadian political culture focuses on the distinctions between regions within English-speaking Canada. It accepts, of course, that French Canada has a distinctive political culture, generally associated with the region of Quebec. But it also insists that the different histories of regions in English Canada, including their different demographic and economic characteristics, have created distinct regional political cultures. The precise number of these regions is a matter for debate. Some go so far as to argue that each of the 10 provinces deserves to be treated as a distinct political culture. More commonly, however, there are said to be four or five main regional political cultures: Ontario, Quebec, the West (or British Columbia and the Prairies), and Atlantic Canada (although Newfoundland is sometimes treated as a culturally distinct region).

From the standpoint of influence on public policy, all three views of Canada's political culture have been significant, but the two-culture image has tended to be the most important. Indeed, the idea of Canada as a partnership between two founding peoples, English and French, has affected the processes and substance of policy from Confederation to the present. Nationalist spokespersons for French Canada, and since the 1960s for Quebec, have always insisted that the differences between the two founding communities go beyond language and that the constitutional arrangements between French- and English-speaking Canada must allow the francophone population to protect its distinctive traditions.

The two-culture image of Canada has long generated resentment in Western Canada, and to a lesser degree in the East. To depict Canada as a partnership between two founding cultures is inevitably to diminish or even deny the importance not only of regional cultures outside the Ontario–Quebec core but of Aboriginal peoples as well. Westerners in particular have long complained that their interests and distinctive histories have been marginalized by the two-culture narrative, which they say is actually the story of central Canada. The roots of western alienation have been nurtured not only by the West's economic and political grievances against Ottawa and central Canada, but also by a long-standing sense that the region has been excluded from the image of Canada projected by federal policies and institutions, and by central Canadian media and intellectual elites whose centres of gravity are Toronto and Montreal.[5]

There is no doubt that most Canadians in *all* regions and in *both* of the country's two major language communities share many fundamental values and beliefs about politics. The political culture they share is clearly liberal-democratic, with core values that include respect for individual freedom, equality of rights, limited government, and belief in the market economy. These abstract notions are no doubt understood somewhat differently in various parts of Canada, or between sociologically distinct segments of the population. For example, it may well be, as many argue, that the collectivist tradition is stronger in French-speaking Quebec than in the predominantly English-speaking provinces. And it is certainly true that patterns of political participation and political trust, sense of political efficacy, and regional versus national identities vary between the regions of Canada. But one finds the same sorts of variations in the United States, France, Britain, Italy, and elsewhere. Cultural differences linked to region or group identification can coexist with a broad consensus on fundamental values and beliefs.

In the case of Canada, part of this broad consensus, or political tradition, has involved expectations for the state. Philip Resnick, among others, argues that Canada has a *statist* political tradition. This is a political tradition characterized by a relatively strong political executive and by a population that tends to be deferential toward those in power. The adoption of British parliamentary government, first in the colonial legislatures during the mid-1800s and then through the British North America (BNA) Act, mainly reaffirmed the tradition of centralized executive authority that had existed before the elected legislature's approval was needed to pass laws. This reaffirmation of strong executive powers, Resnick argues, is apparent throughout the BNA Act:

> What our Founding Fathers were doing was consolidating an orderly move from direct colonial rule to House Rule. They had a particular kind of [political] order in mind, the parliamentary system as it had evolved in Britain, combining the interests of monarchs, lords and commoners. If by the latter part of the 19th century this system was increasingly responsive to the wishes of an electorate, restricted or enlarged, it was by no means a servant of the electorate.[6]

The institutions of government adopted through the Confederation agreement and, equally important, the expectations of the political elites who controlled the levers of state power shaped the future course of Canadian politics. Parliament was sovereign, but Parliament was not merely the people. It also included the Crown, the traditional seat of state authority whose powers came to be exercised by a prime minister and cabinet with few serious checks from the legislature. 'Parliamentary sovereignty', Resnick claims, 'fostered attitudes in the population which were nominally participatory but maximally deferential towards those exercising political power. The mystique of British Crown and Constitution helped make illegitimate *all* forms of political activity not sanctioned or channeled through parliamentary institutions.'[7] This is an important point. Resnick is arguing that the more deferential political culture of Canada, as compared to the United States, did not simply happen but was to some degree created by parliamentary institutions that discouraged popular participation in politics, beyond the rituals of voting, and that enshrined a sort of top-down philosophy of governance.

Is Resnick right? The evidence suggests that he is. There have, of course, been influential currents of participatory politics in Canadian history, particularly coming out of Western Canada. But these populist inclinations have had to struggle against a parliamentary tradition that concentrates political power in the hands of the prime minister (or premiers) and cabinet. This style of governance is epitomized in the long tradition of elite deal-making that has characterized federal–provincial relations. But it also surfaces when this country's political leaders reject referendums or constituent assemblies on constitutional change as 'un-Canadian' or foreign to our political tradition. Indeed, the statist political tradition fostered by British parliamentary government is apparent in a multitude of ways. 'Our governments', explains Resnick, '. . . become the organizers of our civic consciousness. National celebrations in the vein of Expo have to be staged; nationalist propaganda is transmitted across the airwaves, through the newspapers, along with our social security cheques.'[8] Many argue that the Canadian state's orchestration of culture has been a defensive response to the Americanizing pressures from mass media industries centred in the United States. To some degree this is certainly true. But this explanation of state-centred nationalism in Canada does not pay adequate attention to the possibility that the state's efforts may pre-empt those of groups in civil society and encourage a climate of dependence on governments to, in Resnick's words, 'organize our civic consciousness'.

The statist political tradition that Resnick criticizes is also one that he and others on the left defend when it comes to state provision and financing of social services and various entitlements associated with the welfare state. This became one of the chief battlegrounds in Canadian politics in the 1990s, as governments cut back on social spending while trying not to run afoul of core citizen beliefs concerning equality and the role of government. In this regard the actions of the Liberal government in Ottawa, along with the Conservative governments in Alberta and Ontario, illustrate well how policy-makers react to the constraints of political culture. These three governments were among the most vigorous in cutting government spending, including spending on social programs. But in selling these cuts to their respective electorates, cuts that critics portrayed as a betrayal of fundamental Canadian values, these governments associated their actions with other values that are likewise important to Canadians, including self-reliance, limited government, and what are often labelled 'traditional' family values.[9]

In practice, Canadian cultural policy has two major themes: language and multiculturalism. Since the Royal Commission on Bilingualism and Biculturalism (B&B Commission) issued the final volume of its report,[10] these themes have often been linked in the official rhetoric of federal cultural policy. 'Multiculturalism within a bilingual framework' expresses the efforts of successive federal governments to manage the long-standing tensions in relations between French and English Canada in a way that also satisfies other ethnolinguistic groups' demands for a share in the Canadian symbolic order. In terms of the money devoted to these policy goals and the measures taken to achieve them, there is no question that the emphasis has been on the bilingual framework rather than on multiculturalism.

Multicultural Policy

One of the platitudes of Canadian popular sociology and history is that Canadian society is more tolerant toward ethnic and cultural diversity than is the highly individualistic society of the United States. Thomas Berger writes that 'We in Canada do not share the American goal, often reiterated . . . , of integration and assimilation. We believe that diversity is not inconsistent with a common citizenship.'[11] The familiar metaphors of the Canadian 'mosaic' and the American 'melting pot' are intended to convey this difference in the pressures on minority ethnic group members to discard their distinctive cultures.

What is 'culture' for purposes of multicultural policy? The term connotes membership in a group marked off from others by its origins. In practice, this kind of 'culture' is identical to ethnicity, evoking the traditional beliefs and practices of a biological descent group. As Harold R. Isaacs writes, 'It is the identity made up of what a person is born with or acquires at birth,'[12] an inheritance whose most important features are language, religion, and the characteristic ways of perceiving and evaluating experience that are the product of the group's history. Culture in the sense of ethnic group is exclusionary, demarcating one tribe and its idols from another.[13]

Contrary to the expectations of modernization theory, these ethnic identities persist despite the homogenizing pressures of global communications, modern technology, and urbanization. Indeed, it is popular among students of ethnicity to speak of the resurgence of ethnic cultures and attachments. This resurgence is attributed by many to the inability of individuals to find personal fulfillment in modern societies whose icons—McDonald's arches, the plastic credit card, television, the Internet—glorify uniformity of experience.

Conferring official status on a group's language or devoting public revenue to teaching its children the language of their ancestors provides these groups with obvious material benefits. But as Raymond Breton observes, 'public institutions and their authorities are involved in the distribution of symbols as well as material resources.'[14] He continues:

> They dispense recognition and honour. They allocate possibilities for identification with purposes that have significance beyond an individual's limited experience. They distribute opportunities for meaningful social roles. . . . Accordingly, a well-developed symbolic/cultural system can be perceived as inadequate by particular linguistic or ethnocultural groups, in the sense that they feel disadvantaged relative to other groups as far as possibilities of identification, meaningfulness and recognition are concerned.[15]

In other words, public policy and the very structure of the state may reinforce the self-esteem of members of an ethnocultural group by providing them with a reflection of themselves. The ways this may be accomplished range from the appointment of group 'representatives' to highly visible positions within the state system to incorporating the group's traditions into public events such as Canada Day celebrations.

The psychological significance of such symbolic recognition cannot be denied. Nevertheless, the possibility that multicultural policy may degenerate into mere tokenism and ethnic folk dances is great. The increased representation of minority ethnic groups in the celebrations and institutions of public life may promote a sense of being part of the society. But this is not the same as reducing the barriers to their fuller participation in that society and in its economy. The difference between symbolism and material conditions is dramatically illustrated by the gap between Ottawa's integration of the symbols of Aboriginal culture into public celebrations and even the structure of the state, on the one hand, and on the other the continuing exclusion of Aboriginal Canadians from the economic benefits of society. Soapstone carvings given to foreign dignitaries, conferences on Aboriginal issues, and a monumental Royal Commission on Aboriginal Peoples have not been accompanied by significant improvement in the living standards of Aboriginal Canadians or by resolution of issues relating to land claims and self-government. A cynic might suggest that the concern with symbolic distribution may even act as a substitute for more substantive policy.

It is generally agreed that Ottawa's adoption in 1971 of an official policy of multicul-turalism was a direct response to the concerns expressed by ethnic organizations to the 'two nations' vision of Canada that had been the original focus of the B&B Commis-sion and was explicit in the policy of official bilingualism. Indeed, the fourth volume of the B&B report, titled *The Other Canadians*, emphasized the need for a vision that would go beyond the 'two nations' thesis. As Raymond Breton put it, the concerns of ethnic organizations 'reflected status anxiety—fear of being defined as second-class citizens, marginal to the identity system being redefined'.[16] At the same time as official multiculturalism met the symbolic concerns of ethnic group leaders, it also was a clear refutation of the 'two nations' view of Canada advocated by the supporters of special status or independence for Quebec.[17] Thus, the policy was symbolically important on two fronts. It gave *recognition* to the claims of ethnic organizations while at the same time it deprived Quebec nationalists of the legitimacy that a policy of biculturalism would have bestowed on their particular vision of Canadian pluralism. Interestingly, two studies within three years of the policy's adoption found that only about one in five 'ethnic' Canadians was even aware that such a policy existed, and that Canadians generally rejected the idea of using public money for the promotion of multicultural-ism.[18] Given this low level of both popular awareness and support for multiculturalism, it would appear that the main beneficiaries of the symbolic recognition of non-French, non-British cultures were the ethnic organizations that received status and funding under the policy.

With regard to state expenditures, the amounts spent on multicultural programs are paltry. Most of these programs are financed through the budget of Heritage Canada, whose total spending of about $1.1 billion in 2010 represents less than 1 per cent of all program spending.[19] Only a small portion of this money was devoted to programs intended to promote multiculturalism, including annual funding for national ethno-cultural organizations; the establishment and operation of multicultural associations, centres, and events; language and other instruction for immigrants; language instruc-tion in heritage-language programs administered by some provinces; support for uni-versity teaching and research in ethnic studies; assistance to ethnic writers, publishers, and the performing and visual arts communities; and advertising to promote popular acceptance of ethnic and racial diversity. As is the case with most other areas of cultural support, final approval of all grants administered under Ottawa's multiculturalism pro-gram lies with cabinet rather than with an independent agency, which leaves open the possibility that funding decisions may be influenced by partisan considerations. Even in the absence of obvious political interference, the existing system for funding ethno-cultural organizations and activities clearly contains a built-in bias toward established ethnic organizations that have received funding in the past and toward those groups that are the most articulate and best organized.

The fact that multiculturalism is part of the lexicon of Canadian politics reflects the ethnically diverse character of Canadian society. The share of the population with nei-ther British nor French origins has increased steadily since the post–World War II wave of immigration to Canada, from about one-fifth in 1951 to around one-third today. This increase reflects both the changing mix of immigration and, more recently, the higher birth rates among 'new' Canadians in comparison to those of British and French origins. One of the most striking aspects of immigration over the past two decades has been the dramatic increase in people with non-European origins. Whereas European immigrants accounted for 78.8 per cent of all immigration to Canada in 1959, they accounted for only 16.6 per cent in 2009. Today more than half of Canada's immigrants come from Asia: 56 per cent in 2009.[20] The shift in immigration patterns over the last six decades can be seen in Figure 3.1. From 1959 to 1979, European immigrants to Canada dropped by half from the previous decade. By contrast, the number of people from Asia immigrating to Canada went from 5.2 per cent to 41.8 per cent during that same time period. This pattern has led to a marked increase in the size of Canada's 'visible minority' population. In response to incidents of interracial tension in some major urban centres—particularly Toronto, Montreal, and Vancouver, where much of the non-white immigrant population is located—and to studies suggesting that racist attitudes are widespread in Canada,[21] the federal government and some provincial governments have made the elimination of racial discrimination a major component of multicultural policy.

Unlike the policy of official multiculturalism adopted by Ottawa in 1971, policy on racial discrimination aims to provide both material and symbolic benefits to visible minorities. The emphasis is less on promoting cultural expression than on removing the barriers to the equal participation of racial minorities in the economy and in society. In practice this means that the private sector is a major target of this more recent thrust of multicultural policy. Human rights legislation that prohibits racial discrimination in areas such as employment and accommodation is one of the instruments for dealing

FIGURE 3.1 Main Regions of Birth for Immigrants to Canada, 1959–2009

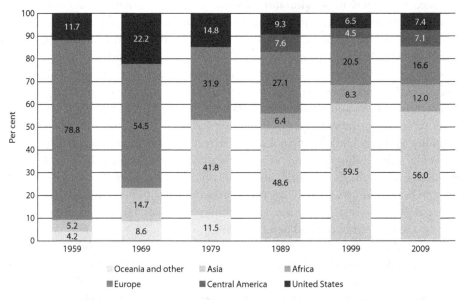

Source: CANSIM Tables, 'Immigrants to Canada by Country of Last Permanent Residence, Quarterly (Persons)', Volumes 16, 17, 27, 33, 34, 37, 38, 39, 40.

with racial inequality in the private sector. This is, however, an *ex post facto* remedy in that it comes into play only after an alleged incident of discrimination has taken place. In relying on the possibility of legal penalties against those who are found guilty of racial discrimination, this approach does not address the racist attitudes at the root of such behaviour. The pervasiveness of racism in grosser or subtler forms in societies around the world suggests that such attitudes are not easily changed and that public spending on media campaigns to promote racial harmony probably has a marginal impact at best. As in the case of state subsidies to ethnocultural organizations, spending on television advertisements, posters, and other visual portrayals of a multiracial society is best understood as an investment in symbolic politics, intended to affect the distribution of symbolic rather than material benefits in society.

Following the long-standing American practice of affirmative action for racial minorities, both Ottawa and some provincial governments have adopted a policy of increasing the representation of visible minorities in the public service. At the federal level this policy is administered through the Public Service Commission. During the 1980s, **affirmative action** was pursued mainly through a system of employment *targets* and *incentives* for departments to meet, instead of through *mandatory quotas* on group representation.

Governments in Canada continue to use targets and incentives, but in addition some of them now have mandatory quota systems (generally labelled 'employment equity' policies). For example, an RCMP memo came to light in 1991 indicating that all new hirings should be of women and targeted minorities. The Metropolitan Toronto Police force has a similar policy in place. It is well known that some governments (e.g., the NDP government of Ontario, 1990–5) have also discriminated against white males, although they have denied having any mandatory affirmative action policy. Parapublic institutions such as colleges and universities and private-sector companies that do business with the federal government have adopted affirmative action policies partly in response to the requirements of the Federal Contractors Program. This requires organizations receiving federal contracts to develop a census of their workforce, indicating such things as gender and visible minority representation, and to implement affirmative action programs under federal supervision.

2. The Constitution

As befits Canada's historical circumstances as a former colony of Great Britain and a geographic and, in many ways, sociological extension of the United States, the Canadian Constitution represents a synthesis of principles developed from the experiences of these other countries. From Great Britain the founders took parliamentary government and the host of conventions governing relations among the executive, legislative, and judicial branches of the state. The federal form of government, by contrast, is clearly based on the American model. Unlike American federalism, the Canadian version included a number of provisions that appeared to, and certainly in the minds of the founders were intended to, establish a centralized form of federalism.[22] A combination of economic and social pressures, aided by some 'imaginative' court decisions during the first several decades of this country's history, produced a very different reality.

A **constitution** is the fundamental law of a political system. It is a set of rules, either written down in documents like the Constitution Act, 1867, and the Constitution Act, 1982,[23] or in the form of unwritten conventions such as the principle that the leader of the party commanding the greatest number of seats in the legislature is called on to become the prime minister. A constitution regulates the relationships between parts of the state system and between the government and the governed. In a federal political system, in which the constitution establishes two levels of government, each possessing exclusive authority to legislate regarding certain subjects, the constitution also regulates relations between the national and regional state systems. An essential feature of constitutional democracies is an independent judiciary whose role is to interpret the constitution when its meaning is in dispute.

Canada's Constitution includes both written documents and unwritten **conventions**.[24] The unwritten conventions of the Canadian Constitution can be divided into two categories: those regulating relations between parts of the state system, and those regulating federal–provincial relations. Canada inherited from Great Britain a number of customary rules and traditional practices pertaining to the powers of and relations between parts of the state system. This British parliamentary inheritance is expressed in the preamble to the Constitution Act, 1867 (formerly known as the British North America Act), which states that the new country has adopted 'a Constitution similar in Principle to that of the United Kingdom'.

Among the most important of these conventions of parliamentary government are the following:

1. *Those pertaining to the prime minister and cabinet.* Examples include the conventions that the leader of the political party with the most seats in the legislature becomes prime minister and has the right to appoint a cabinet, that members of the cabinet will not publicly dissent from government policy, and that any minister who does dissent must resign from the cabinet.
2. *Those pertaining to the relationship between the government and the legislature.* Most important of these is the principle of **responsible government**. This is a convention requiring that a government must enjoy the support of a majority of members of the legislature to govern. If this support is lost, as on a vote of non-confidence or a vote on spending legislation, the government is obligated to resign.
3. *Those pertaining to the relationship between the Crown, represented in Canada by the Governor General, and the government.* Since the 1926 conflict between Governor General Lord Byng and prime minister Mackenzie King, it has become accepted that the Governor General is required to accept the 'advice' of the prime minister regarding the dissolution of Parliament and the calling of an election.
4. *Those pertaining to relations between the government and the bureaucracy.* Particularly important here are the requirements that the bureaucracy be non-partisan and that it serve the government of the day.
5. *Those pertaining to the internal operations of Parliament.* These conventions include the rights of the opposition parties in Parliament and the privilege of parliamentary immunity enjoyed by all legislators.

Since the United Kingdom is not a federal state, Canada's British parliamentary inheritance provides no guidance for the relationship between the federal and provincial governments. Here one must look to the written Constitution and the practices that have come to define the responsibilities and resources of each level of government in Canada and the procedures they follow in dealing with one another.

Having two levels of government—each with its own bases of legislative authority and sources of revenue, independent of the other—does not in itself complicate the policy-making process. Countries with unitary state systems may also be characterized by significant regional divisions that surface in policy-making in other forms (France, Great Britain, and Italy are good examples). In those countries interregional conflict is expressed through national political institutions, such as the legislature, or through extra-governmental components of the political system, such as political parties and social movements. In fact, national institutions may be the principal channels for the expression and mediation of regional interests even in federalized state systems. This is the case in the United States, where members of Congress, especially senators and committee chairpersons, are often more effective advocates of regional interests than most state governors.

The significance of federalism, particularly in a country where the regional states have substantial law-making and taxing powers, is that it is more likely than a unitary state system to reinforce the regional divisions that were likely responsible for the adoption of federalism in the first place. Canadian political scientist Alan Cairns argues that Canada's decentralized version of federalism is 'a function not of societies but of the constitution, and more importantly of the governments that work the constitution'.[25] He writes:

> Governing elites view their task as the injection of provincial or federal meaning into society, giving it a degree of coherence and a pattern of interdependence more suited for government purposes than would emerge from the unhindered working of social and market forces . . . . each government transmits cues and pressures to the environment, thus tending to group the interests manipulated by its policies into webs of interdependence springing from the particular version of socio-economic integration it is pursuing. Provincial governments work toward the creation of limited versions of a politically created provincial society and economy, and the national government works toward the creation of a country-wide society and economy.[26]

Cairns is saying that it is rational for politicians and bureaucrats at each level of government to behave in ways that are likely to increase their control over the factors relevant to the future of the organizations they belong to. These factors would include sources of revenue, the authority to regulate social and economic activity, and the support of citizens and organized interests.

Federal–provincial relations are regulated by both the written Constitution and the unwritten conventions that have developed over time. Canadian federalism is characterized by overlapping jurisdictions, shared revenue sources, and a high degree of administrative co-operation and executive interaction between the federal and provincial states. This is so despite a Constitution that includes a lengthy enumeration of the 'exclusive' legislative powers of each level of government. The founders' clear intention to assign the national government 'ample authority for the great task of nation-building entrusted to it',[27] leaving to the provincial governments what at the time appeared to be relatively unimportant powers over social, cultural, and local matters, was soon undermined by a combination of assertive provincial governments and decentralist constitutional rulings by the Judicial Committee of the Privy Council in Great Britain.[28]

Constitutional conventions are of vital importance for the financial dimension of federalism, for the process of intergovernmental relations, and for the making and implementation of foreign policy. The division of powers set down in the Canadian Constitution and interpreted by the courts is complicated by the intricate network of financial and administrative agreements negotiated between Ottawa and the provinces. Some of the most important of these agreements are in the area of social policy, where the federal government annually transfers billions of dollars to the provinces in aid of provincially administered services. The process by which negotiation on such matters takes place is not established by constitutional law. Instead, it is bounded by certain conventional practices such as the annual meetings of the prime minister and the provincial premiers. In the case of foreign policy, consultation with provincial governments and in some cases provincial representation on the Canadian negotiating team are conventional practices followed in making policy. These practices are necessitated by the fact that although only the federal government has the authority to enter into agreements with other sovereign states, the subject matter of such agreements may fall within provincial jurisdiction; implementation of those agreements may therefore require provincial concurrence.[29]

Federal–provincial relations in Canada involve a continuous and multi-level process of consultation and bargaining between policy-makers representing Ottawa and the provinces. The term **executive federalism** is commonly used to refer to this process. As Richard Simeon has argued, it often resembles the bargaining that occurs in international politics between sovereign governments.[30] It is a process from which legislatures are almost entirely excluded, except when they are called on to ratify an agreement reached between executives of the two levels of government.

Canada's Constitution has two main effects on the policy-making process. The British parliamentary system concentrates power with the cabinet, which is the prism through which virtually all important policy decisions must pass and which generally is able to control the legislative agenda. Because the policy agenda is determined chiefly by the cabinet, those with an interest in influencing policy often focus their efforts on the cabinet and those parts of the state system that influence the cabinet's choices or implement its decisions.

The second main effect that Canada's Constitution has on the policy process is to magnify the significance of regional divisions. The legislative powers the Constitution assigns to the provinces have turned out to be very important. Combined with the relative weakness of national institutions for representing regional interests, this has meant that the provincial governments emerged early as the main spokespersons for these regionally based interests. Consequently, regional conflicts are usually jurisdictional conflicts. The particular character of Canada's Constitution has meant that the ways in which policy issues are defined and conflicts played out tend to highlight regional divisions.

A major reform of the Canadian Constitution took place in 1982, when the Charter of Rights and Freedoms became law. The Charter is widely seen as a major step toward the democratization of the Constitution and policy-making. Alan Cairns has described it as the basis for what he called a 'citizens' constitution', as opposed to the old 'governments' constitution' of federalism. Those older parts of the Constitution are still with us, of course. Cairns's point is simply this: Whereas during the pre-Charter era the Canadian Constitution was primarily about the 'rights' of governments, since 1982 much of our constitutional discourse and activity has focused on the rights of individuals and groups—rights that may take precedence over the legislative powers of governments. This would appear to be a blow to the elitist style of policy-making that was nurtured under the governments' constitution of federalism.

Cairns is right, but only to a point. The real beginning of what he calls the era of the citizens' constitution was Ottawa's 1992 decision—a decision that it made late and reluctantly—to hold a national referendum on the Charlottetown Accord. The Accord itself was the product of a pluralistic policy-making style that broadened the range of consultation, originally limited to first ministers, to include the leaders of groups representing Aboriginal Canadians, women, labour, business, official-language minorities, ethnic and racial minorities, and so on. Yet despite the unprecedented breadth of this consultation process, many believed that the constitution-making process remained highly elitist for two reasons. First, greater consultation and the informal participation of non-state elites in the negotiations on constitutional reform did not mean that popular consent, expressed directly by the people, had been accepted as an indispensible condition of the amendment process. Second, the form of politics that emerged in Canada under the influence of the Charter of Rights and Freedoms, and that was so much in evidence between the demise of the Meech Lake Accord in 1987 and the signing of the Charlottetown Accord in 1992, was still highly elitist. Cairns's assertion that the Charter has encouraged citizens to think of themselves as rights-bearers, and that this has generated a 'political culture increasingly sympathetic to constitutional participation by citizens, at least when their own status and rights are likely to be affected',[31] implies a new populism; until the actual referendum campaign, however, that populism was stifled by the special interest politics that the Charter had encouraged.

Ted Morton and Rainer Knopff make this point in explaining what they believe to be the true character of Charter politics. They note the proliferation and heightened public profile of 'the new citizens interest groups that have sprung up around *their* sections of the Charter'.[32] Morton and Knopff call these groups the 'Court Party' because they rely on the courts and quasi-judicial human rights tribunals to achieve their goals. But these groups also use the media to influence the terms and trajectory of political discourse. Indeed, there are broad affinities of ideological outlook, education, and socioeconomic background, as well as a complementarity of interests, between the media and these rights-seeking groups. The 'rights talk' they generate and their apparent ability to speak on behalf of grassroots constituencies create the impression that Canadian politics has been democratized and made more participatory by the Charter. This impression is false. As Morton argues:

> [The Charter] has shifted responsibility for a growing sphere of policy issues into a new arena where the costs of participation are prohibitive and debate is conducted in a foreign language—*Charterese*, a dialect of *legalese*. Politically [this] represents a horizontal transfer of power to a new elite, not a vertical transfer of power to the people.[33]

The same may be said of the more specialized case of constitutional reform. The apparent opening up of the policy-making process after the elitist debacle of the Meech Lake Accord represented a shift toward polyarchy, not an embrace of populist democracy. The message of the negotiations that produced the 1992 Charlottetown Accord was that consent has a group basis—a message consistent with Canada's deferential political culture. Groups purporting to represent various citizen identities encouraged by Charter politics staked out their right to a voice in the process of constitutional reform. But public opinion and citizens qua citizens remained at a distant remove from the policy-making process.

3. Social and Economic Characteristics

Protection for the French language in Canada has been on the policy agenda since before Confederation. It remains on the agenda because more than one-fifth of the Canadian population is francophone and about 80 per cent of these French-speakers reside in Quebec.[34] This is an obvious example of how the social characteristics of a country can influence its politics, including the issues that get onto the policy agenda. But there is no guarantee that every important social or economic issue will reach that agenda. The political cleavages and controversies that exist within any given society are determined by a number of factors, including the structural features of the political system, the political culture, and the society's history.

Policy issues do not just come into being; they have to be defined. Likewise, interests and identities require learning and mobilization. This being said, it nevertheless is the case that the social and economic characteristics of a society make the emergence of certain issues more likely than others. Donald Smiley once wrote that Canadian politics has had three main axes: the relations between its French- and English-speaking communities, the Canada–United States relationship, and the regional dimensions of Canadian political life.[35] These correspond to three of the country's most prominent social and economic characteristics: the existence and historically unequal circumstances of two major language communities; close economic, cultural, and political ties to the United States; and the economic diversity and disparities between regions of Canada.

Language Policy

The origins of present-day language policy in Canada lie in developments in Quebec during the 1960s. The 'Quiet Revolution' is the label generally used to describe the various institutional reforms put in place in Quebec during this decade, including the creation of several important state enterprises and the transfer of authority over the province's educational system from the Roman Catholic Church to the state. More important, however, the term expresses the revolutionary shift away from a traditional ideology that had stressed the *preservation* of the distinctive cultural values and social characteristics of French-speaking Quebec, including the French language, the Catholic religion, and the centrality of rural life to the ideal of French Canada.

Successive federal governments since the 1960s have pursued a language policy based on a conception of French and English Canada that cuts across provincial borders. Responding to the new assertive nationalism of the Quiet Revolution—the signs of which ranged from Quebec's demands for greater taxation powers and less federal interference in areas of provincial constitutional responsibility to the bombs placed in mailboxes and public monuments—the Liberal government of Lester Pearson established the Royal Commission on Bilingualism and Biculturalism. As Eric Waddell writes, 'The federal government was facing a legitimacy crisis in the 1960s and 1970s and had the immediate task of proposing a Canadian alternative to Quebec nationalism.'[36] The B&B Commission was a first step toward the federal government's adoption of a policy of official bilingualism. This policy was intended to defuse the *indépendantiste* sentiment building in Quebec, especially among young francophones, in part by opening Ottawa as a field of career opportunities to rival the Quebec public service, the growth and professionalization of which had been central to the Quiet Revolution.

The alternative that Ottawa offered, expressed in the federalist philosophy of Pierre Trudeau, was a Canada in which language rights would be guaranteed to the individual and protected by national institutions. In practical terms this meant changing the overwhelmingly anglophone character of the federal state so that francophones would no longer have reason to see it as an 'alien' level of government from which they were largely excluded. These changes have been carried out on two main fronts. First, what Raymond Breton refers to as the 'Canadian symbolic order' has been transformed since the 1960s.[37] A new flag, the proclamation of 'O Canada' as the official national anthem, new designs for stamps and currency, and the language-neutering of some federal institutions, documents, and celebrations (for example, Trans-Canada Airlines became Air Canada, the BNA Act is now officially titled the Constitution Act, and Dominion Day was renamed Canada Day) were all part of a deliberate effort to create symbols that would not alienate French Canadians by reminding them of the colonial past and British domination. Second, the passage of the Official Languages Act (1969) gave statutory expression to the policy of bilingualism that had first begun to take shape under prime minister lester Pearson. This Act established the Office of the Commissioner of Official Languages as a watchdog agency to monitor the three main components of language equality set forth in the Act:

- Canadians' right to be served by the federal government in the official language of their choice;
- equitable representation of francophones and anglophones in the federal public service; and

- the right of public servants of both language groups to work in the language of their choice.

The fact that francophones' representation in the federal state was less than their share of the national population was the situation the Official Languages Act was intended to redress. Francophone under-representation was greatest in managerial, scientific, and technical job categories. Moreover, the language of the public service—the language that officials worked in and, in most parts of the country, the one that citizens could realistically be expected to be served in—was English. In view of these circumstances, Ottawa's claim to represent the interests of francophones lacked credibility.

Among the main actions taken to increase the bilingual character of the federal bureaucracy were the designation of an increasing share of positions as bilingual, language training for public servants, and the creation of the National Capital Region as the office blocks of the federal government spread into Hull, Quebec, during the 1970s. Since two of the objectives of the Official Languages Act were to increase the number of francophones recruited into the public service and to improve francophones' opportunities for upward mobility within it, the designation of positions according to their linguistic requirements has been the most significant feature of Ottawa's language policy. As of March 31, 2004, 39 per cent of positions in the public service were designated bilingual.[38] The popular perception that one must be bilingual to be hired by the federal public service is quite simply wrong. In fact, outside Quebec and the Ottawa–Hull region there are comparatively few positions in the federal bureaucracy that require mastery of both French and English.

Evidence on recruitment to the federal public service and upward mobility within it demonstrate that the linguistic designation of positions *has* worked to the advantage of francophones. A clear majority of bilingual positions are filled by francophones, and 79 per cent of francophones in the public service perform bilingual functions.[39] But as various Commissioners of Official Languages regularly observed, increased representation of francophones should not be taken as an indication that French and English are approaching greater equality as *languages of work* in the federal state. Outside of federal departments and agencies located in Quebec, the language of work remains predominantly English. The domination of English as the lingua franca of the bureaucracy persists even in the National Capital Region. This led the former Commissioner, D'Iberville Fortier, to conclude that French had become a valuable attribute from the standpoint of career advancement, without becoming a working language on par with English.[40] Box 3.1 outlines some of the struggles the Canadian Forces have had in ensuring that they are respecting the official-languages preferences of their personnel.

Ottawa's language policy received two additional thrusts in the 1970s. The first of these involved financial assistance for organizations and individuals seeking to defend or expand the rights of official-language minorities and for local francophone cultural organizations outside Quebec, including financial support for court challenges to provincial laws affecting language rights. Among the challenges financed by Ottawa were Supreme Court decisions in 1979 and 1985 that established the official status of French in the province of Manitoba[41] and successful challenges to the restrictions on

---

BOX 3.1   Audit of the Individual Training and Education System of the Canadian Forces

---

The Individual Training and Education System allows the Canadian Forces to effectively fulfill its mandate in Canada and abroad and is an essential part of the career path of all military personnel. Respect for official languages under this system is therefore crucial.

Objective

The purpose of the audit was to determine whether military personnel in both language groups have access to training in the official language of their choice, and to ensure that there are no barriers to employment or advancement because of their choice of language of instruction.

Data Collection

The audit began in June 2008 and data were collected between September 2008 and January 2009. During visits in Canadian Forces training establishments and at National Defence Headquarters, the audit team met with more than 600 people, including 250 students, from all elements of the Canadian Forces.

Findings

During the audit, we assessed four major areas related to official languages in the Individual Training and Education System:
- strategic and operational planning
- governance
- recruitment, posting and advancement of military personnel
- second-language training

Our audit showed that the Canadian Forces has still not been able to resolve certain instruction and education issues, which prevents it from being fully compliant with the Official Languages Act. While there have been encouraging signs of change, some long-standing problems still remain.

Main Issues
- Shortcomings in strategic and operational planning make it difficult for the Canadian Forces to effectively evaluate how many courses are needed in both official languages.
- Waiting times are often long for courses in military members' official language of choice.
- There is a significant shortage of instructors who can give courses in both official languages.
- Official languages are not considered to be an essential component of the Individual Training and Education System management framework.

- The Canadian Forces is not always able to provide teaching materials in both official languages.
- The Canadian Forces has serious difficulties posting military personnel who have completed their training in one language and who wish to continue their career in the same language.
- There are too many senior officers who still do not meet the language requirements of their rank, including commandants of national training establishments.
- Official languages must be taken into consideration when developing new curricula and when establishing performance measures.
- Second-language training needs should be better integrated into Individual Training and Education System planning as well as career management.

To address these issues, the Commissioner of Official Languages has made 20 recommendations to the Canadian Forces. These recommendations are aimed at better integrating official languages into the planning, management and processes related to the Individual Training and Education System.

The Canadian Forces has submitted an action plan to support its commitment to implement the Commissioner's recommendations. The Office of the Commissioner intends to carry out the necessary follow-up on the various Canadian Forces initiatives.

Source: Office of the Commissioner of Official Languages, 'Backgrounder: Audit of the Individual Training and Education System of the Canadian Forces'. www.ocol-clo.gc.ca/html/audit_verification_forces_e.php.

education and public signs and advertising contained in Quebec's Bill 101.[42] Until 1985, language rights cases were the only ones supported by Ottawa under its Court Challenges Program.[43]

A second thrust of federal policy to promote bilingualism in Canadian society has been through financial assistance for second-language instruction and minority-language schools controlled by the provinces, including French immersion schools throughout Canada and summer immersion programs based mainly in Quebec. The number of kindergarten to grade 12 schools offering French immersion programs decreased from 1197 in 1970–1, with 444,942 students enrolled, to 1039 schools and 251,993 students in 1999–2000.[44] Enrolment has been increasing over the past decade with an average increase of 2 per cent per year. In 2007–8, 311,051 students were enrolled in French immersion across the country. Fifty-one per cent of immersion students are in Ontario.[45]

Even though some non-francophone parents perceive that bilingualism would give their children an edge in the future competition for good jobs, the policy has not been widely embraced. And the perception of greater opportunities for bilingual workers, at least in the private sector, remains to be substantiated. A 2002 survey of 'Attitudes and Perceptions Toward Canada's Official Languages' found that 76 per cent of young anglophone Canadians believed that having two official languages gives Canada an economic advantage.[46] However, the 2006 census showed that only about 17.4 per cent of Canadians (up slightly from 1996) claimed to be able to carry on a conversation in both French and English. The percentage for young Canadians living in Quebec was roughly three times greater than for their counterparts elsewhere in Canada.[47] Moreover, studies of immersion graduates demonstrate that the experience tends to produce 'receptive' bilinguals: people who neither initiate conversations in French nor consume French-language newspapers, radio, or television after leaving immersion. Bilingualism becomes in some sense a badge of social distinction rather than a part of their lifestyle.

Living in the Shadow of a Giant

In the late nineteenth century, Canada was a dependent society with close ties to the British economic system. During the twentieth century Canada shifted into the economic and cultural orbit of an ascendant power, the United States. This shift was due in part to transformations in the world economy, including the decline in Britain's economic stature and the relative increase in that of the United States. The transatlantic dependence based on the export of certain resource commodities and the import of debt capital to finance the infrastructure of the resource-exporting economy was winding down. It was replaced by a continentalist dependence based on the export of natural resources to the United States and the integration of Canadian industry into the American economy through ownership and imports of production technology. The shift was accompanied by transformations in the structure of economic and political power in Canada, notably a decline in the importance of financial and railway interests and an increase in that of the industrial subsidiaries—mainly American—that established themselves behind Canadian tariff walls. Thus, just at a time when Canada was shaking off the vestiges of its colonial status within the British Empire and establishing itself as a politically sovereign nation, its capacity for independent public policy was being undermined by its economic integration into the empire of American capitalism.

Canada's economic ties to the United States take several forms. Among the most significant in terms of their impact on public policy are those involving trade (which will be examined in our discussion of globalization, later in this chapter), investment, capital markets, and treaties.

Investment. Much of the Canadian economy is owned by foreigners, and most of those foreigners are American. Roughly one-third of the 100 largest non-financial corporations in Canada are foreign owned, and several of the most important sectors of the Canadian economy, including the automobile industry, the petroleum and petrochemicals sector, and important segments of the food-processing industry, are dominated by American-based companies.

The roots of American investment in the Canadian economy go back to the National Policy of 1879. The high tariffs imposed on manufactured imports encouraged American companies to establish Canadian subsidiaries—branch plants, as they are often called—that would produce exclusively for the Canadian market, thus 'jumping' the tariff wall. Michael Bliss estimates that by 1913 about 450 subsidiaries, mainly

American, had been established in Canada. The level of foreign investment peaked in the 1970s at about 37 per cent of total economic assets in Canada. Today the level stands at about one-quarter, about two-thirds of which is based in the United States.[48]

The consequences of such high levels of foreign ownership—levels unmatched in any other advanced industrial democracy—have been debated since the 1950s. To some it is self-evident that Canadians have benefited from the billions of dollars that have been invested in our economy, mainly by Americans; but others think it equally self-evident that the costs have outweighed any putative benefits. What is beyond doubt is that the high level of mainly American foreign ownership has increased the integration of the Canadian economy into the orbit of the United States and, moreover, has rendered Canadian policy-makers more vulnerable to the foreign investment policies of the US government.

This vulnerability was highlighted during the 1990s in the dispute over the Helms–Burton Act. In pursuit of the United States' policy of not trading with Cuba, the US Congress passed legislation prohibiting the foreign-based subsidiaries of American companies from doing business with that country. The Canadian and Western European governments protested that this represented a violation of international law. For many countries their protest was little more than perfunctory indignation. But for Canada, which has extensive trade ties to Cuba and is in fact the single largest foreign investor in the Cuban economy, the extraterritorial application of American law through US-owned subsidiaries in Canada represented a more serious matter.

For all of its history Canada has been a net importer of investment capital. However, since the 1980s the volume of Canadian foreign investment, chiefly in the United States, has increased enormously. By 2009 the stock of foreign direct investment in Canada stood at an estimated $549 billion, while Canadian direct investment abroad was $593 billion. The downward trend continued in 2009 when Canada had a $39.2 billion decline in the difference between what Canadians invested abroad and foreign direct investment in Canada. The value of Canadian investment abroad declined $25.9 billion, while foreign direct investment in Canada increased by $15.2 billion during the same time.[49] Canadian companies have participated in the globalization of investment capital. Nevertheless, as Elizabeth Smythe observes:

> globalization, in Canada's case, has really meant ever closer economic integration with the United States in the 1980s and 1990s. In the light of the great disparities in the size of the two economies and their dependence on trade, this trend has given the United States additional means of influencing Canadian policies in the event of investment disputes.[50]

Capital markets. Canadian companies, governments, and government agencies often borrow money. In the case of governments and government agencies, much of this money is loaned to them by foreign investors. In fact, roughly one-third of Ottawa's $566 billion in indebtedness is owed to non-Canadians. Provincial governments and their agents, such as Hydro One in Ontario and Hydro-Québec, are also heavily indebted to foreign investors. Most of this debt is owed to Americans. This helps to explain the soothing noises that Canadian politicians, federal and provincial, regularly make when they visit the temple of Mammon, New York, and the fact that any pronouncement on Canada's creditworthiness by the oracles of international finance, Standard & Poor's and Moody's, is considered front-page news in this country.

In recent years the possibility of Quebec's separating from Canada has had a particularly unnerving effect on foreign moneylenders. During the 1995 Quebec referendum on sovereignty, foreign investors' reaction to a yes vote, and how this would affect the credit ratings of Canada and Quebec, figured prominently in the debate. The episode provided yet another illustration of how Canada's economic ties to the United States serve to constrain policy-makers. At the same time, when the American dollar weakens, as happened in the spring and summer of 2002 and again starting in 2006, the Canadian dollar strengthens.

Treaties. The ties of trade, investment, and borrowing that exist between Canada and the United States have been cemented by treaties. These treaties have a long history. In fact, the Americans' abrogation of the Reciprocity Treaty (1854–66) that existed between the United States and Great Britain's North American colonies was an important catalyst for Confederation. Even before the Canada–United States Free Trade Agreement (FTA) came into effect in 1989, sectoral free trade existed between the two countries. The Defence Production Sharing Agreement of 1958 formalized sectoral free trade in defence-related products that had existed since World War II. More important, the Auto Pact of 1965 created free trade in automobiles and automotive parts. In addition to bilateral treaties, Canada and the United States were original members of the multilateral General Agreement on Tariffs and Trade (GATT), signed in 1947, which committed them both to the lowering of trade barriers and to a code of conduct regarding imports and exports within the GATT community.

The FTA and the North American Free Trade Agreement (NAFTA), which included Mexico and came into effect in 1994, have eliminated most of the barriers to the free movement of goods, sources, and capital in North America (although restrictions on the movement of people still exist, which is not the case in the European Union). Moreover, the World Trade Organization (WTO), the more highly structured and institutionalized trade regime that replaced the GATT at the completion of the Uruguay Round of the GATT in December 1993, joins the Canadian and American economies under the same multilateral trade umbrella. Multilateral trade commitments have often been seen as representing a potential counterweight to the inevitable dominance of the United States in bilateral Canadian–American trade relations. The constraints imposed on Canadian policy-makers by the WTO are much less restrictive than the obligations imposed by membership in the FTA and NAFTA. These free trade treaties reinforce Canada's economic dependence on the United States, guaranteeing access to the American market in exchange for restrictions on the ability of Canadian governments to favour domestic producers and investors over their American counterparts.

The ties that bind Canada to the United States are not only economic. Militarily, the two countries have been joined by treaty obligations since the Ogdensburg Agreement (1940) and the Hyde Park Declaration (1941). The North Atlantic Treaty Organization (1949), the North American Air Defense Command (1958), and the Canada–United

States Test and Evaluation Program (1983) deepened the military alliance between Canada and the United States.

Canadian nationalists and critics of American defence policy have often expressed the hope that Canada could free itself from its military alliance with the United States and develop the sort of non-aligned status that Sweden has long maintained. Prime minister Pierre Trudeau took some tentative steps in this direction during the late 1960s and early 1970s, only to find that the political costs exceeded whatever nationalist satisfaction an autonomous defence posture might provide. The problem is simply this: Canada is not Sweden. Its geographic position and economic dependence on the United States rule out the possibility of military non-alignment. So while there is margin for independent manoeuvre in some matters, such as international peacekeeping, and even some room for minor criticism of American defence policies, there is no real possibility of Canada pursuing an autonomous line on the big issues of global security and the defence of North America.

Regionalism and Provincialism in Canadian Policy-Making

Provincial governments sometimes claim to speak on behalf of regionally distinct societies. This claim was forcefully expressed by Claude Morin, a constitutionalist and one-time member of the Parti Québécois government, in a book entitled *Quebec versus Ottawa*.[51] Morin argued that the interests of Quebec society, by which he meant the francophone majority of that province, can never be protected by a federal Parliament in which Quebecers will always be in the minority. Basing his argument on this simple proposition, he suggested that only the Quebec government was capable of protecting the interests of the provincial society because it was not compelled to make concessions to the interests of other regions. Spokespersons from other provinces generally have been less extreme in arguing their cases for provincial distinctiveness, but it is nonetheless true that every provincial government, regardless of partisan stripe, inherits a set of 'fairly durable and persisting interests'[52] that largely determine the demands they make on federalism. These interests, and what Alan Cairns has called the institutional self-interest of provincial state elites, are more important than culture in shaping the demands of the predominantly anglophone provinces.[53]

There are wide differences between the provinces in their predominant economic activities. Provinces also vary enormously in their trade relations with other provinces and their relationships to markets outside Canada. Nevertheless, these interprovincial economic differences are no greater than those that exist between, say, New York and Nebraska or Ohio and Texas in the United States. How, then, does one explain the fact that in Canada the decentralizing pressures on the federal system appear to be far greater than those to which American federalism is subject? Various explanations have been suggested, including a greater sense of national identity in American society.[54] A second line of explanation points to the existence in the United States of national political institutions, notably the Senate, that are able to act as forums for the expression of regional demands. These national institutions play a role that in Canada is assumed primarily by provincial governments. A third explanation involves American Supreme Court decisions that have given an expansive interpretation to the United States government's power to regulate interstate commerce. In Canada, the courts historically imposed a more restrictive interpretation on Ottawa's trade and commerce and general legislative powers, at least until the 1970s. While the significance of any of these factors should not be dismissed, the key to understanding Canada's decentralized federal system lies in the divisions between the central provinces—Canada's manufacturing and financial core—and the western and eastern peripheries, and in the weakness of national political institutions in representing regional interests.

The uneven regional distribution of economic activity and power in Canada is confirmed by data on the interprovincial distribution of businesses by the size of firms and the location of head offices for the largest industrial corporations in Canada. Not surprisingly, the majority of large businesses are based in Ontario and Quebec. Thus, corporate decision-making power is not evenly distributed across the country. It is still concentrated in central Canada, especially Ontario, although the last several years have seen a shift in the locus of corporate power toward Alberta and British Columbia. A bare handful of the largest companies are based in the Atlantic provinces (see Table 3.2).

TABLE 3.2 Interprovincial Distribution of Corporate Head Offices for the 100 Largest Industrial Firms in Canada, 2010

Province	Total
Ontario	38
Quebec	25
Alberta	17
British Columbia	8
Manitoba	3
Saskatchewan	4
New Brunswick	0
Nova Scotia	2
Newfoundland/Labrador and PEI	1
	98

Note: In 2010, two of Canada's top 100 corporations did not have their head offices in Canada, so totals do not add up to 100.
Source: Compiled from information provided in the *Financial Post*, FP 500, 2009. Material reprinted with the express permission of National Post Inc.

The unequal distribution of economic activity across Canada would not in itself constitute a source of decentralizing pressure on the federal system. These inequalities, however, combine with relatively weak structures for the expression of regional interests at the national level, and with a Constitution that gives provincial governments numerous levers for regulating their economies, to fragment the policy process along regional lines. Regionally oriented business interests have often viewed the provincial state as an ally in protecting and promoting their economic interests.

Decentralist tendencies in Canadian federalism and policy-making also reflect the influences of the Constitution and Quebec nationalism. In the case of the

Constitution, the provinces possess important levers for regulating economic activity within their boundaries: They have wide-ranging taxing and borrowing powers, and they have jurisdiction over most areas of social policy. The Constitution therefore provides significant jurisdictional opportunities for provincial intervention, though the provinces differ in their ability and willingness to take advantage of them.

The assertion of provincial powers under the Constitution has a long tradition. During the first decades after Confederation the Ontario government of Oliver Mowat was a major force in resisting the centralist vision of federalism held by Ottawa under Sir John A. Macdonald.[55] Conflict between Ottawa's nation-building designs and the development goals of provincial governments led to the federal government using its powers of reservation and disallowance of provincial legislation on numerous occasions during this early period. Even when Canadian federalism was most centralized—during the two world wars and during the Great Depression, when the provinces were financially at their weakest—the transfer of constitutional powers from the provincial to the federal level of government was resisted. The only occasion when the federal division of powers has been changed to the advantage of the national government was in 1941 when an amendment to the British North America Act, agreed to by all the provinces, assigned legislative authority over unemployment insurance to Ottawa.[56]

While the scope of state intervention has increased at all levels of government during the post-war era, such growth has been greatest at the provincial level. This reflects both the escalating costs of provincially administered social programs and a restructuring of the financial relationship between the two levels of government. The extensive network of conditional grants erected in the 1950s and 1960s has been dismantled in favour of block transfers from Ottawa to the provinces (see the discussion of social policy in Chapter 7). Moreover, the relative taxing power of the two levels of government has shifted dramatically. In 1950 the federal government collected about two-thirds of all public revenues. Today the provinces and municipalities collect more than half of all tax revenues. Nonetheless, some provincial governments remain heavily dependent on transfer payments from Ottawa. Newfoundland is the extreme case, with about 50 per cent of its total revenues coming from the federal government.

Not unexpectedly, growth in provincial state spending has been accompanied by an increase in the sheer size of provincial bureaucracies. From the standpoint of public policy-making this expansion in the size of the provincial state and in the scope of its powers is significant because of the natural tendency of regional governments, elected by regional electorates, to give expression to a narrower set of interests than are politically significant at the national level. Differences in culture, demographics, and economic structure between regions in Canada acquire a more comprehensive political importance than they would have in a unitary state. The reason lies in the fact that these differences are organized into politics around provincial governments that have extensive constitutional powers and that have developed large and complex state structures to rival those of the federal government.[57]

4. Globalization and Its Consequences in Canada

The central feature of Canada's economic condition is the degree to which it is dependent on markets outside Canadian borders. In some ways this has always been true. From the arrival 500 years ago of European fishermen who trolled the cod-rich waters off the coast of Newfoundland until the middle of the twentieth century, Canada's economic prosperity depended on the exploitation and export of a succession of natural resources—fish, fur, timber, and wheat—to markets abroad, and on the import of people, capital, and finished goods. From the time Europeans began to be seriously interested in what would become Canada, sending it ships, settlers, and goods, the Canadian economy was integrated into larger patterns of trade and shaped by forces beyond its borders.

At some point, however, there developed a hope and even an expectation that Canada would shake off this dependence and become the master of its economic destiny. One sees this in Sir John A. Macdonald's ambitious National Policy of 1879, the first (and only) coherent and explicit economic development strategy that Canada had known before the late 1980s, when the decision was made to embrace free trade (and therefore dependence) as the Canadian fate. One sees it also in Sir Wilfrid Laurier's optimistic prediction that the twentieth century would belong to Canada, a prediction that must surely have been based on Laurier's belief that the remarkable pace of industrialization and population growth, which had made the United States the world's leading economy by the beginning of the twentieth century, would be repeated in Canada. And one sees it in the rise of economic nationalism in Canada, particularly from the 1950s to the beginning of the 1980s, which was marked by a series of policies and institutions designed to limit American influence in the Canadian economy and promote indigenous capital.

Some of these nationalistic hopes still survive, although they have come to appear increasingly atavistic in a world characterized by unprecedented levels of economic interdependence and globalized communication. Today the serious debate is not about whether the forces of globalization can be rolled back, but how and in what circumstances they should be controlled. In Canada the question of globalization is inseparable from that of Canada's relationship to the United States. For Canada, at least, globalization has meant an enormous intensification in economic and other ties to the world's dominant superpower. Whether, on balance, this is a good thing is certainly one of the leading issues in Canadian public life.

The Chrysler minivan that rolls off the assembly line at Windsor, Ontario, appears to be the very embodiment of what economic globalization is about. Assembled in Canada by a Canadian workforce, the vehicle includes parts and component systems from the United States, Mexico, and China. The plastics and metals in these parts come from an even broader set of countries. Many of these components move across the Canada–US border along the hundreds of railroad tracks whose daily destination is the Windsor minivan plant. Decisions about the design and marketing of the vehicle are made principally at Chrysler Group LLC headquarters, about an hour's drive away in Michigan. The company has a global strategic alliance with Fiat, based in Italy, but individual and institutional shareholders in DaimlerChrysler are spread across Canada, the United States, and Europe.

Globalized production, sourcing, and investment have forced us to rethink what were, until fairly recently, firmly established ideas about what is Canadian. The case of the Chrysler minivan is merely one example—though a particularly important one in terms of its employment and income implications—of the new economic realities that characterize Canadian industry. Products exported from companies operating in Canada routinely include foreign content, and imported products will often include content produced in Canada. Moreover, every Canadian province except PEI does more business with economies outside of Canada than it does with the rest of the Canadian economy. Thus, not only is the old idea of a 'Canadian product' cast in doubt, but the very notion of a Canadian economy comes to seem a bit outdated, given the extent of this country's dependence on international (i.e., American) trade.

The essential fact to keep in mind, however, is that in Canada's case economic globalization has really meant greater integration with and dependence on the economy of the United States. The numbers are quite astounding. The total value of Canada–US trade in merchandise, services, and investment makes this easily the largest bilateral trading relationship in the world (although the Mexico–US relationship is deepening dramatically). More than 85 per cent of Canadian exports go to the United States, accounting for about 35 per cent of Canada's total GDP. The share of Canada's substantial import trade that comes from the United States is only slightly smaller, at about three-quarters of total imports. Canada has been the major export market for American goods for more than half a century and is today the leading export market for about three-quarters of all state economies. The United States has long been the largest source of foreign investment in Canada, currently accounting for close to two-thirds of all foreign investment, and roughly half of all Canadian direct investments abroad are located there.

This bilateral trading relationship has a long history, but in recent years it has achieved an unprecedented level of intimacy. The real value of total transactions between the Canadian and American economies has more than doubled since the FTA took effect in 1989, increasing gradually at first and then more dramatically since NAFTA came into effect. For Canada, more trade with the rest of the world has in fact meant more trade with the United States (see Figure 3.2).

This relationship has never been one of equals, and is no more equal today than it was in the past. Revealingly, when the Canadian media were full of stories about the imposition of American duties on Canadian softwood lumber imports in the spring of 2002, there was barely any attention to the issue in the American media. Canada–US trade disputes that lead the national news in Canada are lucky if they receive a mention in the American press, particularly outside the border states that might be more immediately affected. The trading relationship is not only huge, it is hugely asymmetrical, affecting Canada's vital interests far more than it does those of the United States (see Table 3.3).

FIGURE 3.2 US Trade with Canada: Exports and Imports, 1988–2009 ($US billions)

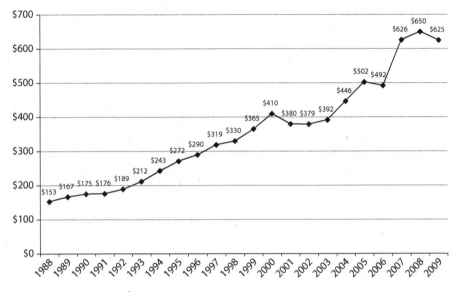

Source: US Department of Commerce.

TABLE 3.3 An Asymmetrical Economic Relationship, 2011

	Canada	United States
	%	%
Share of total exports going to the other country	75.1	19.4
Share of total imports coming from the other country	51.1	14.2

Source: *The World Factbook 2011* (Washington, DC: CIA, 2011). www.cia.gov/library/publications/the-world-factbook/index.html. See 'Economy' and 'Exports—partners' and 'Imports—partners' for Canada and United States.

It would be an overstatement to say that Canada has no leverage in this relationship. After all, Canada—not Saudi Arabia!—is the single largest source of energy imports to the United States and is the destination for over half the value of all US automotive exports. The Canadian economy is extremely important—even strategically important—to the United States. But the influence that this might otherwise give Canadian negotiators in trade disputes with Washington is diluted by Canada's far greater across-the-board dependence on the American economy. For example, an end to petroleum exports from Alberta to the United States would bring Alberta's economy to its knees and ripple through the rest of the Canadian economy in various ways, but this would represent a drop of only 8 per cent in the total supply of petroleum products consumed in the United States.[58] Likewise, if the American border were to be closed to automobiles, trucks, and auto parts from Canada, this would represent a loss of almost

30 per cent of total Canadian exports, or about 12 per cent of GDP. The impact on the Ontario economy would be as devastating as the hypothesized loss of Alberta's oil and gas exports to the United States. The economies of states like Michigan and Ohio would experience serious losses from the end of automotive trade with Canada, but the total value of American automotive imports from Canada represents a little under 1 per cent of American GDP. This enormous and unavoidable imbalance in the Canada–US trade relationship was one of the chief arguments put forward in the 1980s by the Canadian advocates of free trade. The federal government's official policy of reducing Canada's reliance on trade and investment with the United States—a policy called the Third Option, adopted in the early 1970s—had proven about as effective as a statute repealing the law of gravity. A decade later, Canada was even more dependent on the American economy as a destination for exports and a source of imports. Canada's major manufacturers, but also important exporters of natural resources like wood products, oil and gas, and hydroelectricity, recognized that their growth prospects depended on access to the American market. The Canadian Manufacturers' Association (since renamed Canadian Manufacturers and Exporters), which began life a century earlier calling for protectionist tariffs, became a convert to and a politically weighty advocate of a Canada–US free trade agreement. A growing wave of protectionist sentiment in the American Congress during the 1980s seemed to lend urgency to Canadian free traders' case—a case whose momentum was given a major boost by the pro–free trade recommendations of the Royal Commission on the Economic Union and Development Prospects for Canada (Macdonald Commission, 1981–5)—that Canada's best economic hope lay in tighter formal economic integration with the United States. The political argument that this would help shield Canadian industries from Congress's protectionist moods proved widely persuasive, even among many of those who were dubious about some of the economic claims made for free trade.

The Canada–US Free Trade Agreement took effect on January 1, 1989. It was followed several years later by the North American Free Trade Agreement, which brought Canada, the United States, and Mexico together in a free trade zone that encompasses most industries and forms of investment. Both agreements create an architecture of dispute settlement rules, agencies, and monitoring requirements that have not taken the politics out of trade disputes, but that provide rather different forums for their resolution. Experience has demonstrated that these new forums do not replace earlier forums and channels for the making of trade policy. The latter still matter, as does the World Trade Organization. But on the whole it is fair to say that the rules and the dispute settlement mechanisms created under the FTA and NAFTA make it more difficult for member governments to pursue trade policies that favour their domestic interests. They may still do so, but they run the risk of eventually having to pay the cost of sanctions if their policies are found to violate these agreements.

Public Opinion and Canada–US Economic Relations

From the standpoint of Canadian nationalists, the last couple of decades have provided little reason to celebrate. On the contrary, as virtually all will admit, the trajectory of events has been anything but kind to nationalists and their agenda. Economic integration has increased, barriers to American culture and incentives for the generation of Canadian cultural alternatives have proven to be largely ineffective, the 'brain drain'— a phenomenon that Canadians have fretted over, off and on, for a century[59]— has become an issue of public controversy, and Canadians increasingly appear to be indifferent toward the appeals and policies of those who champion the nationalist cause.

Some will challenge this claim. I would suggest, however, that the weight and variety of evidence overwhelmingly demonstrates that the nationalist message resonates more weakly today than at any point over the last half-century. Moreover, among those groups historically most receptive to the nationalist message there has been a softening of support. Public opinion polls appear to show increased resignation, though perhaps not enthusiasm, for greater economic integration with the United States.

It would, of course, be desirable to have time-series data tracking Canadian attitudes on these matters over the last few decades. Unfortunately, no such data exist. Similarly worded polls on the impact of free trade have been conducted over the past decade, however, and they suggest a trend of strengthening ties between Canada and the United States. As Figure 3.3 shows, Canadians have slowly but steadily come to a more positive assessment of the impact of free trade, as more believe it has been positive than those who believe it has been negative. In a 1997 COMPAS poll, less than half of Canadians expressed a view of free trade with the United States that was either very positive or somewhat positive. Yet by 2003 an Ipsos Reid poll found that 51 per cent of Canadians thought that NAFTA had benefited Canada. Most recently, during the 2008 federal election campaign, the Canadian Election Study (CES) found that 62 per cent of Canadians strongly or somewhat agreed that Canada had benefited from free trade with the United States. This was unchanged from the 2006 election survey. Taking into account the fact that the CES did not offer respondents a neutral position, this figure may be somewhat inflated, but it does confirm that Canadians are becoming more satisfied with free trade over time.

The relationship between Canada and the United States is a two-way street, and there are increasing indications that Americans are becoming more likely to see the benefit of closer ties with Canada. An Ipsos Reid poll conducted for the Canada Institute on North American Issues (CINAI) in September 2006 found clear signs of friendship between the two countries:

- When asked who they consider to be Canada's closest friend and ally, 58 per cent of Canadians, unprompted, pointed to the United States. Americans viewed Canada as their second-best friend, just after the United Kingdom.
- At the same time, 90 per cent of Americans said they considered Canada to be more a friend and ally of the United States and its policies than a foe; 85 per cent of Canadians shared this view (an increase of 12 percentage points from 2005).
- Despite popular media portrayals of anti-Americanism after 9/11, in response to the 'war on terror', when asked about the last couple of months, three-quarters of Americans (77 per cent) and two-thirds of Canadians (65 per cent) thought that the relationship between Canada and the United States had either improved or stayed the same.

FIGURE 3.3 Public Assessment of Free Trade

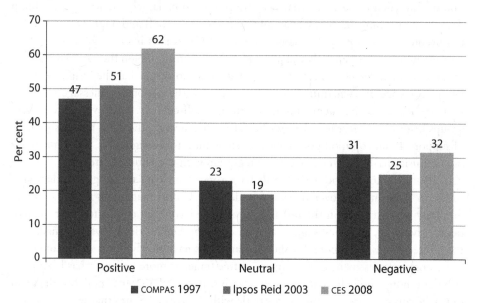

Sources: COMPAS for the *Financial Post*, 1997: 'Would you say that the contribution of the North American Free Trade Accord has been very positive, somewhat positive, essentially neutral, somewhat negative or very negative?' 'Very positive' and 'somewhat positive' were combined as 'positive'; 'somewhat negative' and 'very negative' were combined as 'negative' in the figure.

Ipsos Reid for *The Globe and Mail* and CTV, June 2003: 'Canada has been part of the North American Free Trade Agreement since 1994. So far, do you think this free trade agreement has benefited Canada, hurt Canada, or do you think it hasn't had any impact one way or the other?'

Canada Election Study 2008: 'Do you strongly agree, somewhat agree, somewhat disagree or strongly disagree that, overall, free trade with the US has been good for the Canadian economy?' 'Strongly agree' and 'somewhat agree' were combined as 'positive', 'strongly disagree' and 'somewhat disagree' were combined as 'negative' in the figure.

- Ninety-one per cent of Americans and 78 per cent of Canadians agreed with the statement 'While we may disagree on some issues, Canadians and Americans will always find common ground to work together.'
- The fight against global terrorism was seen as one of the top priorities for the two countries, with 28 per cent of Americans and 19 per cent of Canadians ranking it as their top priority.
- More than half of the respondents on both sides of the border (59 per cent of Canadians and 55 per cent of Americans) agreed that 'The Canadian government has done enough to secure the border between our two countries to protect against terrorist attacks'—an increase of 10 points in Canada and 8 points in the United States over the previous year.[60]

Support for closer economic ties with the United States was greatest among the highest-income earners. This finding confirms other studies that have found the more affluent and highly educated strata of the population to be the strongest supporters of trade liberalization.[61]

Mark Twain once famously declared that rumours of his death were greatly exaggerated. In the case of Canadian nationalism it would be a bit of a stretch to suggest that the patient is certifiably dead, but there is little doubt that the state life support on which it has long depended is no longer up to the task of keeping the patient alive in more than a technical sense. 'The state or the United States' has long been the rallying cry of Canadian nationalists, but these days it does not seem to rally many, except for fairly predictable elements in academe, the state-dependent cultural community, the labour elite, and social activists. The only avowedly nationalist political party, the NDP, saw its popular support drop to single-digit levels nationally during the 1990s. It was only when the NDP shifted its policy focus away from criticism of free trade toward domestic issues such as health care that its support began to increase, to 15.7 per cent of the popular vote in the 2004 election, 17.5 per cent in 2006, 18.2 per cent in 2008, and 30.6 per cent in 2011. Canada's counterpart to what David Brooks calls the 'bobos'[62]—the new knowledge elite in high-tech, information technology (IT), and finance—are supporters of trade liberalization. Canadians have never been as integrated—culturally, economically, and politically—into the American orbit as they are today. And while it might be going too far to say that they welcome this development, it is probably fair to say that they increasingly accept it.

The consequences of globalization for policy and policy-making in Canada go beyond the intensification and formalization of our trade relations with the United States. Doern and his colleagues have identified several distinct ways in which policy-making has been affected by globalization.[63] First, policy discourse has been internationalized. The way policy issues are framed has changed; matters that previously were thought of as purely or chiefly domestic are now discussed in a context of influences and norms that are transnational. Aboriginal rights, for example, have been discussed in the context of United Nations declarations on human rights and the self-determination of peoples. Since the 1991 armed standoff between the Canadian military and Mohawk warriors at Oka, Quebec, it has been fairly routine for Aboriginal groups in Canada to call for UN or some other international involvement in disputes with federal or provincial governments. Moreover, Aboriginal leaders draw on an international discourse of human rights and Aboriginal rights that is kept in circulation through non-governmental organizations (NGOs), international bodies, conferences, and websites that contribute to the contextualization of such rights as matters that transcend domestic politics.

The number of such examples may be multiplied almost without limit. Both the ways and the forums in which issues such as fur trapping or forestry methods in British Columbia are discussed make it clear that their ramifications extend beyond Canada. Education policies and performance are discussed in terms of their meaning for Canada's (or a province's) international competitiveness. Trade considerations are ubiquitous, whether the matter on the agenda is reform of social policy, national unity, environmental regulation, culture, or anything else.

A key aspect of the internationalization of policy discourse is the establishment of international norms and standards and their importation into domestic policy-making. This is obviously true in the case of trade and investment, where the rules set under the FTA and NAFTA and by the WTO became the benchmarks for assessing the actions of governments in Canada. But it is also true of matters such as the status of women, poverty, and human rights, where the meetings and reports of international bodies and forums do much to shape the contours of policy discourse in Canada.

The internationalization of policy discourse challenges the concept of national sovereignty. But despite the erosion of the idea that domestic conditions are matters of national interest only—indeed of the notion that there can be any purely domestic matter—the concept of national sovereignty is far from dead. Nor, as a practical matter, have governments lost all capacity for independent policy-making, although this independence is clearly attenuated. What is certain, however, is that policy issues today are often framed in ways that are indifferent to national boundaries, and that the traditional integrity of policy fields has been breached and invaded by ideas and interests from outside the domestic sphere.

In a study of globalization and provincial government spending in Canada, Mark Pickup found that 'trade liberalization has not made political and regional determinants of government spending subservient to economic considerations.'[64] Rather, increasing trade openness since the early 1990s has been accompanied by increases in provincial transfers to individuals.

Interest groups and their strategies have been internationalized. Some interest groups are international by their very nature; examples include Greenpeace, Amnesty International, International Physicians for the Prevention of Nuclear War, and the World Wildlife Federation. Today, however, many groups whose organization and finances have been restricted to a single country are seeking alliances and support from outside their national borders. For example, Leslie Pal and Andrew Cooper note that three Canadian groups appeared before the UN Committee on Economic, Social, and Cultural Rights in 1995, complaining that Ottawa's decision to repeal the Canada Assistance Plan constituted a violation of the UN Covenant on Human Rights.[65] Attempting to embarrass the government at home by making noise abroad has become a fairly routine tactic in the arsenal of many interest groups, particularly environmental, Aboriginal, human rights, women's, and anti-poverty groups. Such tactics can prove effective not only because the national media in Canada are usually eager to report such stories, but also because the machinery of policy-making in Canada has become more open with respect to the norms and decisions of international bodies. The Canadian and provincial human rights commissions take them seriously, as do various bureaucratic agencies and departments, such as the Human Rights Program in the Department of Canadian Heritage and the departments of Justice and Health.

The traditional separation between foreign policy-making and domestic policy-making has been undermined. And as the definition of foreign policy has changed, so too has the role of Canada's foreign affairs bureaucracy. Historically, foreign policy concerned itself chiefly with trade, national security, international peace, and what might be called humanitarian matters. Today, the definition of foreign policy encompasses these traditional concerns plus environmental concerns, human rights issues, social policy, women's issues, telecommunications and culture, finance, and more. The Department of Foreign Affairs and International Trade (DFAIT) has seen its authority broadened by these developments, but also limited. In areas like agriculture, the environment, and telecommunications, DFAIT must share responsibility for policy-making with departments that have deeper technical expertise and established relationships with industry and interest groups. In some matters that have acquired foreign policy dimensions, such as banking and social policy, DFAIT is not a player.[66]

The broadening of foreign policy also has implications for federalism. Bruce Doern and John Kirton argue that because of provincial budget cuts, including the termination of international trade offices and missions by all provinces except Quebec, 'there has been a shift in foreign affairs capacity from the provincial to the federal level.'[67] We need to distinguish, however, between what they call 'foreign affairs capacity' and actual involvement in foreign policy-making. It may well be that the dismantling of provincial trade offices abroad has rendered the provinces more dependent on Ottawa for export-promotion and investment-attracting activities. This view probably over-values, by taking at face value, the boastful and self-serving claims of results from trade/investment missions such as the 'Team Canada' trips abroad. Some observers doubt that these government-sponsored missions and trade offices have much impact at all, and their elimination by the Ontario government, for example, certainly owed something to this belief. Moreover, even if the provinces, except Quebec, now rely more on Ottawa's formal machinery for trade negotiations and diplomacy, the broadening of foreign policy to include matters in which provincial governments have a clear jurisdictional stake—the environment, social policy, telecommunications, and agriculture, for example—has also extended the range of foreign policy matters requiring provincial government input, cooperation, or even formal agreement for implementation. It may be premature, therefore, to conclude that the role of the provinces in foreign policy-making has declined.

The mixture of policy instruments used by governments has changed. During the last several years Canada has been on the receiving end of a number of direct and indirect hits targeted at long-standing policy instruments. For example, a 1997 WTO decision ruled that protectionist measures used to support Canadian-owned magazines violated the rules on trade. WTO rules and decisions have also required Canada and other member countries to reduce domestic and export subsidies to agricultural producers. Spending instruments and direct subsidies have been squeezed by pressures, often from foreign investors, to reduce budget deficits and public-sector debt. Liberalized trade has meant deregulation in some sectors, such as telecommunications and air travel, that traditionally have been closely regulated by the state. Canada's participation in international treaties and organizations, from the Group of Eight and the WTO to the United Nations Commission on Human Rights and international forums on the environment and the status of women, has increasingly affected policy-making in Canada by producing agreements and rules that serve as touchstones for domestic policy.

Doern and his colleagues caution that generalization about the effects of globalization on the choice of policy instruments is made difficult by the fact that the traditional patterns of policy instruments varied widely between policy sectors (e.g., industrial policy relied heavily on direct subsidies, export promotion, and direct state ownership, whereas environmental policy relied on regulation and monitoring). Nevertheless, they suggest that spending instruments have declined in importance while various forms of regulation and government exhortation have become more important.[68] Pal demonstrates elsewhere that globalization, through its effects on policy networks, draws non-governmental organizations into the policy-making process in novel ways and in some cases transforms them into policy instruments.[69]

Key Terms

affirmative action An employment policy that uses targets, incentives, or mandatory quotas to increase the representation of a designated group or groups, such as women, Aboriginal people, and visible minorities.

constitution The formal establishment of a state that describes the roles and responsibilities of the regime to its citizens.

contextual influences Factors that constitute the background of policy-making.

convention Customary rules and traditional practices pertaining to the powers of and relations between parts of the state system.

executive federalism A continuous and multi-level process of consultation and bargaining between the policy-makers representing the federal government and those that represent the provinces that generally does not include elected representatives of opposition parties.

fragment theory Developed by Louis Hartz, it characterizes English-speaking Canada as a liberal society with Tory 'touches' and French-speaking Canada as a pre-liberal feudal society whose democratization and liberalization were retarded by its feudal past.

political culture The dominant and relatively durable beliefs and values about political life that characterize a society.

proximate influences The machinery of government, political parties, interest groups, and so on whose impact on policy is more direct than is the case with contextual influences.

responsible government A constitutional convention according to which a government must have the support of a majority of the members of the legislature to govern. In other words, the executive branch of government is 'responsible' to the legislative branch.

Discussion Questions

1. Box 3.1 examines some significant gaps in language training for the Canadian Forces. Does the finding that the government has not provided sufficient second-language training point to a failure in the official languages policy?
2. Apart from the English–French cleavage discussed in the text, how might other examples of political culture influence policy-making in Canada?
3. How have the courts changed the policy-making process in Canada? Could they eclipse some other influence?
4. Is Canadian nationalism threatened or strengthened by globalization? Many Canadians fear that the increasing quantities of American consumer products,

entertainment choices, and messages filtering into Canada are undermining our identity. Do you agree? Or is it possible that globalization is leading to greater appreciation of our regional cultures?

5. The chapter takes issue with many of the critiques of globalization. Much of this discussion notes the many different ways of measuring things such as poverty and income differentials. Are disparities between the wealthy and the poor good measures of the success or failure of globalization? What might other measures of poverty look like? How could you find a measure that would appeal to both the defenders and critics of trade liberalization?

Websites

The following sites offer further insights into various influences on policy-making.

Canadian Research Institute for the Advancement of Women (CRIAW)
www.criaw-icref.ca
CRIAW focuses it research on issues of importance to women in Canadian society and uses that research to build community capacity and shape positive social change through policy debate.

Canadian Heritage (Official Languages)
www.pch.gc.ca/eng/1266246388710/1266202941626
A government site, Canadian Heritage outlines the nation's bilingual language policy and opportunities for promoting French and English in Canadian society.

Council of Canadians
www.canadians.org
One of the best-known nationalist groups in the country, the Council of Canadians seeks to protect Canada's independence by promoting progressive policies on issues of social and economic concern, including trade, water, energy security, and public health care.

Global Economic Integration: Opportunities and Challenges
www.federalreserve.gov/boarddocs/speeches/2000/20000825.htm
A speech on global economic integration given on August 25, 2000, by the former chairman of the US Federal Reserve Board, Alan Greenspan.

Global Trade Watch (GTW)
www.citizen.org/trade
GTW was created in 1995 to promote government and corporate accountability in the arena of international trade.

Multiculturalism Policy
www.cic.gc.ca/english/multiculturalism/citizenship.asp
This government site is designed to increase awareness of multiculturalism initiatives.

NAFTA Secretariat

www.nafta-sec-alena.org

The Secretariat administers the mechanisms specified under NAFTA to resolve trade disputes between national industries and/or governments.

World Trade Organization

www.wto.org

The WTO is the only global organization dealing with the rules of trade between nations.

CHAPTER 4
Policy Implementation

Introduction

It used to be thought that implementation was what happened after all the hard stuff was finished. Forging agreement on a policy, getting it embodied in a bill (i.e., a proposed law), and navigating that bill through the various stages of the legislative process (and past the sniping of opposition politicians, the media, and hostile interest groups) were thought to be the tough parts of policy-making. Once all that had been accomplished, surely lawmakers could heave a sigh of relief, knowing that their intentions would be translated into action by bureaucrats whose job was to do precisely that.

Some students of policy-making, however, noticed that the translation of politicians' decisions into administrative action was not as automatic as the academic neglect of the implementation stage might suggest. As time went on, the matters covered by legislation became increasingly technical, but the wording of that legislation was often very general, with the result that it was increasingly left to non-elected officials to determine how the law would be applied. These bureaucrats, like all human beings, had values that influenced the way they implemented policies. Bureaucratic discretion and the impossibility of keeping values out of the administrative process are problems as old as the modern study of public administration.[1] They are what we today would call implementation problems. But they are not the only or even the major source of discrepancies between what governments decide and what actually happens—or does not happen.

Today, no one who knows anything about policy-making takes implementation for granted. To understand why this is so, consider the following three cases:

- *Regional economic development.* Since the 1960s, the federal government has pumped billions of dollars into the economies of the less prosperous eastern provinces. In 1965 the per capita income of the average Newfoundlander, excluding government transfer payments, was about 60 per cent of the Canadian average. During the 1980s, when incomes in New Brunswick, Nova Scotia, and PEI were growing faster than incomes in the rest of Canada, Newfoundland stagnated.

Incomes in the province have improved since 2000, however, because of the strong showing of the oil sector.[2]

- *Affordable housing.* In response to shortages of low- and moderately priced accommodation during the inflationary 1970s, many provincial governments slapped rent controls on landlords. The ostensible aim was to ensure a supply of reasonably priced housing for low-income earners, but in many areas the result was a decrease in vacancies at the low end of the market; in some metropolitan regions, the shortage of low-income housing became acute.

- *Control of toxic chemicals.* The Canadian Environmental Protection Act (CEPA; 1988) includes provisions for the regulation of toxic chemicals used in industry. Spokespersons for Environment Canada describe these provisions as representing 'cradle-to-grave' management of industrial toxins and a major step forward in protecting the health and environment of Canadians. Rules were established giving any Canadian the right to request an investigation of the environmental effects of a particular substance and requiring Environment Canada to respond. But several years after CEPA's passage, only a few dozen of the perhaps 100,000 chemicals in commercial use in Canada had been placed on Environment Canada's Priority Substance List. The list includes those chemicals whose production, use, and disposal are closely monitored under CEPA. A review conducted in the 1990s found the Act to be deficient. The legislation was revised in 1999 to define toxic levels of chemicals. But in 2006 it was still found to be deficient, and the government announced yet another amendment to include additional chemicals that had not been considered in the previous versions of the Act.

Policies often fail to accomplish their goals. Such failure may not be total, and in many cases it might be blamed on badly designed or ill-chosen programs rather than problems of implementation. But the study of policy implementation is not simply the study of failed policies. Policies can, after all, achieve their goals. Sometimes they produce results that, although desirable from someone's point of view, were not quite what the policy-makers had in mind. Before we examine the dynamics of policy implementation, let us pin down what the term means and where it fits into the policy-making process.

What Is Policy Implementation?

'To implement' means to complete, fulfill, or put into effect.[3] Implementation, therefore, is about doing, accomplishing a task, achieving a goal. **Policy implementation** is the process of transforming the goals of a policy into results. It follows the actual setting of goals and is necessary for their attainment. The rational model of policy-making, outlined in Chapter 3, places the implementation stage toward the end of the policy sequence. As Figure 4.1 shows, implementation is considered to be what happens between the adoption and evaluation of policy.

This appears to be very simple and straightforward. But the reality is a bit more complicated. To understand why, recall the formal distinction made in Chapter 1 between policies and programs. Policies, I said, are broad statements of goals that may

FIGURE 4.1 Stages of the Policy-Making Process

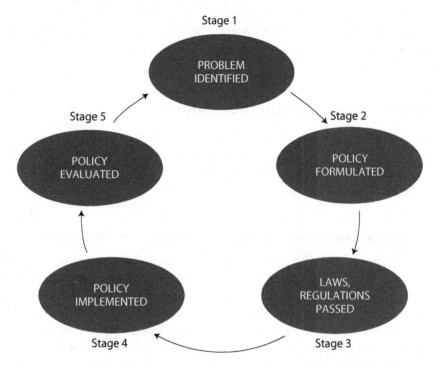

assume two forms: general goals and operational goals. Programs are the measures taken to achieve those goals, to implement those policies. Implementation is what happens at the program stage and is chiefly the task of bureaucrats. But what if program administrators actually establish the operational goals of policy, as they often do? What happens then to our claim that implementation 'follows the actual setting of goals'? Or what about a policy where the means chosen are virtually indistinguishable from the ends? Suppose that a policy of deregulating a particular industry requires the lifting of various existing controls on firms in that industry. In this case the measures taken to implement the policy are identical to the policy itself. Or take the case of a policy that seeks to increase the representation of some targeted group(s) in the workforce of a public agency to some specified level by a particular date. Is there any useful distinction to be made between such a policy of affirmative action and the means selected to accomplish it? Although there is room for manoeuvre in the precise measures used to implement this goal, a policy of affirmative action means hiring more people who have certain characteristics and so is inseparable from the hiring process that implements affirmative action.

A definition of implementation as the process of transforming policy goals into results cannot capture the messy reality of policy-making. Although logic and democratic beliefs tell us that policy formation precedes and is separate from policy implementation, the process is not always so neatly linear. What we can say is that policy implementation involves activities such as the application of rules, the interpretation of regulations, the enforcement of laws, and the delivery of services to the public and is carried out by a variety of officials who derive their authority and function from the law: bureaucrats, regulators, commissioners, inspectors, police officers, firefighters, postal workers, hospital administrators, health-care workers, and teachers, to mention a few.

Why Worry about Implementation?

There are two main reasons why implementation has long concerned those who study policy-making. One relates to democracy, the other to efficiency. The concern regarding democracy has a somewhat longer history than the one regarding efficiency, but both are prominent in contemporary work on policy implementation.

1. Democratic Dilemmas: The Politics/Administration Dichotomy

Democratic theory holds that all just government rests on the consent of the people. For practical reasons the people do not rule themselves. Instead, they assign this function to elected representatives. Policy decisions—which necessarily involve choices and compromises between competing values and interests—should be made by the people's elected representatives. The reason for this is simple enough: If citizens do not like the policies of their government they can replace those who govern them at the next election. Competitive elections held every few years are the key to ensuring that governments are responsive to the public will and accountable to the citizens for its actions (or inaction).

The role of the bureaucracy is to implement policies decided by the people's elected representatives, serving impartially regardless of which political party is in power. The bureaucracy is the machinery for translating political choices into action. It does not determine the *ends* of governance, but merely provides the *means* for accomplishing them.

The reality has always been rather different from the ideal. Indeed, the first modern writings on bureaucracy expressed concern over the discretionary powers of bureaucrats and their influence on policy.[4] Bureaucrats, it was believed, had a tendency to act in their own interests, which meant behaving in ways that might not be in the public's interest. Moreover, the fact that bureaucrats could have something to say about *what* things got done (not simply *how*) confused the lines of democratic accountability and produced opportunities for arbitrary government. Any shift in power from the elected politicians to the unelected bureaucrats would weaken popular control over the government, and public authority would become increasingly arbitrary because it would no longer be firmly anchored in the democratic process.

The fear that bureaucrats may usurp powers that properly belong to elected officials is an old one. Its roots lie in the realization that unelected officials have considerable power to affect policy and, moreover, that their values and interests may not be identical to those of their political masters (to say nothing of citizens). Implementation, according to this view, may subvert democracy. The likelihood of this happening increases as the discretionary powers of the bureaucracy grow.

2. Efficiency Dilemmas

Not only do we expect that policy goals will be accomplished; we also expect them to be achieved at a reasonable cost and without undue delay. In other words, we expect implementation to be efficient—but we also expect to be disappointed. There is a long tradition of considering public-sector bureaucracy to be a form of organized inefficiency, suffering from seemingly incurable pathologies whose symptoms include waste, duplication, delay, and inflexibility. This tradition is kept alive by bureaucracy-bashing journalists and politicians, popular stereotypes of bureaucratic dithering and incompetence, and the regular criticisms of governments' own efficiency watchdogs, such as the Auditor General of Canada and the Government Accountability Office in the United States.

The search for more efficient methods of implementation goes back to the late nineteenth century. Politics at that time was largely about patronage and the distribution of the spoils of power once a candidate or party was elected to office. Administrative positions from deputy minister to customs clerk were among the spoils distributed at the discretion of elected politicians. Administration by amateurs—men and women (not many of the latter) appointed to public service jobs because of their party and individual connections rather than their qualifications—became less and less acceptable as governance became increasingly complex and technical. The inefficiencies in policy implementation generated by the patronage system became a matter of concern in all the Anglo-American democracies, each of which combined patronage and expertise in its own way.

Replacing amateurs with specialists did not eliminate concern with the efficiency of implementation. The focus merely shifted to other sources of bureaucratic inefficiency. Many of these came to be defined as problems of implementation. They include the following:

- goal uncertainty;
- coordination;
- organizational culture;
- non-measurability of outputs;
- 'bureaupathic' behaviour; and
- too much/too little authority in the wrong places.

Rationality and Its Illusions

In the rational model of policy-making, shown in Figure 4.2, implementation involves three hierarchical steps: *instrument choice*, *communication*, and *program delivery*.

As Nakamura and Smallwood note,[5] this rational–hierarchical model rests on some rather fanciful assumptions about the real world of policy-making. Among them are the following:

- Policy formation and policy implementation are separate activities that occur sequentially.
- Policy-makers set goals and policy implementers carry them out.

FIGURE 4.2 The Rational–Hierarchical Model of Implementation

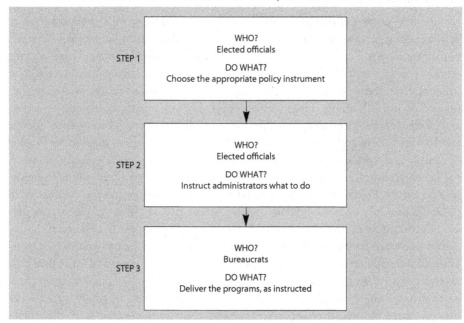

- Policy-makers are capable of formulating precise goals that are communicated to implementers in the form of unambiguous directives.
- Policy implementers possess both the technical skills and the will to carry out the instructions of policy-makers.
- Policy implementation is unaffected by the external environment of the implementers—the organizations and groups they deal with, the political pressures on them, media scrutiny of their activities, and a host of factors over which they have no control.
- Implementation is *technical* and *non-political*.

To understand why these assumptions are false, we need to return to the three steps in the rational–hierarchical model: instrument choice, communication, and program delivery. At each of these steps the premises that underlie the model are undermined by some inconvenient realities. Let's examine them.

1. Instrument Choice

In deciding how best to accomplish a policy goal (or a set of related goals), policy-makers consider a number of factors. Only some of these have to do with the cost-effectiveness or technical efficiency of the instrument chosen to implement a particular policy. Political considerations, past experience, bureaucratic preferences, and random factors like the personal values of key decision makers may all play a role in the selection of the means to accomplish some policy goal(s). Indeed, simple efficiency considerations, such as how to maximize the achievement of value 'X' at the least cost to taxpayers, are likely to be overshadowed by these rival concerns.

Does this mean that instrument choice is usually irrational? Not at all. What it means, in fact, is that there are often three sorts of rationality at play in deciding how to implement a policy. We may label these **technical rationality**, **political rationality**, and **bureaucratic rationality**.

Technical rationality. This is the classical–rational model of decision making that we described earlier. In selecting the means to achieve given ends, it asks two main questions: 'What measures are most likely to achieve these goals?' and 'How can these goals be accomplished at least cost?' The key decision makers here are technical experts: engineers, accountants, surveyors, economists, systems analysts, and so on. The decision-making process that leads to technically rational decisions is characterized by studies, interdepartmental committees, impact assessments, and perhaps commissions and task forces that solicit and distill expert opinion.

Although the two tests of technical rationality listed above may be applied to any policy decision, in practice these considerations seldom dictate instrument choice. This is particularly true in the following circumstances:

- when government is subject to many conflicting demands as to what should be done and therefore must seek compromises both on goals and on how to attain them;
- when the goals and means of policy are not clearly distinct, so that non-technical considerations affecting the choice of goals necessarily influence the choice of means;
- when policy goals are vague, allowing administrators a large margin of discretion, and the interest groups with a stake in how these goals are implemented are well organized and politically active; and
- when government already knows what interest groups it wants to listen to and what it wants to do, but is legally and/or politically required to go through the motions of respecting technical advice.

Technical rationality is most likely to determine the choice of policy instrument when policy goals are uncontroversial, intrabureaucratic rivalries are low, or the policy matter in question is relatively obscure, and experts are therefore able to dominate the decision-making process.

Political rationality. A decision to locate a new government office in Windsor rather than Mississauga because of the perception that the governing party will benefit more—perhaps by electing a new member or by strengthening its support in a swing constituency that it currently holds—is perfectly rational. It makes sense from the standpoint of the policy-makers taking the decision, if not from that of taxpayers footing the bill. We do not have to look very far for evidence that these sorts of considerations often determine the selection of policy instrument. Nor are politically motivated choices necessarily 'bad' ones.

Take the case of a government decision to award a major contract to a Montreal-based company rather than a Winnipeg-based one, even though the Winnipeg company's bid is technically superior (which actually happened in 1988, when the maintenance contract for the CF-18 fighter plane was awarded to Bombardier over Bristol Aerospace). If this choice is influenced by unity considerations—that is, a desire to show Quebeckers what they gain from their membership in Canada—or is based on simple distributive considerations like 'It's Quebec's turn for a piece of the public pie,' who is to say that such a choice is bad? What might be a poor choice from an accountant's or engineer's perspective may be a good one when viewed from the perspective of that slippery concept known as the 'national interest'. Or maybe not. The point is that political considerations are often legitimate ones in instrument selection, and not simply when choosing goals.

Bureaucratic rationality. Why is it that bureaucrats rarely propose policy measures that do not involve government intervention of some sort? After all, it is not inconceivable that the best solution to a social or economic problem might be to lighten the hand of government—a solution that does not require any new program, budget, or staff. When the Canadian government decided to launch a program of privatizing some state-owned companies, thus downsizing government, it set up a new administrative agency to oversee the project. More government to reduce government! In fairness, some bureaucratic agencies do not approach public policy with the assumption that a program or regulatory approach is necessary to deal with a public policy problem. Financial watchdog agencies such as the Office of the Auditor General, the Treasury Board, and the Department of Finance are most likely to be skeptical about the effectiveness of new or existing programs. But as a general rule it is unwise to count on bureaucrats for non-bureaucratic solutions to public policy problems.

This is neither surprising nor nefarious. Bureaucrats, according to the public choice model discussed in Chapter 2, are motivated by a desire to hang on to what they have and, if possible, increase their budgets, staffs, program responsibilities, and prestige. Whether or not one accepts what public choice has to say about bureaucratic behaviour, there are other reasons for expecting bureaucrats to bring their own special rationality to policy problems, including the choice of policy instrument. This involves the *roles and rules* within which they operate. These include the following:

- shared professional norms;
- the imperatives of administrative coordination;
- the organizational 'culture' of a particular bureaucratic agency; and
- unresolved political conflicts and imprecise directions to the implementing agency (the two often occur together).

We will elaborate on these factors in a later section on problems of implementation.

2. Communication

In the rational model of policy-making there is no slippage or distortion between the instructions of those who make policy and the actions of those who implement it. In other words, communication is not a problem. The reality, as anyone who has worked in a complex organization of any sort knows, is otherwise. Between the top and the bottom of an organization much can happen to change or stymie the intentions of those at the beginning of the chain of communication. The same is true when communication between organizations is required to coordinate policy implementation.

There are several reasons why communication is a problem. First, the goals established by policy-makers are often extremely vague, expressed in language that is ambiguous and open to interpretation. For example, the Bank of Canada Act includes the following statement of the Bank's goals:

> . . . to regulate credit and currency in the best interests of the nation, to control and protect the external value of the national monetary unit and to mitigate by its influence fluctuations in the general level of production, trade, prices and employment, so far as may be possible within the scope of monetary action, and generally to promote the economic and financial welfare of Canada.[6]

Politicians typically establish the *general* goals of an agency or program, leaving the *operational* goals to be determined by those entrusted with the implementation of policy. The distinction between general and operational goals is explained by James Q. Wilson:

> By goal I mean an image of a desired future state of affairs. If that image can be compared unambiguously to an actual state of affairs, it is an operational goal. If it cannot be so compared, and thus we cannot make verifiable statements about whether the goal has been attained, it is a general goal.[7]

A law that says 'Fifty per cent of television programming between the hours of 7:00 p.m. to 11:00 p.m. will be Canadian,' and that also defines what constitutes Canadian programming, would set down operational goals for those who implement broadcasting policy. But the Broadcasting Act is not so precise, declaring instead that the Canadian Radio-television and Telecommunications Commission (CRTC) should regulate broadcasters so as to 'safeguard, enrich and strengthen the cultural, political, social and economic fabric of Canada'.[8] In other words, policy-makers have established very general goals, leaving the operational goals up to those who will implement the law.

This lack of precision creates room for confusion, misunderstanding, and simple disagreement between politicians and administrators. Although various formal and informal mechanisms exist to ensure that what elected officials intend is what administrators do, they seldom eliminate ambiguity.

Communication problems are also created by differences in norms, perspectives, and jargon. Administrators do not all speak the same language. An agency staffed by accountants is likely to define the problems of social assistance programs differently from an agency staffed by social workers. Differences in professional norms and jargon can impede communication between agencies, creating confusion and misunderstanding, and widely divergent professional perspectives can produce impenetrable barriers to co-operation. A good example is provided by Leslie Pal in his

1988 study of what was then known as the unemployment insurance program (UI; now employment insurance). Pal shows that those who administered this program during its first few decades viewed it in actuarial terms, as essentially an insurance program that should be financed on an actuarially sound basis. But policy-makers associated with other agencies, such as the Ministry of Labour, frequently proposed extensions and modifications of UI that would have compromised what Pal calls the 'actuarial ideology' of UI officials, generating conflict over both the goals and the implementation of the program.[9]

Communication problems are related to those of coordination within and between organizations. They also include problems of individual motivation, informal relations and networks within organizations, and what we might call the 'permeability' of organizations. By this we mean that the behaviour of those within an organization is often affected by their exchanges with individuals and groups outside their organization. For example, some administrative agencies are in daily contact with the private sector whose actions they regulate. In such circumstances it is quite normal, and not at all surprising, that a clientelistic relationship develops between regulators and regulated—a relationship characterized by close and formalized interaction, dependence of administrators on information provided by the regulated parties, and shared outlooks. These communications may have a greater influence on program implementers' behaviour than either the stated goals of the program or the formal lines of authority within the program's bureaucracy.

3. Delivery

At the third step of the rational–hierarchical model of implementation, administrators deliver the goods: issue the cheques; inspect the premises, product, process, or files; decide who is eligible and who is not; process the applications; and so on. In short, they carry out the policy. But as in the case of the other two stages of the implementation process, things are not so simple. Program delivery is affected by several factors. Among the most important of these is the problem of coordination.

Program delivery typically requires the involvement of many participants whose preferences have to be taken into account, and many decisions and agreements must be reached before the 'output' is produced. Jeffrey Pressman and Aaron Wildavsky demonstrate that even an apparently straightforward program, where the goals are agreed upon and money has been allotted, can experience a long and troublesome delivery because of what they call the *complexity of joint action*.[10]

Virtually all programs depend on some level of joint action. In other words, the efforts of some number of people must be coordinated to accomplish a program's objectives. Often not appreciated, Pressman and Wildavsky argue, are

> the number of steps involved, the number of participants whose preferences have to be taken into account, the number of separate decisions that are part of what we think of as a simple one. Least of all do we appreciate the geometric growth of interdependencies over time where each negotiation involves a number of participants with decisions to make, whose implications ramify over time.[11]

They postulate that as the number of separate decisions that must be taken increases, the likelihood of successful implementation (whatever 'successful' might mean) decreases.

If nothing else, the complexities of joint action tend to produce delay because the preferences of different organizations whose efforts must be coordinated, or even of different individuals within an agency, are unlikely to be identical. Nor is their level of interest in a program likely to be the same. What is a burning priority for one agency may be a peripheral concern for another whose co-operation is necessary for program delivery. Moreover, the resources they are able or willing to devote to the program in question are unlikely to be equal.

Compromise is the first cousin of delay. 'Everyone wants coordination', note Pressman and Wildavsky, 'on his own terms.'[12] The reality, of course, is that coordination carries a price in terms of the compromises that must be made to bridge the varying agendas, timeliness, and resources of those whose joint efforts are required at the program delivery stage. The results may seem to be more or less what policy-makers and societal stakeholders had in mind when the program was first launched. Or they may not. What is certain is that the requirement of joint action introduces additional uncertainties into policy implementation, on top of those we have already discussed.

The Problems of Implementation

In the early summer of 1952, before the heat of the coming election campaign, US President Harry S. Truman used to contemplate the problems that General Eisenhower would face should he win the presidency. 'He'll sit here,' Truman would remark (tapping his desk for emphasis), 'and he'll say "Do this! Do that!" And nothing will happen. Poor Ike—it won't be a bit like the Army. He'll find it very frustrating.'[13]

We have touched on several features of implementation that may produce 'slippage' between what lawmakers decide and what ultimately happens. In this section we will elaborate on several of these and examine some additional problems of implementation.

The focus here (and throughout this chapter) on the problematic characteristics of implementation should not be interpreted to mean that interactions are never clear and that policy is never translated into straightforward action. Instead, our goal is to demonstrate that what are often labelled implementation problems—and therefore mistakenly assumed to be problems of bureaucracy per se—are often governance problems for which there are no administrative 'quick fixes'.[14]

1. Attitudes and Beliefs of Administrators

Administrators are not bloodless ciphers. They often have strongly held ideas about what they should be doing, how they should be doing it, and what is in the 'public interest'—or at least in the interest of that segment of the public with which they deal. They may have served under a particular political party for years and grown comfortable with the policies implemented under its direction. So what happens if their ideas are out of sync with what elected officials expect them to do? This occasionally does happen, but it happens much less often than one might suspect. While it is tempting to imagine that attitudes determine behaviour, psychologists have not found much evidence for this claim. Situational factors often appear to be more important. 'Our behaviour toward an object', observed James Q. Wilson, 'will be influenced not only by our evaluation of it but by the rewards and penalties associated with alternative courses of action.'[15] The tug of personal beliefs can be rather weak compared with these situational imperatives.

This is not to say that attitudes and beliefs are irrelevant. The influence of administrators' values on their behaviour appears to be greatest when the formal rules defining their roles and how their job should be done are weakly defined. In these circumstances the norms developed as a result of specialized training and membership in a professional group may be significant determinants of behaviour. Likewise, the ideological predilections of administrators are allowed greater scope when roles and rules are weakly defined. Even so, empirical studies suggest that the political views of bureaucrats are more likely to correspond to the positions they occupy within the bureaucracy—their agency affiliation and their role within it—than by their social background. An American study found that the social origins of senior-level bureaucrats explained only about 5 per cent of the variation in their opinions, while their agency affiliation—a situational factor—explained far more.[16]

There remains the possibility that the behaviour of those entrusted with the task of implementing policy will be influenced by what might be called the **bureaucratic personality**. The idea of the bureaucratic personality was developed by sociologist Robert K. Merton.[17] He argued that administrators acquire certain dispositions because of the nature of work in a bureaucratic organization. If they appear to be cautious, inflexible, rule-bound, and conformist it is because these personality traits are reinforced by the reward-and-punishment systems of bureaucracies. Through a process of 'goal displacement', Merton argues, administrators will come to value means above ends. The bureaucratic personality is more preoccupied with behaving according to the rules than with achieving the goals that are supposed to be the organization's raison d'être.

2. Turf and Autonomy

Human beings are territorial animals. They are reluctant to give up that which they consider to be theirs, whether that is a bit of land, their office and status at work, or the affection or respect of those around them. They tend to protect their turf, and some may even be imperialistic, seeking to take over the turf of others.

Bureaucrats are human beings and exhibit these same territorial qualities. One of the most common assertions about bureaucrats and their agencies is that they are constantly struggling to acquire larger budgets, a bigger staff, and more prestige. In addition, so the argument goes, they are driven by expansionist tendencies. This makes for a rather neat behavioural generalization, satisfying both those who like their social science simple and others (sometimes the same people) who are ideologically disposed against bureaucracy and 'big government'. Unfortunately, the facts do not support this claim. Various studies have shown that bureaucratic agencies and their chiefs often resist the imposition of new tasks that would increase their resources, and in some cases they even part with a division or program without regret.[18] Does this mean that *homo bureaucratus* is less concerned than other human beings with defending his or her turf? Not at all. Philip Selznick argues that what organizations and those within them really seek is autonomy. What Selznick means by 'autonomy' is a 'condition of independence sufficient to permit a group to work out and maintain a distinctive identity'.[19] In other words, bureaucrats do not crave turf per se, but the resources and conditions that enable them to protect what they see as their domain and their agency's mission (identity). This is a more sophisticated interpretation of the 'territorial behaviour' of bureaucratic agencies, and one that allows us to make sense of those occasions—admittedly infrequent—when an agency accepts a budget cut or program loss without protest.

Concern with protecting turf and autonomy creates problems from the standpoint of coordinating the work of different agencies. Coordination, by its very nature, involves some loss of autonomy for the involved parties. When program implementation requires that the efforts of different agencies, and sometimes different levels of government, be coordinated, one may expect to observe some amount of what Merton called 'goal displacement'.[20] The *policy* goals associated with the program may have to compete with the *organizational* goals of those involved in its implementation.

3. Interests

In a classic study of policy implementation, Philip Selznick argued that bureaucratic agencies that are given a large margin of discretion in carrying out policy will be vulnerable to capture by interest groups.[21] The agency's conception of its role and the way it administers the law are likely to be strongly influenced by pressures coming from the key external stakeholders affected by the agency's action. Selznick called this **co-optation**. Others who have focused on regulatory agencies have observed a similar phenomenon: Agencies originally established to serve the public interest end up becoming the compliant tools of the private interests they were supposed to regulate.[22] The lesson seems clear: Beware the influence of interest groups at the implementation stage of the policy process.

The problem of external stakeholders influencing the behaviour of an agency is greatest in the case of *client agencies*. An example of a client agency would be the Canadian Transportation Agency, which, among other things, approves the rates that may be charged and the routes that may be served by the handful of airlines in Canada. The provincial energy boards that must approve the prices charged by local natural gas monopolies are also client agencies. Without going so far as to say that agencies like these become 'captured' by the interests they regulate, it is reasonable to expect that the information provided by the regulated interests will have a significant impact on the decisions of the regulator. The ability of an agency to verify its information independently, and its willingness to do so, will vary.

As Wilson notes, client relationships between bureaucratic agencies and societal interests are not limited to the business sector.[23] The National Research Council, for example, is a grants agency whose clientele consists mainly of professors interested in research in the natural and applied sciences. The Canada Council for the Arts and its provincial counterparts have clientelistic relationships with groups in the arts community. It comes as no surprise to find that the views of these agencies generally reflect those of the clients who depend on the programs they administer.

Other agencies may also be significantly affected by external stakeholders. The policy community of which an agency is the focal point will often include a number of interest groups, representing a diverse and perhaps contradictory range of demands. This may help to liberate the agency from the clutches of any particular interest group, or it may simply ensure that whatever the agency does will be criticized by somebody. What is certain is that the presence of highly organized external stakeholders is a factor that will affect the behaviour of agencies responsible for policy implementation.

4. Culture: Organizational and Political

'Every organization has a culture', argues Wilson, '. . . a persistent, patterned way of thinking about the central tasks of and human relationships within an organization.'[24] Philip Selznick called this the 'distinctive competence of an organization'.[25] An agency's culture—or cultures, because it is not unusual for an organization to include more than one distinct culture—is produced by a number of factors. These include the professional and ideological norms of its members, the techniques and practices commonly used in performing the organization's tasks, and the situational imperatives it faces. The vaguer the stated goals of a government organization, and therefore the more discretion it is allowed, the greater the influence of organizational culture on how an agency's members define their roles and implement policy.

For example, consider the case of provincial human rights commissions. Their mandate is typically quite vague but generally involves hearing complaints of actions alleged to violate the province's human rights code and then issuing orders for remedial action. Those who work for such agencies often have backgrounds in law, social work, and other social sciences. Their ideological dispositions, one may safely say, tend to be left of centre.

Given the background and leanings of their staff members and the fairly wide latitude these agencies enjoy in determining how they will carry out their vaguely defined tasks, it comes as no surprise when human rights commissions act as outspoken advocates for the rights of women, visible minorities, Aboriginal Canadians, and the disabled. One would expect such an agency to be critical of government policies and social practices and of institutions that are accused of being discriminatory. We are not saying that the culture of the agency—the dominant norms of those within it—determine agency behaviour in a predictable way. In this particular case, the structural imperatives of a human rights commission—the legislation establishing it and its institutional role as a body to hear and adjudicate instances of alleged discrimination—create a web of expectations for the agency, not only among those within it but in the eyes of external stakeholders such as the media, rights-oriented interest groups, legislators, and police forces. What we are saying is that the norms shared by an agency's personnel, and often the predispositions of its chief administrator(s), can have a crucial impact on how policy is implemented.

Two concrete examples will illustrate this point. Les Pal describes how the orientation of the Department of the Secretary of State (SOS) was strongly influenced by the individuals who staffed key departmental positions during the 1960s and 1970s.[26] Many of those who held leadership positions in SOS, particularly in its citizenship branch, had been active in the Company of Young Canadians (CYC), a government-sponsored agency for social activism that was shut down only years after its creation because of what the government interpreted as excessive radicalism. The CYC 'alumni' who went into SOS carried with them a commitment to the activist agenda of the 1960s and a desire to transform the department into the vehicle for improving the status and political participation of disadvantaged groups. As Sandra Gwyn observed of a couple of these radicals-turned-bureaucrats, they

> turned the Citizenship [Branch] into a flamboyant, free-spending *animateur sociale* [*sic*]. Traditional, father-knows-best groups were upstaged. Instead, massive grants went out to militant native groups, tenants' associations and other putative aliens of the 1970s.[27]

In the words of one former radical turned SOS administrator, the citizenship branch was 'the only part of government that seemed human'.[28]

The point is that there was nothing inevitable about the social activism that characterized the agency's approach during the late 1960s and early 1970s. The sense of mission that imbued SOS, in particular its citizenship branch, came largely from the administrators themselves. They carried into SOS a commitment to 'social action', what Pal describes as the deliberate mobilization of social sentiment in desired directions.[29] But desired by whom, and for what purposes? These matters were determined by the dominant culture of SOS's citizenship branch in those heady days.

A final example of how organizational culture affects policy implementation involves the Department of Finance. The department is widely acknowledged to be the most influential agency within the federal bureaucracy, a status it has long enjoyed. As such, it attracts the 'best and the brightest', ambitious civil servants who recognize that Finance is where the action is. 'The department', writes Alan Freeman, 'has developed a corporate culture unparalleled in government. Staff members routinely work 12 hour days, seven days a week, to prepare a budget or develop [a policy like] the goods and services tax.'[30] A former high-ranking official in Finance compares the agency to a monastic order, committed to fiscal responsibility and debt reduction, and motivated by the belief that the Finance point of view is the one that should prevail in government policy-making.

How does this affect implementation? Finance administers virtually nothing, having been shorn of its program responsibilities in the 1960s when the Treasury Board became a separate agency. Nevertheless, Finance is able to influence policy implementation throughout government because of its key role in budget-making and its dominant status—rivalled only by the Bank of Canada—in economic policy-making. In the words of one federal economist, 'Finance wants to monopolize economic thinking in government. There is just no debate about alternatives.'[31] The organizational culture that nurtures this jealous hoarding of economic power apparently has resulted in struggles between Finance and other agencies, such as Statistics Canada, that have wanted to carry out economic analysis. Some Ottawa insiders argue that the 1992 decision to eliminate the Economic Council of Canada, Finance's chief rival in analyzing economic trends and making policy recommendations, was influenced by Finance's desire to eliminate a competitor whose views were not always in tune with its own.[32] These claims suggest that Finance, like other agencies, is motivated by territorialism. But they also illustrate the impact that organizational culture can have on the behaviour of an agency.

Key Terms

bureaucratic personality A concept developed by sociologist Robert K. Merton to describe administrators who become cautious and conformist because of the nature of working in a bureaucracy. The bureaucratic personality values means over ends and considers following rules more important than achieving goals.

bureaucratic rationality One of three types of reasoning used in deciding how a policy should be implemented. Bureaucratic rationality leads bureaucrats to favour measures that involve increased government intervention on the grounds that more bureaucracy will be needed to carry them out.

co-optation An agency's conception of its role and the way it administers the law are likely to be strongly influenced by pressures coming from the key external stakeholders affected by the agency's action.

policy implementation The process of transforming the goals associated with a policy into results.

political rationality The reasoning behind implementation decisions that will benefit the governing party—for example, by strengthening its popular support in a particular region.

technical rationality The classical–rational model of decision making, based on two main considerations: which measures are most likely to achieve the desired goals and how those goals can be accomplished at the least cost.

BOX 4.1   Lax Rules on Political Financing No. 1 Global Corruption Threat: Report

The unregulated flow of money into the political process remains the biggest corruption threat facing a majority of countries, regardless of income levels, according to a new report released Wednesday.

The annual report, the fourth since 2004 prepared by Global Integrity, a Washington DC-based independent think tank, tracked corruption trends around the world.

It rated 57 countries, including Canada, on anti-corruption mechanisms and government accountability.

Canada Ranked 5th out of 57

Canada ranked fifth overall behind Poland, Bulgaria, Japan, and Romania, respectively. Somalia was last.

Overall, Canada moved up from eighth place on the list last year. However, it posted a slight 'downward tick' based on secrecy surrounding political financing and gaps in government accountability, managing director Nathaniel Heller said in a teleconference with reporters Wednesday.

'Canada is a really interesting case,' he said. While the country's overall positive rating is not surprising, there are 'unique gaps in the system that are strange', he said.

For example, senators and judges are not required to disclose assets. Political financing loans to candidates are confidential.

That does not mean there is rampant corruption, but rather there is the potential for problems down the road, said Heller.

Loopholes Undermine Canada's Integrity

The Ottawa-based group Democracy Watch echoed those concerns in a press release Wednesday.

'Canada's federal government has significant loopholes in its government accountability system when compared to other countries and has a lot of work to do to become the world's leading democracy,' said coordinator Duff Conacher.

'Government integrity continues to be undermined by loopholes that allow secret donations to some candidates, and allow for excessive government secrecy including secret, unethical lobbying, as well as by cabinet patronage appointments, lack of judicial and Senate accountability, and weak government accountability lapdog agencies.'

The gap between perception and the Global Integrity's positive assessment of these countries 'may signal the presence of a dynamic civil society and media, which are capable of bringing issues of good governance into the public spotlight', the report said.

'A lack of scandals, on the other hand, would not necessarily be a positive sign and could reflect a more repressive environment in which watchdogs are pressured into avoiding sensitive investigations.'

In another example, organized crime issues play a major (if not dominant) role in shaping perceptions of corruption in Bulgaria but are not reflected in the battery of indicators fielded by the report.

The group did not measure actual corruption.

'That would be impossible. How can you measure what you can't see?' Heller said. Rather, the results point to how well countries are handling corruption issues, he added.

Source: CBC News, February 18, 2009. www.cbc.ca/news/canada/story/2009/02/18/corruption.html (this is an edited version of the original article).

Discussion Questions

1. When political parties campaign on platforms such as reduction of government waste, does this increase the efficiency dilemmas described in the chapter? Or do you think that bureaucrats ignore policy platforms and continue their programs regardless of which party takes the reins of power?
2. Does the article in Box 4.1 reflect any or all of the problems of implementation discussed in the chapter? Does any one problem seem to be more central than the others?

Websites

The following sites provide a sense of different non-governmental agencies that try to foster relationships with the government.

Institute for Citizen-Centred Service (ICCS)
www.iccs-isac.org
The ICCS works with public and government bodies to promote high levels of citizen satisfaction with delivery of public sector services—in other words, ensuring that when implemented, policy does its job of serving those it was created for.

The Institute of Public Administration of Canada (IPAC)
www.ipac.ca
IPAC is an association of public servants, academics, and others interested in public administration who work together to promote excellence in the field of public service. The aim is to ensure that policy is administered to the best of public servants' abilities.

Human Resources and Skills Development Canada (HRSDC)
www.rhdcc-hrsdc.gc.ca
Part of this federal department's mission is ongoing improvement of service delivery to Canadians.

Voluntary Sector Initiative (VSI)
www.vsi-isbc.org
The VSI was created in June 2000 to improve the relationship between the voluntary sector and the federal government and to strengthen the sector's overall operation. The voluntary sector plays an important role in the development and delivery of policies, services, and programs designed to enhance society nationwide.

CHAPTER 5

Policy Evaluation

Introduction

Once we have crafted and implemented policy the work is not over. A key component of the policy cycle involves evaluation of the policy. **Evaluation** is the term used for the measurement of an agency's performance, and it is an important part of policy implementation. Evaluation is the step that enables us to know how well we are accomplishing what we set out to do, and it is a function that has been institutionalized throughout government. Some agencies are specialized evaluation watchdogs with responsibility over a specific policy field (e.g., the Commissioner of Official Languages, who is responsible for monitoring the implementation of federal bilingualism policies) or aspect of policy-making (e.g., the Auditor General of Canada, who is responsible for ensuring that public money is spent as authorized and that taxpayers receive 'value-for-money').

Virtually all government departments, and many smaller agencies such as the Canadian International Development Agency, have in-house program evaluation bureaus. **Program evaluation** is part of the budgetary process that requires all departments and agencies to justify their spending requests to the Treasury Board in terms of how their programs met the policy goals established by cabinet. Evaluation before policy implementation is also legally required under the 1985 Canadian Environmental Protection Act to determine whether a government project will have adverse environmental consequences. This is a form of evaluation known as **impact assessment**. However, it is more accurately described as policy analysis as it attempts to predict the impact a proposed policy might have on the environment.[1] Finally, evaluation of existing programs and assessment of proposed task forces, Royal Commissions, parliamentary committees, and other permanent or temporary government bodies frequently do program evaluations.

The Government of Canada has recently updated its policy on evaluation from 2001. The objective of the new policy, which was put in effect on April 1, 2009, is 'to create a comprehensive and reliable base of evaluation evidence that is used to support policy and program improvement, expenditure management, Cabinet decision making and public reporting'.[2] These elements deserve explanation, which we will do in this chapter.

Policy and Program Improvement

Public policy is never over. In crafting policy, one must acknowledge that the process involves negotiation between various stakeholders and that compromise results in less than ideal policy. With an eye for improvement, all policies are evaluated to see where progress can be made in the future. Often the most vocal critics of a particular policy are those who felt that the compromises reached left their perspective out of the original plan.

The Canadian Charter of Rights and Freedoms is a classic example of how policy is never finished. When the Charter was being crafted many stakeholder groups sought to ensure that particular rights and freedoms were enshrined in the constitution. Women, visible minorities, Aboriginal groups, and many others all sought to have the Charter say something about their particular needs and concerns. The compromise was to list rights for certain individuals and groups who got special protection under section 15 of the Charter.[3] Groups not listed, such as homosexuals, felt that the oversight diminished their rights, especially with respect to spousal issues and children. To make their case, a number of individuals first sought legislative remedy. When Parliament and legislative assemblies failed to provide the changes the groups felt were necessary they sought remedy through the courts. Numerous court cases, in effect, acted as policy evaluations of the section. In *Egan v. Canada*, the court ruled that the Charter should have included homosexuals in section 15 and decided to read homosexuals into the Charter. The Charter case is somewhat unique in that amendments to the constitution are difficult to achieve through legislatures, but nonetheless policy evaluation and revision can occur.

Most policy evaluation is not done in such open and dramatic fashion. Instead, policy evaluation typically involves a systematic approach from within the government department that examines several aspects of the policy. The primary focus is financial, asking the question of whether the policy provides **value-for-money**. However, other questions are also asked, such as whether the policy 'aligns with and supports the departmental Management, Resources and Results Structure'.[4] At the core of this policy evaluation is that it be 'a neutral assessment' of the department.

Expenditure Management

Policy evaluation has been given an increasingly important role in the policy-making process with the rise of value-for-money evaluations. Considering the massive allocation of resources toward public ends, there always remains the crucial question of whether the policy expenditure was worth the money spent. During the 1960s, the Johnson Administration in the United States faced heavy criticism when its unprecedented spending and vast number of programs designed to reduce poverty had not achieved its goals. Rather than reducing poverty, in many instances more and more people were seeking government assistance and, in addition, communities were fraught with other social ills such as increasing crime, violence, and parentless children. Thus, policy evaluation was born in the United States to develop a basis for decoding what needs to be done about a particular problem and as a way to develop a deeper understanding of the social problems that require public action.

As with many reforms, Canadian policy evaluation developed after the American lead. Nonetheless, Canada does have a long history of focusing on 'accountability' of the government managing taxpayer dollars. The agency most associated with expenditure management is the Office of the Auditor General. The Auditor General is mandated by Parliament to provide 'objective, fact-based information . . . to hold the federal government accountable for its stewardship of public funds'.[5] While the Office of the Auditor General dates back to 1878, the role of the office has changed significantly throughout the centuries. Initially, the Auditor General had two roles: to 'examine and report on past transactions, and to approve or reject the issuance of government cheques'.[6] In 1931, the cheque-writing responsibility was transferred to the Comptroller of the Treasury. This change allowed the Auditor General to become more independent by 'examining and reporting on how the funds were handled'.[7] For the next 20 years, the Auditor General mostly looked at whether payments made by the government were productive. In 1977, the Auditor General Act gave the office an expanded mandate that allowed it to examine the way in which the government managed its affairs. With these changes, the scope of the Auditor General was broadened to look at how policies were implemented by other levels of government.

Just as the policies that the Auditor General evaluates have changed, so too has the Auditor General's role been expanded over time. In 1994, the Act was amended to allow for up to three reports per year in addition to the annual report. The 1994 amendment also established the Commissioner of the Environment and Sustainable Development within the office of the Auditor General. The most recent changes to the role and duties outlined in the Auditor General Act passed in 2009 with the Budget Implementation Act. This Act allows the Auditor General to examine foundations that receive public money. In addition, seven Crown corporations are now part of the special examination requirement of the Financial Administration Act.

There are three types of audits that the Auditor General conducts: performance audits, financial audits, and special examinations of Crown corporations.

Performance Audit

The **performance audit**, initially based on the concept of value-for-money audits, answers two questions:

1. Are programs being run with due regard for economy, efficiency, and environmental impact?
2. Does the government have the means in place to measure a program's effectiveness?

In this manner the audit is non-political in that it provides no judgment or evaluation of whether the government should or should not pursue a particular policy. This type of audit looks at the practices, controls, and reporting systems in place to ensure best practices. Probably the most famous non-performance audit of recent memory was the request by the Auditor General to conduct a performance review of Parliament. When a House of Commons committee rejected the Auditor General's request, media reports suggested that Parliament was not ready to allow MP expenses to be audited. As Auditor General Sheila Fraser remarked at the time, 'It was never suggested that it would be an audit of MPs or MP's expenses, and certainly never, never an audit or any kind of assessment of MP's performance.' What Sheila Fraser wanted to do was 'a performance audit of the administration of the House of Commons in such areas as contracting, human resource management, management of information technology and security'.[8]

It is understandable that most people would be confused about the nature of the audit. The popular culture reference to 'audit' typically invokes images of financial accounting and money management. While the Auditor General certainly looks at whether money is properly accounted for, the performance audit examines whether the system itself is running efficiently and whether or not changes can be made to save money in the long run. For example, in a performance audit of the Treasury Board's information technology (IT) system, several risks associated with having aging IT infrastructure were identified. The Auditor General recommended that the Treasury Board begin by collecting information to assess the IT systems across government. The Auditor General also advised the Treasury Board to create plans to ensure that the risks associated with IT be managed on a sustainable basis.[9] Rather than asking directly for cost-cutting measures, the Auditor General is encouraging the government to make key investments to manage the risks associated with the ever-increasing reliance on information technology. Thus, performance audits do not look narrowly at whether every line item in a budget is properly allocated, but rather whether the system put in place will provide Canadians the necessary services they need at an appropriate level of risk.

Financial Audit

Despite the value of the performance audit, the most frequently mentioned audit that the Auditor General conducts is a **financial audit**. These audits answer the question, 'Is the government keeping proper accounts and records and presenting its financial information fairly?' This is the most common use of the term 'audit', and most Canadians probably understand it as being the same thing as an accountant auditing a tax return or other financial information. This type of audit ensures that the transactions conform to laws and regulations. It also allows the Auditor General to report on matters that Parliament should be made aware of.

This type of audit does provide a valuable service to Parliament as many items that can fall between the cracks in normal day-to-day activities are brought to wider attention. For example, the 2010 Fall Report of the Auditor General brought to the public's attention that the procurement of helicopters from National Defence had 'gaps in oversight and approval by senior boards'.[10] The audit not only identified disparities in the procurement process and the complexity of such large expenditures, but it also provided recommendations on how to improve accountability for the future. In addition, key departments were given the opportunity to respond to the recommendations. For example, one passage in the 2010 Fall Report recommends the following:

> 6.75 Recommendation. National Defence should undertake a review of lessons learned in the use of long-term in-service support contracts before amending the contract in 2013 with Boeing, in order to ensure that risks are appropriately identified and managed, costs are properly determined, and alternative service delivery options are considered.

Immediately after the recommendation was published, the Department of National Defence responded:

> Agreed. National Defence will continue to collect the lessons learned in the use of long-term in-service support contracts prior to amending the contract in 2013 with Boeing. This would include reviewing the existing in-service support contracts for the airlift capability project—tactical (ACP-T), maritime helicopter project and medium- to heavy-lift helicopter project, discussing the lessons learned with project managers from the three environments (Air, Land, and Sea), validating in-service support cost models, and communicating the findings to the proper in-service support policy owners for policy amendments. The aim is to ensure that risks are appropriately identified and managed, costs are properly determined, and alternatives are considered.[11]

Thus, while the popular press often writes dramatic headlines about Auditor General reports that imply the office is chiding the government, the reality is often quite different. True, the Auditor General reports often are critical of the way in which the government operates, but that is the nature of the job. The Auditor General is paid to find out where things do not work and offer suggestions for improvement. Departments may not like to be the centre of public scrutiny, but a key element in the reports is for those same departments to justify past decisions and set out mechanisms for constant improvement.

Special Examination of Crown Corporations

The Auditor General also audits most Crown corporations at least once every 10 years. Much like the performance audit, the special examination of Crown corporations scrutinizes the management of the Crown corporation as a whole. Rather than report directly to Parliament, the special examination of the Crown corporation is reported to the board of directors of the Crown, and within 30 days the corporation is required to make the report available to the Treasury Board. From then the corporation is given

60 days to make the report available to the public. Typically these reports are posted on the agency's website with the response to the audit. At the start of the audit the Auditor General's office identifies the systems and practices used for the examination, and the criteria by which they are to be examined is delineated.[12]

Cabinet Decision Making

In addition to the reports of the Auditor General, in 2003 the federal government created the Expenditure Review Committee (ERC) to review all federal spending. The committee is chaired by the president of the Treasury Board and is composed of senior government ministers. The mandate 'is to ensure that government spending remains under control, is accountable, is closely aligned with the priorities of Canadians, and that every tax dollar is invested with care to achieve results for Canadians'.[13]

There are seven criteria that the ERC assesses for existing programs and government spending:

- Public interest: Does the program area or activity continue to serve the public interest?
- Role of government: Is there a legitimate and necessary role for the government in this program area or activity?
- Federalism: Is the current role of the federal government appropriate, or is the program a candidate for realignment with the provinces?
- Partnership: What activities or programs should or could be transferred in whole or in part to the private/voluntary sector?
- Value-for-money: Are Canadians getting value for their tax dollars?
- Efficiency: If the program or activity continues, how could its efficiency be improved?
- Affordability: Is the resultant package of programs and activities affordable? If not, what programs or activities would be abandoned?[14]

While financial accountability is a key component to policy evaluation, the rules by which the Auditor General is governed purposely do not deal with other matters of evaluation. Answers to the above questions help underpin proposals made to the cabinet. In order to ensure such reporting is done, the responsibility for monitoring the evaluations is held by the Treasury Board; the Treasury Board is mandated to ensure that evaluations are done in a timely manner and reported to Parliament.

Public Reporting

Once a report has gone through the appropriate channels within the government it is made available to the public by reports submitted to Parliament. In this manner, Members of Parliament may comment on the evaluation and use the report as fodder for debate. In addition, the Treasury Board makes reports available directly to the public on its government web page.

Limitations to Evaluation

Even if we assume that the policy goal is clearly defined per se, one of the central problems of policy evaluation is determining all the consequences of policy decisions. In the social sciences we are very rarely in a position to isolate the effects of one particular policy in one particular field, and then evaluate them in separation from the economic and political environment (other policies and factors). Unlike the natural sciences, in which the behaviour of the phenomena analyzed can be reliably modelled and even predicted since there are generally some magnitudes that can be held constant, in the social sciences we are dealing with the 'complex phenomena' that include permanent interactions between conscious subjects—people—which makes the introduction of any constants impossible. Even though some laws or social sciences can be deemed as valid as those of natural sciences, we cannot use them to predict the exact results of social interactions. More importantly, it is difficult to say with certainty that a particular policy improved the lives of the people it was meant to help.

For example, although the laws of supply and demand are equally universally true as the law of gravity, the former laws do not allow us to predict anything in terms of numerical values of prices for any given moment in time. All they can produce is a 'model theory' that says that ***ceteris paribus*** (all things being equal), an increase in the supply of a commodity will result in a decrease in its price. But we cannot predict that an increase in the supply of money will bring about a decrease in prices, even less by how much, because increased supply could be offset by the effect of increased demand, yielding the flat or even increasing price trend. Of course, that does not mean that the theory that a supply increase creates the downward pressure on prices is incorrect; it only means that we cannot observe empirically the causal relationships between the supply of money and price movements in isolation from other effects and other polices that impact the prices.[15]

The notion about predicting how policies will affect the problems they were meant to solve is technically the purview of policy analysis. As Iris Geva-May and Leslie Pal point out, 'evaluation is a subset or phase of policy analysis that is primarily research oriented.'[16] This research involves answering questions in an empirical manner. If we want to know the effect of a particular policy, an evaluator needs to document that effect with evidence from the real world.

This has profound implications for policy evaluation. One way to look at it is to argue that any kind of public policy is a use of government force that interferes in one way or another with the spontaneous working of the free co-operation of the people. In contrast, governments often argue that intervention is needed because, left to this spontaneous order, some people fall through the cracks. In other words, governments maintain that the capitalist system is not perfect and that it requires 'correction' on the part of the government to smooth out the imperfections. Regardless of the general desirability of any given policy, the central problem of evaluation is to determine to what extent any policy yielded the results intended. However, this is the critical conundrum: How does one evaluate those effects? To do so we must be able to separate them from the effects of other policies on the same problem, or from the effect of simply changed circumstances.

Let's imagine, for example, that we wish to increase the minimum wage to help low-wage earners. The expected outcome that would indicate the success of our policy would be the increased wage rates for the lowest paid wage earners with no decline in the employment rate overall. However, even if it occurs, this increase could be a product of many different factors besides our minimum wage policy change, including increased investment of capital, larger consumer confidence, or other social policy measures. These other factors could mask the real impact of our policy, deceiving us into believing it reduced the unemployment rate while in reality it increased it. We have no way of directly measuring this impact of our policy. The only thing we can obtain by the econometric or statistical averaging of the data are aggregates, not causal explanations of the relationships between the individual magnitudes that comprise these aggregates.[17]

Many economists would say that increasing the minimum wage will increase unemployment by crowding the low-income earners out of the labour market. We would expect to detect empirically the increased unemployment as a consequence of the increased minimum wage rates. However, if investment rises in the same time period, detrimental effects of a minimum wage increase on unemployment would be masked; we would statistically detect a decline (rather than a predicted increase) in unemployment and conclude that our policy did not have any negative impact on unemployment. In reality, it did, but the effect was 'masked' by the general positive economic trend.[18] Without the minimum wage increase, the unemployment rate would have been even lower than it currently is. But we cannot observe that lower quantity empirically because it never came into existence. And we give the minimum wage increase policy a positive evaluation, even though we should not.[19]

In other cases, there is not only a problem of isolating the effects of a policy from other effects (experimentally 'controlling' for these effects), but also a problem with understanding and identifying the policy outcome conceptually. For example, let's look at merger controls in anti-trust policy, a policy aimed at preventing a large concentration in any particular industry. The usual rationale for this policy is that if industries are too concentrated, the private firms would gain monopoly power and reduce the level of competition by increasing the producer's surplus and profit at the expense of the consumer.[20] This is called **allocative inefficiency**. However, in the same time period, mergers between two firms can have a beneficial effect, for example, by reducing the costs per unit of product, as a consequence of the economies of scale; a larger factory, larger number of employees, and lower costs of coordination of production all reduce costs, and hence the price, and therefore can have clearly pro-competitive effects.[21] What is usually assumed that anti-trust agencies should do is make an *ex ante* **cost-benefit analysis** of any proposed merger between two firms, and approve only those in which the cost savings from economies of scale provided by a larger organization exceed the allocative welfare loss stemming from the more concentrated industrial structure.

This sounds nice at the surface. Who would object to the competent cost-benefit assessment of public projects in the best interests of consumers? But when we try to define costs and benefits in this context we discover peculiar difficulties. For example, it is assumed that bureaucrats can know *ex ante* the extent of welfare losses from mergers and compare them with cost savings. In other words, it is assumed that they are able to know the counterfactual history—what the cost margin, pricing behaviour, cost savings, and managerial efficiency of this new larger firm will be compared to what these variables would be for the two separate firms—and that they are able to determine which of these two worlds is 'better' in terms of prices and quality of the final product for the consumer.[22] However, if bureaucrats were able to do this then the market would be completely unnecessary. If they were capable of predicting, independently from the market evaluation via prices, whether two firms would achieve superior aggregate results as separate entities or as a merged, bigger firm, they (bureaucrats) would then be able to collect all necessary knowledge to centrally plan the whole economy. Uncertainty and insufficient knowledge will be ruled out in principle.[23] However, as a consequence, bureaucrats would not only have to stop the mergers that are 'harmful' to consumers, but they would also have to force the mergers that private investors do not want to carry out but that they, the bureaucrats, predict will have the useful effects.

Once we realize that this is impossible—that government bureaucrats are incapable of collecting and using knowledge about economic data that private actors do not have—we confront the difficult problem of justifying the merger policy and, equally so, evaluating the effectiveness of this policy. When an agency allows a merger and the evaluation for this policy is given, for example, two years later, the evaluator has only prices and quantities of a merged firm to consider. She does not have access to the prices, quantities, and product quality of the two separate firms that would continue to operate if the merger had not been approved.[24] To be able to evaluate this policy successfully we must have knowledge about the future without experiencing it—basically, government regulators must be prophets. But if they are prophets, then the market is redundant since these prophets can plan much better.[25]

The key methodological problems in evaluating economic policies are reflected in these examples. The policy outcomes cannot be evaluated in the same manner that the results of scientific experiments are evaluated because causal lines are blurred in the social sciences. But the prevailing economic methodology in today's social sciences is almost entirely borrowed from the natural sciences. Scientific methodology is thought of as both formulating the individual hypotheses and providing the sufficient empirical data for the hypotheses to be validated or falsified. The tools of statistics and econometrics are abundantly used, and quality of proof is associated not with the logical soundness of the argument but with the amount and quality of empirical material.[26] By the same token, the evaluation of any policy proposal is tightly connected with the collection of sufficient empirical evidence that the policy had favourable or negative effects. But the data that are, in many cases, obtained this way are just guesswork expressed in sophisticated mathematical language.

Quantity does not, of course, mean quality. The fact that policy analysis before implementation and policy evaluation after implementation are permanent and pervasive features of modern policy-making does not mean that governments have a much clearer idea of how well they are meeting their objectives than they did in the days before formal evaluation. One reason for this was identified by the Ministerial Task

Force on Program Review (1985). Its final report noted that most program evaluations are carried out by the implementers themselves, raising serious questions about the objectivity of such studies. The possibility that results will be disclosed under the Access to Information Act is another factor that, according to the task force, reduces the frankness of many evaluations.[27]

A second reason why evaluation may fail to produce accurate and useful measures of performance has to do with the vague character of many public policy goals. The objectives of government programs often include things such as promoting Canadian culture, protecting the environment, improving the quality of life for some group or community, or promoting national unity. While it is possible to measure all these things, measurement often requires considerable ingenuity and the final result is unlikely to convince everyone. Take, for example, an environmental program that establishes a wilderness park in an area of harvestable timber. The economic costs, as these are conventionally calculated, are easily determined on the basis of the dollar value of the timber that could have been harvested and sold. By contrast, the benefits of a wilderness protection program are rather slippery. Economists are not comfortable with values that cannot be expressed in terms of dollars. The best measure of satisfaction, they argue, is the price users would be willing to pay for a good or service. Thus, economists would probably measure the value of the benefits provided by wilderness protection by estimating what visitors to the park would be willing to pay if this 'good' were sold on a competitive market. If, as seems likely, the opportunity cost of not logging the area far exceeds the value of benefits derived by future users of the wilderness area, does that mean that the program is inefficient?

Environmentalists would argue, of course, that things such as wilderness and species diversity have intrinsic value that cannot be reduced to dollar amounts. Animal rights activists would make a similar case, arguing that conventional economics does not take into account the rights of non-human life, except to calculate its consumption value for humans. Many policy analysts—not necessarily environmentalists or animal rights activists—would object to the idea that different policies, intended to achieve different goals, can be rendered commensurable by expressing all impacts in terms of dollars. This approach, they would argue, is biased in favour of programs that produce easily measurable benefits and tends to underestimate those values whose measurement is more elusive.

A third factor that limits the usefulness of performance measurement involves politics. Who has an interest in hard numbers on how well programs are meeting their objectives and how efficiently they are being implemented? Who, on the other hand, has an interest in fuzziness, ambiguity, and soft data that 'prove' the worth of a program? The stakeholders with an interest in hard measures include taxpayers; various state agencies whose *raison d'être* is efficiency in government, such as the Office of the Comptroller General and the Auditor General; and perhaps the clientele of the program in question. The stakeholders with an interest in soft measures include the departments and agencies that implement programs; the responsible cabinet minister and the government of the day, who probably have little if anything to gain but something to lose from exposure of ineffective or wasteful programs; and perhaps the program's clientele, who may be comfortable with a program that is run inefficiently from the general taxpayer's point of view or that serves goals that are not exactly what lawmakers expected the agency to promote. The bottom line is this: Program evaluation tends to take place on the periphery of the policy-making process without powerful supportive constituencies among political and bureaucratic elites.

Measuring Success

How do we know when a program is working? How can we be sure that the results achieved by program administrators have been accomplished as efficiently as possible? What is the litmus test (or what are the tests) of success in the public sector? These questions are crucial, because without some benchmarks for evaluating performance, policy implementation may be misdirected, counterproductive, or wasteful—or all three at once!

Measuring success—both in accomplishing goals and in doing so in an efficient manner—is no simple task. It is, however, easier in the private sector than in the public sector. The bottom lines that typically define organizational success in the private sector—profits, market share, share value, credit rating, and the like—are much more elusive in the public sector. Nevertheless, one thing is clear: *When public and private organizations perform similar tasks, private ones generally perform them more efficiently.* An enormous amount of empirical research supports this generalization.[28]

Why does this difference exist? James Wilson[29] identifies three main reasons:

1. *Situational ambiguity.* Public officials are less able than their private counterparts to define an efficient course of action. This is because they are often expected to achieve multiple goals with little or no guidance—or worse, in an environment of conflicting signals—about how to manage the trade-offs between these goals. For example, what is the goal of Canada Post? If you answered 'delivering the mail as promptly and efficiently as possible' you are only partly right. Canada Post is also expected to operate in Canada's two official languages, serve customers in sparsely populated rural areas, carry out door-to-door delivery in residential districts built before the early 1980s, and implement employment equity policies. These goals do not burden Purolator or FedEx.

2. *Incentives.* Public officials tend to be less motivated than their private-sector counterparts to identify an efficient course of action. This is not because they are lazier or less intelligent. Rather, the difference reflects the fact that private-sector managers will often profit personally from improving the efficiency of their organization, whereas these sorts of payoffs are much less common and less considerable in the public sector.

3. *Authority.* Even if a public-sector agency is staffed by efficiency zealots whose greatest fulfillment comes from finding ways to do more with less, they often lack the authority to carry out their efficiency improvement schemes. Their ability to hire and fire and determine compensation levels for employees is far less than that

of their private-sector counterparts. Government agencies usually depend entirely on the budgets allocated to them by the legislature and do not have the freedom to impose user fees for their services or to raise money in ways not authorized by elected politicians. Nor can they redesign program delivery, close or relocate regional offices, or alter the internal structure of the agency without the approval of other parts of government. And even when such approval is granted, the process is likely to take longer than it would in the private sector.

The Process of Policy Evaluation

Notwithstanding the inherent difficulties with establishing causes and effects of policies, policy evaluation must be conducted. What is probably most frustrating to those who conduct such analyses is that 'Politics, not evaluation results, determine which policies are to be adopted, continued or terminated.'[30] In an attempt to take politics out of the evaluation process, policy manuals dealing with the evaluation standards stress both evaluator skills and values. For example, in the *Professional Ethics and Standards for the Evaluation Community in the Government of Canada*, it is recommended that 'Evaluators need to have a certain mindset and be able to draw on different skills and techniques as they deem appropriate to any specific assignment. Evaluation in the policy context goes beyond research and analysis—it involves a blend of research, interpretation and critical thinking.'[31] At the same time the code of ethics for federal employees states that the ethical values of the government include '*Acting at all times in such a way as to uphold the public trust.*' Within that subsection, public servants are instructed to 'give honest and impartial advice and make all information relevant to a decision available to Ministers'.[32]

Reading evaluation reports made public by the Treasury Board may raise questions regarding how well government agencies have been able to fulfill these goals. To answer this question, in 2004 the Treasury Board reviewed federal evaluation reports on a number of criteria to determine whether there was an acceptable level of review. They concluded that most of the reports were acceptable; however, 23 per cent were rated as inadequate.[33] Most troublesome were two findings:

1. Only 26 per cent of evaluations provided findings on alternative, potentially more cost-effective approaches, though coverage of this issue has increased in more recent reports (31 per cent post–April 2002 versus 16 per cent pre–April 2002).
2. No reports presented evidence indicating that a program was not relevant or not needed.[34]

While the Treasury Board is silent on why there is a lack of critical analysis, it is not difficult to imagine why government agencies do not recommend policy termination. Despite the rhetoric regarding objectivity, neutrality, and professionalism, self-review will inevitably lead to justifying a program rather than arguing for its termination. Moreover, while the civil service is expected to be neutral, policy-making and policy evaluation is inherently political. Take, for example, the government's response to the recession in 2008–9. Initially the government stated in its economic update that it wished to lower taxes and reduce government spending to ensure a speedy recovery. When faced with a confidence motion by the opposition parties and the real threat of being replaced by a coalition government, the federal Conservatives quickly revised their plan and instead put forth a $33.7 billion deficit.[35] This deficit was in fact slightly larger than the one planned by the coalition partners that the government warned would result in economic hardship. Once the stimulus budget was passed and dollars began flowing across the country, would it be possible for the government to say that the stimulus did not work, despite the fact that the predicted $33.7 billion deficit had actually reached $53.8 billion by the time all the accounting had been completed?[36] Having committed to the spending, even with it being a temporary measure, the government now concluded that the stimulus worked and was the reason for the relative speedy economic recovery in Canada. For example, on January 31, 2011, Finance Minister Jim Flaherty stated, 'The Economic Action Plan continues to create jobs and economic growth with more than 26,000 projects underway or completed. With the economic recovery still fragile, our top priority will continue to be the economy.'[37]

Yet others, especially those outside the government, have been less convinced that the stimulus funding produced the results. According to the Fraser Institute's analysis of GDP growth and contribution from government stimulus, 'whether the economy was shrinking, stagnant, or growing, the contributions of government infrastructure investment and government spending to economic growth had little effect on changes in GDP growth.'[38] The government's response to the evaluation was to argue that the Fraser Institute economists used the wrong metric. But that tends to be the problem with evaluations: They depend on who is doing the measurement and the way in which the benchmarks are set. A free market think tank such as the Fraser Institute will evaluate government spending very differently from a labour think tank such as the Canadian Centre for Policy Alternatives (CCPA). Indeed, while the conclusion of the Fraser Institute was that the stimulus funding was too expensive for what it delivered, the CCPA argued that the government should have spent more on stimulus to make it work.[39] While the Auditor General evaluated the stimulus program on its efficiency, the report is silent on whether the funds achieved their desired effect (see Box 5.1).

While governments have routinized and codified policy evaluation, the fact remains that government bureaucrats criticize the policy at the margins and tend to use the evaluations to justify public spending. It is, therefore, only with the change in government and legislators that true policy evaluation is conducted. New governments, no longer bound by previous decisions, are much more likely to provide real evaluation of previous policy and are able to make effective changes to the machinery of government. Policy evaluation done in the political arena is by far the best reason why we have elections and can revise and sometimes terminate policy.

Although policy evaluation is a key element of the policy-making process, it is nonetheless subject to all the same political posturing as other parts of the policy process.

BOX 5.1 Report Applauds Stimulus Program

OTTAWA—Auditor General Sheila Fraser says the federal government was generally successful in rushing out $47 billion in stimulus money, but it sacrificed strict environmental controls and its tracking of job creation to the need for speed.

The first instalment of Fraser's stimulus audit finds that the myriad government departments involved in the Economic Action Plan hired extra people, put in many extra hours, and threw all their available resources at getting the money out the door as quickly as possible.

As a result, Fraser says the approval time for infrastructure programs was dramatically reduced to just two months from six months.

But even though the main goal of the unprecedented government spending was to create jobs, Fraser finds that there has been no serious attempt to determine how much employment has actually resulted from the stimulus.

Her observation adds weight to criticism from opposition parties—that there is no credible way to assess how effective the stimulus plan was in alleviating the effects of the recession or enabling recovery.

Fraser also points out that in their rush, government officials did not look closely enough at projects to see if they should have undergone an environmental assessment.

Instead, they relied on simple statements signed by the applicants for government money. Well over half the approved projects examined in the audit did not have enough information to show whether or not an exemption from environmental assessment was warranted.

'Decisions on whether an environmental assessment was required for some projects were made on the basis of insufficient information gathered from applicants,' she writes. 'As a result, it is unclear whether some projects that were approved should have undergone an environmental assessment.'

She says she might revisit the issue in her next audit of the stimulus program, which will look at how well the money was spent.

The federal government has now made its streamlined requirements for environmental assessments permanent, in an attempt to cut red tape.

Absent from Fraser's report is any mention of political interference leading to money for friends to build bridges to nowhere, as opposition critics have suggested. An analysis by The Canadian Press of the early stages of the stimulus program found that funding favoured Conservative ridings and paid little heed to areas struggling with high unemployment.

The auditors note that all the stimulus programs they examined were heavily oversubscribed, but they did not look deeply into whether the rejected project proposals deserved to be tossed.

Rather, they point out that in most programs cabinet ministers made the final call, as set out in the structure of the Economic Action Plan. The Office of the

Auditor General does not have the scope to dig into policy decisions made by cabinet ministers.

The audit did look at whether the building projects were significantly delayed, a key concern for many municipal organizations who argue that Ottawa should extend its funding past the deadline of next March so that unfinished projects aren't left in the lurch.

Fraser found that many infrastructure projects did not start on time, for many reasons, and some of them missed an entire building season.

'Project delays increase the risk that projects will not meet the completion deadline of March 31, 2011,' the report warns.

The government has responded by increasing its monitoring of delayed projects. The stimulus rules allow Ottawa to cancel the project outright if the deadline is not going to be met.

Fraser also criticizes the government for its shallow reporting to Parliament.

The quarterly reports were required in response to a demand of the Opposition Liberals, but the government larded the reports with anecdotes and amounts of money spent, instead of accounts of job creation.

'As a result, we found the reports presented an incomplete picture of project-level jobs created or maintained,' the audit says.

The Finance Department has been using an economic model to estimate how many jobs might be created, explaining that any jobs-creation data that may have been collected by program administrators was not reliable.

Finance has agreed to prepare a summary report for Parliament about the Economic Action Plan's impact, but that report, like earlier versions, will still be based on modelling.

In a news conference, Fraser said that without a firm jobs count, it will be hard for the government to evaluate which of its programs were most effective in fighting off the recession.

'What it will not be able to do, in all likelihood, is establish which particular programs were most successful and what can be learned from that.'

Generally, though, Fraser was impressed with the attention public servants paid to properly implementing such a large and complex program.

'This report is evidence that when senior officials give priority to large initiatives like the Economic Action Plan, public servants rise to the challenge,' she wrote.

'I would say I would give the government high marks for how they managed the initial phase of the plan,' she said in the news conference.

Source: Heather Scoffield, 'Report Applauds Stimulus Program', The Canadian Press, October 26, 2010. www.thestar.com/business/article/881421--report-applauds-stimulus-program.

Key Terms

allocative inefficiency A theoretical measure of the benefit or utility obtained from a proposed or actual choice in the distribution of resources.

ceteris paribus A Latin term meaning 'all things being equal'.

cost-benefit analysis A technique used to identify all the potential costs and benefits of a proposed or actual policy and then derive the net result. Ideally a net benefit will result in policy adoption, a net negative will result in policy rejection.

evaluation The measurement of an agency's performance.

ex ante A Latin term meaning an analysis done before adoption of a policy.

financial audits These audits ask the question, 'Is the government keeping proper accounts and records and presenting its financial information fairly?'

impact assessment An analysis typically done before policy adoption to determine what impacts the proposed policy will have on the environment.

performance audit These audits examine whether the system itself is running efficiently and whether or not changes can be made to save money in the long run.

program evaluation Part of the budgetary process that requires all departments and agencies to justify their spending requests to the Treasury Board in terms of how their programs met the policy goals established by cabinet.

value-for-money Closely related to allocative efficiency, in government value-for-money audits ask whether the government's use of money was worthwhile.

Discussion Questions

1. This chapter discusses the thorny issue of whether there can truly be an impartial policy evaluation. Is it possible for a government department to be objective when assessing its own policy performance?
2. Performance audits done by the Auditor General examine the overall efficiency of a government, agency, or policy. Can you think of any performance audits that recommended the government spend more to achieve value-for-money?

Websites

The following sites provide further examples of policy evaluation done by the government and private sector.

The Office of the Auditor General of Canada

www.oag-bvg.gc.ca

The Office of the Auditor General (OAG) audits federal government operations and reports its findings to the House of Commons, providing the independent information and advice necessary to hold the government accountable for its stewardship of public funds.

Canadian Public Policy

http://economics.ca/cpp

Based out of Montreal and focused on economic and social policy in Canada, this bilingual journal sparks research into and discussion of public policy problems in Canada. It appeals to a wide readership, including decision makers and consultants in business and government as well as researchers in both public and private institutions of learning.

Canadian Review of Social Policy (CRSP)

www.yorku.ca/crsp

This bilingual journal of progressive social policy is based out of York University and publishes analyses of historical and current development, issues, debates, and publication reviews to its audience of those working in education, the public sector, and social movements in the field of Canadian social policy and administration.

Department of Justice

www.justice.gc.ca

The Department of Justice provides a searchable database of most Acts of Parliament and is a useful resource for examining statutes.

Laurier Institute for the Study of Public Opinion and Policy (LISPOP)

www.wlu.ca/lispop

Based out of Wilfrid Laurier University, LISPOP studies issues related to the creation, use, and representation of public opinion on the policy process. The Institute is also an educational resource for academics and the community at large on these issues.

Simon Fraser University School of Public Policy

www.sfu.ca/mpp

Comprising the Master of Public Policy program (MPP) and the Centre for Public Policy Research (CPPR), Simon Fraser's School of Public Policy places an emphasis on educating public policy analysts and managers to assess problems, synthesize data, and evaluate alternative approaches en route to suggesting appropriate courses of action on issues of policy.

Treasury Board of Canada Secretariat

www.tbs-sct.gc.ca

The Treasury Board is responsible for accountability and ethics; financial, personnel administrative management; comptrollership; approving regulations; and most orders-in-council.

— PART II —

Policy Fields

CHAPTER 6

Macroeconomic Policy

Introduction

Economics is often called the 'dismal science'. No doubt many survivors of introductory economics courses will agree that the description is appropriate. Nevertheless, economic matters touch all of us in profound ways. The science of economics examines how wealth is created, what is needed to create jobs, why people spend, why they save, and why they invest. In other words, its subject matter consists of all the human transactions in which services and goods are exchanged either for money or for other services and goods. Most of us are (or will eventually be) workers, consumers, savers (however unlikely that may seem to students who face the prospect of repaying thousands of dollars of debt after graduation!), and investors, and so the concerns and categories of economics matter to us in very personal ways. Likewise, what governments do—or neglect to do—to protect and promote economic activity matters to us all. The dismal character of economic science should never blind us to this truth.

   Most if not all readers of this book will have heard the terms 'budget deficit', 'Bank of Canada rate', 'money supply', 'trade surplus/deficit', and 'the business cycle'. Each of these refers either to an aspect of the economy as a whole or to government action intended to influence the overall state of the economy. They are part of the lexicon of macroeconomics and macroeconomic policy. *Macroeconomics* deals with the behaviour of the economy as a whole, and thus with large aggregate phenomena like employment, investment, inflation, growth, and trade. The distinction between macroeconomics and microeconomics is one of emphasis. *Microeconomics* focuses on components of the overall economy, such as markets, industries, firms, and consumers. Likewise, the distinction between macroeconomic policy and sectoral economic policy is not sharp or absolute, although there are important differences in terms of the policy instruments that governments employ. Macroeconomic policy is sometimes referred to as *economic stabilization policy*—a description that clearly conveys the expectations that have developed for the state's role in maintaining acceptable levels of growth and employment.

Changing Paradigms in Macroeconomic Policy-Making

1. The Keynesian Consensus

The beginning of modern macroeconomics is usually dated from the publication of John Maynard Keynes's *The General Theory of Employment, Interest and Money* (1936). Keynes created a rift in the economics community with his view of the role that government could or should play in the economy. Prior to Keynes, classical economic thought conceived of the market as a place with internal corrective measures and saw little if any role for government intervention. The dominant view in economics was that supply created its own demand. The law of supply and demand holds that if supply does not meet demand, then one of those two elements will change until there is equilibrium. This means that in the absence of uncompetitive practices on the part of businesses, labour, or government, an economy will tend toward equilibrium (demand matched by supply) and full employment. In seventeenth-century Europe, for example, the demand for tulip bulbs was so great that bulb producers could not keep up the supply. To deal with the shortfall of supply, a seller had only to show a piece of paper saying that he or she owned a bulb to sell it at a higher price. Not only did the price increase, but so did the trade in tulips. At the height of 'tulipomania' the number of. bulbs on the market was 10 million. The tulip market finally collapsed on April 27, 1637, when a decree was issued declaring that the purchase and sale of tulip bulbs was to be conducted in the same way as any other business. Speculation ceased and, though many people were ruined, prices fell to reasonable levels. Today gardeners still plant tulip bulbs and the price reflects the supply and demand.

The supply and demand theory, or classical economics, was associated with laissez-faire economic policies. It did not deny the existence of cyclical fluctuations in economic activity, but it maintained that deviations from equilibrium were temporary and self-correcting. It therefore followed that government intervention, no matter how well intentioned, would inevitably aggravate economic disruptions by interfering with the natural harmony of the price mechanism and markets.

Keynes argued that equilibrium might be reached at points other than full employment and focused on aggregate demand as the chief determinant of the level of economic activity. Calling into question the classical assumption that a free-market economy is inherently stable, Keynes argued that the sum of consumer, business, and government demand might be insufficient to maintain full employment, in which case governments should step in to increase the level of aggregate demand. The main tools of demand management that he suggested were measures to encourage private expenditure and government spending on public works.[1] **Keynesianism** quickly came to be the general label for government interference in the market, especially government policies intended to reduce the severity and duration of downturns in the business cycle.

The business cycle that concerned Keynes was what economists call the intermediate cycle, determined by the rate of capital investment (I will have more to say about business cycles later in this section). Keynes argued that the level of capital investment, upon which growth and full employment depended, was determined by the marginal efficiency of capital. When the rate of return on new capital investment weakened, the government could play a compensatory role either through investment in public works or through taxation policies designed to make private capital investment more attractive than it would otherwise be (i.e., policies like investment tax credits and the removal or reduction of taxes on the purchase of new machinery or building materials to make new capital investment less costly). These government responses to observed and anticipated trends in economic activity came to be called **discretionary stabilization measures.** In addition, governments adopted **automatic stabilizers** intended to moderate the fluctuations in the business cycle. Among the most significant of these were the income maintenance programs that constituted the foundations of the emerging welfare state. To cite a Canadian example, it appears that the main impetus behind the introduction of the universal family allowance in 1945 came from Keynesian economists in the federal bureaucracy who believed that such payments would help maintain a high level of purchasing power in the economy.[2] In this way social policy was harnessed for purposes of economic management. However, it would be a distortion to attribute the emergence of the welfare state to the prior conversion of governments to Keynesian economic policies.

The theories and policies that came to be described as Keynesian dominated in the economics profession and among state elites in capitalist societies until roughly the early 1970s. Indeed, Milton Friedman, who would become associated with the monetarist 'alternative' to Keynesian policies, acknowledged this consensus when in 1965 he observed, 'We are all Keynesians now.'[3] The basis for this consensus was the apparent success of Keynesian policies. The annual rate of real economic growth for member countries of the Organisation for Economic Co-operation and Development (OECD) averaged more than 5 per cent between 1950 and 1970. Unemployment and inflation rates both averaged in the 2–3 per cent range. The trade-off between employment and inflation expressed in the Phillips curve—developed by the British economist A.W. Phillips in the late 1950s—was widely accepted. Evidence from the real world at least did not contradict the idea that government action to stimulate growth, and therefore employment, would also result in upward pressure on prices because demand would increase.

The first cracks in the Keynesian consensus began to emerge around 1970, largely, though not exclusively, in response to evidence of the increasing unmanageability of capitalist economies. Between 1974 and 1983 the rate of annual growth in real GNP for OECD countries was 2.1 per cent, while inflation averaged 9.7 per cent and unemployment, about 6 per cent.[4] The phenomenon of **stagflation**—low or no real economic growth, accompanied by high levels of inflation—called into question the conventional wisdom regarding the government's ability to manage the economy through taxation and public spending (i.e., fiscal policy). This economic disorder provided the impetus for the development of alternative theoretical models in macroeconomics, the most important of which have been monetarism and neo-classical economics. It is likely, however, that both the 'success' and subsequent 'failure' of Keynesian policies have been exaggerated. An important part of the explanation for both the general buoyancy of capitalist economies until the early 1970s and the comparatively unstable economic conditions that seem to have existed since then lies in changes in the conditions for economic growth, what we will call **structural changes**. These changes have not passed unnoticed by some economists, although both the mainstream of that profession and governments appear oblivious to them.

The Keynesian paradigm is interventionist. It provides a basis in economic theory for the **positive state**, a state dedicated to maintaining high levels of employment and economic growth. It is also a state that believes only government intervention in the economy can achieve those goals. In order to stabilize economic activity, two conditions are necessary. First, it must be possible to identify economic trends, particularly in business investment and consumer expenditure, before their consequences—either low growth and increased unemployment or excess demand and inflation—are experienced. Second, if a shortage in effective demand is acknowledged to be the cause of economic recession and unemployment, governments must be willing to use demand policies (i.e., fiscal policies) to remedy market failure. Conversely, a government can cool an overheated economy by either increasing taxes or withdrawing some deductions enjoyed by business. Thus, Keynesianism sees the state as potentially part of the solution to the periodic failure of the market to produce adequate business investment and full employment. The main challengers to Keynesian economics, however, argue that the state is part of the problem.

2. The Monetarist and Neo-Classical Challenges

The reasons for the unravelling of the Keynesian consensus were found both in the real world of economic phenomena and within the economics profession itself. As unemployment and inflation reached levels unprecedented in the post-war period, and as economic growth slowed in several of the main capitalist economies, the effectiveness of the discretionary fiscal policies that were the key weapons in the Keynesian arsenal were increasingly questioned. The fragmentation of the Keynesian consensus provided the intellectual opportunity for challenges to the demand management model, and in some political systems it also created receptive conditions for alternative economic policies. At the same time, the discipline of economics was developing in a more abstract direction, using mathematical models and emphasizing the logical coherence of theory over the accuracy of its assumptions about human behaviour. The advance of this trend in the discipline has not been slowed by frequent criticism from some distinguished economists, including Nobel laureates Wassily Leontief and James Tobin. Leontief's comments are typical: 'Page after page of professional economic journals are filled with mathematical formulas leading the reader from sets of more or less plausible, but entirely arbitrary, assumptions to precisely stated but irrelevant conclusions.'[5]

Of the two main challenges to Keynesianism, monetarism has certainly had the greatest influence on economic policy. Monetarist economic policies were adopted in both the United States and the United Kingdom at the end of the 1970s (more on this shortly). Partly because of its association with the Thatcher government in the UK and with the anti-interventionist political views of its main economics advocate, Milton Friedman, the term 'monetarism' has acquired connotations of political conservatism.

Before considering whether this is a fair ideological characterization of the policy prescriptions that follow from the monetarist model, it is necessary to understand what monetarism says about the determinants of economic activity. This is not a simple matter. Monetarism is frequently misunderstood as the use of credit policy (i.e., interest rates) to influence levels of demand and hence economic growth and inflation. In fact, the major monetarist economists, such as Friedman and Karl Brunner, argue *against* the use of monetary policy to counter short-term fluctuations in economic activity.[6]

Monetarism has a fundamental principle from which all else follows: Changes in the money supply (currency and deposits against which cheques can be written) entail changes in economic activity. In Friedman's words, 'Erratic monetary growth almost always produces erratic economic growth.'[7] Basing his analysis on historical studies of the American economy, Friedman concluded that periods of economic growth and inflation were associated with expansion of the money supply, while decreases in the stock of money were associated with economic recession and, occasionally, a fall in real prices. Friedman and other monetarists generally dismiss the influence of fiscal policy, taxation, and government spending on economic activity, although they maintain that these factors do play an important role in determining the size of government (too big) and its role in the economy (too interventionist). But they also argue against the deliberate manipulation of the money supply as a means of stabilizing the economy on the grounds that the real effects of changes in the money supply are experienced only after a time lag. Friedman, using evidence from the American economy, estimates this lag at anywhere from six months to two years. By the time a government-induced increase in the money supply has its intended effect, therefore, the economic conditions that prompted the policy are likely to have changed. What was intended to be stabilizing may in fact have destabilizing consequences.

What, then, do monetarists propose as an appropriate macroeconomic policy? Monetarists argue that the money supply should be increased at a gradual and constant rate, perhaps 3–4 per cent annually. This policy prescription, known as the monetary rule, is based on the belief that the private sector is inherently stable, a belief that has as a corollary the view that the main cause of adverse economic conditions is discretionary government policy. Monetarists advocate a predictable institutional framework for economic activity. The reasoning behind proposals for such a framework—what Brunner calls a 'policy regime'—is that it would minimize the effort that private agents (consumers, businesses, and investors) must make to acquire information about the probable consequences of their behaviour. If the future is predictable, this reduces the risk that the economy will suffer as a result of misperceptions (which monetarists argue are the chief consequences of discretionary policy) or unexpected events. An emphasis on the continuity of economic policy, as expressed in the monetary rule, is fundamentally at odds with the Keynesian argument that government policy should change as often as necessary to compensate for significant fluctuations in the level of business investment and aggregate demand. It is, however, very similar to the emphasis on policy 'rules' advocated by the new classical economics.

The **new classical economics** is sometimes, and misleadingly, referred to as the 'rational expectations' school. It is distinguished by two main microeconomic assumptions that have important consequences for its analysis of the overall economy and, therefore, the policies it advocates:

1. Consumers, workers, firms, and businesses operate from a position of perfect knowledge about the consequences of their behaviour and always seek to maximize their utility (the rational expectations assumption).
2. Markets clear rapidly; in other words, the equilibrium of supply and demand will always re-establish itself within a short time (the equilibrium assumption).

The 'rational expectations' assumption, though often derided as obviously unrealistic, is acknowledged by many leading neo-Keynesian and monetarist economists to be a useful hypothesis for model-building and possibly even the most accurate behavioural assumption for the long run.[8] The second assumption, that markets clear rapidly and therefore the economy is constantly in a moving equilibrium, is the main point of contention between the new classical economics and its critics.

Stated very simply the problem is this: If markets do clear rapidly and the economy is usually in equilibrium, how is one to explain the persistence of high unemployment rates in the 1990s? The new classical economists answer this question by arguing that the 'natural rate' of unemployment has increased as a result of state benefits that are generous enough to cause many workers to choose to be unemployed (monetarists agree with this proposition that the level of 'voluntary' unemployment has increased significantly). A second part of this model's explanation of unemployment argues that workers may *temporarily* price themselves out of jobs by miscalculating the equilibrium wage. This argument is associated with Robert Lucas, one of the major figures in new classical economics. It stresses imperfect information and uncertainty as the sources of workers' misperceptions about the appropriate price for their labour. According to the new classical model, these misperceptions will not persist because workers will quickly adjust their expectations to the new equilibrium wage. Discretionary economic policy is identified as one of the major sources of uncertainty in the economy and is seen by the new classical economists as having a destabilizing effect (the exact opposite of the role that Keynesians attribute to it).

One might be tempted to conclude that the new classical economics explains unemployment by explaining it away—by denying the existence (or persistence) of involuntary unemployment. But this conclusion would be incorrect. Some economists, such as Robert Lucas, have said that the unemployment of the Great Depression could be explained as a problem of worker misperceptions:

> If you look back at the 1929 to 1933 episode, there were a lot of decisions made that, after the fact, people wished they had not made; there were a lot of jobs people quit that they wished they had hung on to; there were job offers that people turned down because they thought the wage offer was crappy. Then three

months later they wished they had grabbed [those jobs] . . . . People are making this kind of mistake all the time.[9]

Other economists, however, point to government intervention as a cause of involuntary unemployment. Taxation policies often have unintended consequences, they say, and may sometimes be counterproductive. For example, payroll taxes such as employment insurance (EI) are often criticized as job killers because they increase the cost to the employer of every employee hired—thus, a company might want to hire ten workers but not be able to afford more than nine. While the workers currently employed have a cushion, should they become temporarily unemployed, more people are in the market looking for work who might already be employed if the government did not impose employment taxes.

3. Rules versus Discretion

Monetarist and new classical economists have much in common in what they say about the government's appropriate relationship to the economy. Both emphasize predictability in government behaviour; therefore both oppose the use of discretionary policies to influence demand and investment on the grounds that these policies are either ineffective or actually destabilizing (because of the uncertainty they provoke). Neither monetarists nor the new classical economists advocate complete laissez-faire macroeconomic policy. Instead, they argue for policy rules, like Friedman's monetary rule, intended 'to lower the burden of the information problem imposed by discretionary policy-making on agents'.[10] Without denying that cyclical fluctuations in economic activity occur, both monetarists and new classical economists maintain that the private sector is inherently stable and that economies tend toward full employment. They differ on the time required for prices and wages to adjust to market-clearing levels—monetarists argue that this may take years. In the end, however, neither school is troubled by current levels of unemployment, since both believe that the availability of state benefits increases the proportion of people who are voluntarily unemployed.

The Keynesian position is very different. Economists like James Tobin, Franco Modegliani, and Alan Blinder attribute the prosperity and relative economic stability of the 1950s and 1960s to the use of active (discretionary) fiscal and monetary policies to compensate for fluctuations in the business cycle.[11] The economic disorder of the 1970s caused Keynesians to re-examine their theoretical understanding of the economy, but it did not undermine their faith in the capacity of government policy to stabilize economic activity through the application of measures designed to raise or lower demand. It is hard to escape the conclusion that the difference between the Keynesian position that markets do not clear (except perhaps in the long run) and the belief of monetarists and new classical economists in the inherent stability of the private sector reflects a difference in political values as well. Asked about this connection, the Nobel laureate and prominent Keynesian James Tobin responded: 'Logically there need not be any. But there is a correlation. A neo-Keynesian seems to be more concerned about employment, jobs, and producing goods than people who have a great faith in market processes.'[12]

4. Three Business Cycles and a Political Cycle

The causes and even the existence of business cycles are matters of disagreement among economists. There can be no doubt, however, that both the language of macroeconomic policy (expansion/contraction, peak/trough, recession/recovery) and the behaviour of policy-makers reflect a belief in the periodic and more-or-less regular occurrence of fluctuations in the overall level of economic activity. The data from industrial capitalist countries tend to confirm the existence of cyclical variations in the degree to which both labour and capital are used, and thus in the rate of economic growth. Despite the evidence,[13] many contemporary textbooks in macroeconomics devote only passing attention to business cycles, and then in the context of stabilization policies that, logically, could be intended to compensate for random economic disturbances rather than cyclical variations. It should come as no surprise to find that neo-Keynesian economists like Paul Samuelson tend to take business cycles more seriously, because of their weaker belief in the inherent stability of the private sector, than do monetarists or new classical economists. The latter, because they assume the economy to be in a moving equilibrium, basically ignore the issue of business cycles. Monetarists like Friedman acknowledge the existence of cycles (which he attributes to fluctuations in the rate of growth of the money supply), but argue that government policies have actually aggravated the severity of economic fluctuations.[14]

The historical evidence suggests the existence of three distinct cyclical tendencies of different average durations: short (3–4 years), intermediate (7–10 years), and long (40–60 years). The short and intermediate cycles are the least controversial in terms of their causes and therefore in terms of the sorts of government policies that would be appropriate to compensate for the fluctuations they entail.

The short cycle is usually referred to as the *inventory cycle* and is a reflection of producers' responses to changes in the rate of consumer expenditure. The basic idea is that retailers respond to a decline in consumer spending—registered in excessive inventories—by cutting their orders for future stock in an effort both to adjust to the reduction in consumer spending and to reduce costly inventories. As a result, they tend to overreact, cutting more, or more quickly, than they should. By the time consumer spending begins to recover, their inventories have been so depleted that once again they overreact, ordering more than the market can absorb. In other words, the rate of increase in supply (and therefore the utilization of existing productive capacity in the economy) outpaces the recovery in consumer spending. If the level of consumer spending did not vary, the inventory cycle would not occur. However, the evidence suggests that variations in consumer spending, related in part to short-term trends in consumers' optimism or pessimism about the economy, are inevitable.

The short duration of the inventory cycle presents problems for policy-makers in their efforts to reduce the extent of these business swings. To be effective, policy measures must be timely (implemented at the beginning of a contraction or expansion to reduce its amplitude); they must be specific in their effects (aimed directly at the factors—particularly consumer spending on durable goods and producer inventories—that determine the length of the cycle); and they must be retractable (capable of being changed or eliminated when the economy enters another phase of the cycle). This would suggest that the best way of dealing with the short cycle is through compensatory policies such as temporary reductions in the sales tax on durable consumer goods or special tax credits for business intended to reduce the costs of carrying inventories larger than warranted by a declining rate of consumer expenditure. Reliable forecasts of trends in consumer expenditure and business inventories are necessary to ensure that the timing of compensatory policy is appropriate. Otherwise, what was intended as a stabilization measure will in fact add to the severity of a swing in the cycle.

The intermediate cycle has received the most attention from economists. It is a reflection of both investment in new productive capacity and the periodic replacement of machinery and other durable goods. As Paul Samuelson observes, 'it is the durable or capital-goods sectors which show by far the greatest cyclical fluctuations.'[15] The reason is that this sort of spending can be deferred during periods of weak economic activity, but is subject to 'bunching' in good times, when businesses are most likely to invest in fixed capital (new plant, machinery, and equipment).

The causes of swings in the intermediate cycle are different from those that generate the short cycle. Consequently, different compensatory policies are appropriate. These may include government spending on public works, roads, harbours, buildings, and so on—projects that will take up the slack during periods of weak capital investment. A policy of public works spending was recommended by Keynes, but this is subject to a number of practical difficulties (to be considered below, in our discussion of the political business cycle). Probably the most suitable policy is one that increases the marginal efficiency of capital (i.e., that increases the profitability of new capital investment). The reduction or elimination of sales taxes on the purchase of machinery and construction materials, tax changes to allow the more rapid amortization of the costs of new capital investment against corporate taxes, and investment tax credits are all measures that would have the effect of reducing the cost of capital investment. If the problem is excessive investment generating inflationary pressures, the same policy instruments could be used in the opposite direction (e.g., sales taxes could be increased) to make capital expenditures less attractive. In either case, if countercyclical policy measures are to be effective they must remain *discretionary*. For example, if a reduction in the sales tax on purchases of new machinery becomes 'permanent' as a result of the political influence of the business interests that benefit from it, the usefulness of this particular lever of economic management will be lost.

The most controversial of the three cycles is the long cycle. These are often referred to as Kondratieff long waves, after the Russian economist Nikolai Kondratieff. The idea that capitalist economies experience long phases of relative expansion and contraction was popularized among English-speaking economists by Joseph Schumpeter[16] and Alvin Hansen.[17] After several decades of general neglect, the theory of long waves of economic activity has attracted renewed interest since the 1970s, in part because of dissatisfaction with conventional explanations for the weaker economic growth and higher levels of unemployment that have characterized most Western economies since the early 1970s. The empirical evidence for the existence of the long cycle is not conclusive. Some maintain that sustained periods of growth are not cyclical at all, but the product of historical accidents such as inventions and the 'discovery' and exploitation of new territories. If, however, the modern proponents of the long wave are correct in their claims (1) that industrial economies typically experience long periods of above-average growth followed by decades of below-average growth, and (2) that these historical swings are not random but can be linked to recurring characteristics of economic development, the implications for economic policy are significant.

The theory that explains the long cycle has two main components. The first emphasizes the role of major technological innovations like the internal combustion engine in providing the impetus for a general increase in investment in new industries created by (and existing industries transformed by) the new technology. It appears, as Schumpeter argued, that major technological change has tended to occur in clusters and that the growth industries spawned by these innovations have led the general economic expansion that characterizes the upswing of the long cycle. As the new technologies spread throughout the economy in the form of new products and/or production processes and their innovative possibilities approach exhaustion (i.e., the technological revolution reaches maturity), the general level of investment also begins to weaken. In this way the peak of the long cycle is reached. What follows is an extended period of lower economic growth caused by the weakened inducement to invest.

The second part of the theoretical explanation for long waves of investment involves what the American Marxist economist David Gordon has called the 'social structure of accumulation',[18] which might also be described more simply as the social climate of economic activity. The social climate characterizing a particular generation is influenced by the phase of the long cycle during which that generation's attitudes toward work and business are formed and also has an independent effect on the trend of economic activity. Maurice Lamontagne puts it this way:

> Generations reaching adulthood during hard times are more likely to respect the work ethic, to be more disciplined and to produce a harmonious social environment based on a broad consensus favouring economic growth. Generations reaching adulthood during prosperous times are more likely to be 'spoiled' by affluence, to be less motivated by the work ethic, to be more aggressive in the pursuit of their varied 'cultural' goals and to create an antagonistic social environment inimical to economic growth.[19]

Lamontagne is arguing that the downswing in the long cycle, in part brought on by the weakened social consensus in support of business values, gives rise toward the bottom of the cycle to a changed social climate that provides receptive ground for the next long phase of economic expansion.

This theory is logically tidy and certainly suggestive, given that the advent of weaker economic growth in most Western economies coincided with the emergence of the so-called 'Me generation'. Moreover, the concept of a relationship between generational experiences, social values, and the propensity to invest may help to explain what economists call labour market rigidities and 'stickiness' in wages during periods when the general level of unemployment is high, and unemployment for young adults tends to be about twice the general level. The theory needs rigorous testing in several societies before it can be accepted as a real phenomenon. Still, if we assume that decades-long fluctuations in the propensity to invest do exist, and that they are linked to revolutionary 'bunches' of technological innovation and to the level of social consensus on the primacy of business values, the implications for economic policy are profound. Measures appropriate for countering swings in the short and intermediate cycles would not be suitable for dealing with the causes of the long cycle. In fact, short of replacing the market entirely with some sort of centrally planned economy, it is difficult to see how economic policy could be more than a palliative measure aimed at avoiding a full-blown depression as the long cycle approaches its trough.

If the heirs to Keynes are correct in their belief that the discretionary policies of governments can have a stabilizing effect on overall economic activity, it remains the case that the success of such policies depends on their timely application and on the selection of suitable policy instruments. Otherwise, what was intended as a stabilization measure may in fact have destabilizing consequences. For example, if businesses are cutting back on production and laying off workers because of excessive inventories, a decrease in the bank rate intended to stimulate consumer demand for durable and nondurable goods may be the wrong measure to address what is a short-term source of instability. By the time the government recognizes the recessionary conditions, implements the interest rate changes, and waits for the economy to respond, the recessionary pressures may well have worked themselves out. Suppose, for instance, that the initial government decision making takes six months to complete. The market response could take an additional six months, and then it may take the government another six months to recognize that change. By now 18 months have passed, and in that time other policies may have been adopted that will influence the government's response (e.g., it may have signed a new trade agreement). Errors in the selection and timing of discretionary economic policies may sometimes be due to inaccurate forecasting of economic trends and to incorrect diagnoses of the causes of economic instability.

Another cause of failure in governments' attempts to manage their economies, however, may be what is often referred to as the **political business cycle**. Proponents of this argument point out that governments often use economic policies, particularly spending and tax measures, to improve their chances of re-election. The Swiss political economist Bruno Frey showed that governments in Britain and the United States pursued expansionary policies leading up to elections where the outcome seemed uncertain.[20] It is well known that government decisions on where and when to spend money on public works are often influenced by their desire to secure re-election. The Keynesian principle that governments should use public works to stimulate the intermediate investment cycle suggests an assumption that policy-makers act in response to economic signals. In the real world, however, they are also sensitive to political signals, particularly in the lead-up to elections.

Another explanation of the political business cycle is associated with the Polish economist Michal Kalecki. He maintains that there is a fundamental contradiction between full employment and price stability, and that the only way governments can deal with the resulting 'cost-push' inflation when the economy is at full employment is to engineer a deliberate economic slowdown. Such a policy is likely to have adverse consequences for a government's public support. Consequently, it will be rejected or at least not implemented with the necessary vigour. The outcome, so Kalecki and contemporary economists such as Paul Samuelson argue, is an 'increasing bias toward rising prices rather than stable prices' and a situation in which 'larger and larger amounts of unemployment are needed today to have the same wage and price restraining effect as in the past.'[21]

The Goals of Macroeconomic Policy in Canada: A Case of Diminishing Expectations

The 'official' adoption of Keynesian stabilization policy in Canada is generally traced to the federal government's 1945 White Paper on Employment and Income, and the Liberal party's election platform of that year. In the words of the White Paper:

> The Government will be prepared, in periods when unemployment threatens, to incur deficits and increases in the national debt resulting from its employment and income policy, whether that policy in the circumstances is best applied through increased expenditures or reduced taxation. In periods of buoyant employment and income, budget plans will call for surpluses.[22]

The White Paper and the Liberal party's election platform explicitly committed the government to maintaining high and stable levels of employment. Two aspects of this early commitment to macroeconomic stabilization are noteworthy for their differences from the more recently stated goals of government policy. First is the emphasis on employment and the general neglect of price stability as a goal of economic policy. This reflected the preoccupations of a generation whose ideas of what could go wrong with the capitalist economy were shaped by the Great Depression—when unemployment rates reached 20 per cent and prices actually declined. Inflation had averaged only 0.1 per cent per annum between 1927 and 1946, but unemployment had averaged 8.1 per cent. Second, the faith in fiscal policy, including budget deficits, as an instrument for achieving economic growth and full employment is in sharp contrast to much recent thinking on macroeconomic policy. In 1934 Keynes was confronted with the question, 'Can America spend its way into recovery?' His answer was unequivocal: 'Why, obviously! . . . We produce in order to sell. In other words, we produce in response to spending. It is impossible to suppose that we can stimulate production and employment by *refraining* from spending.'[23] Compare Keynes's answer to the following statement from the mid-1980s by Canada's finance minister at the time, Michael Wilson:

> Ten years of stimulation and deficits have not solved our problems. They have stimulated only a mountain of debt—a mountain of debt which is now growing twice as fast as the economy. Even worse, not only did 10 years of attempting to solve our problems this way fail to produce the desired growth and jobs, but now, as a result, we have less and less flexibility to deal with pressing public priorities.[24]

A heightened concern with price stability and budget deficits distinguishes recent thinking on macroeconomic policy from its counterpart during the decades of the

Keynesian consensus. Nevertheless, the official goals of government policy have remained substantially unchanged. These were summarized in the *Report of the Royal Commission on Banking and Finance*[25] as (1) rising productivity; (2) a high and stable level of employment; (3) price stability; and (4) a sound balance of payments. In its first annual review, the Economic Council of Canada added a fifth goal to this list: an equitable distribution of income.[26] This does not, however, appear to have been an important goal of Canadian macroeconomic policy. Instead, the distributional aspects of taxation and spending policies are considered in our analysis of social policy (Chapter 7). The other four goals continue to be the main pillars of both the policy and the rhetoric of governments, though their relative importance has changed and so has the thinking about the appropriate means for achieving them.

The most important change has been a retreat from the high employment objective that was a main pillar of Keynesian stabilization policy. Although political parties continue to repeat the mantra of 'Jobs, jobs, jobs!', particularly around election time, when in power they have shown a much greater tolerance for unemployment than would have been considered appropriate a couple of decades ago. Notwithstanding the Liberal government's National Infrastructure Program, initiated after the 1993 election, job creation has been the result of factors outside the Canadian economy. In other words, prior to the most recent recession, the past 15 years have demonstrated that Canada has benefited from the positive end of the business cycle. In 2007 Canada recorded its lowest level of unemployment in 30 years, leading some to claim that the market economy reduced the huge swings in the business cycle. Issues like the deficit, accumulated public-sector debt, Canada's international competitiveness, and price stability appeared to take priority over employment in recent years.

The diminishing expectations held for government as a guarantor of employment were suggested by the 1993 'Red Book', in which the Liberal party set out its policy commitments. It stated:

> The role of government in the economy is twofold: to establish the overall framework, which includes monetary and fiscal policy, federal–provincial fiscal relations, and trade policy; and to work in partnership with provincial governments, business, labour, and non-governmental institutions to achieve national economic objectives.[27]

The role of government, according to the Red Book, was to establish a framework for economic activity. This was a less active, and many would say a more realistic, role for government than the optimistic Keynesianism of the 1945 White Paper. This role was outlined even more clearly in the Liberal government's 1994 document *A New Framework for Economic Policy*, in which government indebtedness was identified as the primary cause of economic malaise, including high unemployment.

The critics of this scaled-down economic role for government, including many within the NDP, labour activists, and generally those on the left, argued that it reflected the agenda of the Canadian corporate elite and international capital. The banks and Canada's chief monetary institution, the Bank of Canada, came in for particular vilification because high real interest rates served the interests of investors at the expense of employment creation. Jim Stanford's argument was representative of this point of view: 'Monetary institutions . . . must be reformed to reflect a better balance of the needs of the whole macro economy, rather than (as at present) just the interests of the owners of financial wealth.'[28] Stanford and others on the left spoke of a 'permanent recession' and the 'socialization of capital'.

To describe the circumstances of the 1990s as a state of 'permanent recession' was rather a stretch. The fact was that Canada's job-creation record had been one of the best among advanced industrialized democracies since the recession of 1981–3 and, moreover, the personal cost of being unemployed is lower today than it was before the welfare state reforms of the 1960s. In addition, the labour force participation rate, that is, the proportion of people of working age who want jobs, is higher today than during the heyday of Keynesian economics. Keynesianism always implied a level of national economic autonomy that has become impossible in the global economy. Finally, those who hearken back to the golden years of 3–5 per cent unemployment appear to assume that the government's economic management policies were largely responsible, when in fact no such cause–effect relationship has ever been established. It may well be, then, that the diminished expectations held today for the government's economic role constitute a realistic response to contemporary circumstances. The experience of the past decade has shown that there need not be a trade-off between inflation and jobs; Canada has sustained an inflation rate between 1 and 3 per cent.[29]

Despite the move away from Keynesian economic policy during the 1990s and into the first decade of the 2000s, the global recession triggered by the sub-prime lending crisis in the United States provided the impetus to dust off Keynesian policies. Canada, along with most of the world, entered into a deep recession starting in 2008. In Canada, the unemployment rate jumped from 6.2 per cent in October 2008 to 7.2 per cent in January 2009. The rate has remained in the 8 per cent range throughout 2009 and 2010.[30] To deal with the recession, the Conservative federal government adopted classic Keynesian policies of government spending in its 2009 budget. Examples include an $8.3 billion infusion to skills and job training, $7.8 billion to stimulate the construction industry, and $12 billion for new infrastructure programs. In all, the government planned to spend $51.6 billion over two years to kick-start the economy.[31] While the Conservative government outlined a plan in its 2010 budget to get out of deficit by 2015, there remains pressure from the NDP and the Liberals to continue stimulus spending because of the jobless recovery.

1. The Macroeconomic Record: Performance and Policy

Like most Western capitalist economies, Canada has experienced higher levels of unemployment and price inflation and a more erratic record of growth since the early 1970s than it did in the previous two decades. At the same time the size of the federal government's debt (leaving aside that of the provinces) as a share of national income doubled during the 1990s. At its height it amounted to about one-third of gross national expenditure. Although total government debt has been reduced from 131 per cent of GDP in 1996, in 2007 it amounted to 65.2 per cent of GDP and today it has risen again to 81.6 per cent.[32] Whether or not government debt affects the economy's performance is a matter of dispute. It is, however, considered part of the problem by much of the public, the media, many politicians, and some (not all) economists, and for this reason we examine the deficit issue separately.

While the Canadian trends are broadly similar to their counterparts in the United States and other Western economies, Canada's labour productivity historically has been consistently lower than the OECD average and usually lower than that of its largest trading partner. This is despite the fact that Canada's record of economic growth as a measure of GDP has been slightly better than the OECD and American averages. In addition, historically Canada has had consistently higher unemployment rates than the United States in particular. However, the most recent recession has changed that dynamic, with Canada now posting slightly lower unemployment rates than the United States. For example, in October 2010 Canada's unemployment rate was 7.9 per cent compared with the US rate of 9.6 per cent.[33] The IMF estimates that Canada's unemployment rate will continue to be lower than that of the United States until 2015.[34]

Furthermore, unemployment rates have been going down in recent years, and some regions have even experienced labour shortages—not only Alberta, but British Columbia and, increasingly, Saskatchewan. The other positive factor to consider is the resilience suggested by the fact that the output gap for 1996–2005 averaged out to zero. This means that after an economic shock Canada tends to adjust more rapidly than many other OECD countries.

For the student of public policy the relevant question is what, if any, influence government policies have had on the performance of the economy. The output gap in particular has been linked to the structural reforms that took place in Canada beginning in the 1980s. However unpopular they may have been, the FTA and NAFTA, the GST, and the Bank of Canada's low-inflation policy have all been credited with improving our ability to withstand market shocks.[35] Mancur Olson examined the relationship between rates of economic growth and levels of government spending (final consumption and transfers) in the developed Western economies and Japan for the period 1950–79. He concluded that, 'except for Japan, there is no clear relation between the extent of government spending and transfers and the rate of growth.'[36]

There is a consensus among both mainstream and radical economists that the generally buoyant conditions of the 1950s and 1960s were propelled by internal forces within post-war Western economies rather than 'caused' by government policies. Economists W. Arthur Lewis (1954), C.P. Kindleberger (1967), and Nicholas Kaldor (1966) are associated with the idea that the existence of a large supply of labour available for employment in the expanding manufacturing sector of the economy was the principal factor that fuelled this economic growth. So long as the supply of labour remained abundant (as workers moved from the primary to other sectors of the economy) and upward pressure on wages therefore remained low, profitability in the expanding sectors of the economy continued to attract new capital investment. However, Andrea Boltho suggests that cheap raw materials for industrial processes and business confidence (promoted by governments' Keynesian and post-war reconstruction policies) also contributed to the buoyancy of this period.[37]

Marxist economists such as Ernest Mandel do not fundamentally disagree with this explanation of the extended post-war boom, although Mandel considers business confidence to be a consequence rather than a cause of the post-war expansion. Where the Marxists and the mainstream economists part company is in their explanations of why this expansion came to an end and their answers to the question of whether the much less propitious economic conditions of the 1970s and 1980s constitute a basic crisis in the capitalist system. There are four main explanations for the end of the full employment/steady, growth/stable prices phase of the 1950s and 1960s:

1. *The labour market.* This explanation points to the decreasing supply of labour and increasing wage demands, as well as to reduced flexibility in shifting workers between jobs and industries. The reduction in flexibility is greater in Western European economies than in North America. It is reinforced by legislation that makes layoffs and plant closures difficult, as well as state subsidies to declining industries, high levels of unionization, and rigidities in real wage rates.

2. *Unusual shocks.* Some argue that the general downturn that hit industrialized countries in the early 1970s was brought on by abnormal events that did not reflect fundamental flaws in these economies. The inflationary effects of American government spending on the Vietnam War and the OPEC price increases are commonly mentioned destabilizing events. In the words of a study commissioned by the OECD, 'our reading of recent history (1971–5) is that the most important feature was an unusual bunching of unfortunate disturbances unlikely to be repeated on the same scale, the impact of which was compounded by some avoidable errors in economic policy.'[38]

3. *Contradictions of capitalism.* Marxist analysts maintain that what conventional economists typically regard as unusual events, and originating from outside the economy, are in fact the structural outcomes of relationships within the world capitalist system. They interpret both the Vietnam War and the OPEC price shocks not as temporary and accidental occurrences but 'as a part of the challenge to US domination in the world economy'.[39] Marxists see the 'crisis' of Western capitalism as the result of conflict in the world economic order. They emphasize what they argue to be the inherent contradiction between what the state must do to support business profitability and the concessions it must make to the working class to maintain popular support for a social order grounded on economic inequality. To put this in more concrete terms, as long as conditions allowed for a general expansion of Western economies the governments of these countries could afford to 'buy off the working class through reforms, among which full employment and social security policies played a key role'.[40] When these conditions no longer existed (and here Marxists accept the relevance of factors such as changes in the labour supply and the availability of cheap raw materials), governments resorted to measures intended to restore the rate of business profitability. (This is not an absolute rate, but depends on the rates of return on capital available elsewhere.) Profitability assumed priority over full employment.

4. *The world economy in transition.* This explanation comes in a number of Marxist and non-Marxist varieties. We will focus on one non-Marxist version associated

with economist Michael Beenstock. He argues that the economic slowdown in the Western economies has been caused by the transfer of manufacturing capacity from developed countries (DCs) to less-developed countries (LDCs). Beenstock accepts the view that the growth in manufacturing fuelled the long post-war expansion. In response to factors such as the rise of the multinational corporation as the instrument for the transfer of technology from the DCs to the LDCs, and the availability of a cheaper and more flexible labour force in the LDCs, industrialization took hold in these economies. The result was a shift in the world economy as the higher marginal return on capital in the LDCs attracted an increasing share of new investment in manufacturing. Beenstock shows that the LDCs' share of world trade in manufactured products increased from 4 per cent in 1960 to 9 per cent in 1980, and that their share of world value-added trade in manufacturing grew from 9 to 14 per cent over the same period.[41] His conclusion that 'the economic upheavals that have taken place since about 1970 have been a consequence of a major realignment in the balance of world economic power'[42] might appear something of an overstatement in light of these figures. Combined with the increasing import penetration in the Western DCs of Japanese manufacturers, however, and with some of the internal developments mentioned in the previous three explanations of the economic downturn, the shift of manufacturing production to the LDCs probably has contributed to the weaker economic performance of the DCs. It certainly has contributed to increased political pressures on Western governments to protect domestic producers and jobs.

All of these explanations for the decline in stability and growth generally experienced in Western economies after about 1970 point to non-cyclical causes. Yet in their responses to these unfamiliar circumstances, governments initially continued to behave as though the countercyclical policies that had become the standard repertoire of macroeconomic intervention could do the job. In several countries, including Canada, the United States, and Great Britain, governments resorted to various temporary systems of wage and price controls. They did this in the belief that unusual interference with the price-setting mechanisms of the market (which economists such as John Kenneth Galbraith considered to be seriously flawed anyway), but particularly with wage increases, was necessary to bring inflation under control. By the mid-1970s many Western governments, including Canada's, had concluded that the main economic problem was persistent inflation and that the Keynesian repertoire of demand management techniques was not adequate to deal with it.

Disillusionment with Keynesianism did not result in a wholesale intellectual conversion to a different philosophy of economic management or a different set of discretionary tools. Instead, confronted with the same disorienting circumstances that undermined the Keynesian consensus among academic economists, policy-makers responded with an increased openness to new approaches for stabilizing the economy. When inflation came to be regarded by governments in several countries as the most debilitating problem confronting their economies, the emphasis in stabilization policy shifted from spending and taxation instruments to control over the money supply. Monetarism, which stressed gradual expansion of the money supply, the announcement of long-term targets for monetary growth, and thus an increased policy role for the central bank, was embraced with varying degrees of enthusiasm by the United States, Great Britain, West Germany, and Canada.

In the Canadian case, the Bank of Canada's *Annual Report* for 1973 had expressed sympathy for the Friedmanite policy of steady and predetermined increases in the money supply.[43] It was not until November 1975, however, that the Bank began to announce targets for the annual growth of the money supply, accompanied by a policy of gradually reducing the rate of increase in the money stock. As we have seen, the argument for monetary targets and policies intended to slow the growth of the money supply is that such measures are most likely to succeed in restraining demand and thereby bringing inflation under control. Given that the annual rate of inflation did not drop below 7.5 per cent during the Bank of Canada's seven-year experiment with monetarism (1975–82), one might be tempted to conclude that there is little empirical evidence to support this claim. Evaluating the effectiveness of monetarist policies, however, is complicated by at least two factors.

First, Canada's open economy, closely integrated with that of the United States through trade and financial markets, meant that the Canadian rate of inflation and overall level of economic activity were vulnerable to developments in the American economy. The high inflation of 1980–2 was to some extent 'imported' from the United States, particularly as a result of the policy of high interest rates pursued by the Federal Reserve Board (the monetary authority in that country). The Bank of Canada followed the Federal Reserve Board's lead for fear that failure to keep pace in interest rates would result in downward pressure on the Canadian dollar and therefore in inflationary pressure from an increase in the cost of goods imported into Canada.

Second, the Bank of Canada and some supporters of monetarism argue that the persistence of high levels of inflation after the adoption of a monetarist strategy is not proof that the theory is wrong. But it may indicate that monetarism was not applied properly. Speaking in 1980 before the House of Commons Standing Committee on Finance, Trade and Economic Affairs, the governor of the Bank, Gerald Bouey, maintained that the Bank's policy of *gradually* reducing the growth in the money supply was at fault. A more radical policy of restraint, he argued, would have been more effective.

Studies on whether monetarist policies in such countries as the United States, Great Britain, and Canada actually had an impact on inflation have reached mixed conclusions.[44] What is not in doubt is that the shift to monetarism meant that price stability was the chief priority of macroeconomic policy, at the expense of short-term employment. Statements by the Bank of Canada made this point time and again during the late 1970s and early 1980s. The intellectual guru of monetarism, Milton Friedman, has acknowledged that 'monetary policy is not an effective instrument for achieving directly either full employment or economic growth.'[45] It is not intended to be a solution to the problem of weak economic growth and high levels of unemployment. It is fair to conclude, therefore, that monetarism represents not simply a change in policy instrument but also a reorientation in economic priorities away from traditional Keynesian concerns with full employment.

Since 1982, when it abandoned the use of targets for growth in the money supply, the Bank of Canada has made price stability its principal goal. Under the current governor,

Mark Carney, the Bank has aimed to keep inflation at a 2 per cent target, the midway point between a 1 and 3 per cent inflation control target range. Indeed, two of Carney's predecessors, Gordon Thiessen and John Crow, often stated that the goal of Canadian monetary policy was zero inflation.[46] During the 1990s this meant that the Bank followed a policy of high real interest rates to dampen inflationary pressures. But the Bank of Canada, while quite independent from the government of the day, is subject to influences that restrict its margin for manoeuvre. In Thiessen's words:

> the widely held view that the Bank of Canada controls the spectrum of interest rates in Canada . . . is a holdover from the days when financial markets here and elsewhere were subject to controls and restrictions of various sorts, and the pressures in markets tended to show up in limitations on the availability of funds rather than in interest rates. These days, markets are more open, more international, and, as a result, much more efficient. But it does mean that interest rates in Canada will move around in response to international events or domestic developments that alter market expectations.[47]

Theissen might have added that one international influence of particular significance is the United States Federal Reserve Board, whose policies are able to influence interest rates and economic activity internationally, but especially in Canada because of the extent of trade and capital market integration between the two countries. In October 2002, for example, even though the inflation rate rose above the 2 per cent target, the Bank of Canada did not raise interest rates. The dichotomy was explained in a press release of October 16, 2002:

> The strong expansion of the Canadian economy is continuing, with domestic demand growth fuelled by the substantial monetary stimulus in the economy. Core and total CPI [consumer price index] inflation have risen appreciably above the Bank's 2 per cent target for inflation control, largely because of a number of relative price movements. At the same time, the outlook for global economic activity has weakened, reflecting uncertainty about economic, financial, and geopolitical developments, as well as a reduced tolerance for risk in global financial markets. These uncertainties and the weaker global outlook may dampen growth in aggregate demand for Canadian output in the near term. The Bank has therefore decided to leave the target for the overnight rate unchanged at this time.[48]

2. The Deficit/Surplus and the Economy

Canadian governments have been less concerned with price stability since the early 1990s, when annual inflation rates fell to their lowest levels since 1971–2. Concern with inflation was replaced by an increasing preoccupation with the size and persistence of government deficits and the amount of government spending—currently about 12.6 per cent of all federal program spending—that goes to servicing accumulated federal debt.[49] A *deficit* is, quite simply, a shortfall between what a government raises from taxes and other sources of revenue during a given year and what it spends. Economists distinguish between a deficit's cyclical and structural components. The **cyclical deficit** is that part of the shortfall caused by variations in expenditures and taxes that are related to the state of the economy. The **structural deficit**, or cyclically adjusted deficit as it is often called, is the shortfall that would have occurred if the level of economic activity had been 'normal'—that is, if fluctuations in the business cycle were ironed out.

This distinction is a crucial one for two reasons. First, the cyclically adjusted deficit provides the correct measure of a government's *discretionary* fiscal policy. It eliminates the automatic increase in government spending that results when weaker than 'normal' economic circumstances lead to lower tax revenues and higher claims on public spending (through statutory income maintenance programs such as unemployment insurance and welfare). In other words, the fact that the size of a government's budget deficit has increased by 10 per cent from one year to the next does not necessarily mean that its fiscal policy has been countercyclical (i.e., spending to compensate for weakened demand). It could be that the entire increase in the deficit was due to automatic changes in government revenue and spending linked to the state of the economy. Or the increase could have resulted from a rise in the interest rates that governments, like other borrowers, must pay on the new debts they assumed during that year. The cyclically adjusted deficit is often much smaller than the overall deficit.

The deficit became the symbol of economic mismanagement for conservative critics of government, some of whom argued that annual revenues and expenditures should be constitutionally required to balance. Their opponents countered that such a requirement was not only unrealistic but potentially harmful for the economy and that it would cause unnecessary hardship. If fluctuations in the level of economic activity are unavoidable, then the income the state receives from individuals and corporations will vary with the health of the economy, as will its expenditures on statutory income maintenance programs. If the budget were required to balance, the level of taxation and/or the level of benefits paid to individuals would have to be constantly readjusted. The political and administrative impracticability was considered clear. In addition, many argued that any automatic increase in taxation or cut in state benefits to offset the deficit resulting from weak economic circumstances would only aggravate the severity of an economic downturn. Thus, in addition to the Keynesian argument that deficit financing can be used as an instrument of macroeconomic stabilization, it was argued that governments should be free to run deficits if necessary to allow for greater stability in taxation rates and social programs. Despite these misgivings, however, the anti-deficit argument was accepted in a large part by the Liberal government of Jean Chrétien, whose lasting legacy was not only deficit elimination under Finance Minister Paul Martin but consistent budget surpluses since 1997.

One reason for the Liberal government's acceptance of deficit elimination was the burden of interest payments on an accumulated federal debt of more than $600 billion. This was seen as a major problem for four reasons. First, debt represents a transfer of the burden of paying for current consumption onto the shoulders of future generations, and therefore involves intergenerational inequities. Second, given a limit on available savings, government borrowing may displace other, potentially more productive, uses for investors' money. In fact, because a significant share of the money that Canadian governments and their agents borrow is raised outside the country—about one-fifth of Ottawa's debt is owed to foreigners—this investment displacement effect is less than it would be in a closed economy; nevertheless, foreign indebtedness makes Canada vulnerable to the preferences of non-Canadian agents. Third, if a large share of what the government spends must go toward paying the interest on its debts, a non-discretionary expenditure item, this reduces the government's ability to finance new activities and maintain current ones. Finally, debt has a psychological dimension: If investors *perceive* the government's debt to be excessive,[50] they become less willing to invest.

How large was the deficit in Canada and what were its causes? Figure 6.1 shows a widening gap between Ottawa's expenditures and revenues during the early to mid-1980s. Its main cause was the fact that weak government revenues during the 1981–3 recession led the government to take on additional debt at a time when interest rates were exceptionally high. By 1997, however, the deficit had been eliminated and since that time the federal government has been posting surpluses achieved in part by reducing transfer payments to provincial governments, by increasing equalization payments from 'have' to 'have-not' provinces, and by increasing employment insurance (EI) premiums while reducing benefits.[51] Once surpluses became the norm, the new policy challenge was what to do with the windfall. During the 2000 federal election, for example, the Liberal government campaigned on a 'balanced' approach, promising to divide the surplus among tax cuts, debt financing, and new spending on social programs. Thereafter, continuing budget surpluses enabled the Liberals to announce new spending initiatives, including a national daycare program and additional funding for the military as well as municipalities. By the 2006 federal election, the Liberal government under Paul Martin was able to boast eight consecutive balanced budgets. Although the Conservative opposition argued that the Liberals intentionally underestimated their surpluses to have the financial room to make politically advantageous new spending announcements, since the Harper government came to power it too had planned budget surpluses. Instead, during the most recent recession, the federal government has gone into deficit spending as a result of stimulus and reduced revenues. In more recent budget announcements the finance minister has set forward a plan to return to balanced budgets; however, this is not expected to occur until 2015 (see Figure 6.1).

As a percentage of GDP, the federal deficit shrank considerably compared with the mid-1980s, falling from 7 per cent in 1984 to about half of 1 per cent in 1997. But at the same time the size of the federal government's accumulated debt climbed to more than $600 billion (and provincial and municipal debt added almost $300 billion more to the total). As Figure 6.2 shows, Ottawa's debt-to-GDP ratio declined rapidly during the late 1990s and beginning of the twenty-first century. However, it still exceeds that of the provinces and territories. In 2010, about one-tenth (10.7 per cent) of every dollar spent by the federal government still goes to paying interest on the accumulated debt. That figure represents a considerable improvement over recent years, as the debt charges in the 1990s went as high as 29 per cent. Despite the deficit and additional debt charges incurred as a result of stimulus spending to combat the recession, Canada still fares well on its debt-to-GDP ratio, especially in comparison with other industrialized nations.

FIGURE 6.1 The Federal Deficit/Surplus, 1980–2015 (estimated)

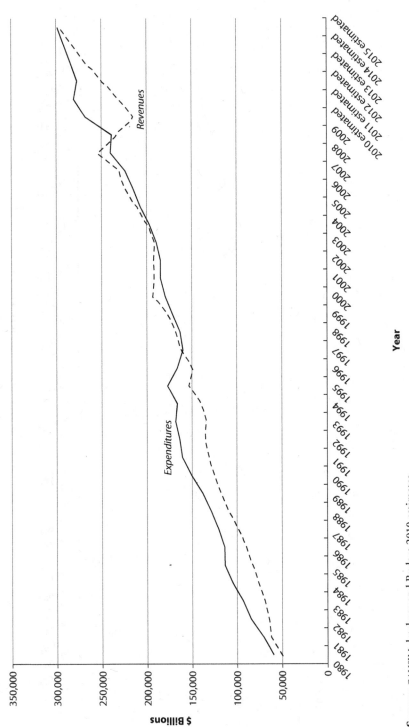

$ Billions

Revenues

Expenditures

Year

350,000

300,000

250,000

200,000

150,000

100,000

50,000

0

1980
1981
1982
1983
1984
1985
1986
1987
1988
1989
1990
1991
1992
1993
1994
1995
1996
1997
1998
1999
2000
2001
2002
2003
2004
2005
2006
2007
2008
2009
2010 estimated
2011 estimated
2012 estimated
2013 estimated
2014 estimated
2015 estimated

Source: CANSIM database and Budget 2010 estimates.

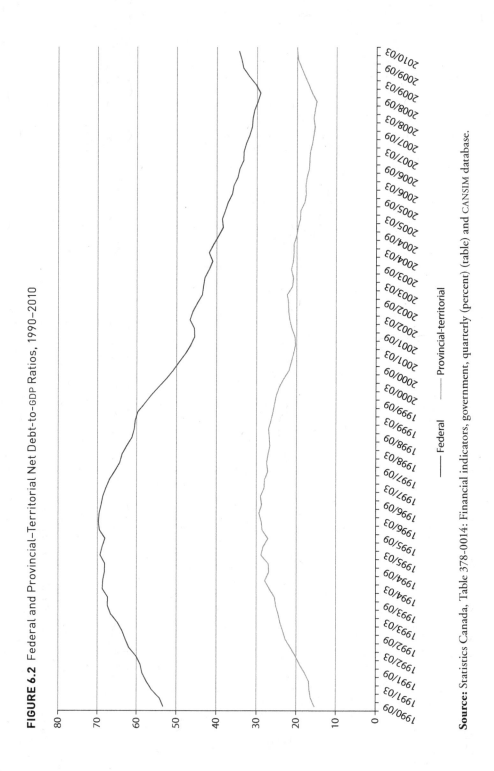

FIGURE 6.2 Federal and Provincial–Territorial Net Debt-to-GDP Ratios, 1990–2010

Federal ——— Provincial-territorial ———

Source: Statistics Canada, Table 378-0014: Financial indicators, government, quarterly (percent) (table) and CANSIM database.

Those who emphasize spending cuts as the solution to chronic deficits suggest that the debt problem is one of excessively generous social programs and government waste. This was the perspective presented by the Harper Conservatives when they first came into office. At the time, the government boasted that 'federal program spending as a share of GDP has declined significantly since 1983–84' and, more important, 'As a result of spending restraint and strong economic growth, the ratio of federal program spending to GDP declined steadily throughout the latter half of the 1980s.'[52] It is the rate of spending to GDP that government officials point to when they attempt to justify increasing Canadians' debt load during the recession. A case in point is the budget documents from 2010 where the federal government justified the deficit by saying, 'over the long term, the private sector is and should be the primary source of jobs and growth. Governments have an important role to play in creating the right conditions for Canadians and businesses to thrive.'[53] The current government believes that they have struck the right balance of targeted spending and net debt-to-GDP ratios that places Canada in the best fiscal position in the G7. According to the IMF, Canada has a projected increase of net debt from 2007 to 2014 of 5.9 per cent compared to Japan's 63.1 or the United States' 42.6 per cent. Moreover, as can be seen in Figure 6.3, the current account deficit as a per cent of GDP is one of the lowest of the G7 and is projected to continue into 2015.

Provincial governments had also reduced their spending until the most recent recession. Five provinces forecast either balanced budgets or surpluses in 2009. As

FIGURE 6.3 Current Account Balance (per cent of GDP)

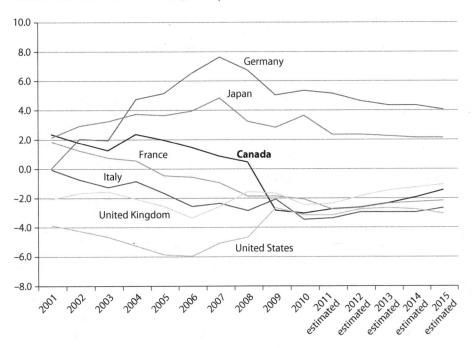

Data source: IMF, *World Economic Outlook* report, April 2011.

can be seen in Table 6.1, only Newfoundland, Manitoba, Saskatchewan, Alberta, and Nunavut had budget surpluses in 2009.

TABLE 6.1 Budgetary Balances in Recent Years

	2002	2005	2009
	(Millions of Dollars)		
Federal	**7347**	**5117**	**883**
N.L.	−468	−489	1057
P.E.I.	−17	−34	−121
N.S.	113	165	−89
N.B.	79	242	−320
Que.	22	−664	−2810
Ont.	375	−1555	−8148
Man.	63	405	78
Sask.	1	383	2680
Alta.	1081	5175	1198
B.C.	−1184	2575	−1725
Y.T.	−21	5	−16
N.W.T.	120	−17	−143
Nun.	−47	−8	5
Total provincial-territorial	**117**	**6183**	**−8354**

Note: Provincial net debt not available for 2009–10.
Source: Statistics Canada, *Canada Year Book*, volumes covering years 2001–2010 (fiscal year ending March 31).

The External Dimension of Macroeconomic Policy

From time to time news media report that 'The Bank of Canada today made large purchases of Canadian dollars to defend the dollar's value' or that 'The Canadian prime rate has moved upwards in response to recent increases in American interest rates.' Several important features of macroeconomic policy are conveyed in these statements. At the most general level, they suggest that Canada's economy is a very open one, easily influenced by events beyond our borders. The reference to defending the dollar implies that the international valuation of a country's currency (particularly the rate of exchange between its currency and those of its major trading partners) is a matter of some policy importance. At a more specific level, such stories point to a major policy-making role for the central bank (the Bank of Canada) and underline the dependence of the Canadian economy on developments in the United States. If an economy were closed—if it were entirely self-sufficient in what it sells and buys and in financing the expenditure requirements of both the private and public sectors—management of the overall economy would focus exclusively on internal factors. But of course every modern economy is to some degree open to external influences. In comparison with other developed capitalist economies, Canada falls around the middle of the spectrum, with the value of exports and imports together amounting to about a quarter of the value of gross domestic product. Where the Canadian economy is exceptional is in how much of its trade is conducted with a single partner—close to one-fifth of Canada's GDP is accounted for by exports to the United States.

The transactions between one economy and another are expressed in a country's balance of payments. This is an account of all the income flows entering (credits) and leaving (debits) the economy. The balance of payments is closely, but not perfectly, related to the value of a nation's currency (i.e., the exchange rate). For a simplified illustration, suppose that a Canadian corporation purchases a shipment of radios from a Japanese corporation. The Japanese exporter will naturally expect to be paid in yen, Japan's national currency. Likewise, a Canadian exporter of coal to a Japanese electrical utility will expect to be paid in Canadian dollars. If the sum of all transactions in this bilateral trade relationship is not in balance—if Canadian businesses and individuals buy $1 billion more from Japan than our economy sells to the Japanese—this shortfall must be covered through the purchase of yen. This introduces two complications. First, Canadians who need yen for their vacations in Tokyo, or businesses that require yen to pay for the Japanese merchandise they are importing, exchange their dollars for yen at banks. Thus, the problem of trade imbalances is not experienced individually by people or corporations. Rather, it is felt at the level of the national financial system in terms of reserves of foreign currencies in demand. Second, if Canadian demand for the yen is persistently greater than Japanese demand for the dollar, the value of the yen will increase vis-à-vis the dollar. This means that the cost of goods imported to Canada from Japan will rise, while the cost of Canadian goods in Japan will fall.

With imports becoming dearer and exports cheaper, it might appear that a change in the value of a nation's currency in relation to that of one or more of its trading partners is not a matter of great importance. This is not the case. First of all, if an economy experiences a chronic deficit in its balance of payments, its government will likely come under pressure to devalue the national currency to bring the value of what it buys from the outside world into line with what it sells there. Second, a decline in the value of a nation's currency relative to that of its main trading partners may produce inflationary pressures if the foreign goods and services that now cost more to buy are ones whose consumption is not easily or quickly reduced (if they are, in the economist's jargon, relatively demand-inelastic). Since 1971 the capitalist world has been on what economists call a 'managed floating' exchange-rate system. The relative value of national currencies is allowed to float in response to supply and demand. But the state, through the central bank, may interfere with the market for the national currency by, for example, buying the currency when demand for it is weak and imports are becoming increasingly expensive. Because of their effects on domestic price levels and employment, the foreign exchange rate and the balance of payments are matters of public policy in all capitalist societies.

These general observations on the relationship between trade and macroeconomic policy are uncontroversial. In the Canadian case, however, controversy surrounds the particular profile of our trade with other economies and the concentration of that trade with the United States. As the earlier example of Japanese radios and Canadian coal implied, trade involves transactions in commodities. In fact, a significant portion of trade takes the form of foreign ownership-related transactions such as dividends paid to the foreign shareholders of corporations in Canada, income transfers from Canadian subsidiaries to their foreign parent corporations, and payments such as licensing fees for the use of technology owned outside of Canada. In the terminology of the national accounts, these are **service transactions**. In addition to the items just mentioned, service transactions include tourism and interest paid to the foreign holders of Canadian debt. Trade in commodities is referred to as **merchandise transactions**. Together these make up what is called the **current account**. Although the annual value of Canadian merchandise exports usually exceeds the value of imported commodities, Canada has registered a deficit in service transactions every year since 1950. The significance of chronic balance-of-payments deficits for public policy is explained by Maureen Molot and Glen Williams:

> Ideally, governments would like to ensure that the value of what is brought into the country is less than, or only as much as, the value of what is sent out. Otherwise, the resulting international indebtedness will force policy-makers to divert energy and capital into a search for the means to repay the deficit.[54]

The two largest negative contributors to Canada's balance of trade are the payments associated with foreign ownership of economic assets in Canada and, more important, the interest paid to the foreign holders of Canadian debt. Short of placing serious restrictions on foreign ownership or imposing currency controls to stem the flow of profits leaving the country—measures that, aside from being political non-starters, would violate Canada's obligations under the FTA, NAFTA, and the WTO—nothing much can be done about the first drain on the balance of payments. As for the outflow of money to the foreign holders of Canadian debt, it is clear that reneging on those obligations is not an option. The fact that 16 per cent of public-sector debt is held by non-Canadians means that the interest paid on this debt represents a significant drain on the Canadian economy. But it also increases the influence of external investors and credit-rating agencies whose judgments affect the level of interest that governments must pay to attract buyers of their debt. The only way out of this circle of debt and dependence would seem to be to borrow less abroad.

Walls, Doors, and Plans: Economic Policy in an International Context

The influence of external economic and political circumstances on the performance of the Canadian economy has been significant from the time of the initial European settlement of this country. Indeed, the Canadian economy began as a colonial extension of the French and, after 1760, British commercial empires. The country's history has been punctuated with questions about the appropriate response to economic challenges from the outside world, from the debate over annexation to the United States in the 1840s, the National Policy of 1879, the national election of 1911 (fought largely on the issue of free trade with the United States), the foreign ownership debate of the 1960s and early 1970s, and the 'Third Option' policy of the 1970s (the aim of which was to diversify Canada's external trade) to the FTA (1989), NAFTA (1993), and Canada's participation in the General Agreement on Trade and Tariffs (GATT; the forerunner of the World Trade Organization).

There are three general approaches that a country like Canada can take regarding the international economic system of which it is a part: **protectionism** (tariffs on imports and subsidies for domestic producers), *free trade,* and *economic planning.* A fourth approach, which we will not discuss because it has not been relevant in the modern economic history of Canada, is *territorial expansionism* motivated by economic factors.[55] In reality, none of these approaches is found in a pure form. Since any nation's economic policy invariably combines elements from at least two of them, they might be more appropriately described as policy orientations.

Protectionist measures have a long history in Canada. The first 'made-in-Canada' tariff (as opposed to one set by the British Colonial Office) was imposed in 1858.[56] The National Policy of 1879 elevated tariff protection to a major component of Ottawa's economic development strategy. Whether the Conservative government of John A. Macdonald was acting principally on a vision of the country's economic future or on more crass considerations of popular support and business pressures is an open question (though most studies by economists and historians point to the political power of business interests as a major factor, especially in determining the tariff rates applied to particular commodities).[57] What is not in dispute is that the 1879 tariffs and their successors were intended primarily to protect domestic producers rather than to raise public revenue. The average rate of the 1879 tariffs was 28 per cent, and the highest rate was applied to manufactured items such as agricultural implements, railway equipment, iron, and clothing.[58] Tariff walls remained high until World War II. Since then they have declined significantly, and under the FTA, tariffs between Canada and the United States have been virtually eliminated.

But tariffs are only one of the means that governments may use to protect their domestic industries. As the general level of tariff protection has fallen, the world trading system has seen a proliferation of non-tariff barriers such as voluntary export restraints negotiated between countries, import quotas, technical and administrative barriers to the free entry of imports, marketing boards, and subsidies to domestic producers. The numerous forms (and Byzantine complexity) associated with non-tariff barriers, along with disagreements between governments over what is and is not a restrictive trade policy, have created more trouble for trade negotiators than tariffs ever did.

Other interests, however, have always preferred the idea of 'doors' rather than 'walls', at least in relations with the part of the world that is of the greatest economic importance to Canada. Free trade is also the approach favoured by most economists. They argue that the best way to maximize a nation's wealth is to pursue its **comparative advantage** in the world trading system: exporting those goods and services that it can produce at a relatively low cost because it is abundantly endowed with the necessary factors of production, and importing those products that require factors of production with which it is poorly endowed. Canadian exports are more skewed toward non-manufactured goods than is true of other advanced capitalist economies. On the other hand, our imports are overwhelmingly skewed toward manufactured products that require a relatively higher level of skilled labour and technical knowledge. This suggests that Canada's comparative advantage lies in its natural resource industries.

The policy implications of the theory of comparative advantage are potentially disturbing. First, the theory suggests that the current profile of Canada's international trade is rational from the standpoint of maximizing the nation's wealth, regardless of any attendant problems. Second, and relatedly, if Canada has a relative cost advantage in natural resources, this might be taken as an argument for government to channel investment into megaprojects such as gas and oil pipelines, freshwater exports, hydroelectric exports, and offshore oil. The case for megaprojects rests on the expectation that the construction phase will generate activity in other sectors of the economy and that a substantial export market will exist for the resource in question. The downside is that such a strategy increases the economy's vulnerability to fluctuations in international markets for the targeted resources. This was clearly demonstrated by the precipitous drop in the world price of oil and gas during the 1980s, which resulted in the cancellation of plans for a gas pipeline from the Canadian Arctic to American markets as well as a number of synthetic oil projects in Alberta, and uncertainty over the future of the Hibernia oil reserves off the coast of Newfoundland. The Hibernia project continued because the government invested some $420 million in it when Gulf Canada pulled out. This investment has paid off for the government and private investors alike as the price of oil has increased in the last few years. The offshore oil sector today accounts for 40 per cent of the nominal GDP in Newfoundland and Labrador, and approximately 35 per cent of Canada's conventional light crude production.[59] When the advocates of freer trade between Canada and the United States made their case during the 1980s, however, they did not rely on the comparative advantage argument. Instead, they argued that the domestic market was too small to encourage Canadian producers to improve their competitive performance and that free access to the American market would encourage domestic firms producing behind tariff walls to become more efficient. They also claimed that protectionism resulted in a transfer of income from Canadian consumers to the businesses (many of them foreign owned) protected by tariffs and non-tariff barriers. In addition to these economic arguments, the advocates of free trade put forward a political one: Pointing to mounting protectionist sentiment in the US Congress, which erupted in a number of sectoral trade disputes between the two countries during the 1980s, they argued that a free trade agreement would provide political security against any escalation of trade hostilities that would harm Canada more than the United States.

The case for free trade rested on a combination of the economic benefits it promised together with its claim to represent hard-headed political realism. Its opponents made three main counterclaims.[60] First, they argued that the costs of economic adjustment—

businesses closing and workers becoming unemployed—were likely to be greater than free-traders estimated. A second argument focused on the longer-term economic costs, maintaining that free trade would result in a permanent shift of production facilities to the United States, in possible downward pressure on wages in Canada, and in a reduction of research and development activity in this country. The third objection against free trade was that it would undermine Canada's political sovereignty. According to this view, greater economic integration would ultimately lead to greater pressure on Canadian governments to bring their policies into line with those of the United States. This claim is not easily proved or disproved. It resonates, however, with some very old fears about Canada's national identity and our ability to maintain it in the face of Americanizing pressures.

Four years after the FTA came into effect, the Conservative government signed a treaty with the United States and Mexico that created NAFTA. Like the FTA, NAFTA generated enormous controversy in Canada and was even more controversial in the United States—a fact that generally was not appreciated in Canada. The fears associated with NAFTA were rather different. Because this free trade partnership involved two wealthy developed countries and one poor developing economy, the chief concern was that investment and jobs would flee the relatively high-wage economies of Canada and the United States for the paradise of the *maquiladoras*, the industrial enclaves just below the US–Mexico border where low labour costs attract foreign manufacturers. 'That giant sucking sound' was how American billionaire Ross Perot described this expected flood of dollars and jobs. Lax environmental regulations, rudimentary labour laws, and lower taxes on business were additional factors expected to lure capital from Canada and the United States to Mexico. To make matters worse, said the critics, ordinary Mexicans would not even benefit from this surge of investment and economic activity. Instead, NAFTA would put them at the mercy of rapacious capitalists, paying them low wages while pouring filth into Mexico's air and rivers. Defenders of NAFTA argued that the trade deal would make Mexicans richer and thereby enable them to buy more goods from Canada and the United States. Moreover, they said, the growth of a middle class in Mexico would put increasing pressure on that country's authorities to protect the environment and improve working conditions. In response to fears about NAFTA's possible consequences for the environment in Mexico and the very real gap between labour standards in that country and those in Canada and the United States, side agreements on these matters were negotiated. These side agreements are generally acknowledged to be toothless.

How has Canada fared under the FTA and NAFTA? The answer depends on whom you ask. On the whole, those who supported free trade before these deals were signed continue to stand by it, while those who opposed it say that their worst fears have come true. The bottom line is that any fair-minded assessment of the agreements' economic, social, and political effects must take into account a multitude of other influences. These include interest rates, business cycles, international economic developments, government's focus on deficit and debt management, and federal–provincial relations, to mention some of the more important ones. There are no easy answers about who wins and who loses under free trade.

But several things are clear. First, even supporters of free trade have been disappointed over the continuation—even escalation—of trade skirmishes between Canada and the United States over a range of goods from softwood lumber to salmon. The dispute settlement mechanisms established under the FTA have not taken the politics out of cross-border trade wars. American policy continues to be as protectionist as it was before the FTA—a testament to the ability of interest groups to take advantage of the fragmentation that characterizes the American policy-making system.

Second, naysayers' claims that the FTA was responsible for the job losses experienced during the recession that followed its implementation were exaggerated. The timing of the deal was unfortunate for free-trade boosters, coinciding as it did with the beginning of a recession in the United States, which inevitably pulled the Canadian economy into recession as well. High interest rates in 1989–90 and the rising value of the Canadian dollar, which made Canadian exports more expensive in the United States, almost certainly overshadowed whatever impact free trade had on employment and investment in Canada at that time. However, the longer term analysis suggests that as of 2006 NAFTA has resulted in a net total of 3.1 million new jobs, representing an increase of 125.5 per cent over pre-NAFTA employment.[61] The naysayers concede that we have gained jobs since NAFTA, but they question what kinds of jobs they are. The auto sector in Canada and the United States has been undergoing severe restructuring. In any event, the migration of manufacturing jobs from Canada to lower-wage locations in the American South, Mexico, and elsewhere began before the FTA. And though some argue that the pace of this outflow was increased by the FTA, and has accelerated even further under NAFTA, such claims are difficult to prove.

It is also difficult to substantiate predictions that the FTA and NAFTA undermine Canadian social programs, culture, and political sovereignty. Social programs have been under enormous pressure in recent years, but for reasons that have little to do with the free trade agreements—at least not in a direct sense. Rather, these agreements are more properly viewed as the political products of the same broader forces of economic globalization that have, in Keith Banting's words, 'placed enormous pressure on the welfare state, creating contradictory pressures for the expansion of the redistributive role of the state, and for its contraction and redesign.'[62] There is a sense among decision-making elites and the more affluent strata of Canadian society that globalization is an inevitability to which governments must adapt by reducing the role of government and increasing the competitiveness of Canadian business. The general population appears not to share this enthusiasm and is more likely than the elites to see freer trade as threatening their incomes and job security.[63] While the ideology of free trade has less secure roots among average citizens than in the corridors of power and privilege, ordinary Canadians do respond to claims that their governments spend and tax too much and that public-sector deficits and debt are serious problems. The cuts to social spending that began gradually under the Conservatives in the 1980s and accelerated under the Liberals in the 1990s—to say nothing of those implemented by provincial governments—owe more to domestic political forces than to the free trade bogeyman.

In regard to cultural sovereignty—a value that has never set the pulses of ordinary Canadians racing—the FTA and NAFTA are far less significant than Hollywood, the

Internet, Disney World culture, and *the preferences of ordinary Canadians*. Canada's protectionist cultural policies were never the product of popular demand, although nationalist elites have always tried to portray them in this light. When the WTO decides, as it did in the summer of 1997, that the Canadian government's long-standing policy of favouring Canadian-owned magazines violates WTO trade rules, it would seem ridiculous to point an accusing finger at the FTA.

Dissenters from the dogma of free trade, including many in the NDP, labour leaders, social activists, cultural nationalists, and left-wing academics, are not unanimous in the alternatives they propose. But none of them seriously suggests protectionism as an option. In the era of globalization, the word has virtually disappeared from the lexicon of economics. According to the OECD, Japan, the European area, the United States, and the United Kingdom have all been moving in the direction of deregulation since the mid-1980s. Canada is positioned in the middle of this group, having made a significant shift toward deregulation in the late 1980s under the FTA and later continuing with NAFTA. To attempt to resist this trend would seriously undermine Canada's ability to compete in the world market.[64]

Canada's heavy dependence on international trade and its participation in global trade liberalization (through the GATT and, more recently, the WTO) rule out protectionism as a framework for economic policy. Instead, the opponents of free trade tend to support the adoption of an industrial strategy or planning option. This would not be inconsistent with limited free trade for particular industrial sectors, as existed under the Auto Pact from 1965 until it was overturned by the WTO in 2000. However, advocates of the planning option must have faith in the state's capacity to coordinate the development of the economy, and the obstacles to planning are significant:

1. *Coordination between governments*. The federal division of powers, under which provincial governments control a number of important levers for influencing economic activity, means that either the provinces would have to give up some of the powers they currently have (an improbability to say the least) or the mechanisms for coordinating federal–provincial economic activity would have to be strengthened. This second possibility seems only slightly less remote than the first.

2. *The electoral cycle*. It is axiomatic that all governments in liberal democracies are influenced to greater or lesser degrees by short-term considerations related to electoral expediency and the desire for political support, at the expense of long-term economic strategies.

3. *Social structures*. Canadian society is characterized by an almost complete absence of umbrella institutions representing labour organizations and businesses. In countries such as Germany and Sweden, these institutions have operated to generate social consensus on the objectives of economic policy, and therefore to overcome the 'short-termism' of electoral politics.

4. *Inertia of the past*. Past policies and government inaction have contributed to a level of integration between the Canadian and American economies that is unparalleled. From a practical standpoint this means that any attempt at state planning would likely encounter vigorous opposition from those American and domestic

economic interests that have developed around continentalist trade linkages. American opposition would be all the more likely given that a relatively high degree of state intervention in the economy would be required, and that Canadian interests would determine the goals of the government's economic policy.

5. *Existing free trade obligations.* Canada is currently a member of the FTA, NAFTA, and the WTO. Although negotiations toward the creation of a Free Trade Area of the Americas faltered after five Latin American countries refused to sign on, the Canadian government has also signed a free trade agreement with Chile (2003), and bilateral negotiations on freer trade between Canada and the European Union have been ongoing for a number of years. In short, a web of treaty commitments and trade institutions locks Canadian governments into the free trade orbit. These commitments are not easily cast aside or changed. Indeed, it is hard to imagine the circumstances under which the Canadian government would invoke the termination clause of the FTA or demand major reforms to the FTA or NAFTA that its partners would not be willing to concede. This reality is nowhere more evident than in the fact that despite the Liberal party's explicit campaign against the FTA in 1988 and its expressions of disapproval during the 1993 campaign, upon taking office the Chrétien Liberal government ratified NAFTA.

In view of these obstacles, it seems unlikely that planning represents a realistic alternative for Canada. At a minimum, planning would require significant institutional changes in the way policy is made, including the creation of state structures capable of representing and accommodating regional and functional (particularly business and labour) interests. But institutional change not grounded in receptive attitudinal and social conditions is useless. As Hugh Thorburn has observed:

> even before this [institutional change] comes the leap of faith—the decision and collective will to set up the machinery around which a consensus can be built on a basis of rational planning for agreed-upon objectives. If we cannot agree to do that, then we cannot do anything.[65]

There is little in Canada's contemporary history to suggest that such a 'collective will' is on the horizon. The fractious character of federal–provincial relations in itself is sufficient to cast serious doubt on the viability of economic planning. Moreover, elite decision makers in both the public and private sectors tend to favour a smaller rather than larger role for government.[66] Given the forces ranged against it, the state planning option is clearly a non-starter.

Key Terms

automatic stabilizers Measures intended to moderate the fluctuations in the business cycle.

comparative advantage A strategy whereby a country will export goods and services with which it is abundantly endowed and will import those products that rely on factors of production with which it is poorly endowed.

current account The combination of service and merchandise transactions.

cyclical deficit That part of a budgetary shortfall caused by variations in expenditures and taxes that are related to the state of the economy.

discretionary stabilization measures Government responses to observed and anticipated trends in economic activity.

Keynesianism Economic theory espoused by British economist John Maynard Keynes, according to which the government can and should play an active role in the economy by using demand management policies to encourage spending during economic downturns and to reduce spending when the economy is growing so fast as to cause serious inflation.

merchandise transactions Trade in commodities.

monetarism Economic theory maintaining that levels of real economic activity change with changes in the money supply.

new classical economics Distinguished by two main microeconomic assumptions: (1) that consumers, workers, firms, and businesses act from a position of perfect knowledge about the consequences of their behaviour and they attempt to maximize their utility (the rational expectations assumption), and (2) that markets clear rapidly (the equilibrium assumption).

political business cycle A reference to the fact that governments typically use economic policies, particularly spending and tax measures, to improve their chances of re-election.

positive state A state dedicated to maintaining high levels of employment and economic growth.

protectionism A policy intended to assist domestic producers by offering them subsidies and imposing tariffs on imports.

service transactions Tourism dollars spent abroad, interest paid to the foreign holders of a country's debt, licensing fees for technology owned outside a country, dividends paid to foreign shareholders, and income transfers from subsidiaries to foreign parent companies.

stagflation Stagnant real economic growth at a time of high inflation.

structural changes Changes in the conditions for economic growth; since the 1970s, structural changes seem to have led to higher unemployment and an unstable economy.

structural deficit The shortfall that would have occurred if the level of economic activity had been 'normal', that is, if fluctuations in the business cycle were ironed out; also called the cyclically adjusted deficit.

BOX 6.1   Canada's Balance of International Payments: Second Quarter, 2010

Canada's overall current account deficit (on a seasonally adjusted basis) widened by $2.6 billion to reach $11.0 billion in the second quarter, marking the seventh straight quarter of deficit. Export growth for goods slowed while import growth remained strong, which led to a deterioration in the merchandise trade balance. At the same time, a lower deficit on investment income flows with non-residents was partially offset by a higher deficit on international trade in services.

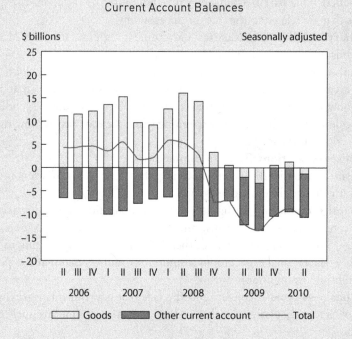

Current Account Balances

Cross-border financial transactions (unadjusted for seasonal variation) resulted in further significant inflows of funds to the Canadian economy in the second quarter, led again by foreign purchases of Canadian securities. Non-residents acquired Canadian bonds at an unprecedented rate and foreign investment in Canadian stocks rebounded.

Swing in the Goods Balance Led by Trade Flows with the United States

The balance on trade in goods declined $2.5 billion in the second quarter to return to a deficit position, following two quarters of surplus. Exports advanced by less than imports, largely reflecting trade results with the United States. The goods surplus with the United States shrank by $2.3 billion, following two quarters of gains.

Exports of goods rose by $1.2 billion, substantially less than in the previous quarter. Energy products and industrial goods were the two main contributors to the recovery in goods exported during the previous three quarters, but they both declined in the second quarter of 2010.

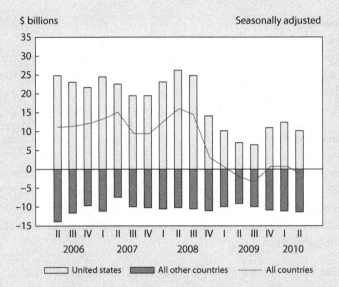

Goods Balances by Geographic Area

Source: Adapted from Statistics Canada, Canada's Balance of International Payments, *The Daily*, 11-001-XWE, August 30, 2010; http://www.statcan.gc.ca/daily-quotidien/100830/dq100830a-eng.htm

Discussion Questions

1. Given the global financial crisis and the worsening current account deficit with the United States, do you think the two economies are too closely linked?
2. With the stalling of the Free Trade of the Americas talks in 2005, do you think the idea of hemispheric free trade is completely dead?
3. What role should the government play in the economy? Does government policy make the economy stronger or weaker?

Websites

There are many different sources of economic data and analysis. The following are some easily accessible sites, Canadian and otherwise, that provide information on current economic conditions.

Department of Finance Canada
www.fin.gc.ca
This website provides current information on recent budgets, economic and fiscal information, international issues, and taxes and transfer payments to provinces. In

addition to communicating the government's priorities, it makes available publications and research documents on the Canadian economy.

The Economist
www.economist.com
This is the premier online source for the analysis of world business and current affairs, providing authoritative insight and opinion on international news, world politics, business, finance, science and technology, as well as overviews of cultural trends and regular industry, business, and country surveys.

International Monetary Fund
www.imf.org
The International Monetary Fund (IMF) is an organization of 187 countries, working to foster global monetary co-operation, secure financial stability, facilitate international trade, promote high employment and sustainable economic growth, and reduce poverty around the world. The IMF also publishes a wide range of time-series data on financial indicators for member countries.

Organisation for Economic Co-operation and Development (OECD)
www.oecd.org
The OECD is a group of 30 countries committed to democratic government and the market economy. Active relationships with some 70 other countries, non-governmental organizations, and civil society give it a global reach. Best known for its publications and statistics, the OECD covers a broad range of economic and social issues from macroeconomics to trade, education, development, and science and innovation.

Statistics Canada: CANSIM
http://cansim2.statcan.ca
CANSIM is Statistics Canada's key socioeconomic database. Updated daily, it provides fast and easy access to a large range of the latest and most up-to-date statistics available in Canada. The main website usually requires some nominal payment for data and tables, but most Canadian universities have subscriptions that allow students and researchers to access the information free through their library accounts.

Polaris Institute
www.polarisinstitute.org
Formed in response to the two major free trade agreements that had an impact on the Canadian economy in the last two decades of the twentieth century, the institute supports citizen movements in developing strategies and tactics to challenge what it sees as the corporate power driving public policy on economic as well as social and environmental issues.

Montreal Economic Institute
www.iedm.org
This Quebec non-profit group advocates for the use of market mechanisms in its proposed reforms to Quebec and Canadian economic policy.

Institute of Public Economics
www.uofaweb.ualberta.ca/ipe
Affiliated with the University of Alberta, the institute promotes research and teaching in the field of public economics, which is the study of the public sector and its influence on the economy and society.

CHAPTER 7

Social Policy

Introduction

Many of the most expensive functions carried out by the state in advanced capitalist societies are associated with social policy. These functions include public education, health-care services, publicly subsidized housing, and the provision of various forms of income support to segments of the population such as the unemployed, the aged, and the disabled. Together these functions constitute the dimension of state activity that is conventionally labelled the welfare state. The sphere of activity of the welfare state is generally understood to include state interference with the operation of market forces to protect or promote the material well-being of individuals, families, or groups on grounds of fairness, compassion, or justice.

Few people are opposed to fairness, compassion, and justice. Nevertheless, the term 'welfare state' carries negative connotations in our society. There are two main reasons for this. First, ours is an individualistic culture that values self-reliance and tends to reject the notion that society has an obligation to support those who are capable of working. While Canadians tend to be less individualistic than Americans, they are less collectivist than, say, Swedes, Danes, or Belgians. Second, although the welfare state is associated with compassion for society's least privileged elements and with the redistribution of wealth from those who can afford to pay to those in need, many people also associate it with inefficiency, disincentives to work, and even fraud. For these reasons few Canadian politicians dare to utter the words 'welfare state' unless they have something bad to say about it. Even the friends of the welfare state tend to avoid using the term itself because of the unfavourable baggage it carries in our society; instead they use a kind of code, speaking of 'social justice', 'the caring society', or 'Putting People First'.[1]

Yet the term 'welfare state' is worth retaining as a shorthand for that area of state intervention that involves social policy. There can be no doubt that the state's role in the provision of social services and the share of national income devoted to welfare-state policies have increased enormously during the past century. Social programs account for just over 40 per cent of federal spending, but closer to 60 per cent of all program expenditure. Expressed as a percentage of GDP, welfare-state spending currently ranges from a high of about 29 per cent in Sweden to a low of about 7 per cent in Korea.[2] Canada, at 16.5 per cent, ranks below the OECD average, although international comparisons are complicated by the fact that some kinds of social benefits do not appear on the state's expenditure books.

Many have argued that the relatively high levels of social spending in Western European countries, compared with North America, can be attributed to the fact that their populations are older. One way of controlling for the effects of differences in the age profiles of societies is to count only social spending on the working-age share of the population. For all but a few countries the majority of this spending takes the form of expenditures on forms of unemployment insurance. Spending on people of working age varies widely, from a high of about 13 per cent in the Netherlands and Finland to a low of about 1 per cent in Japan. Canada is just slightly below the average at about 7 per cent.[3] Yet, as Figure 7.1 shows, Canada's transfers to seniors greatly exceed the transfers to other groups, including single-parent families. Government transfers make up a large proportion of income received by Canada's seniors. In 2008, 48.5 per cent of the income received by elderly families came from government transfers.

Although the sheer growth in social spending is beyond dispute, there is considerable disagreement over the causes and significance of welfare-state expansion.

FIGURE 7.1 Income Source in Canada, 2008

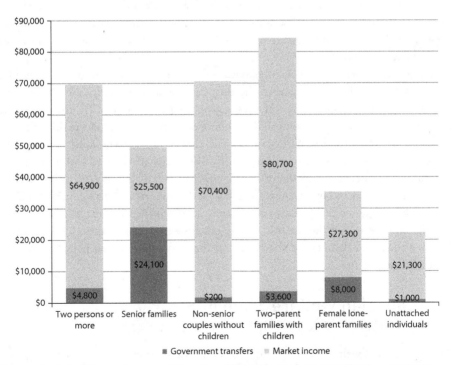

Source: Statistics Canada, Income of Canadians 2008, *The Daily*, 11-001-XIE, June 17, 2010; http://www.statcan.gc.ca/daily-quotidien/100617/tdq100617-eng.htm

The conventional view maintains that the welfare state has emerged as a result of the socioeconomic pressures and political demands produced by industrialization and urbanization. Developments in the economy and in the way society is organized are accompanied by the political mobilization of the general population. This political mobilization takes a variety of forms, including the extension of universal voting rights, unionization, the emergence of mass political parties, and the proliferation of interest groups. Thus, industrialization and urbanization confront policy-makers with a new set of problems and popular expectations, and the extension of mass democracy increases governments' responsiveness to popular demands. Precisely how each government responds will depend on the particular structures of association (churches, labour organizations, co-operative societies, and so on) and cultural values that characterize the society. But although the timing and extent of welfare-state reforms are influenced by the particular characteristics of each society, the pressures for their introduction can be attributed to socioeconomic changes and the political democratization experienced in all advanced capitalist societies.

An alternative interpretation of the welfare state argues that the introduction of social reforms in capitalist societies is intended primarily to defuse social tension and thus to protect the interests of capital. The American Marxist James O'Connor describes this purpose of such reforms in terms of **legitimization**: Welfare spending is used to promote social harmony and to legitimize the existing economic system in the eyes of those who benefit least from its operations. It is perfectly reasonable to accept O'Connor's claim that the welfare state has the *effect* of smoothing over the social frictions generated by the capitalist system of production without having to accept the suggestion that those who manage the state consciously set out to protect the interests of the capitalist class.

Policy-makers, whatever their ideological bent, must occasionally balance popular demands against the preferences of the business/investment community in circumstances where the reconciliation of these competing interests is difficult, to say the least. The historical record shows that they have often come down on the side of popular demands, instituting welfare-state policies that have been vigorously opposed by powerful elements of the business community. But they have done so within the limits of business confidence (limits that vary among societies) and in ways that minimize the cost burden shouldered by business. In other words, the welfare state is neither purely the result of democratic pressures nor purely a contrivance for anaesthetizing class conflict and protecting the interests of capital. Instead, it is produced by the tension between the state's democratic character and the limits imposed on policy-makers by the capitalist system.

The Canadian Welfare State in Comparative Perspective

The defenders of welfare-state spending usually base their case on society's obligation to alleviate the financial hardship suffered by its least privileged members and on the desirability of narrowing the inequalities in wealth generated by the market economy.

It is therefore worth considering both the extent of economic hardship in Canada and the distribution of income. These data provide the background for any evaluation of the need for and success of social expenditures. One way of looking at this background is to compare Canada to other advanced capitalist societies. The problem with this approach is that an unemployed single mother in Halifax is unlikely to be impressed by news that she is better off than her counterpart in Louisville, Kentucky. For someone experiencing economic hardship the relevant measure of his or her condition is that of others within the same society. This does not mean that international comparisons are beside the point; what it does mean is that these comparisons cannot be the sole basis for assessing the extent of the social needs to which welfare spending responds.

It has become popular to portray Canada as a society whose standard of living has been overtaken and even surpassed by that of countries such as Austria, the Netherlands, and Ireland over the past two decades. But if a measure of real purchasing power—what economists call 'purchasing power parities'—is used rather than nominal income, one finds that few countries surpass Canada in their standard of living. For decades, only the United States had a higher average real purchasing power than Canada. In recent years Canada has declined in the rankings, but it is still among the handful of wealthiest countries (see Figure 7.2).

Of course, 'averages' may conceal inequalities in the extent to which a relatively high standard of living is shared by different segments of the population. Various studies of the distribution of income in Canada compared to that in other developed capitalist societies all point to the same conclusion: Canada falls somewhere in the middle. The distribution of income is more equal than in the United States or France, but less equal than in Japan, Sweden, or Norway.

FIGURE 7.2 Per Capita Purchasing Power Parities for Selected OECD Countries, 1999 and 2008

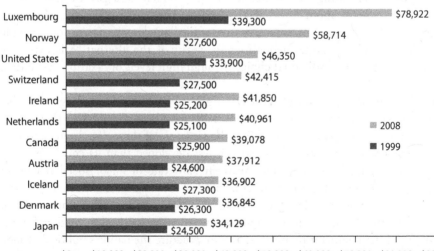

Source: OECD, *OECD Observer,* June 2000; The World Bank (2010).

The well-being of a society obviously cannot be reduced to the purchasing power of its 'average' member and the distribution of income. This is not the place for a long discussion of the material and psychological components of personal well-being, but it should at least be acknowledged that measures of the quality of life (QOL) need to be included in any attempt to compare the levels of welfare in different societies. Since the QOL cannot be measured directly, it must be inferred from one or more factors that, arguably, reflect some dimension of life experience.

This gets us onto controversial terrain. For several consecutive years the United Nations Development Program ranked Canada first in the world on its Human Development Index—a composite measure that included real purchasing power, life expectancy, adult literacy, and mean years of schooling. For the past few years Canada has slipped, and in 2010 it was ranked eighth. The United Nations cautions that this does not mean that Canada has become a worse place to live—only that other countries have improved. Indeed, one of the most recent reports found that over the past 40 years 'many of the poorest countries posted the greatest gains'[4]. Canadians have grown used to hearing that the UN rates their country as one of the best places in the world to live. Canada does less well in the UN's ranking of countries when gender equality and inequalities in the distribution of income are added to the picture, but still places in the top 10. One can take issue with the validity of the UN's Human Development Index, but it would take a churlish disposition or the blindness of an ideological malcontent to deny that Canada is a pretty good place to live—for most people.

In terms of the state's response to social needs, governments in Canada together spend less on welfare than do many Western European countries. To note this is not to imply that the 'right' level of welfare expenditure is higher than Canada's. Comparisons like this do not take into account demographic differences, nor do they tell us anything about how efficiently the money is being spent (i.e., how much a given level of spending contributes to the achievement of a government's social policy objectives) or about how social spending affects the economy. Moreover, getting it 'right', in this context, is a matter of ideological preference. Some people are willing to tolerate large inequalities in wealth if the alternative is extensive state interference with individual choice through high levels of taxation and public spending.

Leaving aside the question of what the 'right' level of social spending might be, one can at least say that Canadian governments have been slower than their Western European counterparts in assembling the structure of the welfare state, and that the contemporary Canadian welfare state is less developed than its counterparts in many other capitalist societies. The relatively slow rate of major social reform in Canada probably owes less to the level of need in Canada than it does to political factors. These would include the comparative weakness of the labour movement in this country, the absence of an electorally strong left-wing party on the national stage, the ability of the dominant political parties to structure the nation's political agenda around non-class divisions like language and region, and even the nature of Canada's federal Constitution.

The Extent of Social Need in Canada

Social policy is essentially a response to inequality. Indeed, payments made to individuals and families who are in financial need are the cornerstone of the welfare state. Such need may be temporary, related to fluctuations in the economy, to declining demand for the individual's particular skills, or to a stage in an individual's life cycle (e.g., maternity leave or retirement). Or the need may be chronic, as in the case of those who because of sickness, injury, or some other condition are unemployable, or for those whose employment incomes are insufficient to maintain what the state has determined to be a socially acceptable standard of living. These are usually assumed to be **redistributive payments**—transfers of money from those who can afford to pay to those who are in need. Yet the distribution of income has changed relatively little despite the implementation of major social security programs. In 1951 the top 20 per cent of income earners in Canada accounted for 42.8 per cent of total money income and the bottom 20 per cent of income earners accounted for 4.4 per cent. In 2008 the top quintile accounted for 42.2 per cent of money income and the lowest quintile for 9.8 per cent.[5] When social security benefits are excluded from the picture, the inequality gap is much wider.

The distribution of income is, of course, only part of the story in any assessment of social well-being. The other part involves the extent of poverty. The distribution of wealth in a society may be very unequal. But if the material condition of society's least privileged members is high enough that they are able to afford life's necessities and maintain their personal dignity, it would seem capricious to speak of poverty. This condition of universal (if unequal) affluence was the vision that American president Lyndon Johnson expressed in the 1960s in the slogan 'The Great Society' and that Pierre Trudeau promised when he spoke of 'The Just Society'. The reality, of course, is that poverty has not been erased from the social landscape in the United States, Canada, or any other capitalist society.

It is true that what is meant by the term 'poverty' suggests something different in these advanced capitalist countries than it would in Bangladesh or Mexico. Poverty is a relative concept. This is reflected in the fact that poverty is defined by organizations like Statistics Canada, the National Council of Welfare, and the Canadian Council on Social Development (CCSD) in terms of the share of household income spent on food, shelter, and clothing.[6] There is nothing sacred about a poverty line that is set in this way. Indeed, among those who study poverty there has been considerable controversy in recent years over the methodology used to measure this condition.[7] These debates are not merely academic, for the simple reason that statistics on poverty are routinely reported by the media and are used by individuals and groups in debating social conditions and social policy. Many journalists, academics, politicians, and interest groups have come to refer to the **low-income cut-off lines** (LICOs) set by Statistics Canada as 'poverty lines' because the latter term has more political punch. Here, however, is what Statistics Canada says about the nature and appropriate interpretation of its low-income cut-offs:

> Low-income cut-offs (LICOs) are established using data from Statistics Canada's Family Expenditure Survey. They are intended to convey the income level at

which a family may be in straitened circumstances because it has to spend a greater proportion of its income on the basics (food, shelter and clothing) than the average family of similar size. The LICO varies by family size and by size of community. Although LICOs are often referred to as poverty lines, they have no official status as such, and Statistics Canada does not recommend their use for this purpose.[8]

Keeping in mind the controversy associated with the measurement of poverty, we will use Statistics Canada measures of low income in analyzing social need in Canada. Traditionally, the low-income cut-off line—not the 'poverty line'—is 43 per cent or more of gross household income spent on food, shelter, and clothing. This is about 20 percentage points above the national average of household income spent on life's essentials. In 1991, Statistics Canada began publishing before and after low-income measures (LIMs). These are used to make international comparisons. In addition, Human Resources and Skills Development Canada (HRSDC) developed a Market Basket Measure (MBM) that takes into account the standard of living costs across the country. Statistics Canada states that no one measure is better than another, but all three provide different ways to examine the same issue.

Four main facts emerge from an analysis of statistics on poverty in Canada. First, the number of people living in poverty depends a lot on how you take the measure. As of 2008, 9.4 per cent, or 3 million Canadians, were living below the low-income cut-offs measured by after-tax income or by the market basket measure.[9] Using the LIM, the number increases to 4.3 million Canadians. No matter how you measure it, these figures represent an improvement over poverty levels of a couple of decades ago;[10] in 1969, 23.1 per cent of Canadians were living below the low-income cut-off line.[11] For 2007, the 'lowest rate of low income ever captured by Statistics Canada' was reported.[12] Second, poverty is not distributed equally. The likelihood of being poor is greater for families led by women, elderly single women, and single people aged 25 or less. The National Council of Welfare uses the term the 'feminization of poverty' to make the point that women account for a larger share of the poor in most age and family status categories than men. However, the general trend toward a decrease in the poverty rate is also evident in the case of single-parent families led by women. In 1981 the poverty rate for these families was about 53 per cent, and by 1996 it had increased to 55.8 per cent. But in the last decade the proportion of female-led single-parent households with incomes below the LICO has fallen to roughly 26.6 per cent.[13] Third, according to John Richards, the poverty rate among children in female lone-parent families fell from 56 per cent in 1996 to 33 per cent in 2005.[14] Fourth, for those individuals and families without employment or a private source of income, the social assistance benefits they are eligible to receive leaves them below the LICO. Because of provincial differences in eligibility requirements and in benefit levels for provincially administered welfare and social services, the extent of this shortfall varies across the country. Table 7.1 shows the welfare income paid by each province in 2008 to single employable persons, disabled persons, and couples with two children as a percentage of the Statistics Canada LICOs. When the value of the child tax benefit, the GST rebate, and in-kind transfers such as

TABLE 7.1 Welfare Income as a Percentage of LICOs, 2008

	Single Employable		Person with a Disability		Couple with Two Children Aged 10 and 15	
	Basic Social Assistance	Total Income	Basic Social Assistance	Total Income	Basic Social Assistance	Total Income
Newfoundland and Labrador	51	71	51	71	44	72
Prince Edward Island	41	56	55	56	54	64
Nova Scotia	39	59	57	59	42	63
New Brunswick	22	55	47	55	36	58
Quebec	44	68	67	68	36	71
Ontario	43	81	77	81	44	78
Manitoba	40	60	48	60	48	64
Saskatchewan	50	67	60	67	51	71
Alberta	33	86	84	86	45	81
British Columbia	47	73	70	73	45	83

Source: National Council of Welfare, Welfare Incomes 2008, Bulletins 1–4.

subsidized housing is added to these welfare levels, they increase by about 20 per cent but still remain below the low-income cut-off in most provinces.

Three Pillars of Social Policy

There are three pillars of Canadian social policy: (1) income security; (2) health care; and (3) redistribution. In this chapter we examine income security and redistribution. The next chapter focuses on health care.

1. The Income Security System

The income security system consists of those programs intended to protect or supplement the incomes of individuals and families. Some of these involve direct money transfers to those who meet specific eligibility criteria. Old Age Security (OAS) payments, the Guaranteed Income Supplement (GIS), employment insurance (EI) benefits, and social assistance are examples of these. Others involve benefits received through the tax system, such as Registered Retirement Savings Plan (RRSP) deductions and marital, child, and age exemptions. Spending on social policy, of which income security programs constitute the major share, accounts for about 40 per cent of all federal spending and more than 60 per cent of all program spending by Ottawa. After payments on the public debt, this has been the most rapidly growing area of federal spending. A number of factors suggest that the demand pressures on the income security system will continue to grow in the future.

Among these factors is Canada's aging population. According to the most recent census, the national median age increased from 37.6 years in 2001 to reach an all-time ·high of 39.5 years in 2009. Seniors account for 13.9 per cent of Canada's population.[15] This translates into increased demands on the OAS and CPP/QPP systems, not to mention additional pressures on the health-care system because the elderly are society's heaviest consumers of health services.

Changes to the family have also increased the pressure on the income security system. Since the 1968 reform of Canada's Divorce Act, the number of single-parent families has increased steadily. More than four-fifths of these families are headed by women. We have already seen that female-led single-parent families experience a high rate of poverty—about five times higher than that for male single-parent families. To put this a bit differently, even though single-parent mothers with children made up only 3 per cent of Canadian households in 2008, they accounted for 23 per cent of the families falling below Statistics Canada's LICOs. This high rate of poverty among single-parent families headed by women indicates a major failing of the existing income security system. There is no reason to expect the prevalence of single-parent families (especially female-led) to decline in the future—although it is encouraging to see that, as John Richards points out, the proportion of such families falling below the LICO has decreased significantly in recent years.[16]

A third factor that has increased demands on the social safety net has to do with economic change. While Canada's job creation record has been quite good compared to most other advanced capitalist economies, some of these new jobs have been in low-paying service occupations—'McJobs', as they are sometimes disparagingly called. Some argue that much of the growth in service-sector employment involves part-time jobs, and therefore part-time pay as well as no benefits. While it is true that from the mid-1990s to 2000 an increasing number of Canadians fell into the category of the working poor—people who are employed for some or even all of the year but whose incomes leave them at or below social assistance levels—that trend has reversed direction in recent years. In fact, the thesis that the proportion of well-paid jobs has decreased over the last two decades is not borne out by the data. Even more encouraging is the finding that low-paying jobs (those paying less than $10.00 per hour) have not increased since the second half of the 1990s.[17]

In response to the challenge posed by the increasing costs of social programs, an old debate has resurfaced. It pits those who support universal eligibility for social benefits against those who argue for selective eligibility based on some sort of income test. Those on the political left view social benefits as entitlements that go with citizenship. They oppose selectivity on the grounds that means-tested benefits carry a social stigma that is repugnant in a society that values equality. Those on the right are more likely to support selectively paid social benefits on the grounds that this is a more efficient way to target benefits where they are most needed. The most important universal income security program is OAS. But although there is no means test to determine eligibility, OAS payments are treated as income for tax purposes. This means that lower-income recipients retain a larger share of those benefits than do higher-income recipients. In this way a program that is universal in terms of eligibility is actually geared to income in its application.

Programs directed at elderly Canadians are an important part of the income security system. Federal spending on these programs came to about $34.6 billion in 2009–10.[18] In addition, several of the provinces have income supplement programs for the elderly that, like the federal Guaranteed Income Supplement, are income tested and thus are targeted at those with little or no private income. Housing subsidies, subsidized drugs, and various tax credits represent other ways in which provincial governments provide benefits to the elderly.

Aside from the inevitability of rising program costs associated with an aging population, two other major policy issues are raised by the existing retirement income security system. One relates to equity. Thomas Courchene demonstrates that elderly Canadians with significant private income gain most from the current system of benefits.[19] This is because the value of the deductions for occupational pension plans and RRSPs under the tax system increases with one's income. '[T]he main result', argues the National Council of Welfare, 'is to enhance the tax advantages of the rich.'[20] Consequently, even though the universally paid OAS benefits are progressive because they count as taxable income, this progressivity is offset by the regressive impact of benefits received by the elderly through the tax system.

Another issue associated with income security for the elderly involves the Canada and Quebec Pension Plans. It became widely recognized in the mid-1980s that the CPP faced a funding crisis. The benefits paid to pensioners under the plan were supposed to be financed by contributions and the plan's investment income. But in 1985 the benefits paid by the CPP exceeded contributions to the fund for the first time. A Department of Finance study published that same year indicated that if the contribution rate, which is split evenly between employees and their employers, remained unchanged the CPP would be bankrupt by 2004.[21] Estimates indicated that if university graduates entering the labour force in the 1980s were to collect the level of benefits currently received by CPP recipients, the contribution rate would have to increase about 200 per cent by the time these graduates reach retirement age (from about 6 per cent of earnings in 1997 to about 12 per cent by the year 2040). Consequently, in 1997 the federal government reformed the CPP program not only to ensure current funding but also to provide funding for future generations. It is now estimated that the CPP is sustainable for the next 75 years using the current contribution rate.[22]

Canada's unemployment rate has been on the decline for the better part of the last decade. Providing income assistance to people who are temporarily out of work because of layoffs continues to be a spending priority of the government, but changes in the makeup of the workforce have dramatically influenced the way in which employment insurance is collected and distributed. Probably the biggest changes have been the increase in the number of women in the labour force and the extension of the program to cover parental and adoption benefits. As can be seen in Figure 7.3, the highest average weekly amounts go to those receiving adoption benefits. The average weekly benefit for the regular EI beneficiary is $348, compared with $355 for parental and

FIGURE 7.3 Average Weekly Employment Insurance Benefits (dollars)

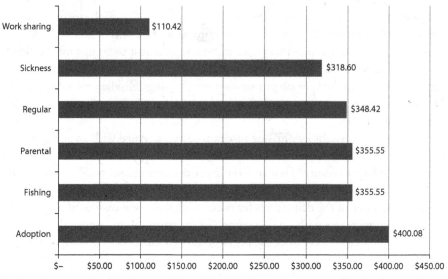

Source: Statistics Canada, CANSIM table 276-0016.

$400 for adoption leave. In contrast, those who are eligible for sickness benefits receive $318, while those in the fishing industry receive $355.

Employment insurance is funded through the contributions of employees and employers, as well as by money from the federal government. It provides most claimants with benefits equal to 55 per cent of their income up to $43,200 prior to becoming unemployed for a period of up to 45 consecutive weeks. The main policy issues involve the way benefits are distributed and the effects of this program on the labour force (and therefore on economic performance). Unlike social assistance, EI is not targeted at the poor. But EI does have a couple of redistributive effects, operating to redistribute income between regions and between sectors of the economy. Provinces with the highest rates of unemployment derive the greatest benefits from EI, receiving transfers in excess of their contributions to the program. Moreover, the period of employment prior to collecting EI also tends to be shorter in these high-unemployment provinces. EI is a normal part of annual income for a large part of the labour force, particularly in the Atlantic provinces. Most economists argue that EI benefits, which are paid to individuals, have the same economic effect as equalization payments from Ottawa to the less affluent provinces; both serve as disincentives for people to move from areas with weak economies to more economically vibrant parts of the country.

Some sectors of the economy, including fishing, forestry, tourism, and the construction trades, are characterized by seasonal unemployment. As it happens, some of the high-unemployment provinces—including Prince Edward Island, Newfoundland, and New Brunswick—are also provinces in which seasonal industries account for a large share of provincial economic activity. In a very real sense EI subsidizes these industries because the contribution rate is the same for employees and employers in all sectors of the economy, even though the risk of becoming unemployed varies greatly between sectors. As Figure 7.4, shows, more favourable economic conditions in Western Canada mean that EI contributions from those provinces help to pay the benefits received by unemployed people from Quebec east to Newfoundland and Labrador. The existence of EI makes it less costly for individuals to remain in industries characterized by erratic employment or seasonal layoffs.

This raises the question of how social policy may affect economic performance. Both the Macdonald Commission (1985) and the Forget Commission (1986) recommended that what was then called unemployment insurance (UI) should be reformed to eliminate disincentives to work and to labour mobility. While their diagnoses of the effects of UI on economic performance were the same, their prescriptions for change were different. The Macdonald Commission recommended raising eligibility requirements, lowering the level of benefits, and gearing employer/employee contributions to the risk of layoff in each industry. These cost-saving measures were accompanied by a recommendation that a 'Transitional Adjustment Assistance Plan' be created to subsidize the incomes of those moving between sectors and regions of the economy.[23] The Forget Commission took a different line, recommending that claimants be automatically entitled to the full 50 weeks of benefits, but that the level of benefits received be based on the claimant's earnings during the entire year prior to filing the claim. The Commission recommended that this change, known as annualization, be accompanied by a form of guaranteed annual income designed to supplement the earnings of low-income households.[24]

In 1994 the Liberal government released a discussion paper entitled *Agenda for Jobs and Growth: Improving Social Security in Canada*. The 'Green Book', as it was dubbed, argued that the existing unemployment insurance system was an important

FIGURE 7.4 National Unemployment Rate, October 2010

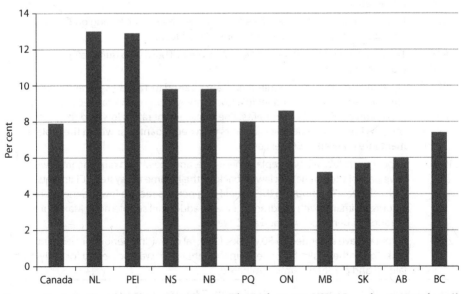

Source: Statistics Canada, Labour Force Survey, *The Daily*, 11-001-XIE, November 5, 2010; http://www.statcan.gc.ca/daily-quotien/101105/tdq101105-eng.htm

cause of unemployment, creating rigidity in Canadian labour markets and slowing adjustment to economic change. This view was repeated several months later in the government's 1995 budget when Minister of Finance Paul Martin stated that 'a key job for unemployment insurance in the future must be to help Canadians stay off unemployment insurance.'[25] When reforms to the system were finally brought in about one year later, they involved a combination of tightening and redirected spending. On the tightening side, benefits were lowered, especially for repeat claimants, eligibility was made more difficult, and premiums were reduced to encourage businesses to take on new workers. The redirected spending involved job training programs intended to improve the employability of those receiving EI benefits. Table 7.2 shows the evolution of unemployment/employment insurance over the past several decades. The most significant reforms occurred in 1996, which involved cutting benefits, increasing the weeks of work required to obtain EI, and reducing the number of weeks a potential recipient could receive EI. As a result of these reforms, studies have shown that the 'proportion of the unemployed who actually received unemployment benefits dropped from 83 per cent in 1990 to 44 per cent in 2004'.[26]

TABLE 7.2 Evolution of the Unemployment Insurance System Since 1971

Main Changes	
1971	The 1971 UI Act is passed. Coverage is extended to virtually all employees, the replacement rate is increased to 67 per cent, and benefit durations are increased and made a function of local and national unemployment rates.
1977	The minimum weeks of work needed to claim UI (the entrance requirement) is increased from 8 weeks to 10–14 weeks, depending on the local unemployment rate.
1979	The replacement rate is lowered to 60 per cent. New entrants to the labour market and repeat claimants are required to have extra weeks of work to qualify for benefits.
1990	Entrance requirements are increased to 10–20 weeks, depending on the local unemployment rate. Benefit durations are reduced.
1993	The replacement rate is lowered to 57 per cent. Those who quit their jobs are made ineligible for UI.
1994	The minimum entrance requirement rate is raised to 12 weeks. Benefit durations are reduced, so that a claimant in a low-employment region can receive a maximum of 36 weeks of benefits. The replacement rate is lowered to 55 per cent, except for low-income claimants with dependants, for whom the replacement rate is raised to 60 per cent.
1996	Repeat users face a lower replacement rate, and those with high incomes will have part of their benefits clawed back by the income tax system. Claimants with relatively few hours in their qualifying periods receive lower benefits. Low-income claimants with children receive an additional supplement. Maximum duration of benefits is capped at 45 weeks.
2000	Parental leave extended to 50 weeks. Deferral of waiting period for claimants making another claim for benefits in the same year. Waiting period for individuals laid off and parental claims eliminated.

Sources: OECD, *OECD Economic Survey, Canada 1996,* 78; HRDC information.

Employment insurance was a key element of the federal government's Economic Action Plan. The government pledged more than $4 billion in additional benefits, training opportunities, and EI premium relief as a mean to protect jobs. Part of the temporary changes included an extra five weeks of employment insurance benefits, enhanced work sharing, extended benefits for long-tenured workers, and wage earner protection.[27]

Social assistance—or welfare, as it is commonly referred to—used to be funded on a 50–50 basis by Ottawa and the provinces. Beginning in 1990, however, the federal government 'capped' its contributions to Ontario, British Columbia, and Alberta. Then in 1995 the previous cost-sharing formula was replaced by the Canada Health and Social Transfer, which is not tied to provincial spending levels. Eligibility for welfare, unlike EI, is determined by a means test. Both eligibility requirements and the levels of welfare benefits to be paid are determined provincially; thus, benefits vary significantly between provinces (see Table 7.1).

The total cost of social assistance has roughly quadrupled in real terms since the Canada Assistance Plan (CAP) was launched in 1966. This growth can be attributed to a couple of factors. First, because Ottawa covered half the costs of the assistance and the various social services provided under the plan, the provincial governments that actually administered welfare programs felt less pressure to control spending increases than they would have felt if they had had to bear the full cost of financing these programs. Second and more important is the fact that demand for welfare increases during recessions. As in the case of EI, spending on welfare is related to the level of unemployment. The number of welfare recipients rises and falls in step with changes in the unemployment rate. Since the late 1980s the number of people receiving social assistance has tended to be greater than the number of people receiving EI—a troubling fact that reflects an increase in the number of 'employable unemployed'.[28] As the unemployment rate decreased during the late 1990s, so did the percentage of people receiving both unemployment benefits and social assistance. Part of the reduction in social assistance had to do with reforms many provinces initiated during this time to make it more difficult to claim and receive social assistance benefits. Interestingly, not only did the unemployment rate decrease, but the number of workers increased. Contrary to the beliefs of social welfare activists, the welfare reforms in Alberta and Ontario produced an increase in jobs and a decrease in dependence.

We have already seen that benefit levels paid under social assistance are not adequate to enable recipients to maintain a standard of living above Statistics Canada's low-income cut-off. The large increase in the number of 'employables' receiving welfare has focused attention on a rather different aspect of this program: whether social assistance is designed in a way that discourages the employable unemployed from seeking work. Leaving aside the question of the appropriate balance between society's obligation to the individual and the individual's personal responsibility for his or her material well-being, it appears that the current welfare system may discourage some of those who are compelled to seek social assistance from re-entering the labour force. The reason for this is that the marginal taxation rate for people who go off welfare to take a low-paying job is extremely high. In other words, if a person on welfare accepts a low-paying job, thus becoming disqualified from receiving social assistance benefits, the effective rate of taxation on that person's earned income is extremely high. What this means in concrete terms is that the transition from welfare to work may not actually result in any improvement at all in one's standard of living. Even if welfare levels are not compatible with what most Canadians would consider a decent standard of living, it makes economic sense for many whose employment prospects are limited to low-paying jobs to stay on welfare. This reality is sometimes referred to as 'the poverty trap'.

While the 'poverty trap' remains a problem for many Canadians, the job growth in recent years, especially in Western Canada, has taken many people out of the cycle of poverty. Both the general level of poverty in Canada and the number of 'working poor' have declined over time. In 1976, 46 per cent of families with incomes below the LICO had some employment income. In 1999 the figure was 59 per cent, and more than one-quarter of these families included someone who was employed for the entire year. By 2003, however, that figure had dropped to 47 per cent.[29] In 2007, 34 per cent of Canadians with low income relied on a low-income wage.[30] This still represents a large proportion of people, but it also indicates a change in the right direction. For a single mother faced with the choice between remaining on welfare and accepting a job at the provincial minimum wage, it may not make economic sense to take the job. All provinces allow welfare recipients to earn a certain amount without any reduction in their welfare benefits. And some provinces allow earnings exemptions for work-related expenses like child care. Measures like these are intended to reduce the disincentives to work that have plagued the welfare system.

But do they work? The idea behind letting welfare recipients keep all or part of their earnings is, of course, to eliminate financial disincentives to work and, ultimately, to wean people from welfare dependence. Yet a number of studies suggest that instead of reducing the number of people on welfare, this approach may actually contribute to an increase in the welfare rolls, since the opportunity to collect welfare benefits and retain more earned income will attract more people into the welfare system while doing little to discourage those already in the system from leaving it.[31]

2. Redistribution: Class and Regional Dimensions

It is widely assumed that the welfare state involves some significant redistribution of income from those who can afford to pay to those who are in need. It is often assumed that the vehicle for this redistribution is the tax system, particularly the progressive personal income tax. On the expenditure side, income security programs are believed to comprise a social 'safety net' that provides greater benefits to the poor than to those who are well-off. In fact, however, those who study the distributive effects of taxation and public spending disagree on the question of whether the growth of the state has been accompanied by a significant narrowing of income inequalities.

The tax system does *not* redistribute income from the wealthy to the poor all by itself. The reason for this is that only some forms of taxation are what can be called **progressive taxes** (designed so that the rate of taxation increases with one's income). Other forms, notably sales and property taxes, health insurance premiums (which still exist in Alberta and British Columbia and were reintroduced in Ontario in 2004), and the GST/HST (except for the least well-off), are **regressive taxes**. They weigh more heavily on those with lower incomes because the amount of the tax that one pays does not depend on one's income. When income transfers from the state to individuals and families are left out of the picture, the overall distributional impact of taxation is regressive. Lower-income groups pay a much larger share of their income in taxes than do high-income groups. Separate studies by Gillespie, Maslove, Dodge, Gray, and the National Council of Welfare all find that the highest effective rate of taxation is experienced by the lowest-income earners.[32] If this is the case, why do governments place such a burden on the lowest-income earners? The reason has to do with the disincentives that taxes place on the economy. A recent study of 21 OECD countries found that income taxes cause lower economic growth than consumption or property taxes.[33] Thus, while a society may want to ease the burden from the poorest in its midst, they must balance that desire with the consequence of the taxation policy. Much of Canada's tax reforms have involved moving away from income tax toward consumption tax to avoid a reduction in the GDP. In doing so, the argument goes, the poor will have more opportunities for employment and thus be able to lift themselves out of poverty, thereby reducing the need for transfers from government.

One should not conclude from this evidence of regressivity in the burden of taxation that the state is a sort of perverse Robin Hood: taking from the poor instead of the rich. Any proper assessment of the distributional impact of government policies must include the income benefits from public spending. There is no doubt that the total effect of the money transfers received under income security programs and public spending on education, housing, health care, transportation, and a host of other programs favours the poor. Only when we combine the distributional consequences of taxation with those of public expenditure can we judge whether government policies in fact promote greater equality of income. Based on 1969 income data, Irwin Gillespie concluded that the total fiscal incidence (i.e., distributional impact) of taxation and spending by all levels of government in Canada was favourable to the poor.[34] This redistribution was attributable to public expenditures, not the tax system.

There is evidence, however, that the taxation side of the public finance equation has become more favourable toward the poor since Gillespie's earlier studies. Based on a comparison of the tax and transfer systems from 1985–2000, Marc Frenette, David Green, and Kevin Milligan found that after 1995 the system has become 'more redistributive than any other one that we investigated over this two-decade period'.[35] They note that many of these changes can be attributed to provincial policy as well as the expansion of the child tax benefit system.

Another way of looking at the distributional effects of public policy is to consider the relative importance of different sources of public revenue. What one finds is that since the early 1950s, when revenues from personal and corporate taxation were roughly in balance, the share of public revenue accounted for by taxation of personal income has increased while the importance of corporate income taxation has fallen dramatically. Personal income tax revenues today account for 32 per cent of total government revenue.[36] The burden of this increase has fallen mainly on middle-income earners. The conclusion is inescapable: The welfare state has been financed mainly by the users of public education, public health services, and income security programs. While many on the left often argue in favour of increased corporate taxes to offset the burden faced by middle-income earners, governments have increasingly moved away from that policy. The reason is that for every 10 per cent increase in the corporate tax rate, there is a reduction in investment to GDP by 2 percentage points.[37] In other words, corporate taxes result in a reduction in the economy because businesses are more flexible in regard to where they locate than are individuals. If one jurisdiction imposes a high corporate tax, the company will seek a region with a more favorable business climate. This results in both investment and job losses for the countries with higher corporate tax rates.

No discussion of redistribution in Canada can ignore the ways the federal government has attempted to address regional inequalities in income. These efforts have taken three main forms: (1) equalization payments from Ottawa to the less affluent provinces, intended to ensure 'that provincial governments have sufficient revenues to provide reasonably comparable levels of public service at reasonably comparable levels of taxation';[38] (2) income transfers from Ottawa to individuals, which (as we saw in our discussion of EI) are a major source of income in communities where employment opportunities tend to be seasonal; and (3) industrial assistance programs that subsidize businesses in economically depressed regions.

Economists have tended to be critical of these regionally redistributive programs on the grounds that they reduce the incentive for people to move to more prosperous regions of the country where jobs are more plentiful. The overall efficiency of the economy, they argue, suffers as a result of programs intended to subsidize incomes and public services in economically weak regions. The usual rebuttal to this economic efficiency argument is that the price of these programs is worth paying to achieve the goals of fairness—no Canadian should be seriously disadvantaged from the standpoint of educational opportunities, health care, and other public services as a result of where he or she lives—and national unity. Moreover, some economists contend that equalization can actually *promote* efficiency. Robin Boadway and Frank Flatters, for instance, argue that without equalization payments there might be too many people moving from the poorer to the richer provinces in search of higher levels of services (which are, after all, real economic benefits) than are available in the poorer provinces. They argue that migration based on these considerations, rather than market factors, could be costly to the overall economy.[39]

Leaving aside the economic arguments for and against programs that transfer resources from more affluent to less affluent parts of the country, it has long been recognized that the Constitution assigns the responsibility for expensive social programs to the provinces. However, the capacity to raise revenues to finance these responsibilities varies widely among the provinces. Equalization is intended to address the inequality in provincial fiscal capacity and to do so in a way that does not interfere with the constitutional right of provincial governments to determine their policy priorities. It is clear that the approximately $14.3 billion per year that Ottawa devotes to equalization—money that comes without strings attached as to how recipient provinces must spend it—does help to equalize provinces' financial capacities to offer 'reasonably comparable' levels of social services. As can be seen in Table 7.3, Ottawa's transfers to the provinces, under the Canada Health and Social Transfer and equalization payments, have increased in recent years.

TABLE 7.3 Federal Support to the Provinces and Territories (in millions of dollars)

Major Transfers	2005–6	2006–7	2007–8	2008–9	2009–10	2010–11
Canada Health Transfer	20,310	20,140	21,688	22,639	23,987	25,426
Canada Social Transfer	8,415	8,500	9,857	10,560	10,865	11,186
Children			1,100	1,100	1,133	1,167
Post-Secondary Education			2,435	3,235	3,332	3,432
Social Programs			6,202	6,202	6,388	6,579
Equalization	10,907	11,535	12,925	13,462	14,185	14,372
Offshore Accords	219	386	552	663	645	616
Territorial Formula Financing	2,058	2,118	2,279	2,313	2,498	2,664
Other Payments					563	739
Total	**41,909**	**42,679**	**57,038**	**60,174**	**63,596**	**66,181**

Source: Data from Department of Finance Canada. Reproduced with the permission of the Minister of Public Works and Government Services, 2011.

Globalization and Welfare Policy

One of the key critiques of trade liberalization and globalization focuses on the potential negative effects of these factors on social programs. Labour leaders, poverty groups, and anti-globalization activists maintain that closer trade between Canada and less-developed countries will inevitably lead to a race to the bottom. For example, during the NAFTA debate, Bob Rae, who was then Ontario's NDP premier, argued that trade liberalization with Mexico would

> put downward pressure on wages and labour standards. Under NAFTA, we believe companies in Ontario will insist that if they are to compete with enterprises in Mexico, Ontario workers must reduce their wages or face job losses. Under NAFTA, we believe companies in Ontario increasingly will think about diverting their investments and relocating to Mexico, where the enforcement of labour standards is lax.[40]

In particular, critics of NAFTA held that it would lead to wage cuts, job losses, the erosion of labour standards, and the harmonization of labour laws to the lowest common denominator. The link between jobs and social programs is clear. An increase in joblessness would inevitably result in higher numbers of people seeking employment insurance or social assistance. And if trade liberalization also results in reductions in social spending, the entire polity will be in jeopardy.

Similar claims surfaced during the debate on a Free Trade Area of the Americas (FTAA). Maude Barlow of the Council of Canadians warned that trade liberalization would result in social welfare declines. Barlow argued that Canadians had

> already seen a steady erosion of their social security under the new rules of economic globalization and trade agreements like NAFTA and the WTO, as Canada's economy has merged into the American orbit and American rules. Socially, Canada now looks more like the US than in any time in its history, with its huge gaps between haves and have-nots. In Canada, as in the US, while great prosperity abounds in some quarters, great poverty is growing in others.[41]

Notwithstanding claims such as these, the effect of trade on social programs has been benign. It is true that free trade affects employment—but not in the way Bob Rae predicted. According to Parbudyal Singh's review of the literature, the overall impacts of NAFTA were positive but small for both Canada and the United States. Gains were made in employment in Mexico, but they did not take away from its trading partners.[42] Rather than the agreement eroding labour standards in Canada and the United States, it has in fact led to 'positive effects in protecting labour rights, and the cooperative activities have served to educate and highlight labour practices and policies in the region'.[43]

As for social programs, when welfare policies of Canada and the United States are compared we find that Canada's policies did not change as a result of the trade agreement. In 1998, roughly a decade after the FTA came into effect, the Hoover Institute noted that 'Canada's welfare policy continues to be significantly more generous than America's,' and this is still the case today.[44] Cuts to social programs are the not the result of trade liberalization, but of the economic policies adopted by the provincial governments. That is why there is no uniform social welfare program in Canada. While Conservative governments in Alberta and Ontario tried to reduce the number and the amount of welfare claims, left-of-centre governments in British Columbia and Quebec increased social welfare spending. Thus, any changes in social welfare spending have little to do with trade liberalization and a great deal to do with the ideological positions of provincial governments.

This is supported by evidence from Northern Europe. Social welfare programs in Sweden, the Netherlands, and Denmark increased significantly in the 1950s and 1960s. At the same time, these countries followed free trade policies. Nonetheless, social democracy flourished with trade liberalization. This led the Hoover Institute to conclude that 'free trade actually helps, not hurts, social welfare programs.'[45] The increase in trade helps to increase the wealth that the country needs to finance the welfare state. As a result, open markets lead to more health services, increased education, and a generous social security system that might otherwise not have been affordable. Willem Thorbeck and Christian Eigen-Zucchi echo this finding in their analysis of NAFTA and Mexico. Instead of producing the 'giant sucking sound' of jobs headed to Mexico that American presidential candidate Ross Perot predicted, free trade led to modest job gains for the United States and huge gains for Mexico. Moreover, trade liberalization in Mexico has been followed by political liberalization. Thorbeck and Eigen-Zucchi point to the fact that after NAFTA, the Institutional Revolutionary Party lost its 71-year monopoly of power in Mexico.[46]

Globalization and trade liberalization do put pressures on governments. Fortunately, these pressures tend to be positive ones. All countries benefit from the increase in jobs: Less-developed countries become politically freer, and developed countries keep their high-paying jobs and strong labour standards while opening themselves up to larger markets.

Key Terms

legitimization The purpose (according to some Marxist critics) of social reforms and welfare spending in capitalist societies.

low-income cut-off lines (LICOs) Income levels used by Statistics Canada, not as 'poverty lines', but to qualify the numbers and characteristics of individuals and families falling into the lowest level of income category—defined in relative terms and taking into account current overall standards of living.

progressive taxes Forms of taxation, such as personal income tax, in which the tax rate increases with one's income.

redistributive payments The transfer of money from those who can afford to pay to those who are in need.

regressive taxes Taxes, such as sales and property taxes and the GST/HST, that weigh more heavily on those with lower incomes because the amount of tax paid is not determined by income.

BOX 7.1 The Big Mac Index: Making a Meal of It

The Big Mac index is based on the theory of purchasing power parity (PPP), according to which exchange rates should adjust to equalize the price of a basket of goods and services around the world. The exchange rate that leaves a Big Mac costing the same in dollars everywhere is our fair-value benchmark. So our lighthearted index shows which countries the foreign-exchange market has blessed with a cheap currency, and which it has burdened with a dear one. Our index shows that Asia remains the cheapest place to enjoy a burger, while those on the hunt for a value meal should steer clear of Scandinavia. The euro, despite its troubles, continues to be expensive when compared with many other rich-world currencies, though the British pound is trading close to its fair value. China's recent decision to increase the 'flexibility' of the yuan has not made much difference yet—the yuan is undervalued on the burger gauge by 48 per cent.

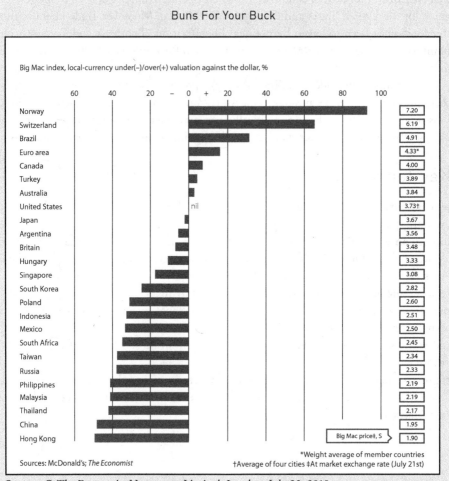

Buns For Your Buck

Big Mac index, local-currency under(−)/over(+) valuation against the dollar, %

Sources: McDonald's; *The Economist*

*Weight average of member countries
†Average of four cities ‡At market exchange rate (July 21st)

Source: © The Economist Newspaper Limited, London, July 23, 2010.

Discussion Questions

1. With the aging of Canada's population, Canadian policy-makers have an enormous challenge. How can they continue to fund cherished social programs such as health care and Old Age Security with fewer people able to work and pay for these programs through the income tax system? Is increasing the mandatory retirement age the answer? Can policy-makers encourage younger Canadians to have more children? Or is immigration the answer?

2. Has Canada become a poorer country since the introduction of free trade? Do the increasing numbers of children being raised in single-parent homes headed by women mean that the country on the whole is more impoverished?

Websites

The following sites all represent private, independent organizations concerned with social policy.

Caledon Institute of Social Policy
www.caledoninst.org
The Caledon Institute undertakes research into areas such as income security, taxation, social spending, and social services in an effort to develop and promote 'concrete, practicable' proposals for reform.

Campaign 2000—End Child and Family Poverty in Canada
www.campaign2000.ca
Campaign 2000 is a network of social organizations across Canada dedicated to research and public education on issues involving children and families.

Canadian Council on Social Development (CCSD)
www.ccsd.ca
The CCSD describes itself as committed to the development and promotion of 'progressive social policies inspired by social justice, equality and the empowerment of individuals and communities'.

The Fraser Institute
www.fraserinstitute.org
The Fraser Institute is a think tank devoted primarily to economic issues. It measures poverty in terms of the basic necessities of life, such as food, clothing, shelter, and other household essentials.

Gapminder
www.gapminder.org
Gapminder bills itself as a 'fact tank' that promotes a fact-based world view. To that end it provides free statistical content that allows users to examine comparisons of most countries around the world. The data provide documentation on major global development trends and provide attractive animated statistics.

Centre for the Study of Living Standards (CSLS)
www.csls.ca
The CSLS is dedicated to researching living standards. Its work offers perspectives on the trends that contribute to policy-making. The centre also advocates on particular issues with the aim of contributing to the public debate on living standards and finding effective ways to raise them.

Citizens for Public Justice (CPJ)
www.cpj.ca
A faith-based organization, CPJ promotes public justice in Canada based on its research, analysis, publications, and public dialogues on important public policy debates surrounding issues such as social justice, economic equity, and environmental integrity.

National Council of Welfare

www.ncw.gc.ca

The National Council of Welfare is a citizens' advisory group reporting to the Minister of Human Resources and Skills Development Canada (HRSDC). Topics of focus include income adequacy; employment programs; the justice system; social services, such as child care and child welfare; poverty; and specific populations, such as single parents and seniors.

CHAPTER 8

Health Policy

Introduction

Canada's health-care system is a jumble of confusing, sometimes conflicting elements and practices. Most doctors work on a fee-for-service basis, operating very much as individual businesspeople. But unlike the owners of most private businesses, they are not paid directly by those to whom they provide services, nor can they determine what they will charge. Provincial governments reimburse doctors for the bills they submit under a schedule of covered services and rates set by the province. The Canadian health-care system generally is characterized as a public system—indeed, its critics sometimes refer to it as socialized medicine—but about one-third of total health-care expenditures in Canada fall outside the public system. Among the health-related procedures, services, treatments, and devices that are not covered by public health insurance are most prescription drugs and dental services, vision correction, and much physiotherapy. Some people have insurance coverage (partial or full) for these services under a private plan, usually provided through their employers, but those who don't have insurance pay out of their own pockets. Canada's Constitution assigns primary jurisdiction over health care to provincial governments, but Ottawa plays an important role in the system in terms of setting some of the rules, providing some of the dollars, and even delivering services to some groups, such as Aboriginal Canadians living on reserves and members of the military. Finally, for decades Canada has suffered enormous losses of doctors and nurses to the United States, though these losses are offset, to some degree, by physicians trained in other countries.

Canadians often complain about their health-care system, and public opinion surveys show that most believe it is in need of either fundamental change or a complete overhaul.[1] Yet when they are asked about their personal experiences, the vast majority claim to have been satisfied with the treatment they received.[2] Public perceptions aside, forces at work within the health-care system as well as Canadian society have ensured that reform of the system is a necessity acknowledged by all. Foremost among these forces has been the steadily escalating cost of health care. Health spending is the single largest program expenditure for provincial governments, having grown from roughly one-quarter of expenditures in the early 1970s to about 32 per cent today. Rising costs would not be a problem if governments could divert financial resources from other programs or increase revenues without paying a political price. But in the real world of Canadian politics, neither of these options is easily available.

Few issues in Canadian politics have been as prominent in recent times as health care. Stories of long waiting periods for elective surgery procedures; overcrowded emergency rooms; a lack of general practitioners and specialists in many communities; doctors, nurses, and medical technicians leaving Canada for the United States; and hospital closings and restructurings have become routine. Canadians believe that something is seriously wrong with their health-care system, but they also seem reluctant to consider reforms that involve anything other than spending more money to restore a status quo ante that may no longer be viable. Political leaders have not been particularly helpful in educating Canadians on the problems that hobble the health-care system, in some cases because they may genuinely believe that the root of the problem is a lack of money, but in other cases because they know that health care is a political minefield in Canada and that a tried-and-true strategy for discrediting someone who proposes a serious rethinking of health policy is to accuse him or her of having a 'hidden agenda' that involves smuggling American-style, two-tiered health care into Canada.

In this chapter we will examine the dilemmas that confront policy-makers in the health-care field. Among the questions that we will explore are the following:

- Is money, or lack of money, the main problem facing the health-care system?
- How does Canada's health-care system compare with those of other countries in terms of performance and citizen satisfaction?
- In what ways does the health-care system reflect the values of Canadians?
- What are the obstacles to and opportunities for reform of the system?

The Constitutional and Legal Parameters

Canada's Constitution assigns the primary responsibility for health care to provincial governments. Section 92, subsection 7, gives to the provincial legislatures the exclusive power to make laws respecting 'The Establishment, Maintenance, and Management of Hospitals, Asylums, Charities and Eleemosynary Institutions in and for the Province, other than Marine Hospitals'. If the language sounds archaic, one reason is that the health-care system and the role played by the state in financing, regulating, and funding health care have changed radically since 1867. At the time of Confederation, and for several decades after, governments spent very little on health care. Hospitals were usually built and run by private organizations, mainly churches and charitable bodies. Their revenue came chiefly from the fees that patients paid for their services, although facilities for the mentally ill received most of their funding— paltry as it was—from the provincial governments. Doctors billed patients directly for their services. Public health boards were gradually established at the local level in response to threats to public health, such as disease epidemics and unsanitary living conditions, and the advent of vaccination campaigns. But a significant state presence in the field of health did not emerge until about the middle of the twentieth century. Indeed, the position of minister of health did not become common at the provincial level until the 1880s, when provincial boards of health were first created, and did not exist federally until 1919 when the Dominion Department of Health was established.

By the early 1960s all Canadian provinces had hospital insurance plans in place that covered standard hospital care. Patients had to pay for upgrades to private or semi-private rooms, but most services were covered by the provincial plan. Ottawa's willingness to share the costs of public hospital insurance was certainly an important factor in the adoption of this popular program. Public insurance for doctors' services and diagnostic and therapeutic procedures began in Saskatchewan in 1962 and extended across Canada by 1972. As in the case of hospital insurance, Ottawa's willingness—even eagerness—to help finance a comprehensive nationwide public health-care system, commonly referred to as **medicare**, helped to persuade the provincial governments that they could weather the opposition they faced from doctors and private insurance companies. Combined with the fact that public opinion generally favoured medicare, the lure of federal dollars made the extension of public health insurance difficult for provincial policy-makers to resist.

The certification of doctors, nurses, therapists, and other health-care workers has always involved a combination of provincial regulation and self-regulation by the practitioners themselves. For example, **provincial medical associations** determine the licensing standards that doctors must meet to practise in a particular province. The supply of physicians is to some degree determined by the number of medical schools at a province's universities and the decisions they make, in consultation with the provincial medical association and government, about how many students to admit. Most doctors' incomes are not set by the government; the exceptions are the minority who work for salary for a public health board or other public-sector agency. Doctors' incomes are significantly influenced, however, by the fact that the provincial regulations determine the fees that doctors may charge the province for specific services, what services they will be paid for, whether they may charge patients more than the billable amount without penalty, and what the upper limit on their billings may be.

In the case of nurses, excluding those who work for private organizations such as the Victorian Order of Nurses and the Red Cross, the conditions of employment are established under collective agreements with provincial governments. Although most nurses work directly for hospitals or clinics, their work responsibilities and opportunities are affected by provincial regulation of matters such as licensing standards and the legally recognized categories within the health-care profession. For example, nurse practitioners make up a relatively new category that is now recognized in most provinces and for which formal degrees are now granted by some schools of nursing; in terms of both responsibilities and pay, they represent an intermediate level between registered nurses and physicians. A different category of health-care professional covers midwives; long recognized and regulated by the state in many European countries, midwives are now licensed in most Canadian provinces.

Ottawa plays no direct role in the licensing and regulation of health-care professionals except for those employed by the federal government on reserves or in the northern territories, or who work for the Canadian armed forces. The federal government does, however, indirectly affect these professions and the conditions of employment in them. The Canada Health Act, 1984, penalizes provinces that allow doctors to bill their patients above what the province's schedule of billable services permits. Ottawa's financial contribution to the provincially administered health-care system is a crucial factor in provincial decisions regarding their health-care workers. Finally, Ottawa's authority in the field of immigration ensures that it plays a role in admitting to Canada the doctors and other health practitioners who are often in short supply in certain regions of the country and some sectors of the health-care system.

The main federal statutes affecting Canada's health-care system are the Medical Care Act, 1966, and the Canada Health Act, 1984. The Medical Care Act set down for the first time the principles that provincial health-care systems had to respect to qualify for federal cost-sharing:

- Provincial health insurance plans must be administered and operated on a non-profit basis by a *public authority*.
- They must provide *universal and equal access* to health services for all insurable residents of the province.
- Provincial health insurance plans must be *comprehensive*, covering all necessary procedures and services.
- Coverage must be *portable*, so that people do not lose their health-care benefits when temporarily absent from their home province.

The meaning of these principles is not self-evident. To say that the health-care system should respect the principle of universality, for example, does not tell us whether this principle is compromised if some people are able to buy superior services or faster delivery than is available to everyone. And does comprehensiveness require that every health-related procedure, service, or device be covered? Eyeglasses, corrective eye surgery for nearsightedness, tooth fillings and extractions, and other devices and services that are very clearly related to health are not covered for most segments of the population. How inclusive the publicly financed health-care system must be before it satisfies the criterion of comprehensiveness is an open question.

The ambiguity associated with these principles became a political problem by the late 1970s when an increasing number of physicians across Canada began to charge their patients a fee on top of the amount paid by provincial health insurance plans. This practice, known as **extra-billing**, was criticized by some as undermining the principle of equally accessible health care. Poorer patients, it was argued, would be less likely to see a doctor for necessary diagnosis or treatment. But even if extra-billing did not dissuade some people from going to the doctor, the burden of such payments—which, it should be said, were quite low—would weigh more heavily on the poor than the affluent, thereby introducing an element of inequality that some considered a violation of the spirit and the letter of medicare.

The Canada Health Act (CHA), 1984, provides for Ottawa to penalize provinces that allow doctors to extra-bill their patients—a practice that was becoming increasingly common before the law's passage. The CHA reiterates the principles of medicare and has become the basis for the often asserted and routinely accepted claim that Ottawa has a responsibility to defend national standards in the delivery of health care. Indeed, over time the principles of medicare have acquired a kind of sacrosanct status in Canadian politics, and any politician who questions them does so at his or her peril.

Despite the widespread conviction that Ottawa has a legitimate role to play in setting and monitoring national standards in health care, it is important to recognize that this role rests on money and public opinion. The federal government's involvement in health care is not mandated by the constitutional division of legislative authority. The Constitution assigns responsibility for health care to the provinces, a fact that

---

BOX 8.1   Milestones in the Development of Medicare

1947	Public hospitalization insurance introduced in Saskatchewan.
1957	Ottawa commits to 50/50 cost-sharing for provincial hospitalization insurance.
1962	Saskatchewan government extends universal, publicly financed insurance to physician services, followed by a doctors' strike that lasts 23 days.
1964	Royal Commission on Health Services recommends publicly funded, universal insurance not only for doctor services, but also for prescription drugs and home care as well as dental and optical services for some groups.
1966	Ottawa introduces the Medical Care Act.
1968–72	Through an intense series of intergovernmental negotiations, all 10 provinces and two territories eventually 'sign on' to medicare, agreeing to provide universal public coverage for hospital and physician care in exchange for matching federal contributions toward the costs of many services. However, 'expenditures on mental and tuberculosis hospitals, home care, certain outpatient diagnostic services, and administration costs were *not* cost-shared.'
1977	Ottawa changes its funding arrangements, replacing cost-sharing.
1984	Ottawa passes the Canada Health Act, penalizing provinces that allow doctors to bill patients more than the amounts payable under public health insurance.
1995	Established programs financing (EPF) transfers are replaced with the Canada Health and Social Transfer (CHST), under which provinces are free to determine what portion of the CHST they devote to health.

Source: Adapted, with additions, from Commissioner Roy J. Romanow, Q.C., *Shape the Future of Health Care: Commission on the Future of Health Care in Canada, Interim Report,* February 2002, 13. http://dsp-psd.pwgsc.gc.ca/Collection/CP32-76-2002E.pdf.

no federal government has questioned. But Ottawa has played a major role in the financing of health-care services since the 1960s, paying as much as 41 per cent[3] of provincial health-care costs at the high point of its commitment to medicare. Moreover, many Canadians have come to share the belief that Ottawa ought to establish and protect national standards in health care—a belief that has been encouraged by federal politicians and many other opinion leaders for the last couple of decades. As Ottawa's financial commitment to provincial health care has diminished, the lever of public opinion has become increasingly important for maintaining whatever clout the federal government retains over health care in the provinces.

It was probably inevitable that the Charter of Rights and Freedoms would eventually be brought to bear on issues of health care. At least this is the opinion of some Charter specialists. In their book *The Charter and Health Care*,[4] former Deputy Minister of Finance Stanley Hartt and law professor Patrick Monahan argue that the Charter provides a constitutional basis for challenging the public-sector monopoly on the provision of health-related services and procedures where delays in treatment have become such that they violate the Charter (s. 7) guarantee of the individual's 'life, liberty and security of the person and the right not to be deprived thereof except in accordance with the principles of fundamental justice'. Hartt and Monahan acknowledge that governments have a right to exclude private health-care providers from the market—but not, they argue, when this exclusion deprives Canadians of Charter-based rights. They point to the 1988 'Morgentaler' ruling on Canada's abortion law, which held that delay in the provision of medically necessary treatment is an unconstitutional violation of an individual's section 7 rights. By depriving an individual of the opportunity to receive treatment in Canada from a health-care provider operating outside the public monopoly system, the effect of the Canada Health Act, although not its intention, is to violate an important Charter guarantee. Hartt and Monahan put it this way:

> The courts have held that laws structured so that they fail to achieve their stated purposes are inconsistent with the principles of fundamental justice under Section 7. In the context of health care, the entire rationale and purpose of the public health-care model is to deliver timely medical services to Canadians. To deny Canadians access to timely medical care in the public system and simultaneously prevent them from using their own resources to access such services is directly contrary to that stated purpose. Thus it cannot be consistent with the principles of fundamental justice.[5]

Are they right? There is still room for debate. However, in the decision in *Chaoulli v. Quebec*, 2005, the Supreme Court invalidated Quebec's prohibition against private insurance for medical procedures that are covered by the public health-care system. One part of the case involved a patient, George Zeloitis, who argued that he should be allowed to purchase private insurance to shorten the wait time for his hip surgery. Whether this decision will be used as a precedent in other provinces remains to be seen. Still, it is worth noting that in some parts of Canada the waiting period for orthopaedic surgery can be as long as 17 weeks.[6] Diagnostic procedures that could identify life-threatening conditions at an early stage, when the prospects for a successful intervention are still good, may be delayed for months under the current system. Given these harsh realities, it is not hard to imagine a constitutional challenge of the sort proposed by Hartt and Monahan, nor is it unthinkable that such a challenge might succeed.

The Financial Picture

Health care is expensive. It is estimated that total public spending on health care in Canada in 2010 was approximately $135.1 billion.[7] Health care is the largest expenditure in the budgets of all provincial governments. In 1974–5 health care accounted for an average of 28 per cent of provincial program spending. By 2010 that figure has increased to roughly 70 per cent. At the high end, Nunuvut devotes about 93.8 per cent of its total program spending to health. But even in the province that devotes the smallest share of its budget to health, Ontario, health care still eats up 67 per cent of program spending.[8]

In real terms, adjusted to take into account inflation over the years, per capita public-sector spending on health care has increased 12-fold over the last generation: from about $401 per person in 1976 to about $3,663 per person in 2010, measured in current dollars. If we go inside the spending envelope we find that, in recent years, this growth has been fuelled by spending on hospitals and physician services (see Figure 8.1).

FIGURE 8.1 Total Health Expenditure, Selected Use of Funds, Canada 1975–2010 (current dollars)

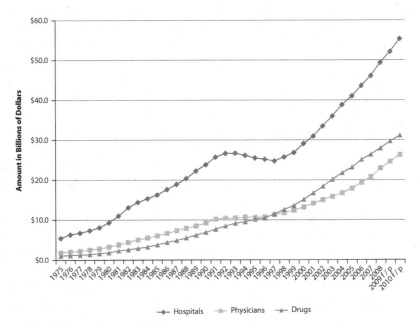

→ Hospitals → Physicians → Drugs

Source: Canadian Institute for Health Information, National Expenditure Database.

An additional fast-growing component of health-care spending has been the increasing costs of drugs, drug therapies, and diagnostic and other medical technology. Even more important, perhaps, is the role played by Canadians' rising expectations. As the *Interim Report* of the Commission on Health Care puts it, 'One of the most significant cost drivers is how our own expectations have grown over the past decades. We expect the best in terms of technology, treatments, facilities, research and drugs, and as a consequence, we may be placing demands on our governments that are not sustainable over time.'[9]

Since the late 1970s Ottawa and the provinces have been locked in a feud over their respective contributions to health-care spending. When this feud erupted, Ottawa provided provincial governments with roughly 50 cents of every dollar they spent on health care. Indeed, provincial spending on health, including hospital construction, had been encouraged by Ottawa's offer to match such spending dollar for dollar. In retrospect it is easy to see that this formula was guaranteed to cause problems. On the financial side, it reduced whatever incentives the provinces might have had to control their spending. And on the accountability side, shared-cost programs in any policy field make it difficult to determine who should be held accountable for the system's performance. Does the fact that Ottawa pays a share of health-care costs mean that it should be held accountable, to some degree at least, for program and service decisions that are made by provincial governments?

These issues became more than academic in 1977, when Ottawa retreated from its commitment to match provincial spending on health. Under the established programs financing (EPF) formula that it imposed on the provinces, the federal contribution to health, as well as to post-secondary education, would be geared to the previous year's level of provincial spending, adjusted to take into account change in a province's gross provincial product. This new formula did not result in a precipitous drop in Ottawa's contributions to provincial health-care budgets, at least not right away. Over time, however, the provinces' share of public health-care spending increased steadily (see Figure 8.2).

Moreover, the form taken by federal health-care transfers to the provinces shifted significantly away from cash toward tax points. Although the amounts transferred have increased somewhat since Ottawa moved from annual budget deficits to surpluses in the late 1990s, there is no disputing the fact that the federal government's share of public spending on health falls short of the levels of the 1970s and 1980s. How far short, whether contribution levels should help to determine federal influence on the shape of health policy, and whether Ottawa should be involved at all in what is, after all, an area of provincial jurisdiction, are matters for debate.

Determining the real extent of Ottawa's contribution to the provinces' financing of health care is complicated by the fact that some of that contribution takes forms other than cash and tax transfers earmarked for health. The main vehicle for Ottawa's contribution is the Canada Health and Social Transfer, which amounted to about $35.6 billion in 2010.[10] Approximately $24.8 billion of that total went to health; however, it is up to each province to decide how it will divide its CHST money among health care, post-secondary education, and social assistance.[11] The federal government is quick to point out that, on top of the CHST, it transfers a significant amount (roughly

FIGURE 8.2 Total Health Expenditure by Provincial and Federal Governments and the Private Sector, 1975–2010 (current dollars)

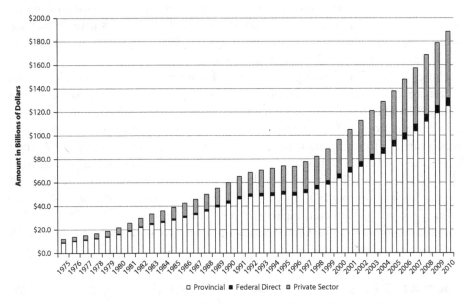

Source: Canadian Institute for Health Information, National Expenditure Database.

$13.4 billion in 2009) every year to the less prosperous provinces in equalization grants, and that some portion of that total also gets spent on provincial health care. In addition, Ottawa spends an estimated $6 billion per year on health services for Aboriginal Canadians and the military, as well as various programs for health promotion, protection, innovation and research, and health information systems.

Thus Ottawa's financial contribution to health care is not inconsequential. Nevertheless, three facts are clear:

- Ottawa's share of total public spending has declined over the last three decades, while the provinces' share has increased.
- The federal contribution is less significant in the provinces that do not receive equalization payments, notably Ontario and Alberta, than it is in those provinces whose ability to finance public services is more dependent on Ottawa.
- To the extent that Ottawa's influence on provincial health policy depends on its ability to use the threat of withholding dollars to induce compliance, this influence may be weakened as Ottawa's contribution to provincial health budgets shrinks.

International Comparisons

Canadian political leaders—at least some of them—often tell us that our health-care system is the envy of the world. The truth is that the rest of the world knows little to nothing about health care in Canada. Nor are Canadians particularly well informed about how health-care systems operate in other countries, with the partial exception of the United States. The exception is only partial because some of what Canadians believe about the American health-care system is inaccurate. An examination of how Canadian health care measures up against other national systems is useful from the standpoint both of arriving at an informed assessment of Canada's performance and of thinking about alternative ways of financing and delivering health care outside the tired box of Canadian–American comparisons.

However Canada's spending on health is measured—whether per capita or as a percentage of the gross domestic product—it ranks near the top internationally (see Figure 8.3). The United States is clearly the world's highest spender on health, followed by a few countries in Western Europe, with Canada in seventh place. Spending on health care is affected by many factors, including the scope of services that fall under the health-care umbrella (e.g., coverage for dental services is universal in Germany, but limited to a small minority in Canada), drug prices, how services are delivered, the pay levels of doctors and other health-care practitioners, and the age distribution of the population. Moreover, higher spending does not necessarily mean a healthier population—otherwise the United States and Germany would have the longest life expectancies and lowest rates of infant mortality, which they do not.

FIGURE 8.3 Total Health Expenditure as a Percentage of GDP, Selected Countries, 2009

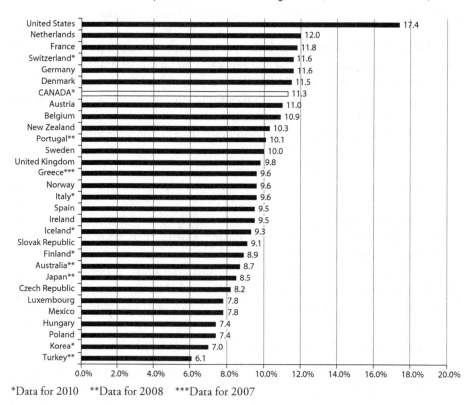

*Data for 2010   **Data for 2008   ***Data for 2007

Source: Data based on OECD (2010), "Total expenditure on health", Health: Key Tables from OECD, No. 1., http://dx.doi.org/10.1787/20758480-2010-table1

As for the share of its total spending on health accounted for by the public sector, Canada is unremarkable. The Scandinavian countries, France, and even the United Kingdom have a higher ratio of public to private spending than Canada (see Table 8.1). Among the world's affluent countries the United States is clearly the outlier, with more private than public spending on health care. At the same time, because it spends so much more on health than other countries, as a percentage of GDP the United States spends more on public health than many other countries, Canada included (see Figure 8.4).

TABLE 8.1 Public Expenditure as a Percentage of Total Health Expenditure, Selected Countries, 2010

Country	Public expend. on health (%)	Country	Public expend. on health (%)
Australia	68.0[1]	Italy	77.6
Austria	77.7[2]	Japan	80.8[1]
Belgium	7.5[2]	Korea	58.3
Canada	70.6	Luxembourg	84.0[2]
Chile	47.4[2]	Mexico	47.3
Czech Republic	84.0[2]	New Zealand	80.5[2]
Denmark	85.0[2]	Norway	84.1[2]
Estonia	75.3[2]	Poland	72.2[2]
Finland	75.1	Portugal	65.1[3]
France	77.9[2]	Slovak Republic	65.7[2]
Germany	76.9[2]	Slovenia	73.4[2]
Greece	60.3[3]	Spain	73.6[2]
Hungary	69.7[2]	Sweden	81.5[2]
Iceland	80.5	Switzerland	59.0
Ireland	75.0[2]	Turkey	73.0[3]
Israel	58.5[2]	United Kingdom	84.1[2]
United States	47.7[2]		

1. 2008 data
2. 2009 data
3. 2007 data
Source: Data based on OECD (2010), "Total expenditure on health", Health: Key Tables from OECD, No. 1., http://dx.doi.org/10.1787/20758480-2010-table1

The number and incomes of people working in the health-care system and the costs of drugs and medical technology are important factors influencing the size of the health-care bill. Canada has fewer physicians per capita than many countries—about two per 1,000 compared to three in France and Germany and almost six in Italy. At the same time, general practitioners in Canada make, on average, about twice as much as their French counterparts but significantly less than comparable physicians in the United States.

FIGURE 8.4 Public-Sector Health Expenditure as a Percentage of GDP, 2008

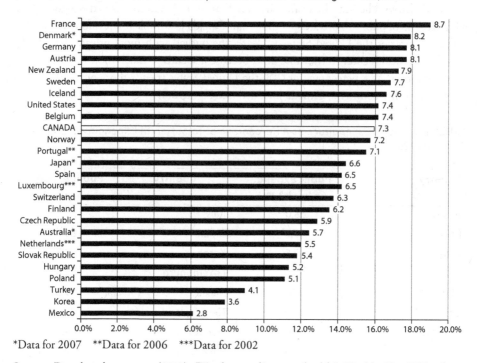

*Data for 2007   **Data for 2006   ***Data for 2002

Source: Data based on OECD (2010), "Total expenditure on health", Health: Key Tables from OECD, No. 1., http://dx.doi.org/10.1787/20758480-2010-table1

Drug prices in Canada are lower than in many other affluent societies, including Germany, the United States, and Sweden, but the overall drug bill for any country is also affected by patterns of prescribing (which vary between societies) and the age distribution of the population (older people being heavier users of prescription drugs).

Canada is not the only wealthy country whose citizens believe that their health-care system is broken and needs to be fixed. A survey conducted in 1998 found that only one in five Canadians believed that the health-care system worked well and needed only minor changes. Close to one-quarter said that the system needed to be rebuilt completely, and 56 per cent said that fundamental changes were needed. This distribution of views was broadly similar to that found in other Anglo-American democracies, the major difference between Canada and these other countries being that Canadians' satisfaction with their system appeared to have fallen dramatically since the late 1980s. Although Canadians were far more satisfied than Americans with their health-care system in 1988, this was no longer the case in 2010 (see Figure 8.5).

It is tempting to conclude that the decline in Canadians' satisfaction with their health-care system is due to a deterioration in the performance of that system. But matters are probably not that simple. It is not clear that waiting lists for various diagnostic and surgical procedures are significantly longer today than they were in the 1980s, or that most hospital emergency rooms are more crowded than they used to be.

FIGURE 8.5 Public Satisfaction with Health Care in Three Countries, 1988, 1998,and 2010

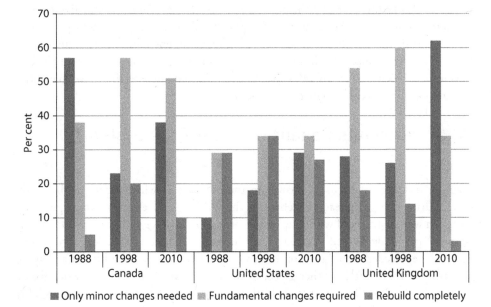

■ Only minor changes needed   ■ Fundamental changes required   ■ Rebuild completely

Source: OECD, *OECD Health Data* and the 2010 Commonwealth Fund International Health Policy Survey.

What is clear, however, is that negative media coverage of the health-care system has increased dramatically since the 1980s. Moreover, the real level of public spending on health care has risen, leading governments to look for ways to rein in this spending. The cuts and restructuring they have undertaken and the reactions of doctors, nurses, and others inside the system to these changes have probably contributed to the increase in negative, sometimes alarmist, coverage and, in turn, to the sharp drop in public satisfaction.

On the other hand, public opinion polls and patterns of media coverage tell us nothing about how the performance of Canada's health-care system measures up internationally. A study undertaken by the World Health Organization in 2000 ranked Canada thirtieth among the WHO's 191 member countries in the quality of its health care.[12] The ranking system involved a combination of health expenditures, average life expectancy, infant mortality rates, and measures of the responsiveness of the health-care system. This latter component of the WHO evaluation was based on surveys of health-care providers that purported to measure qualities such as the health system's respect for persons, client orientation, and treatment of disadvantaged groups. While there is much to question in the methodology of the WHO study, at the very least it provides grounds to reflect on the confident but almost never substantiated claims that are made about the international superiority of Canada's health-care system.

Given that Canada is one of the world's leading spenders on health, and that Canadians are often told Canadian medicare is the envy of the world, most Canadians would be shocked to hear that the performance of their system is only mediocre compared to that in many other countries. Performance is notoriously difficult to measure. At the end of the day, however, what truly matters is not how the performance of Canada's system compares to health care in the United States or any other country, but how it measures up to Canadians' expectations. There are reasons to believe that these expectations have become higher over time.

What Really Ails Canada's Health-Care System?

Money

'Lack of funding' is the usual answer to the question of what's wrong with health care. During the party leaders' debate in the 2000 federal election campaign, Jean Chrétien was the target of withering attacks from all the other party leaders for having 'starved' and 'underfunded' medicare. All the leaders, Chrétien included, agreed that more money needed to be spent on health care. There was barely a hint of a suggestion from anyone that any other aspect of the health-care system needed to be fixed, apart from the Bloc Québécois leader's insistence that Ottawa had no business telling Quebec what should be done in an area of provincial jurisdiction.

But is money the problem? Many of Canada's most prominent health-care experts claim otherwise. Robert Evans and Greg Stoddart, two of the country's foremost health-care economists, argue that health care has been adequately funded but that the system needs to be restructured to perform more efficiently. When asked why Canadians have been hearing for years that the system is crumbling because of underfunding, Stoddart explained:

> There is a tension between the people who pay the bills—provincial governments—and the people who work in the system, such as doctors, nurses and other hospital workers. We often forget that there have been flare-ups over funding ever since medicare began. What's new today is not only is there serious tension over how much money will go into the system, there is also concern over how it will be spent. For the first time provincial governments are not just slowing down the growth in health care spending, they are actually cutting spending. They are also saying, for the first time: 'We have to do more than sign the cheques. We are going to influence how care is provided.' Not surprisingly, this has created an uproar in the system.[13]

Robert Evans makes the same point when he observes that 'There will always be pressure for more from people who make their living in the system. Every dollar that goes into the system becomes somebody's income. . . . People get concerned when their jobs, incomes and established patterns of practice are threatened by spending decisions.'[14]

Neither Stoddart nor Evans proposes user fees or a mixed public/private system, along the lines of the American model, as part of the answer to what they argue are the inefficiencies in Canada's health-care system. Instead, they maintain that the financial resources already in the system can be better managed through reforms to the way health services are delivered. They also argue that those who work in health care are aware that the system can be redesigned to perform more efficiently. 'But the system isn't structured to reward effectiveness or efficiency or to take advantage of their ideas.'[15] Similarly, Paul Stanway argues that Canadians want it both ways: They ask for significant change but then resist that change when it is proposed (see Box 8.2).

BOX 8.2 Health Care Fails because We Don't Really Want Change

The fact that public health care in Alberta, and across Canada for that matter, is plagued by access problems is not news. It's been that way for decades. Rationing of services (waiting lists, lineups) is the default coping mechanism of publicly funded health systems around the world—Alberta included.

The real question is why don't we fix the problem? And after nearly four decades since I first wrote about overcrowded emergency rooms, I'm pretty sure of the answer.

It's us: the public, the voters, the media, the opposition. To oversimplify the problem, it comes down to demanding change . . . and then resisting all significant change. Fix the system, but don't mess with it.

For example, few Albertans would argue that we should spend more on bureaucracy rather than on improving health services, so three years ago the provincial government moved to streamline a system that had nine—nine!—increasingly expensive bureaucracies administering health care for just 3.5 million Albertans—the population of a medium-sized city in most parts of the world.

The former health boards couldn't work together, couldn't live within budgets, and couldn't improve service and outcomes despite ever-larger infusions of taxpayers' dollars. And the opposition parties want to reinstate these monuments to inefficiency! Actually what they want is a political club to beat the government with. And the media, as always, wants a train wreck. So they conspire to scare the starch out of Albertans by putting the worst possible spin on any and all attempts to change the system.

Ron Liepert wants to better direct seniors' health benefits toward those who actually need the help, and he's excoriated for attacking 'needy' seniors and victimizing the elderly.

An Alberta government finally takes the time to prioritize the construction of new health facilities, new beds—responding to need rather than political pressure—and is accused of being out of touch, arrogant and (the ultimate irony) outrageously political!

Canada used to have one of the best public health systems in the world, but this terrified, whining opposition to change has seen us fall to the middle of the pack among developed countries. We're still among the best when it comes to per-capita health spending (only the Americans spend more) and the percentage of our GDP devoted to health care, but more and more we're rationing instead of meeting increased demand.

So what do we do? Who can we learn from?

Well, according to the World Health Organization (WHO), the public health plans that are doing the best are those with the most flexibility—countries like France, Germany, and Japan. They have their problems, but they have all been more successful than Canada in meeting changing needs. In a word, they're more efficient.

They're not all the same—there's no one-size-fits-all solution to health-care challenges. But what they do share is compulsory basic health insurance (either public or private), a combination of public and private delivery of health services, and in most cases the expectation that the patient should pay something toward the cost of services if they can afford to do so.

Compare that to the constipated world of the Canada Health Act, where we prohibit private insurance for 'medically necessary' health care, only governments can be trusted to run hospitals, private delivery of public services is frowned upon, and 'extra-billing' is supposedly illegal.

Famously, only North Korea has a more rigid system of public health care, yet we're actually surprised when our bureaucratic, ring-fenced, self-absorbed health system can't deal with increased demand and changing demographics.

According to the WHO, France has consistently had among the best, most responsive public health systems in the world in recent years. It's the most expensive system in Europe, but per-capita less expensive than Canada. It's not perfect, but survey after survey suggests it meets the needs and expectations of the French people most of the time.

But here's the thing—to get most of what they want most of the time the French accept that the government plan will only reimburse them for about 70 per cent of their health costs, they may be treated in a private facility, they will pay a small fee to see a doctor or specialist, and they will need private, top-up insurance if they don't want to pay cash or flash their credit card.

Can you imagine the response if any of these things were suggested in Alberta?

Actually we can, because all of them have been suggested at one time or another, and then abandoned because of opposition from the public, the media, and special interest groups. Can't you just hear David Eggen of the NDP/Friends of Medicare claiming the end of life as we know it?

Paul Stanway is a veteran Alberta journalist and former director of communications for Premier Ed Stelmach.

Source: Paul Stanway, 'Health Care Fails because We Don't Really Want Change', *Calgary Herald*, November 23, 2010.

To better understand the nature of the problem, consider the following:

- *Emergency room closures.* In a number of communities across Canada, emergency room services at hospitals have been cut back, consolidated, or closed. For example, Windsor, Ontario, has four hospitals, but only one of the four keeps its emergency room open overnight. The result may be longer waiting times for those seeking emergency treatment, but there is no question that this sort of consolidation of services saves money.
- *Hospital restructuring.* In 1996 the Conservative government of Alberta decided to close cardiac care units in a number of the province's hospitals and to centralize these services at certain regional hospitals. The motivation was to save money. Critics argued that people would die as a result of this restructuring, which they claimed would lead to delays and reductions in the quality of diagnosis and treatment. But according to one study, there has been no decline in health performance.[16]
- *Nurse practitioners.* Doctors earn more money than nurses. In recent years a number of provinces have moved to recognize and license nurse practitioners, whose responsibilities and authority go beyond those traditionally associated with nurses to include some functions normally reserved for physicians. Many doctors have objected to this, but there is little doubt that transferring some of the activities of doctors to less expensive practitioners—assuming there is no loss in the quality of service—improves the cost efficiency of the system. Indeed, it could be argued that increasing the number of practitioners available to treat patients means shorter waiting times and therefore improves the quality of service.

Most people assume that closing hospitals or reducing the number of beds in them necessarily means a decline in the performance of the health-care system. The reason for this assumption has little to do with the realities of health care but much to do with politics, media behaviour, and the responses of those who work in the system and whose jobs, duties, and incomes are affected by changes like these. No community likes to lose a hospital, a chronic-care or neonatal ward, or any other health-care service. Politicians will always be found to predict calamitous results from such changes. It is in the nature of the mass media to emphasize the sensational and, through their construction and coverage of stories, to give credibility to claims that may rest on a weak foundation of facts. Those whose jobs and incomes are directly affected by closures and restructuring are usually on the front lines of protest and criticism of such measures.

Yet the fact is that many parts of Canada have experienced the loss of beds and even hospitals, and a track record exists on which to base claims about how access to health care and other aspects of system performance have been affected. The conclusion reached by most experts is that there is not a direct correlation between the number of hospital beds in a community and access to care for patients in need. The explanation for what might appear to be a paradoxical conclusion is that hospitals in jurisdictions across Canada have been carrying out more surgeries on an outpatient basis, significantly reducing the volume of overnight stays. More and more services are now provided at a patient's home, a clinic, or a nursing home, all of which are less expensive than hospitals as sites for the delivery of health services. According to Vivek Goel, a public health physician in Toronto, the number of hospital patient days per 1000 population dropped by about 40 per cent between the mid-1980s and the mid-1990s, from about 1200–1300 to 700–800.[17] The five-year rate shows a decline of 10.3 per cent from 1995 to 2000.[18] Critics often charge that bed and hospital closures, although they may save money, jeopardize the health of patients who need to be treated in a hospital setting or who should be kept overnight rather than treated and discharged the same day. No doubt this is true in some cases; yet studies of the health impact of the reduction in the number of hospital beds do not show it to be a general problem. Based on a study of Winnipeg hospitals carried out by the Manitoba Centre for Health Policy and Evaluation, Dr. Noralou Roos drew the following conclusions:

> [W]e didn't find that shorter lengths of stay in hospital led to more problems after patients went home. Another concern was that the cuts would mean less intensive monitoring of patients after major surgery or heart attacks, leading to patients dying needlessly. We studied three of the most common types of patients: heart attack, hip fracture and cancer surgery. We looked at death rates to see if they went up while the patient was in hospital or afterwards. They didn't. We could find no evidence the cuts hurt quality of care.[19]

No one would suggest that health-care spending can be indiscriminately cut without any adverse consequences; the health of some patients will suffer. Even so, it is not clear that more money is the solution to what ails Canadian health care. Virtually all experts agree that the most important reforms to Canada's health-care system would involve changes in how services are delivered and where resources are targeted. The problem is that reforms of this kind are complex and more difficult to explain to citizens than the idea that the system needs more money.

Measuring Performance and Determining Accountability

How do we know whether our health-care system is performing well or poorly? It sometimes happens that the evidence of failure or success is obvious and dramatic. For example, when people diagnosed with breast or prostate cancer must wait two months before receiving radiation treatment, allowing time for their cancers to spread, we know that things are not working as we would wish. On the other hand, when an organ transplant or a timely diagnosis saves someone's life, we are likely to think that this is how we expect our health system to perform. But most of the time, and for most health services, procedures, and providers, the evidence on which to base an assessment of their performance is sketchy at best.

In most markets and for most products or services, this situation would be considered unacceptable. When buying a car, a Caribbean vacation package, a refrigerator, or the services of an electrician, most of us expect to be given some information as a basis on which to make our choice. Until fairly recently, though, this sort of information was almost entirely unavailable when it came to health services. Furthermore, because of the way most health services are paid for, most people have only a vague idea, if any, of what the services they receive actually cost. This is not a situation that allows for either reliable assessment of performance or accountability on the part of service providers.

The problem of measuring performance was acknowledged by the Commission on the Future of Health Care in Canada. In its *Interim Report* (2002) the Commission observed that 'you cannot improve what you cannot measure' and that 'good, reliable, comparable information on far too many aspects of our health care system—from waiting times, to costs, to treatment outcomes—is woefully lacking'.[20] Both the United States and the United Kingdom have a sort of 'scorecard' system that provides the public with information on the performance of specific hospitals and practitioners in cases involving certain procedures, such as cardiac bypass surgeries or Caesarean births, as well as the waiting times for particular surgeries and procedures. Canada lagged behind both with respect to systematic performance measurement, partly because some in the system resisted this sort of evaluation and partly because political will was lacking to require hospitals to collect and make publicly available information that, in some cases at least, could be interpreted as an indication of substandard performance.

This changed in February 2003, when the First Ministers agreed on an action plan to improve access to timely care across Canada. One of the first steps was to measure and address waiting times. The First Ministers made a commitment to achieve meaningful reductions in waiting times for such priority areas as cancer, heart, diagnostic imaging, joint replacements, and sight restoration by March 31, 2007. To this end a Wait Times Reduction Fund was set up and the First Ministers agreed to collect and make available information on wait times. Most Canadian provinces now provide online access to current waiting times by city and hospital, measured in the number of days a patient must wait between seeing the specialist and the time the procedure is performed. As some critics have pointed out, however, these estimates do not include the time that patients must wait between referral by a family physician and the visit to the specialist; this is often the longest wait of all.

While this new system allows health ministers to boast about reducing wait times and supporters of medicare to show that the system is working, it also quantifies disparities in care from one region to another. Other things being equal, communities like London, Ontario, and Edmonton, Alberta, which have university medical schools and therefore exceptional concentrations of highly trained specialists and high-quality facilities, have an advantage over places like Windsor, Ontario, and Trois-Rivières, Quebec. One would expect more densely populated urban centres to offer a greater range of services, including those of specialists, and to have expensive diagnostic technology and treatment facilities that are less likely to exist in more sparsely populated areas.

One important measure is the waiting time for surgeries and such diagnostic procedures as CAT scans and MRIs. Again, how well a hospital or community does on measures like these will depend in large part on the size of the community and whether or not it has a medical school. But even in relatively well-serviced communities it appears that waiting lists are sometimes so long that the health of some patients may be jeopardized. In the United Kingdom, a Patient's Charter establishes acceptable waiting times for specific services and procedures and is used as a benchmark in evaluating the performance of hospitals. The Commission on the Future of Health Care in Canada identified delays in receiving health-care services as one of the main worries that Canadians express about their health-care system. This worry has existed for years, yet relatively little has been done either to measure and make publicly available information on waiting times or to deal with their causes. Lack of resources—specialists and expensive technology—is one factor contributing to the length of waiting lists, but virtually all studies conclude that waiting times could be shortened and health risks reduced through reforms that do not require more spending. This is no doubt why, in 2005, the Conservatives made introduction of a wait times guarantee a central plank in their election platform. Modelled on the recommendations of a bipartisan senate committee, the Patient Wait Times Guarantee announced by prime minister Harper in April 2007 establishes maximum acceptable waiting times for key treatments and procedures.[21] One component of the guarantee is that patients who cannot get timely care in their own province will be able to travel to another jurisdiction, at the government's expense, to receive the necessary treatment.

Posting wait times on Internet sites is a positive step toward giving citizens the information they need and, ultimately, ensuring accountability on the part of the system to those who use and pay for it. Yet Canadians still have no legal guarantee (provided in the UK under the Patient's Charter) that comparative information on performance will be available. Provincial variations in health-care delivery mean that there is no standardization in what is reported, and true comparison across jurisdictions is therefore impossible. Nor are particular practitioners identified. The usual argument against naming names is that deviations from standard performance may be statistical flukes, and that **outcome-oriented performance indicators** make sense only for the relatively few cases in which high volumes of reasonably similar procedures are performed in a variety of centres. Those in the system tend to prefer **input-oriented performance indicators**, such as the number of practitioners with specific qualifications in a given area, the rate and appropriateness of prescribed diagnostic tests, and similar measures from which probable health outcomes may be inferred.

Input measures of health system performance may well be better than nothing, and output-oriented evaluations that do not identify practitioners at least provide those in the system with comparative information on which to identify possible problems and poor performance. But neither provides the sort of practitioner-specific, publicly accessible information that would allow a woman to choose an obstetrician who often performs C-sections over one who does so much less often, or that would enable a cancer patient to make decisions based on knowledge of the waiting times with different specialists. Of course, the ability to choose also depends on factors such as the referral system (a referral to a specialist must be obtained from a general practitioner), the number of doctors and hospitals in a particular community, and the workloads of different practitioners. Still, making more information available would at least provide a basis for identifying substandard performers in the health-care system. Some will say that this is not a good thing—that apparent weaknesses in the performance of some practitioners or hospitals may be attributable to circumstances that have nothing to do with competence or other quality-of-service factors. In weighing the reputation of hospitals and practitioners against the right of patients to a health-care system that meets certain performance expectations, however, which should come first? Hospital administrators and practitioners can always provide explanations if they feel their performance has been unfairly assessed. Most provinces engage in regular testing of students in particular grades and publish school-by-school rankings of the results. Schools and school boards may protest that below-average results reflect factors other than the quality of instruction, and their explanations may be entirely plausible.

Prevention versus Curative Care

Canada's health-care system is geared primarily toward the identification and treatment of illness. In this respect it is no different from the health-care systems of other rich countries. People come to associate more doctors, bigger and better hospitals, and newer machines with better health. In this they are mistaken. For decades studies have confirmed that the key drivers of health quality are related to lifestyle, the quality of the environment (including public sanitation), access to immunization against contagious diseases, and the availability of antibiotics. These factors, not the medicare system, are primarily responsible for the increased life expectancy and lower infant mortality that the Canadian population has experienced over the last two generations.

Disease prevention and the improvement of conditions that may lead to illness have been goals of public policy since the nineteenth century. When ships carrying immigrants to Canada were required to land at Sable Island so that new arrivals could be checked for tuberculosis and cholera and, if necessary, quarantined, this was a preventative public health measure. The public sanitation laws and workplace safety standards that were gradually put in place beginning in the late 1800s likewise were geared toward ameliorating conditions that jeopardized health. Public immunization campaigns against tuberculosis, polio, and rubella led to enormous improvements in public health in the twentieth century. Alongside these public health measures, the growing affluence of Canadian society made possible improvements in diet and, consequently, stronger immune systems for an increasing share of the population. Affluence has also meant less crowded housing, reducing the prevalence of stress and violence as well as communicable disease. Compared to the amounts spent on **curative care**—practitioners, hospitals, sophisticated medical technology, the latest drugs—the amount of money spent on prevention is relatively small. Virtually all health experts agree, however, that the health return on each dollar invested in preventative measures is comparatively high. This raises the question of why the health system, or more generally public policy, is not more oriented to the prevention of illness.

The answer has two parts. First, to the extent that the conditions that cause illness are the inevitable accompaniments of industrial processes and affluent lifestyles built around the personal automobile, high energy consumption, waste, and stress, these conditions cannot be eliminated or even significantly ameliorated without challenging both the fundamental values on which societies like ours rest and the powerful interests that have developed around these processes and lifestyles. Second, a reorientation of the health-care system from diagnosis and treatment to prevention would require some transfer of resources from existing procedures, organizations, and practitioners to others. For example, if lifestyle changes are part of the key to prevention, more money for education in schools and the workplace and through advertising is certainly important. But such a program would compete for dollars that might otherwise be spent on diagnostic machines or practitioners' fees. With governments spending in the range of $80 billion annually on health care, an additional $1 billion for public education may not seem very significant. But it's important to consider what changes in behaviour, and therefore what health improvements, would be produced by such an investment. Both Ottawa and the provinces already spend money on educational campaigns to promote fitness, discourage smoking, and encourage healthy eating habits. It is virtually impossible to measure the effectiveness of such expenditures. There is little doubt, however, that more coercive measures—for example, mandatory seatbelt legislation, automatic licence suspensions for people exceeding legal blood-alcohol limits, and bans on smoking in public places—are more likely to deliver health results than measures geared toward persuasion.

These more coercive measures run into two obstacles. One involves public opinion and personal freedom. Almost no one believes that punishing someone for driving while intoxicated is a serious breach of that person's freedom. People are divided, however, on whether a total ban on smoking in public places is an acceptable limitation on the freedom either of smokers or of bar and restaurant owners. Some argue that people should be free to choose between smoking and non-smoking establishments. Nonetheless, most provincial governments have imposed smoking bans on all public spaces, including bars, bingo halls, and pubs. Even more people would likely object to a special tax on fatty foods like french fries and hamburgers, a tax that some quite logically propose on the grounds that fat-laden diets have contributed to health problems such as obesity and diabetes. The second obstacle involves the economic interests—not just of business owners but of their employees as well—that are affected by bans and lesser forms of coercion intended to change behaviour. The tobacco industry has waged a long and expensive fight to eliminate or at least to limit restrictions on the distribution and advertising of its products. To this point, however, restrictions on the distribution and advertising of alcohol have not been so stringent, despite abundant evidence of the health risks associated with excessive drinking. And despite widespread awareness of the dangers associated with state-sanctioned gambling—from personal stress to family breakups, addiction, and even suicide—it has proven extremely difficult for communities across North America to resist the revenues generated by casinos or to eliminate them once the tax base and local economy become dependent on them.

Some, like Michael Decter, former Deputy Minister of Health under Ontario's NDP government (1990–5) and now a health policy consultant, go so far as to argue for a complete rethinking of our ideas about what health care involves:

> [W]e need a broader agenda. We need positive action on the issues that pose the greatest threats to life expectancy and health: unemployment, substance abuse, Native poverty and social disintegration, obesity, hunger, poor eating habits, adolescent suicide, AIDS. As social issues, not illnesses, these can't be cured by

doctors in hospitals. Instead, solving them must be the focus of our approach to investing in our health as a nation. If we redirect our spending and follow it up with the right legislation, we can improve health where it is really decided.[22]

There is not much doubt that Decter is right in his claims that illness is related to social conditions and that 'the poor comprise a disproportionate number of our sick.'[23]

But his proposal that health care be reformulated as part of a broader social agenda would almost certainly require considerable increases in both taxation and government regulation. No one seriously disputes the old adage about an ounce of prevention being worth a pound a cure. The politically important questions are how much more taxation and regulation Canadians are prepared to accept to shift the focus from cure to prevention, and what practical steps toward that goal governments should take.

Key Terms

curative care Care aimed at healing injury and curing disease that is provided by medical practitioners, hospitals, sophisticated medical technology, and drug therapies.

extra-billing Charges for services that some physicians billed directly to the patient, on top of the amount they would receive under provincial health insurance plans.

input-oriented performance indicators Measures used to assess the number of practitioners with specific qualifications in a given area, the rate and appropriateness of prescribed diagnostic tests, and similar quantitative factors from which probable health outcomes may be inferred.

medicare A nationwide, comprehensive public health-care system.

outcome-oriented performance indicators Quantitative measurements of the health system that focus on results, such as life expectancy, waiting times for surgery and treatments, and post-treatment effects.

provincial medical associations Professional associations that determine the licensing standards that doctors must meet to practise in a particular province.

Discussion Questions

1. If access to health care is a fundamental right in Canada, is that right violated when health care is rationed or wait times are so long as to jeopardize patients' health? How might Canadians protect their right to health care and ensure that it is timely and accessible?

2. Does it really matter how much money the federal government contributes to the health-care system when determining what the national standards of health care should be?

3. How can public policy be redirected to reduce health-care costs while improving longevity and quality of life? Typical public policy tools include sanctions and regulations. How might incentives be used to encourage Canadians to change their lifestyles and encourage healthier living?

Websites

The following are the provincial websites that provide online information on wait times for certain procedures.

Alberta Wait List Registry
http://waittimes.alberta.ca

British Columbia Surgical Wait Times
www.health.gov.bc.ca/swt/

Saskatchewan Surgical Initiative
www.sasksurgery.ca/wli-wait-list-info.htm

Manitoba Health Services Wait Time Information
www.gov.mb.ca/health/waitlist/index.html

Ontario Wait Times
www.health.gov.on.ca/en/public/programs/waittimes

Quebec Surgery and Treatment Waiting Lists
http://wpp01.msss.gouv.qc.ca/appl/g74web

New Brunswick Surgical Wait Time
http://www1.gnb.ca/0217/surgicalwaittimes/index-e.aspx

Nova Scotia Wait Times
www.gov.ns.ca/health/waittimes

Newfoundland
The Newfoundland and Labrador Department of Health and Community Services does not have an online database for wait times. Instead, it publishes periodic reports in Newfoundland.

Prince Edward Island Wait Times
www.healthpei.ca/waittimes

Other online health resources include the following:

Health Canada, Reports and Publications
www.hc-sc.gc.ca/ahc-asc/pubs/index-eng.php
The Reports and Publications section of Health Canada's website contains a wealth of material on topics related to public health policy, such as access to information and privacy, the Food and Drugs Act, science and research, and First Nations health, to name a few.

Canadian Association for Health Services and Policy Research (CAHSPR)
http://cahspr.ca

A multidisciplinary organization, CAHSPR is committed to improving health and health care in Canada by improving the quality, relevance, and application of research on health services and health policy.

Canadian Healthcare Association (CHA)
www.cha.ca

CHA develops and advocates for health policies that meet the needs of Canadians. Its communications team shapes policy positions on national issues and presents these positions to government, the media, and the public.

CHAPTER 9

Family Policy

Introduction

Depending on one's point of view, developments over the past few decades have represented either a renaissance of the family or its decline into the Dark Ages. Those who subscribe to the renaissance view see little to lament in the demise of the so-called traditional family characterized by a male breadwinner, a financially dependent wife, and children whose legal rights were limited and whose social status was such that they were generally considered little more than the property of their parents. In fact, these people celebrate the new diversity in family forms—same-sex couples, single-parent families, cohabiting partners with or without children—as more in tune with the values of pluralism, tolerance, and individual choice than the *Leave It to Beaver/Father Knows Best* family of the 1950s. The idealized portraits of the nuclear family that dominated television's early decades have been replaced by the caricatures of *The Simpsons* and *Family Guy*, and alternative configurations involving same-sex or single parents. In a society where close to half of all new marriages will end in divorce, single parenthood has become common, and most women with young children work outside the home, traditional notions of family and public policies based on them are no longer appropriate to the times. The clock cannot be turned back, say those who celebrate the changes in family structure, nor should we wish it could be.

Not everyone shares this view, however. Indeed, the same period has seen a backlash against the perceived rottenness of modern society and a resurgence of what are often labelled 'traditional values'. The backlash has taken a variety of forms. At the top end intellectually, it includes the cerebral and carefully argued positions of people such as the sociologist (and US Senator) Daniel Patrick Moynihan, who argued that modern society was 'defining deviancy down' in an effort to accommodate behaviour that would not have been tolerated in the past, and Barbara Dafoe Whitehead, author of a highly controversial analysis of the social, psychological, and economic costs associated with single parenthood. Lower down the scale it finds expression in the social conservatism of people like Pat Buchanan and talk-radio host Dr. Laura Schlessinger in the United States, where the controversy over family and family values has been intense for years.

In Canada, conservative social commentators like David Frum and Ted Byfield provide the intellectual weapons for those who lament the decline of the traditional family, while the Conservative Party of Canada and some of its provincial counterparts—in Ontario and Alberta especially—along with groups like Right to Life and REAL Women have given a political voice to proponents of 'traditional' family values.

Issues involving the family force us to confront some of our most deeply cherished and least questioned beliefs. For most people, the emotional response triggered by mention of the family is much more intense than that associated with any of the other communal groupings to which they belong. People whose eyes might glaze over at the mention of tax policy will often become attentive when the same policy matter is discussed as family policy.

Part of the reason for this is quite simply that we are more likely to pay attention to things when their connection to our own lives is made obvious. But there is more at work here. We are all products of a family—'intact', 'broken', 'traditional', 'nuclear', 'same-sex', 'nurturing units', 'dysfunctional', or however else we choose to characterize it—and we are more likely to have ideas about what constitutes a good family than, say, a good foreign policy. Moreover, for most people family policy—in common with issues such as abortion, capital punishment, and assisted suicide—has a moral component. The emotionally charged character of hot-button issues like these reflects the recognition that they involve fundamental questions about the meaning of human existence and how we should live our lives. In confronting our beliefs about the family, we are, unavoidably, confronting the most fundamental questions about ourselves and the society in which we live.

What Is Family Policy?

Family policy is seldom referred to by this name. Nevertheless, as *The Economist* puts it, 'Governments act in ways that, intentionally or otherwise, affect the family: in this sense every country has a "family policy".'[1] Margrit Eichler makes the same point:

> Family policies are not a clear set of policies since they include all those that affect families. This includes social welfare legislation, policies concerning social services (such as day care), income tax regulations, provisions in civil and criminal codes that determine who is responsible for certain types of dependants, family law, regulations concerning most social benefits, custody decisions, and many other social tools. These and other policies together constitute what we tend to call 'family policy', although not all of them are always considered.[2]

In some societies family policy takes obvious forms, such as the one-child-per-family limit in China. More commonly, however, family policy involves a more subtle combination of measures based on some conception of what constitutes a family and is intended to accomplish certain goals relating to families. These goals may be cultural, social, or economic. For example, laws that do not recognize same-sex couples as families for purposes of social benefits, inheritance rights, adoption rights, and so on embody certain cultural values about the legitimacy of heterosexual relations and the cultural illegitimacy and moral inferiority, in matters relating to the family, of same-sex relationships. A divorce law that makes divorce extremely difficult, such as existed in Canada before 1968, is likely to be based on traditional religious values that hold marriage to be sacred. A law that prescribes the same treatment for married couples and people in common-law relationships is likely to be based on a different set of values. Certainly it sends a different cultural message, as does a family studies curriculum that treats all family configurations as morally equivalent.

The cultural goals that public authorities, whether secular or religious, associate with families overlap with the social expectations held for the family. These expectations often have a taken-for-granted character that depends on cultural norms rather than laws and regulations. For example, it is generally expected that parents or guardians will be primarily responsible for ensuring that their children are adequately fed, clothed, and sheltered. In other words, the costs and responsibilities of child-rearing are considered private matters, to be borne mainly by parents. But the benefits that flow from good child-rearing will be experienced not only by the individuals involved but by the society as a whole. Likewise, the costs of a childhood of deprivation are not entirely private. Society will bear some of the burden of whatever dependencies and behavioural dysfunctions can be traced to an individual's family circumstances.

Families are expected to perform many of the tasks that shape the character, habits, and abilities of those who, in their turn, will become adult members of society. The possibility that they might fail in this awesome responsibility, and that society may be the poorer for their failure, has long been recognized. Plato was convinced that the family was an essentially selfish institution whose narrow interests were often at odds with the collective interests of society. The solution, he argued, was for the state to take over the traditional functions of the family, including that of determining who should be allowed to procreate and overseeing the upbringing of children. In this way society would be guaranteed a virtuous citizenry whose first thoughts would be for the good and glory of their country.

While most of us would reject Plato's proposals for the family, there is a logic in his reasoning that many, if not most of us, would find persuasive. For example, most Canadians believe that health care is a public matter that should be paid for and provided chiefly by the state. Under such a system, should parents-to-be and families be allowed to behave in ways that produce or nurture children who suffer from preventable diseases or conditions that impose costs on all of us? This question arose in a highly dramatic fashion in 1996 when a Winnipeg mother of two, who had a serious record of substance abuse and was on social assistance, became pregnant and refused to attend a substance abuse program that the local Children's Aid Society insisted on. In the United States judges have required certain women—substance abusers or women with records of child abuse—to have contraceptive devices implanted in their arms to prevent further pregnancy. Less dramatically, the idea that would-be parents should be required to take some sort of course on parenting is often proposed, and many people consider it reasonable. Plato would have agreed, although he would likely have thought it a rather pathetic half-measure.

Family policy may also be designed to achieve economic goals. For example, the Swedish tax system provides neither tax benefits for married couples nor deductions for dependent children. This policy goes back to the 1970s when Sweden was experiencing an acute shortage of labour. The government reformed the tax system to encourage more married women to enter the labour force (in addition, state-subsidized daycare, generous maternity leave, and flexible work hours all reduced the cost of having children and remaining in the labour force). The 1945 introduction of family allowances in Canada could not have been sold politically had it not been for the Department of Finance's belief that these payments would be part of a Keynesian fiscal strategy aimed at propping up household purchasing power. Those who advocate a national program of subsidized daycare routinely use economic arguments (among others). Margrit Eichler is typical: 'It would . . . make good economic sense to provide child care for all children who need it. This would generate jobs for the child-care workers and enable mothers to work for pay.'[3]

Despite the fundamental importance of the family and the number of policies that seek to influence its character or behaviour, or that compensate for what may be perceived as its shortcomings, governments in Canada have not created the sort of institutions that one might expect to be associated with weighty policy matters. Most Western European countries have had centralized ministries of the family since shortly after World War II, but Canada relies on an uncoordinated hodgepodge of policies implemented at various levels of government by an assortment of agencies, some governmental and others, like Children's Aid Societies, that are funded by the government but operate independently. We do not mean to imply that such an approach is necessarily a bad thing. The absence of an institutional 'home' for family policy does, however, help to conceal the fact that such a thing as family policy actually exists. Not only does it exist—though often treated as some minor backwater within the field of social policy—but family policy has become in recent years an increasingly important and controversial subject.

Canada's Families: Yesterday and Today

When the law that created the family allowance—the 'baby bonus', as it was called for years—was passed in 1945, the typical Canadian family consisted of a married couple with two children; about one-quarter of families had three or more children. By 1993, when these payments were abolished (they were replaced by a tax credit geared to income), it had become much more problematic to speak of the 'typical' Canadian family. Married couples still predominated. However, many of them were the product of remarriage, the divorce rate having skyrocketed after the 1968 reforms to the Divorce Act. Over a tenth of all couples were living in common-law relationships, a category that Canadian law had not recognized in 1945. Single-parent families, usually headed by women, were comparatively few and were typically the result of abandonment or the premature death of a husband. By 2006 there were 1.4 million single-parent families, accounting for 15.8 per cent of all families.[4] Families today tend to be smaller than in the past, and whereas the vast majority of women with young children did not work outside the home in 1945, a clear majority do today.

The Canadian family has undergone enormous changes over the last two generations. The implications of these changes for Canadian society are the subject of heated debate. Some blame the demise of the traditional family for what they perceive as the moral decay of contemporary society. Others applaud the new family configurations as potentially liberating for women. Virtually everyone agrees that the increasing numbers of single-parent families help to explain poverty levels (a hotly disputed concept, as we noted in Chapter 7). But this agreement does not provide the basis for a consensus on what governments should be doing in relationship to the family.

In his best-selling book *Boom, Bust, and Echo*, demographer David Foot attributes much of the controversy surrounding Canadian families to the changes that have taken place and continue to unfold in their demographic characteristics. Let's examine some of these changes.

1. Number of Families

The vast majority of Canadians continue to live in families. Following the Statistics Canada definition of a family used for census purposes—a currently married or common-law couple with or without never-married children, or a single parent with never-married children, living in the same household—we find that roughly 84 per cent of all Canadians live in families. Although an even greater share of the population lived in families a generation ago—about 87 per cent in 1971—the family remains by far the most typical household in Canadian society. Far more significant than the marginal decline in the percentage of Canadians living in families are the changes that have occurred in the size and marital characteristics of these families.

2. The Shrinking Family

The large family has become a social anomaly. As recently as 1971 about 14 per cent of all families comprised six or more persons; today only about 2 per cent fall into this category. More than half of all husband–wife families have either one or two children, compared with about 40 per cent of such couples in the 1960s. Childless couples have also become more common. Over a third of all families do not have children living at home—an increase of several percentage points from the level of the 1960s. The reasons include deliberate choice, the aging of Canada's population (a higher proportion of older couples means that a higher proportion of their children will likely have left home), and the fact that both marriage and childbirth typically take place later in life today than they did in the past (the older the woman, the more likely she is to have difficulty conceiving).

3. Traditional and Non-Traditional Families

The traditional family consisted of a married man and woman with children. The man was the family's breadwinner and the woman stayed home with the children. This family configuration has not disappeared—indeed, some demographers suggest that it may be making a comeback—but it is much less prominent than it was a couple of generations ago. Childless families, one-parent families, common-law couples with children, and stepfamilies are all more common today than they were in the past.

It is virtually impossible to find out how many children lived in non-traditional families before the 1970s. Census-takers and demographers seldom concerned themselves with this group until changes in social mores and the law cleared the way for a rapid increase in the incidence of divorce, remarriage, and common-law relationships. By contrast, the 2006 census found that roughly two-thirds (65.7 per cent) of Canadian children lived in two-parent families, down nine percentage points from 1996. Fourteen per cent lived in common-law families. Eighteen per cent lived in single-parent families, the vast majority of which were headed by women. It is estimated that close to half a million of Canada's 7.8 million families are stepfamilies—that is, couples with at least one stepchild. And while common-law couples are less likely than their married counterparts to have children, slightly more than 45 per cent of all common-law couples have children living with them; this figure represents more than 530,900 families.

4. Fractured Families

Back in 1951, the ratio of marriages to divorces was 24 to 1. Today the ratio is closer to 3 to 1. The proportion of the population that has been through a divorce has increased by more than 400 per cent since the early 1970s. This means, of course, that an increasing number of children spend at least part of their youth in single-parent families or stepfamilies. The economic consequences of this phenomenon are pretty clear: Children raised in intact families are much less likely to experience poverty than those in fragmented or **fractured families**. The social and psychological consequences of being raised in a single-parent family or a stepfamily, on the other hand, are the subject of enormous disagreement.

There has also been a sharp increase in the number of common-law households, which today account for about 15 per cent of all families. The incidence of common-law relationships varies widely by region. Common-law families are almost three times as common in Quebec (28 per cent of all families, as of 2006) than in PEI or Ontario (10 per cent). Common-law couples are less likely than married ones to have children living in the household but that gap has been narrowing in the last decade.

5. Working Mothers and Children

Another striking change in Canadian families is the enormous increase in the proportion of mothers who work outside the home. Before World War II, fewer than 1 in 10 married women worked outside the home. Today 6 in 10 are part of the labour force. Only about one-quarter of couples with children today conform to the traditional model of male breadwinner and stay-at-home mother. In most couples with children, both parents are employed; this remains true even when the family includes one or more children younger than seven years. Although the OECD notes that 'the presence of children in the household . . . has a significant impact on maternal employment patterns',[5] Statistics Canada reports that among mothers with 'children under the age of 16, the proportion that were employed more than doubled from 1979 to 1999' to an all-time high of 78 per cent in 2006. Figure 9.1 shows labour-force participation rates both for all women and for mothers (broken down by age of children).

The increase in the numbers of working mothers has generated an unprecedented need for alternatives to the traditional mother-at-home child care. In 2002–3, the National Longitudinal Survey of Children and Youth (NLSCY) found that 54 per cent of children under five years were cared for either by other family members or by sitters—an increase of 12 percentage points from 42 per cent eight years earlier. During that time care became more institutionalized, with an increase in use of day-care centres from 20 per cent in 1994–5 to 28 per cent in 2002–3.[6]

The number of licensed daycare spaces in Canada nearly doubled between 1986 to 1996, partly because of higher employment rates among mothers during this time and partly because of a 6.8 per cent increase in the numbers of children aged four and under.[7] Child-care arrangements depend on the age of the child. In 2002–3, few children under one year of age were in child care. Among children aged two to four, however, more than 30 per cent were in a daycare centre, compared to 20 per cent for the other age groups.[8] Despite calls from women's groups and others for a nationally subsidized daycare system, the priority that Ottawa and provincial governments attached to deficit reduction in the 1990s and early 2000s prevented the adoption of such a program. Although the

FIGURE 9.1 Labour-Force Participation, All Women and Mothers (by age of children), 1976–2006

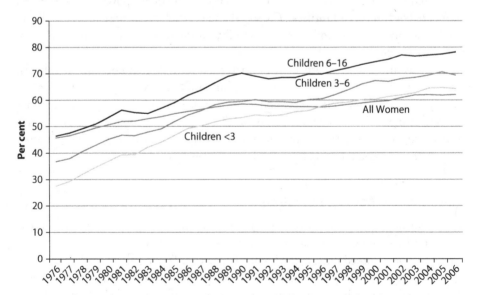

Source: Statistics Canada, Table 282-0002, 'Labour Force Survey Estimates (LFS), by Sex and Detailed Age Group, Annual (personal unless otherwise noted)'; CANSIM database, E-STAT (distributor). http://estat.statcan.gc.ca/cgi-win/cnsmcgi.exe?Lang=E&EST-Fi=EStat/English/CII_ 1-eng.htm, accessed November 23, 2010.

Liberal government in 2005 finally fulfilled its 1993 election campaign promise of a national daycare program, the 2006 Conservative government promised only to fund that program for one additional year and then replace it with a child tax credit and subsidy to local groups to create child-care spaces.

6. Family Incomes: Increasing Polarization?

Family incomes are considerably larger today than they were a generation ago. Measured in 2008 dollars, the average family income climbed from $36,800 in 1976 to $51,000 in 2008; but most of that growth took place in the 1970s. Family incomes had been more or less stagnant since the early 1980s and, by some measures, fell in the mid-1990s.

In recent years it has become popular to claim that a growing percentage of Canadian families fall below Statistics Canada's low-income cut-off lines and that more and more children are raised in poverty. The National Council of Welfare estimated in 1996 that one in five children under the age of 18 years lived below the LICO.[9] Campaign 2000, an advocacy group that has as its focus the elimination of child poverty, states that in 2010 one in ten Canadian children was living below the low-income cut-off. According to Statistics Canada, the persons under the age of 18 living below the low-income cut-offs in 2008 was 610,000—about 9.1 per cent of Canadians in that age group, or one in nine. As Figure 9.2 shows, child poverty levels rise and fall with the economy. In good times, such as the latter 1990s and early 2000s, we can see poverty rates decline compared to the peak of the recession in 1996. It is highly likely that the

FIGURE 9.2 Persons 18 Years and Under in Low Income After Tax (by number and percentage), 1976–2008

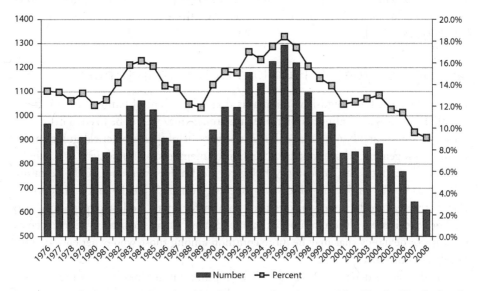

Source: Based on Statistics Canada tables, 'Persons in Low Income After Tax, by Number' and 'Persons in Low Income After Tax, by Prevalence in Percent', CANSIM database.

FIGURE 9.3 Low Income (after tax) by Family Type, in Thousands, 1975–2008

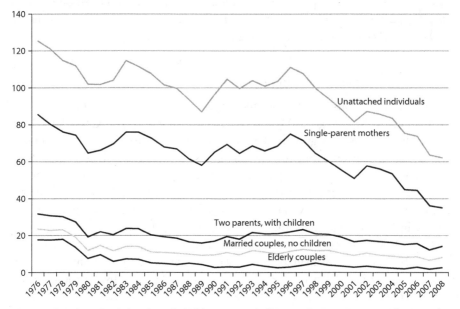

Source: Based on Statistics Canada Table 202-0804, 'Persons in Low Income After Tax, by Economic Family Type'.

positive trend of reducing child poverty in 2008 will be diminished as a consequence of the global recession in 2009. The likelihood that a person will be poor is five times greater in a female-led lone-parent family than in a two-parent family. Figure 9.3 shows the proportions of families falling below the LICOs from 1975–2008 for five different family types.

Are Some Types of Families Better than Others?

Pop psychologist John Bradshaw maintains that 97 per cent of families are 'dysfunctional'. In other words, almost all families are broken and need to be fixed! This makes for an attention-grabbing message, but is not very helpful as a practical guide to the family arrangements that work best for family members or for society as a whole. Emotional serenity and robust psychological health for everyone would certainly be nice, as would families in which everyone loves unconditionally and is supportive. But in the real world policy-makers need to aim for more modest targets (love still cannot be legislated, although support payments can), such as reducing the social costs of forms of deviancy that may be more common among those who experience certain family circumstances.

Is it possible to determine what family configurations are 'best'? Or is the attempt a short path to intolerant and reactionary judgments that end up condemning square pegs simply because they don't fit into holes that someone has decided should be round?

The fact is that an enormous amount of study has been devoted to this question, starting in the 1960s with Daniel Patrick Moynihan's controversial report on the pathology of inner-city black families in the United States. And while some experts and advocates argue that family configuration either does not matter or would not matter if the right social and economic policies were in place, the preponderance of the evidence suggests that they are wrong.

The work that has been done on family structure and its consequences is vast and nuanced. Nevertheless, it is possible (with a bit of crimping) to squeeze this literature into two main camps. One argues that there is nothing inherently better in one particular family configuration than another, and that most or all of the negative consequences attributed to certain family types, such as single-mother families, are spurious; that is, they are caused by factors such as low incomes rather than the family configuration per se. The other camp argues that the heterosexual two-parent family is superior to alternative family structures in virtually all respects: economically, socially, and culturally. Today those who subscribe to this second view base their argument on social scientific evidence rather than the biblical injunctions and moral precepts of earlier generations. So do experts in the first camp. Neither view, however, is free of moral criteria. These criteria are not always acknowledged, in part because in our age—the age of the scientific expert—moral arguments are viewed with suspicion in debates on public policy. Yet moral concerns are always just below the surface of debates that purport to be purely scientific, whether one is talking about the effects of deficit reduction, free trade, environmental regulation, or almost any other policy matter. In examining the two broad camps in the literature on family structure and public policy, therefore, I will consider both the scientific and the moral arguments on both sides.

1. 'It Takes a Village': The Collectivist Model for Family Policy

Many families are able to take care of themselves. They can feed and clothe their children, nurture their self-esteem, teach them values and skills that will enable them to deal competently with life's challenges—in short, these families are able to give their children a future, and in doing so they benefit us all. But many other families are unable or unwilling to provide their children with the material circumstances and nurturing they need to become autonomous and socially well-adjusted adults capable of telling right from wrong, holding a job, and forming healthy relationships with others. In other words, these families either cannot or will not give their children a future, and we all experience the negative consequences of their failure.

This is where the 'village' comes in. In her best-selling book *It Takes a Village, and Other Lessons Children Teach Us*,[10] Hillary Rodham Clinton uses the traditional village society as a model and metaphor for the roles that community organizations, and chiefly the state, must play to help families in need and provide disadvantaged children with a future. The 'village' that Clinton describes in her book 'can no longer be defined as a place on a map, or a list of people or organizations, but its essence remains the same: it is the network of values and relationships that support and affect our lives'.[11] It is not enough, she argues, indeed it is downright harmful, to base family policy on the premise that parents (or guardians) alone are responsible for raising their children; the entire village has a responsibility to *its* children, a responsibility that will in most cases be borne chiefly by parents but that is nonetheless a collective responsibility.

This means greater public investment in health care, education, and income assistance for needy families, as well as measures to improve the safety of neighbourhoods and to provide jobs for all who want them. This approach is familiar enough. It is echoed by Canadian writer and social activist June Callwood, who says the following about child poverty:

> The obvious key to ending child poverty is a collaborative model which brings a community together on behalf of all its children and puts money where its mouth is. It must involve a holistic approach which includes adequate income, quality licensed child care, job training and education upgrades for youth and adults, affordable and decent housing, access to community supports, and at the end of the day, a real job.[12]

Callwood, like Clinton, believes that much of what is wrong with the contemporary family can be fixed if the 'village' assumes its proper responsibility for the well-being of children and other vulnerable members of society. Part of the problem, and the responsibility, is financial, of course. But in what ways is the family itself broken? Here Clinton offers an analysis that, frankly, is not very different from that of people like David Popenoe, James Q. Wilson, and Barbara Dafoe Whitehead, who usually are characterized as 'conservatives' in the debate on family policy. She points to the generally harmful consequences for children of marital breakdown, the inability of many parents to spend adequate time with their children, the negative influence of the mass media, and the problems often associated with teenage pregnancy. Without falling into a syrupy nostalgia for 'the good old days', which Clinton dismisses as largely a fabrication of marketing departments and folks with a conservative ideological agenda, she clearly believes that families and children confront more difficult challenges today than they did a generation or two ago. The way to deal with these challenges, she argues, is not to emphasize a return to a supposedly lost world of 'family values'. Rather, the solution lies in using the 'village'—government agencies, experts, community groups, churches, and so on—to provide the support that is often missing in today's world. Clinton's approach may be best understood from some of her more concrete suggestions for policy reform. Following are three examples:

- *Infant health.* Clinton recognizes that some mothers have lifestyles during pregnancy and/or after childbirth that place their children at particular risk of developing health problems. The 'village' needs to step in. Support and advice from family and friends may not be available or of adequate quality, and in any case, as

Clinton puts it, they 'are no substitute for formal systems that have as their primary mission good health for all women and babies'.[13] She cites approvingly those European countries where a mother's eligibility for state-paid monetary benefits depends on her agreeing to allow home visits by health specialists or to participate in other forms of parent education.

- *Parenting skills and the child's cognitive development.* Clinton emphasizes the importance of early talking, reading, and parent–child interaction for the development of the child's verbal and analytical skills. Summarizing the conclusions of research by Betty Hart and Todd Risley, she observes that 'The biggest difference among the various households . . . was in the sheer amount of talking that occurred. The more money and education parents had, the more they talked to their children, and the more effectively from the point of view of vocabulary development.'[14] While insisting that the amount and quality of parent–child interaction is the determining factor, Clinton acknowledges that working-class and lower-income families are much less likely than more privileged families to offer children the benefits of early language exposure.

  So what, if anything, is to be done? Parent–child talking cannot be legislated, much less what Clinton would consider quality talking. Nevertheless, she says, 'The village can encourage this all important activity.'[15] She points to a government-funded program administered by the American Library Association that attempts to help parents improve their reading skills and emphasizes the role played in children's cognitive development by reading to them at an early age.

- *Marriage breakdown.* Clinton recognizes that the explosion in the divorce rate since the 1960s has had negative social consequences. 'More than anyone else,' she writes, 'children bear the brunt of such massive social transitions . . . studies demonstrate convincingly that while many adults claim to have benefited from divorce and single parenthood, most children have not.'[16]

  What can the 'village' do? Clinton suggests that when children are involved there perhaps should be a mandatory 'cooling off' period before a legal divorce is allowed, during which parents could receive instruction and counselling. She seems to lean toward some form of obligatory counselling when she cites approvingly court rulings that require divorcing parents to attend classes on the potential consequences of divorce for children.

The **collectivist approach** to family policy that Clinton advocates is popular among social workers, sociologists, child psychologists, counsellors of various sorts, and other experts on the family. It is, quite obviously, an approach that requires the professional skills of these people, who in Clinton's view are integral parts of the 'village'. Despite her insistence on the 'personal' character of the village, the support network she describes erases the distinction between relationships that are truly personal and intimate and relationships with people who are essentially strangers— however well-meaning and benign they might be. In the words of Jean Bethke Elshtain:

> Clinton's village [is] a juggernaut of parents, or whatever is left of parents, neighbours, or whatever is left of neighbours, judges, lawyers, the police, all educators everywhere, politicians (the 'non-regressive' ones), the media (good and very bad), doctors, psychiatrists, child welfare bureaus, 'civil society', the food industry, the clothing industry. This is a boundary-less village.[17]

The key to being part of the village is that a person or organization attempts to 'help' families and children. By calling this sprawling network a village, Clinton attempts to give her approach to family policy a human face and thus disarm those who detect in it a justification for meddlesome bureaucracy and the extension of public authority.

Richard Weissbourd echoes Clinton's philosophy in his book *The Vulnerable Child*: 'Important as family and friendships are to children, across the political spectrum there is a growing consensus that both children and parents depend on wider nets of social ties, on communities.'[18] The disintegration of communities under the pressures of modern life has placed children at greater risk, Weissbourd argues. Like Clinton, he places his hope in the new 'village', whose role is to '[create] environments that ease the task of parenting and that provide stimulation and support to children at every stage of development'.[19]

It's hard to disagree with such sentiments. But the question remains: What should be done? At this point one's analysis of the problem—or, more accurately, cluster of problems—facing the family is crucial in determining the sorts of policies most likely to help families and the sorts of help that are actually needed. Clinton parts company from many of her political soulmates when she argues that 'every society requires a critical mass of families that fit the traditional ideal, both to meet the needs of most children and to serve as a model for other adults who are raising children in difficult settings.'[20] And her acknowledgement of the economic and emotional damage that children often suffer as a result of divorce likewise distances her from those who deny that family configuration, per se, is the key reason for the differences in the school performance, social behaviour, and adult lives of children from single-parent families and stepfamilies compared with those from intact ones.

What Clinton does not do, however—and this is a key difference between the collectivist and personal-responsibility approaches to family policy—is point to the traditional intact family as the model. The problem for those who advocate a collectivist approach, as Clinton, Weissbourd, and most family policy specialists do, is that they don't want to stigmatize non-traditional families—which often do work!— by privileging traditional families and/or reducing the ease of divorce when children are involved.

In a Canadian textbook on family policy,[21] sociologist Margrit Eichler goes a step beyond Clinton's 'village'-based model of family policy to propose a more radically collectivist approach. She contrasts what she calls the *individual responsibility model* of the family, on which current policy is based, with the *social responsibility model* that she advocates. Some of the key differences between these models are summarized in Table 9.1.

TABLE 9.1 The Individual Responsibility and Social Responsibility Models of the Family

	Individual Responsibility	Social Responsibility
1. Gender assumptions	Equal status and rights of men and women.	Committed to eliminating as far as possible the real-world inequalities between men and women.
2. Family definition	Families may by created by legal marriage or cohabitation. The law does not distinguish between these types of families, nor between the children produced within or outside of marriage.	Same as under the individual responsibility model.
3. Economic obligations	Married or common-law partners are equally responsible for each other's economic well-being and for that of their dependent children.	All dependency relations are recognized in law, whether or not they are between family members. Adult members of a functioning interdependent unit are responsible for each other's economic well-being.
4. Parental rights and responsibility to provide care	Fathers and mothers are equally responsible.	Mothers and fathers are both responsible. Parents retain responsibilities, though not necessarily rights, toward dependent children with whom they do not live.
5. Appropriate role of public authority.	The state's role vis-à-vis the family and children should be supplementary and temporary. It is assumed that parents will be responsible for the economic welfare and care of family members, and that public authorities enter the picture only when these forms of support are not provided by a family member.	The care and support of dependent children is a responsibility that the public authority shares with parents. The cost of caring for dependent adults is a public responsibility.
6. Sexuality of family units	Same-sex couples are recognized as family units for certain purposes.	No distinction is made between same-sex and opposite-sex couples.

Source: Adapted from Margrit Eichler, *Family Shifts: Family, Policies, and Gender Equality* (Toronto, ON: Oxford University Press, 1997), 14–17.

Eichler argues that the assumptions underlying family policy in Canada have evolved from a patriarchal ideology before the 1970s to an individualist ideology in recent decades. The main principles of the **patriarchal model**, and examples of policies based on these principles, are shown in Table 9.2.

TABLE 9.2 The Patriarchal Family: Principles and Policies

Principles	Policies
1. Legal marriage was the basis for families.	Common-law unions were not accorded the same rights as married couples. Children born out of wedlock did not have the same rights as the offspring of married couples.
2. The husband/father was considered the head of the family and the primary breadwinner.	The law failed to protect women who were discriminated against by employers. The law treated the wife and children as economic dependants of the husband/father.
3. The economic contribution of a husband to a family was assumed to be superior to that of his wife.	Property acquired by a husband during the course of a marriage, and held in his name only, was considered to be his alone. In the event of a divorce his wife had no legal claim on this property.
4. The wife/mother was expected to be the primary caregiver for the children and other members of the household.	No state-subsidized daycare existed, nor were there tax deductions for child-care expenses.
5. The economic welfare of family members was not a public responsibility.	Aside from family allowance payments, which were always rather small, there were no public maternity benefits until the 1970s when the Unemployment Insurance Commission began to pay them to women who took time away from their jobs for childbirth.
6. Families were considered to be heterosexual, by definition.	Until the 1970s, and even the 1980s, it was common to treat homosexuality as a psychological illness. Same-sex couples were not recognized as legal families, nor were the members of such couples eligible for any of the social benefits to which members of opposite-sex couples were entitled.

Changing social values and pressure from the women's movement resulted in a steady erosion of the patriarchal model during the 1960s and 1970s. It was replaced by the **individual responsibility model** of the family, whose capstone would be the guarantee of gender equality in the Charter of Rights and Freedoms. This transition represents undeniable progress toward gender equality within families and has also eliminated the legally privileged status of married over common-law couples. However, Eichler notes that in the real world men and women are not similarly situated when it comes to the raising of children; nor, generally, are the economic opportunities available to women equal to those that men experience. Therefore, she argues that the individual responsibility model of the family does not abolish sexism in family policy. Indeed, the formal equality that the Charter and Canadian laws now guarantee may serve to hide the gender inequalities that policy allows to persist. For example, the average income of a female single parent is only about 60 per cent of that of a male single parent, and female-led single-parent families are several times more likely to depend on social assistance payments than their male-led counterparts. This situation is what critics of the individual responsibility model of the family would characterize as equal in law, unequal in life.

In place of the individual responsibility model of the family, Eichler advocates a **social responsibility model** that would extend enormously government's responsibility for the well-being of families. She identifies six main policy goals associated with this model:

- minimizing social stratification based on sex;
- collective support for all dependants;
- collective support for all those who provide care for dependants;
- social recognition for all those who provide care and support for dependants, regardless of whether they are related;
- facilitating self-support and autonomy for all those who, given adequate means, can take care of themselves; and
- social and legal recognition for same-sex families.[22]

Eichler provides several examples of policies that would be required to promote these goals:

- a nationally financed daycare program;
- longer and financially more generous parental leave provisions;
- a federally organized child support assurance system (essentially a guaranteed minimum income for custodial parents and their children) to insulate children from the loss of income that often accompanies the separation and divorce of parents;
- far greater child benefits through the tax system for low-income families; and
- refundable tax credits for care providers, most of whom are women (this would be a publicly paid form of income for domestic work in families in which there are dependent children or adults).

The philosophy behind Eichler's approach to the family and her recommendations for policy reform is straightforward: 'To the degree that it is socially useful, give it social support.'[23] This is a deceptively simple formula, however. What counts as 'socially useful'? Eichler uses three tests: gender equality, social fairness (between classes), and economic efficiency. Gender equality and social fairness are good in themselves, she argues, but there are often economic efficiency reasons for doing the right thing. For example, Eichler makes the following argument about the economic efficiency of a national daycare system:

> There is a substantial literature that suggests child-care monies are better expended by establishing and supporting public daycare centres than by transferring the monies directly to the parents. It would also make good economic sense to provide child care for all children who need it. This would generate jobs for the child-care workers and enable mothers to work for pay, while allowing children to profit both from the social setting of daycare and the home setting of individualized attention.[24]

The economic good sense of this proposal is not self-evident. As is usually the case with an argument for government spending that is based on the claim that such spending will generate income by producing jobs (in this case, for daycare workers) and enabling more women to enter the labour force, it ignores the fact that such measures would have to be paid for through taxation, which would mean diverting money from uses such as purchasing and investment. One might argue that the measures proposed by Eichler would be economically more productive than those other uses, but this is not obvious.

In answer to the question of what family configuration is best, Eichler would say that none is inherently superior to the others. She certainly does not agree that a legal marriage between a man and a woman constitutes the best circumstances in which to raise children. After reviewing the scientific literature Eichler concludes there is no empirical evidence that legal marriages provide better emotional and material support than common-law unions. She goes on to say that, 'In general, some families (of whatever type) function better than others. Some legal marriages involve emotional, physical, and sexual abuse, as do some common-law unions and some same-sex unions.'[25] At another point she observes that 'there is now solid research evidence that children's well-being is *not* related to the amount of continued contact between fathers and children.'[26]

These claims fly in the face of a massive amount of social scientific research that Eichler alludes to only in passing, completely ignoring many of the most often cited studies on family structures and their consequences for children. These studies form the basis for what we will call the personal responsibility model of the family. Let's examine this model.

2. 'It Takes a Family'[27] (Preferably an Intact One)

David Popenoe is one of the best-known critics of the decline of traditional families and a vigorous advocate of the **nuclear family**. He frames the question this way:

> What family structure, under the conditions of industrial, liberal-democratic nations, is best able to produce offspring who grow up to be both autonomous and socially responsible, while also meeting the adult needs for intimacy and personal attachments that become ever more compelling in an increasingly impersonal world?

His answer is the nuclear family. Before any reader explodes with indignation, it is important to note that Popenoe's definition of the nuclear family is not necessarily the male-breadwinner, stay-at-home-wife model. 'I refer instead', he writes, 'to the nuclear family in more general terms—consisting of a male and female living together, apart from other relatives, who share responsibility for their children and for each other.'[28]

This definition of the nuclear family will probably not cool the rage of readers who spent at least some part of their childhoods in families that did not conform to this model. As Barbara Dafoe Whitehead observes, 'it is nearly impossible to discuss changes in family structure without provoking angry protest.'[29] This is more than unfortunate, because the available social scientific evidence—and there is a lot of it—shows quite clearly that *family structure has an independent effect on the material, emotional, and even physical well-being of children*. By 'independent effect' we mean that these consequences are not simply the result of income or other differences between intact and other families (although these differences certainly widen the well-being gap between different family configurations).

The impact of family breakup and unwed motherhood on the material well-being of women and children is the least controversial component of the literature on the effects of family structure. Most single-parent mothers, and therefore their children, have low incomes. The vast majority of children living below Statistics Canada's low-income cut-off live in single-parent families. In 1995, more than 80 per cent of single-parent families led by women under the age of 25 fell below the LICO. Single mothers between the ages of 25 and 44 years did slightly better, but more than half (just under 60 per cent) still fell below the LICO. The incomes of single mothers as a group increased in the course of the 1990s, but most of the gains went to those over the age of 40; the prospects for those under 25 improved very little.[30]

Separation and divorce usually end with the mother (1) receiving custody of the children and (2) experiencing a significant drop in income. 'Divorce', says Barbara Dafoe Whitehead, 'almost always brings a decline in the standard of living for the mother and children.'[31] The problem of poverty is largely a problem of single parenthood, which in turn is caused by increases in the incidence of divorce and birth outside marriage (about one-quarter of all annual births in Canada). About one-third of all welfare recipients in Canada are single mothers. Evidence from the United States shows that single-mother families experience a form of welfare dependency. Not only do they stay on welfare longer than other recipients (not surprising, given the demands of raising children), but their dependency on welfare tends to be passed on to the next generation. Sociologist Sara McLanahan observes that 'Evidence on intergenerational poverty indicates that, indeed, offspring from [single-mother] families are far more likely to be poor and to form mother-only families than are offspring who live with two parents most of their pre-adult life.'[32] This is true of both whites and blacks.

The issue of child poverty is, in fact, largely a function of changing family structure. David Eggebeen and Daniel Lichter estimate that more than half of the increase in child poverty in the United States during the 1980s was attributable to changes in family structure (i.e., the increase in single-parent families).[33] Given what we know about the economic consequences of single parenthood in Canada—children in single-mother families are about five times more likely to fall below the low-income cut-off than those in intact families—it is probable that Eggebeen and Lichter's conclusion is valid for Canada as well. To the degree that poverty begets poverty, the income discrepancy between single- and two-parent families threatens to become a new class division, separating those whose material circumstances in childhood make it possible for them to lead a middle-class life (vacations, participation in sports or other cultural/recreational activities, post-secondary education, etc.) from those whose early circumstances make this life much more difficult to attain. Investment in education provides an important example of this difference. As Dafoe Whitehead observes, 'The parents in intact families are far more likely to contribute to children's college costs than are those in disrupted families.'[34] Research by Judith Wallerstein, director of the California Children of Divorce Study, supports this not very surprising conclusion.[35] Moreover, it is well known that a significant proportion of first-time home purchases involve help from relatives, usually parents. As in the case of post-secondary education, children from single-parent families (and, according to some research, even those from stepfamilies) are less likely to receive such help. In ways like these the class divide between those from intact and fragmented families is likely to be reinforced over time.

Those who prefer a collectivist approach to family policy respond to these findings by calling for increased public support for single parents and all those who are raising children on low incomes. But the consequences of family breakup and single parenthood are not simply economic. A survey of more than 60,000 children in the United States showed that at every income level except the highest (households with income of more than $50,000/year in 1988), children living with single mothers were considerably worse off than those living in two-parent families.[36] This finding applied to both boys and girls and across racial groups. James Q. Wilson summarizes the study's findings as follows: 'Children living with never-married mothers were more likely to have been expelled or suspended from school, to display emotional problems, and to engage in anti-social behavior.'[37]

This conclusion has been corroborated by numerous studies. Based on longitudinal studies that now span two decades, Sara McLanahan and Gary Sandefur arrive at some dismal findings. In *Uncertain Childhood, Uncertain Future*, they conclude that even after controlling for race, income, and parents' education, being raised in a single-mother family decreases a child's chances of finishing high school, increases a girl's chances of becoming a teenage mother, and increases a boy's chances of becoming a jobless adult.[38] All these risks increase substantially in the case of families headed by teenage mothers. Nicolas Zill and Charlotte Schoenborn report that children from single-parent families are two to three times as likely as those from intact families to have emotional and behavioural problems, and this difference persists after controlling for family income.[39] Studies by Zill and others show that family breakup has a strong impact on school achievement, even after controlling for the effects of family income, race, and religion.[40]

Sociologist Amitai Etzioni, one of the leading communitarian intellectuals in the English-speaking world, offers an explanation for the impact of family disruption on children's academic performance:

> The sequence of divorce followed by a succession of boy or girlfriends, a second marriage, and frequently another divorce and another turnover of partners often means a repeatedly disrupted educational coalition. Each change in participants involves a change in the educational agenda for the child. Each new partner cannot be expected to pick up the previous one's educational post and program. . . . As a result, changes in parenting partners mean, at best, a deep disruption in a child's education, though of course several disruptions cut deeper into the effectiveness of the educational coalition than just one.[41]

These are circumstances that cannot be addressed by increasing income support for single-parent families.

Since Daniel Patrick Moynihan's 1964 report on the crisis of fatherless, low-income black families in the United States, it has been widely recognized that the absence of fathers in single-parent families has negative consequences for children that go beyond the economic ones. In Moynihan's words, a community without fathers 'asks for and gets chaos'.[42] Yet Margrit Eichler claims that 'there is now solid evidence that children's well-being is *not* related to the amount of continued contact between fathers and children.'[43] Who is right?

The preponderance of the evidence comes down on the side of Moynihan and those who argue that fatherlessness tends to have negative consequences for both children and society. *The Economist* summarizes these consequences as follows:

> For boys, the absence of men can induce what sociologist Elijah Anderson calls 'hypermasculinity', characterized by casual, even predatory, sex and violence. Fatherless girls, like their brothers, tend to do less well in school and have greater difficulty in making the transition to adulthood; they are much more likely than girls who grew up with a father to be young and unmarried when they first get pregnant.[44]

It is well known that fatherless boys are much more likely to engage in anti-social behaviour than those who grow up with fathers. In the words of one study, 'The relationship is so strong that controlling for family configuration erases the relationship between race and crime and between low income and crime. This conclusion shows up time and again in the literature.'[45] Studies by Judith Wallerstein, Sara McLanahan, Urie Bronfenbrenner, and Nicolas Zill, among others, confirm that fatherlessness carries both personal and social costs.

Family breakup is often followed by remarriage or cohabitation with another partner. Consequently the numbers of stepfamilies—or what today are often called 'blended families'—have increased dramatically over the last couple of decades. Such families have been celebrated by the Hollywood dream factory at least since the *Brady Bunch* era of the 1970s. But research indicates that the reality of these increasingly common family structures is often less positive than saccharine films and TV shows would suggest. 'In general,' says Barbara Dafoe Whitehead, 'remarriage neither reproduces nor restores the intact family structure, even when it brings more income and a second adult into the household. Quite the contrary.'[46]

David Popenoe cites the findings of the National Child Development Study in Great Britain, which tracked the development of 17,000 children born in 1958. He notes that 'the chances of stepchildren suffering social deprivations before reaching 21 are even greater than those left living after divorce with a lone parent.'[47] Sara McLanahan's research on children in stepfamilies found that their parents hold lower educational aspirations for them and are less involved in their schoolwork than parents in traditional families.[48] It appears, however, that the effects on girls and boys are not the same. Research from the United States suggests that boys often respond positively when their mothers remarry, becoming less likely to drop out of school than boys in single-mother families. By contrast, girls who have close ties to their mothers often perceive the stepfather as a rival and an intruder and are *more* likely than girls in single-mother families to drop out of school.[49]

One of the most disturbing revelations to emerge from recent studies of stepfamilies is that children in such families face a much greater risk of physical abuse, including sexual abuse, than children in intact families. Canadian researchers Martin Daly and Margo Wilson estimate the risk to be 40 times greater for children in stepfamilies. Stepfathers are not the only culprits. Daly and Wilson report that much of the abuse is committed by neighbours, a stepfather's male friends, or some other non-relative. However, they also conclude that stepfathers are far more likely to abuse their stepchildren than their biological children.[50] The risk of sexual abuse is much greater for a girl living with a stepfather than for one who lives with her biological father. As Judith Wallerstein explains, 'The presence of a stepfather can raise the difficult issue of a thinner incest barrier.'[51]

Finally there is the issue of parental time for children. Stanford University economist Victor Fuchs observes that the main sources of social investment in children are their parents. Family breakup often means a significant reduction in the time that parents spend with their children. The involvement of fathers with their children typically declines dramatically. But even the custodial mother's investment of time often declines as she tries to balance child-raising with the need to work outside the home. The problem of time may be more acute in the case of single-parent families, but it also exists in intact families. One researcher estimates that the amount of time parents spend with their children has declined by about one-third since the 1960s.[52] The perceived need for both parents to work outside the home is a chief reason for this decline.

Whether the investment of time that children require is best provided by parents or can be provided as well in institutional settings has been the subject of a long-standing and acrimonious debate. Less controversial is the importance of time for a child's intellectual and emotional development. David Popenoe writes:

> The significance of time in childrearing is highlighted by empirical findings on the promotion of 'prosocial behavior' in children. The development of prosocial behavior—which includes helping, sharing, and concern for others—has been shown to stem from early attachment experiences, from the modeling by children of their parents' prosocial behavior, and from good nurturing, especially the way children are disciplined. At heart, prosocial behavior is based on strong feelings of empathy for other people. The type of discipline that best promotes the development of empathy in children is that which involves reasoning with the child. . . . Discipline with reasoning and explanation is time intensive. . . . Today, when the time devoted to parent-child interaction is decreasing, especially in the father-absent family, it is likely that the teaching of empathy correspondingly suffers.[53]

One conclusion seems to flow inescapably from studies like the ones reviewed in the preceding pages—namely, that intact families tend to be better both for children and for society than single-parent or other configurations. Those who reject this conclusion often point to the undeniable fact that many intact families do a lousy job of raising children. Certainly intact families are not free of pathologies such as incest, physical and emotional abuse, child neglect, alcoholism, and so on. Confronted with the evidence that, as an adult, an individual from a broken family is more likely than one from an intact family to have difficulty maintaining a stable relationship with a partner, many will respond that growing up in a home where parents show no love for one another can be no less damaging for a child than divorce.

Nevertheless, the now voluminous scientific literature on the consequences of family structure for children's development shows that intact families work better, even when those families are not models of domestic bliss. Sara McLanahan identifies three advantages that intact families usually have over other family structures:

- *Household income.* Intact families are less likely than single-parent families to experience poverty. Inasmuch as two incomes are increasingly necessary to sustain a middle-class lifestyle, this particular advantage has grown in importance.
- *Authority structure.* Intact families are more likely than fragmented ones to provide children with a stable structure of authority.
- *Household composition.* Intact families are most likely to provide a stable household environment for children. In fragmented families, by contrast, the departure of one adult household member is often followed by the arrival of a new one. Changes of this kind can undermine children's sense of security and affect their relationships with their parents.[54]

In Canada, family policy has focused primarily on economic issues. Organizations such as the National Council of Welfare and the Vanier Institute of the Family locate the roots of family problems chiefly in low incomes and the inadequacy of the public resources targeted at those families most in need, particularly those led by single mothers. The economic dimension is certainly important, but it is not the whole story. Policies built on the premise that more public dollars will solve the problems afflicting disrupted families ignore the independent effects of family structure. Acknowledging those effects can be personally difficult for some and ideologically inconvenient for others. Serious policy reform must, however, take them into account.

The literature reviewed above forms the basis for what we call the **personal responsibility model** of the family, in contrast to Eichler's social responsibility model. By 'personal responsibility' we mean that this model emphasizes the primary obligation of parents for the welfare of their children and for one another, and that policy ought to be built on the assumption that parents should be the main source of social investment in children. We hesitate to call it the individual responsibility model of the family—a category that Eichler uses—because it does not rest on an individualistic philosophy. On the contrary, it sees in rampant individualism and the ethic of personal fulfillment one of the sources of the problems facing modern families. As Dafoe Whitehead argues, 'Increasingly, political principles of individual rights and choice shape our understanding of family commitment and solidarity. Family relationships are viewed not as permanent or binding but as voluntary and easily terminable.'[55] The family is a communal institution that stands as a bulwark against the sort of corrosive individualism that many, on the right and the left alike, argue is characteristic of our age.

Policy Options for the Family

Generally speaking, family policy in Canada may be characterized as an uncoordinated hodgepodge of policies, based on assumptions that are not always clearly recognized or even consistent, and delivered by an assortment of institutions including not only agencies of all three levels of government but also privately run organizations like provincial Children's Aid Societies, Big Brothers Big Sisters, family planning clinics, and so on. Some provinces have attempted to develop a more systematic approach to family issues, as New Brunswick has done through its Ministry of State for Family and Community Services. For the most part, however, family policy continues to be homeless. Responsibility for matters affecting families is divided between agencies responsible for health, social services, public housing, education, income support, and law enforcement. The courts also play a major role in family policy, particularly in matters relating to divorce, child custody, and the rights of both parents and children.[56]

In itself, the fact that responsibility for matters affecting families is shared by all levels of government and a plethora of agencies is not a problem (unless one believes that central planning and a one-stop-shopping approach to policy delivery are by definition superior to looser, less coordinated approaches to policy-making and implementation). The real problem is the failure of governments to develop a clear vision of the family and of the appropriate balance between family autonomy and social responsibility. In the absence of such a vision, all sorts of assumptions and definitions of the family jockey for public recognition. Should a homosexual couple be recognized in law as a family in matters concerning spousal benefits? Some private companies led the policy debate by treating same-sex couples on a par with heterosexual ones in regard to pension rights and so on. Since 2005 and the passage of Bill C-38, the Civil Marriage Act, same-sex couples have had the same rights as heterosexual couples.

Precisely because the question of what constitutes a family is so controversial, politicians have tended to avoid hard choices that would offend vocal interests. The fate of same-sex benefits legislation in Ontario under the NDP government during the early 1990s illustrates this. Although the NDP had promised to introduce such a law, its commitment wavered in the face of considerable public hostility and the intention of some NDP legislators to vote against it. When the government decided to hold a 'free vote' on the issue—that is, government members were not required to support the bill—the NDP as much as conceded defeat. Since then, however, the battle has shifted to the courts. In 1995, in *Egan v. Canada*, the Supreme Court of Canada rejected a homosexual male's argument that he should be entitled to the same spousal rights as a partner in a heterosexual couple.[57] In June 2002, however, the Quebec government unanimously passed Bill 84, the Civil Union Bill. And the following month the Ontario Superior Court ruled that denying same-sex partners marriage was an unjustifiable violation of the Charter of Rights and Freedoms. Once the courts had begun to find that prohibitions against same-sex marriages were unconstitutional, it became easier for governments to act in the legislature. On June 17, 2003, prime minister Jean Chrétien announced his intention to legalize same-sex unions. While many church leaders and other small-*c* conservative groups objected to the proposed legislation, arguing (among other things) that marriage was a provincial responsibility, the Supreme Court of Canada ruled in December 2004 that the federal government has the exclusive jurisdiction to decide who has the right to marriage in the country. With the Supreme Court's decision and the Bloc Québécois and NDP siding with the minority Liberal government, the same-sex law passed by a vote of 158 to 133 on June 29, 2005.

The same-sex issue is certainly a hot button for many people, and it is an important one in terms of rights and the values we wish to see reflected in our society. But it is far less important in terms of social costs than, for example, the consequences of family breakup, teenage motherhood, child poverty, and many other matters that concern the family. We will examine three policy proposals that address these more pressing issues: public daycare, reform of divorce rules, and guaranteed child support.

1. Daycare versus Home Care

'If you want to open the floodgates of guilt and dissension', writes Hillary Rodham Clinton, 'start talking about child care. It is an issue that brings out all of our conflicted feelings about what parenthood should be and about who should care for children when parents are working or otherwise unable to.'[58] Few people would disagree, or at least few parents who have had to confront the dilemma that Clinton describes. While a clear majority of parents with young children work outside the home—including about 60 per cent of women—public opinion surveys show that an even greater percentage of women would rather stay home with their children than put them in daycare. Moreover, most Canadians believe that the family has suffered as a result of both parents working. Danielle Crittenden refers to this angst as 'the Mother of all problems'.[59]

The issue of publicly subsidized daycare has been one of the chief nodal points in debates on family policy since the 1971 *Report of the Royal Commission on the Status of Women*. In 2002–3, only 28 per cent of preschoolers whose mothers worked outside the home were in a provincially licensed daycare facility.[60] Most parents rely on private child care, provided mainly by sitters or family members. Although the federal and Quebec tax codes permit a deduction from taxable income for child-care expenses, they do not permit a similar deduction for parents who take care of their own children. However, starting in July 2006, the minority Conservative government made good on a pledge to provide direct assistance to parents with children under the age of six. In that month the federal government sent parents a $100 cheque for each child under six. The money was ostensibly to be used to offset child-care costs, but since there were no strings attached, it also benefited parents with no child-care costs and could be used in any way the families saw fit. When this proposal was debated during the 2006 federal election campaign, the NDP and Liberals argued that the money in question was not adequate for the task and that the plan lacked accountability. When Liberal aide Scott Reid suggested on a television talk show that some people might 'blow [the money] on beer and popcorn', the Conservatives took the moral high ground, maintaining that parents know what is best for their children.

In addition, the Conservative government proposed a plan to create new child-care spaces. But this also was hotly contested, especially by those who had supported the previous Liberal government's proposal for a national daycare program. Under the Liberal plan, announced in 2005, the government would have spent $5 billion over five years to create new licensed child-care spaces, and during the 2006 election campaign the Liberals had promised an additional $6 billion starting in 2009. Once the Conservatives came to power, however, they committed to fund the Liberal plan only for the 2006 fiscal year and promised to have their own plan in place by 2007. Critics charged that the Conservative plan fell short of what the federal and provincial governments had finally agreed to provide for Canadian families.

The arguments for and against an expanded system of publicly financed, state-regulated daycare can be grouped under three headings: economics, fairness, and child development.

Economics

As we mentioned earlier in this chapter, advocates of a publicly financed daycare system argue that such an investment would yield economic returns in the form of more jobs for child-care workers and greater opportunity for parents, especially mothers, to participate in the labour force, thus earning income and paying taxes. There are two problems with this argument. First, it ignores the fact that creating such a system is not costless and that the taxes needed to pay for increased spending on daycare represent a diversion of income from taxpayers in general to the users of the public daycare system. It is not self-evident that this use of taxpayers' money is more efficient from the standpoint of creating jobs and generating economic activity than the spending/investment choices that taxpayers themselves would make if the money were left to them to spend.

Second, it is a fallacy to assume that supply creates its own demand. The simple fact that a country has a public daycare system (as several European countries do) may create greater opportunities for parents to participate in the labour force, but it does not guarantee that the number of jobs available will expand to absorb those additional workers. Supply does not create its own demand. On the other hand, a policy designed to increase the supply of available workers would make economic sense if there were an acute labour market shortage, as was the case in Sweden in the 1970s.

Fairness

One of the principal arguments for publicly subsidized daycare is that it enables women, who are far more likely than men to bear the chief responsibility for child-rearing, to continue working even when they have preschool children, thus narrowing the earnings and career-advancement opportunity gaps between men and women. In addition to this gender fairness argument, however, there is a class-based case to be made for publicly financed daycare: Its primary beneficiaries would be parents who cannot afford the cost of private care for their children. A universal system without user fees for higher-income parents would also benefit the affluent, however.

The tax code permits a parent to deduct up to $7000 per child from his or her taxable income for child-care expenses, but no such tax benefit is available to parents who stay home with their children. Some argue that this is unfair in that it provides tax relief to parents who work outside the home and pay someone else to look after their children, but not to those who stay home and care for their children themselves. In May 1996 Liberal MP Paul Szabo presented a motion to amend the tax code to extend this tax relief to parents who stay home with their children. His motion accomplished the remarkable feat of achieving agreement between the Reform party and the Bloc Québécois, both of which supported it.[61] But Finance Minister Paul Martin rejected the proposal, saying that although he was sympathetic to the objectives of the suggested reform, the federal government could not afford the cost of implementing it.

The problem with Szabo's proposal is that parents who stay home with their children already enjoy all the financial benefit of their investment in caring for their children, because the money they would have had to pay someone else stays in their pockets. An identical criticism applies to proposals for a publicly financed homemaker's income that would recognize the undeniable value of work done in the home. What these proposals overlook is the fact that households already enjoy 100 per cent of the value of the domestic labour provided by one or more family members.

Single-earner families (in which one member of the couple stays home to raise the children) sometimes complain that the tax regime is unfair to them because, even though they save on daycare costs, they lose out on the second income. Even more unfair, these families argue, is the fact that the single-earner family pays a higher tax rate than the dual income-earner family. Imagine, for example, two families, each of which has two children and the same gross income. In the first family each partner earns $35,000 for a combined family income of $70,000. Not only do they receive the $7000 deduction for child care, but they pay income taxes individually at the $30,000 level. Their total tax bill is roughly $13,501. (The calculation varies depending on the province where the family lives. It can be as high as $15,612 in Manitoba and as low as $10,410 in Nunavut.) In the second family, where the woman works and earns $70,000 a year while her husband stays at home with the children, the couple's total tax bill is roughly $15,631 (in Newfoundland the tax bill is $17,133; in Alberta it is $14,448; see Table 9.3). On average, then, the single-earner family is paying $2129 more a year in taxes than the double-income family at the same income level.

Child Development

'Imagine a country,' writes Hillary Rodham Clinton, 'in which nearly all children between the ages of three and five attend preschool in sparkling classrooms, with teachers recruited and trained as child care professionals. Imagine a country that conceives of child care as a program to "welcome" children into the larger community and "awaken" their potential for learning and growing.'[62] That country, she says, is France, whose long-standing system of *écoles maternelles* provides a model for what Clinton believes preschool care can and should be.[63] She describes these preschools as 'modern and inviting', with interiors that are 'bright and colorful', and with spaces designed for all the child's physical and affective needs. She argues that the care provided in such settings contributes positively to the emotional, social, and intellectual development of

TABLE 9.3 Tax Bill for a Family of Four with an Income of $60,000, 2010

	Single-Income Family	Dual-Family Income	Increase in Tax Bill from Single-Income Family
Newfoundland	$17,221	$14,332	$2,889
PEI	$17,977	$14,940	$3,037
Nova Scotia	$18,339	$15,112	$3,227
New Brunswick	$16,908	$14,595	$2,313
Quebec*	$15,315	$13,275	$2,040
Ontario	$15,606	$13,133	$2,473
Manitoba	$17,133	$15,612	$1,521
Saskatchewan	$15,053	$13,320	$1,722
Alberta	$14,448	$13,322	$1,126
British Columbia	$14,355	$12,330	$2,025
Yukon	$14,762	$13,838	$924
Northwest Territories	$13,505	$11,292	$2,213
Nunuvut	$12,579	$10,410	$2,169
Average	$15,631	$13,501	$2,129

*__Calcuated__ for 2009 tax year from www.budget.finances.gouv.qc.ca
Source: Compiled by author from www.taxtips.ca/calculators/taxcalculator.htm and www.budget.finances.gouv.qc.ca, accessed November 26, 2010.

children. '[T]he most important thing for a child', she says, 'is the quality of care he receives, not necessarily the setting he receives it in.'[64]

Arguments about the advantages and disadvantages of daycare versus home care for the child's social, emotional, and cognitive development are inevitable when the issue of daycare is debated. Some parents do a good job, others do not. Likewise, some daycare facilities conform to Clinton's glowing description of France's *écoles maternelles* and others are better described as warehouses for kids. No expert would dispute the idea that the quality of care is more important than the setting. The real question is this: What level of public resources would need to be invested in a universal daycare system to provide a developmental experience equivalent to the one that caring, reasonably competent parents can provide in their home? Is it even possible for a public institution to provide a developmental experience equivalent to the one provided by parents? The research on this question is inconclusive.

What is beyond doubt is that the child-care facilities available to the affluent tend to be better—of a higher all-around quality and more appropriate to the age and cognitive needs of the child—than those available to the poor. And so the issue of daycare for children's development has an important class dimension. Just another reason, say advocates of universal publicly financed daycare, for a greater social investment in pre-school care and education to close a developmental gap between affluent and poor children that the existing system reinforces.

2. Divorce

As we have seen, much of the problem of family poverty, including child poverty, is attributable to family breakup. More controversially, the children of divorced parents appear to be at greater risk of developing emotional and behavioural problems, doing poorly at school, running afoul of the law in the case of boys, becoming a teenage mother in the case of girls, and suffering from emotional problems as adults. These elevated risks exist even after controlling for factors such as family income and parents' education. The obvious answer to many of the problems that beset families and children would seem, therefore, to be a reduction in the incidence of divorce. This probably is not a realistic option. Some might even argue that it is not a desirable one, though it's important to recognize that the happiness of parents and the welfare of their children are not always identical in these matters. As David Popenoe writes, 'The central problem is the so-called individualistic divorce when children are involved—typically one partner departs in order to achieve self-fulfillment, leaving the children in the lurch.'[65]

So what, if anything, can be done to reduce the frequency of divorce? A number of proposals have been put forward in recent years:

- *A two-tier system of divorce.* Marriages with no minor children involved would still be easy to dissolve, but for couples with minor children the law could require mandatory marriage counselling and/or a longer waiting period before legal divorce is permitted.
- *Covenant marriage.* A variation on the above principle was adopted in Louisiana in 1997. The state passed a law creating an optional form of marriage called 'covenant marriage' that is harder to enter into and harder to leave than the usual sort. A couple entering a covenant marriage must participate in premarital counselling and may divorce only in the event of circumstances such as abandonment, two years' separation, adultery, physical or sexual abuse, or the sentencing of one of the partners to a lengthy jail term (or death).
- *The 'children first' principle.* Mary Ann Glendon has proposed that, in cases where the terms of a divorce settlement are contested in court, judges should first determine the best possible division of assets and income from the children's point of view.[66] Only then would the judge turn to other contested issues.
- *Value change.* As Popenoe observes, 'the problem is at heart cultural, not political or economic. Married couples must increasingly come to believe that they live in a society where marriage and marital permanence are valued, and where divorce is to be undertaken only as a very last resort.'[67] Barbara Dafoe Whitehead has suggested that the government and the public health community portray divorce as a public health problem, as has been done in the case of smoking. (Certainly it would not take much trouble or imagination to show that the economic costs associated with high levels of divorce are enormous. Furthermore, follow-up research on spouses who had reported their marriages to be unhappy found that, five years later, those who had stayed together were happier than those who had opted for divorce.)[68]

- *Stigma.* The analogy with smoking raises the issue of social stigma. Anti-smoking campaigns in Canada and the United States have attempted to stigmatize smokers, portraying this lifestyle habit as unhealthy, filthy, selfish, unsexy, and generally undesirable from both personal and social points of view. Could, or should, social stigma be enlisted in the cause of reducing divorce? Probably not. But stigmatization is used in some jurisdictions—Massachusetts, for example—to publicly shame parents who fail to meet their legal child-support obligations.
- *Mass media.* The influence role played by television, film, popular music, and the mass media generally in promoting social acceptance of divorce and non-marital childbirth is difficult to establish conclusively; the same is true of the media's impact on other forms of social behaviour. What is beyond dispute is that few media images and messages concerning the family convey any real sense of the negative consequences that tend to be associated with family breakup and single parenthood. It is difficult to see what could be done to change this, short of imposing some unacceptable form of censorship.

3. Guaranteed Income for Families with Children

George Bernard Shaw said that the *want* of money is the root of all evil. And it certainly is true that many of the problems that beset families have their roots in inadequate family incomes. In response to this hard reality, Ottawa and the provincial governments agreed to a revised system of child tax benefits that would target income support primarily at poorer families. The child tax benefit came into effect in 1998.[69]

Critics argue that this benefit does not go far enough. The problem of low family income is one to which single-mother families are especially vulnerable. To address the more acute need of this group, some have proposed a child-support assurance system that would essentially guarantee a minimum level of child support to single-parent families. The non-resident parent would be expected to pay child support, but in cases where he (in rare cases she) fails to meet this obligation, or where the amount paid is less than the guaranteed minimum payment that would be established under this system, taxpayers would cover the difference.

There are several obstacles in the way of a guaranteed income for families with children. The first involves costs. As Frances Woolley, Judith Madill, and Anrdt Vermaeten observed in their 1997 examination of child benefits, 'It is not clear that there is political will on the part of the government or sufficient pressure from the public to find additional funding for child benefits through increased taxes.'[70] They speculated that any increase in public money for single-parent or other low-income families with children would very likely come at the expense of single men and women receiving income assistance. In fact, however, since the federal government increased the child tax benefit in 1997, most provinces and territories have clawed back the increase from parents receiving social assistance and put the money into other programs; Ontario, for instance, directed the clawed-back funds to the work-ing poor.[71] Finally, no guaranteed income program for families with children can work without the co-operation of provincial governments. There is little reason for optimism on this score.

Key Terms

collectivist approach An approach to family policy advocated by those who believe that child-rearing is a collective responsibility and therefore that parents should have public support.

fractured families Families in which the parents have separated or divorced (or never married one another); can also include families of remarriage (often referred to as stepfamilies or blended families).

individual responsibility model The family policy model advocated by those who believe that the state's role vis-à-vis the family and children should never be more than supplemental and temporary.

nuclear family A family unit consisting of one male and one female with their chil-dren who share the responsibility for their children and for each other, living together apart from relatives.

patriarchal model A family model consisting of a male breadwinner, a financially dependent stay-at-home wife, and children who are essentially considered to be the property of their parents.

personal responsibility model The family policy model advocated by those who believe that parents carry the primary responsibility for the welfare of their children as well as one another; built on the assumption that parents are the main sources of social investment in children.

social responsibility model The family policy model that holds that the care and sup-port of dependent children is a responsibility that the public authority shares with parents.

BOX 9.1   The Presidential Glass Ceiling

More women than ever have university degrees, but men still dominate university leadership.

When Elizabeth Cannon showed up for her first day of engineering school in 1979, women made up 5 per cent of the program. Now, as she takes the reins of the University of Calgary, women make up 23 per cent of the school's future engineers and more than half of the university's student population, a trend reflected in schools across Canada.

But as Canadians fret over the feminization of lecture halls and ponder affirma-tive action for males, they seem to have missed the fact that the number of women sitting in the president's chairs remains stubbornly low. In the fall of 2000, 12 of the 68 leaders of Canadian universities—18 per cent—were female. A decade later, just 13 of 70—19 per cent—are women. The United States saw a similar rise and plateau: in 1986, women made up 9 per cent of university and college heads; the number grew to 19 per cent in 1998 before growth stalled again, settling at just 23 per cent today. Female professors are being hired in almost equal numbers to men—45 per cent of new full-time teaching positions were awarded to women in 2008—but the upper ranks are still overwhelmingly male. Just 22 per cent of full-time professors are women, although they make up a majority of education departments and nearly half of arts teachers.

We asked some female university leaders why the growth in female leadership has slowed to almost nothing—and what can be done to fix it. 'The fact that we're getting more women in the academic ranks will increase the number of women at the top,' says Cannon. 'But we can't rely on demographics alone.'

Martha Piper, who oversaw UBC from 1997 to 2006, was surprised to learn that more women aren't leading our universities: 'Wow. My impression was that more women were being appointed than that,' she says. Piper says if women are going to win the top spots, administrations have to actively encourage them. That means identifying women inside the university during succession planning, encouraging them, and hiring from that pool. 'Every time there's a new president, there are these national search teams,' she explains, 'I sit on a couple of corporate boards and they make it their job to figure out who the leaders are and how to develop them. Universities need to start cultivating from within.'

Ramona Lumpkin, who started her term as president of Mount Saint Vincent University this fall, encountered one roadblock in her 33-year career that she suspects is holding other women back. It took her awhile to realize that her less assertive and more collaborative leadership style was equal (if different) to the leadership style of her male colleagues. 'Not everyone speaks in the bass range,' she says, referring to her soft voice that can get lost in a room full of men. Lumpkin says it will take some recognition on the part of administrations that women often lead differently, in order for them to feel comfortable leading male-heavy groups.

Piper says being a mother kept her from moving up sooner. She was encouraged to apply for a vice-president's position at the University of Alberta around 1990, but she decided to focus on parenting instead, and wonders how many women give up on advancement entirely, due to family pressures. 'Probably 80-plus per cent of women decide somewhere mid-career whether they want to throw their hat in the ring to be a head, a dean, or whatever,' says Piper. 'You have to ask what they need at that stage of life.'

Sandra Acker, a sociologist with the University of Toronto (who was an associate dean once herself) studies how women succeed and fail in academic administration. In her recent paper, 'Gendered Games in Academic Leadership', Acker profiled four female academic administrators chosen from 31 interviewees. While she notes that not every academic is a mother, she wrote, 'the most striking similarity is the way that all four women talked about family and relationship issues affecting their choices.' Indeed, one of the women she studied said it was impossible to live up to the expectations of being both a manager and a mother when her boss was working 85-hour weeks. 'I work a lot, but didn't want to be there on a Friday night at nine o'clock. I have a family,' she told Acker. The man's family was in another city, allowing him to work late nights and weekends.

Piper believes that universities should recognize that mothers are often the ones driving kids to music lessons and helping with their homework. 'We look so much at maternity leave, which is important, but early teenagehood is just as demanding and we don't have good supports at that period of time,' she explains. Some female academics may need after-school programs for their children, especially considering that highly mobile academics rarely have extended family members living nearby who can babysit, she says.

As Elizabeth Cannon decides how to shape her school's future, she's already thought about how to nurture women along the way. 'We've tried on campus to increase access to quality daycare, to give [mom] academics peace of mind. Being supportive of women who have returned from maternity leave matters too,' says Cannon. 'But really, it's not just tangible things you can do,' she says. 'It's also the culture that you build.'

Source: Josh Dehaas, 'The Presidential Glass Ceiling', Macleans.ca (November 25, 2010). http://oncampus.macleans.ca/education/2010/11/25/the-presidential-glass-ceiling.

Discussion Questions

1. The article in Box 9.1 suggests that the reason why women do not advance to positions of leadership in universities is because of family commitments. Despite the gains made in the workforce by women, to what extent do you think personal considerations play a part in the advancement of women?
2. Is the state the same as a village? Can we expect any state to play a role in child-rearing equivalent to the role played by private-sector networks of family and friends helping each other?
3. Does the state have a role to play in helping Canadians raise their families? Is its primary role (1) to provide services for families or (2) to use its policy-making power to encourage certain behaviours that are good for families?
4. What role should Canadian tax policy play in helping families with children?

Websites

There are as many institutes and organizations on the family as there are family types. The following list of influential Canadian and American sites is merely a sample.

Canadian Institute of Child Health

www.cich.ca

The Canadian Institute of Child Health works to promote and protect the health, well-being, and rights of children and youth through monitoring, education, and advocacy.

Institute for American Values

www.americanvalues.org

Founded in 1987, the Institute for American Values bills itself as 'a private non-partisan organization that contributes intellectually to strengthening families and civil society in the US and the world'.

Vanier Institute of the Family

www.vifamily.ca

According to this site, the Vanier Institute of the Family's mission is 'to create awareness of, and to provide leadership on, the importance and strengths of families in Canada and the challenges they face in their structural, demographic, economic, cultural and social diversity'.

Institute of Marriage and Family Canada (IMFC)

www.imfcanada.org

The IMFC conducts, compiles, and presents the latest and most accurate research to ensure that marriage and family-friendly policy are foremost in the minds of Canada's decision makers.

Alberta Centre of Child, Family and Community Research

www.research4children.com

Based in Edmonton, this centre's work aids children not only in Alberta but in Canada and internationally. It develops, supports, and integrates research from various sectors and disciplines for promoting effective public policy and service delivery to improve the lives of children, families, and communities.

PLAN Institute

www.planinstitute.ca

With a focus on fostering caring citizenship in Canada, the PLAN Institute works to improve the lives of people with disabilities while supporting their families and communities. Part of their work includes identifying areas for policy change and developing policy innovations to benefit people with disabilities.

CHAPTER 10

Aboriginal Policy

Introduction

'Canadians, and the government of Canada, present themselves around the world as upholders and protectors of human rights,' said Matthew Coon Come, National Chief of the Assembly of First Nations, to the 2001 United Nations World Conference against Racism. 'However', he added, 'at home in Canada the oppression, marginalization and dispossession of indigenous peoples continues.' In a speech that *Globe and Mail* political writer Jeffrey Simpson described as 'incendiary' and that prompted a call for an apology from Canada's Minister of Aboriginal Affairs, Chief Coon Come compared the living conditions of many Aboriginal Canadians to those experienced by indigenous peoples in Mexico, Thailand, and Brazil. Dispossession, systemic discrimination, state-sanctioned violence, and the denial of fundamental human rights were the hallmarks of the Aboriginal policy pursued by successive Canadian governments, he said, a policy that was pushing Aboriginal peoples to the 'edge of extinction'.

As head of the Assembly of First Nations from 2000 to 2003, Chief Coon Come was generally considered to be the leading spokesperson for Aboriginal people across Canada. The firestorm of controversy generated by his UN speech might have been surprising, given that many of the same points had been made several years earlier in the *Report of the Royal Commission on Aboriginal Peoples* and repeated on numerous occasions by other Aboriginal leaders, as well as Canadian intellectuals and some media commentators. The message was not particularly new. But the forum in which it was delivered—a major UN conference at which the Canadian government hoped to showcase its good international citizenship and strong stance against racism—placed Ottawa in the embarrassing position of having to defend its record and policies against charges that it, too, was part of the global problem of racism.

Chief Coon Come's criticisms of Aboriginal policy in Canada and his prescription for change—a prescription that included greater recognition of Aboriginal rights, increased autonomy, more control over land to which Aboriginal communities lay historic claim, and more money from Ottawa—were broadly in line with the 1996 recommendations of Ottawa's own Royal Commission on Aboriginal Peoples. To understand the basis for this sweeping reform agenda, and the reasons why it was so controversial, we need to place it in the context of the history and current circumstances of Aboriginal Canadians and their relationship to the Canadian state. In this chapter we will attempt to provide the background information necessary for readers to arrive at their own conclusions about what reforms are best for Aboriginal Canadians and for all of Canada. More specifically, we will examine

- Aboriginal status;
- the size and characteristics of the Aboriginal population;
- the reserve system;
- the legal status of Aboriginal claims to sovereignty and landownership; and
- the principles underlying Aboriginal policy.

Who Is an Indian?

It has become unfashionable in some circles to use the word 'Indian' when referring to the descendants of those who occupied North America before the arrival of Europeans. 'Amerindian' is an alternative that has long been used by anthropologists and population geographers. 'Aboriginal peoples', 'Native peoples', and more recently, 'pre-contact peoples' and 'First Nations' are also part of the lexicon. However, there are extremely practical reasons for not banning the word 'Indian' from discussions of government policies toward Aboriginal peoples. Under Canada's Indian Act, which has been on the statute books since 1876, a person who qualifies as an Indian under the law has certain entitlements that do not apply to non-Indians. Moreover, Indian bands living on land referred to in law as Indian reserves are subject to a number of special legal provisions. Until the Indian Act and the legal status of 'Indian' are abolished, no analysis of Aboriginal policies can avoid using these terms.

In law, an Indian or **status Indian** is anyone who is officially registered or entitled to be registered under the Indian Act. The defining characteristics are both biological and social. The Indian Act of 1876 stipulated that an Indian was any male person of Indian blood who belonged to a band recognized by the federal government, and any child of such a person or a woman married to such a person. An Indian woman who married a non-Indian lost her legal status as an Indian and the entitlements associated with that status, as did her children.

This changed in 1985. In response to pressure from Aboriginal women, Canada's obligations under the United Nations International Covenant on Civil and Political Rights, and, most important, the sexual equality provisions of the Charter of Rights and Freedoms (sections 15 and 28), the federal government eliminated this obviously discriminatory section of the Indian Act. Since then female Indians, women who marry male Indians, and the children of such women enjoy the same rights under the Act as male persons. Women who lost their Indian status under the pre-1985 provisions of the Indian Act were permitted by this amendment to apply for reinstatement of their band membership and re-registration as status Indians.

The fact that non-Aboriginal women married to Aboriginal men and, since 1985, non-Aboriginal men married to Aboriginal women acquire the right to Indian status indicates that blood is not the only criterion determining who is an Indian under the law. Indeed, the courts have long recognized that a person's 'associations, habits, modes of life, and surroundings' may be important in determining his or her legal status as an Indian.[1] Writing in 1971, Peter Cumming and Neil Mickenberg observed that 'The questions of how much Indian blood a person must have, and of how closely an individual must be associated with a native community before he will be considered a "native person", have not been answered.'[2] This remains true today.

Canadian law also recognizes the Métis and **Inuit** as two other categories of Aboriginal peoples of Canada. Although the Constitution Act, 1867, speaks only of 'Indians, and Lands reserved for Indians' (s. 91, ss. 24), a 1939 decision of the Supreme Court of Canada pronounced the Inuit to be Indians within the meaning of the Constitution.[3] They are excluded, however, from the provisions of the Indian Act. **Métis**, the mixed-blood descendants of Indian women and Scots or French-Canadian traders and settlers in the Red River region of Manitoba, may also be considered Indians under the law if they are the descendants of Métis who were part of Indian communities covered by treaties. Descendants of Métis who received scrip (certificates that could be used to purchase land) or lands from the federal government are excluded from the provisions of the Indian Act. Nevertheless, Métis are considered to be 'Indians' within the meaning of the Constitution, and so Ottawa has the authority to pass laws concerning the members of this group. The Inuit and Métis are grouped with the Indian people of Canada by section 35 of the Constitution Act, 1982, which recognizes and affirms the 'existing aboriginal and treaty rights of the aboriginal peoples of Canada'.

Canada's Aboriginal Population

In recent years the actual size of Canada's Aboriginal population has become a matter of some controversy. It is variously estimated at between 1 and 2 million people, or 3.2 to roughly 8 per cent of the population. Professional demographers are inclined to accept the lower figures, while Aboriginal spokespersons and some politicians maintain that the higher figures are more accurate. The numbers matter for two reasons. First, certain entitlements accompany Indian status under Canadian law, and so the determination of who is an Indian in the eyes of the law has practical and financial consequences. Second, the political weight and even moral authority of a minority group's demands may depend in part on its size. This is especially true when the material stakes are high and some segments of the population stand to lose in proportion to the minority's gains. In such circumstances demography can become a political battleground.

Despite the widely divergent estimates offered for the size of the Aboriginal population, it is possible to arrive at a reasonably accurate assessment of their numbers based on clear criteria. The 2006 census, conducted by Statistics Canada, provides the following numbers:

- 1,172,790 people, representing 3.7 per cent of the Canadian population, gave as their ethnic origins North American Indian, Métis, Inuit, or a combination of one of these with some other ethnic origin.
- 623,780 people, or about 1.9 per cent of the Canadian population, are status Indians (i.e., covered by the Indian Act).
- 342,865 people, representing 1 per cent of the population, live on reserves or in other Aboriginal settlements.

The regional distribution of Canada's Aboriginal population is shown in Figure 10.1.

FIGURE 10.1 Registered Indian Population by Province, 2006

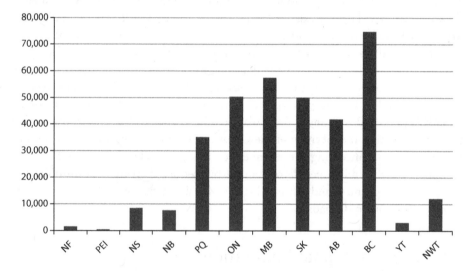

Source: Adapted from Statistics Canada, Aboriginal Peoples, 2006 Census, 97-558-XWE2006006, January 2008; http://www.statcan.gc.ca/bsolc/olc-cel/olc-cel?lang=eng&catno=97-558-X2006006

When the 1981 census was taken, the number of status Indians was estimated at just 335,475, or 1.4 per cent of the national population. It appears, therefore, that this segment of the Aboriginal population grew by an astounding 60 per cent over a decade—a jump that cannot be fully explained by natural increase. Two additional factors contributed to this growth. One was the 1985 amendment to the Indian Act that restored the right to Indian status for those women (and children) who had lost that status as a result of marriage to non-Indians. The other factor was surely the attraction of the increasing benefits, including potential land claims settlements, paid by the federal government to those qualifying for Indian status. Whatever the causes of this dramatic growth in numbers, the Aboriginal component of Canada's total population, including those who are not covered by the Indian Act as well as those who are, is still quite small; many more Canadians claim Italian, German, Chinese, or Ukrainian ethnic origins.

Language is widely believed to be one of the key elements of a culture—perhaps *the* key element—and a reasonable barometer of the real viability of a cultural community. According to the 2006 census, 210,075 Canadians, or considerably less than 1 per cent of the population, claimed an Aboriginal language as their mother tongue. This was down from 359,640 people at the time of the 1971 census. Those who claim an Aboriginal language as their mother tongue are outnumbered by about a 4-to-1 ratio by native speakers of Chinese (852,955) and are outnumbered by native speakers of both Punjabi and Arabic.

The Reserve System

The Indian **reserve system** has sometimes been called Canada's own version of apartheid. Indeed, a South African delegation came to Canada early in the twentieth century to study the pass system used on Canadian reserves as a means of social control.[4] On the face of it the description seems fair. Both income and life expectancy are significantly lower for people who live on reserves than for other Canadian norms. Rates of suicide, alcoholism, violent death, unemployment, and infant mortality are all higher than the Canadian average, in some cases dramatically higher. Moreover, although Aboriginal ancestry is not a necessary condition for residence on a reserve, the reserve system was created to provide a sort of fixed homeland for Indians, and the vast majority of those residing on reserves today are in fact status Indians. When we consider the disparities in living conditions between reserves and the mainstream of society, together with the fact of physical segregation on the basis of 'race', it's hard not to conclude that the reserve system sounds a lot like apartheid. Euro-Canadians who have seen first-hand the squalor and destitution that characterize many of Canada's reserves often wonder how such a system has been allowed to survive in a country that prides itself on being a compassionate democracy.

In 1969 the Liberal government of Pierre Trudeau produced a White Paper on Indian policy that proposed the abolition of reserves along with all the other legal structures that have treated Aboriginal people differently from other Canadians. But Aboriginal leaders charged that this liberal vision of integration was actually one of assimilation and equated it with cultural genocide. As a result the White Paper was abandoned and the paternalistic, racially based system established in colonial times continues today, as does Aboriginal resistance to its abolition. If the reserve system is a form of apartheid, why has it not been rejected outright by the people who are its 'victims'?

The answer is complex. To understand how a racially based system of segregation can survive in a liberal democratic society we must examine the origins and operation of Indian reserves in Canada. We must also consider the goals of today's Aboriginal leaders who are opposed to dismantling the reserve system.

The Indian Act of 1876 defined a reserve as follows:

> The term 'reserve' means any tract or tracts of land set apart by treaty or otherwise for the use or benefit of or granted to a particular band of Indians, of which the legal title is in the Crown, but which is unsurrendered, and includes

all the trees, wood, timber, soil, stone, minerals, metals, or other valuables thereon or therein.

Central to this definition—and to the quandary of the reserve system—is the guardianship relationship established between the federal government and Indians living on reserves. The legal ownership of reserve land belongs to the Crown, but the land and all the resources appertaining to it must be managed for the 'use or benefit' of the particular band residing there. In practice this means that virtually no legal or commercial transaction of consequence may be undertaken by Indians living on a reserve without the permission of the federal government. This is what critics are referring to when they speak of the Indian Act's paternalism. For example:

- Band members may not sell any part of the reserve.
- The federal government retains the ultimate authority to grant timber-cutting licences and to establish their terms.
- Reserve land may not be used as security for loans.

In 2006 there were 2675 Indian reserves in Canada, about two-thirds of them in British Columbia. Together they cover about 2,600,000 hectares (10,000 square miles—an area roughly half the size of Nova Scotia). Most are uninhabited, since many bands have leased their reserve land to non-Indians for purposes such as resource exploitation, rights of way, farming, and recreational uses. Reserve populations vary from two to about 12,000, and most inhabited reserves have populations of fewer than 1000 people. Just over 300,000 Indians live on reserves, or about 60 per cent of all status Indians. Although there are reserves in all regions of the country, most of the lands, and the vast majority of those living on them, are located in rural and remote areas. This has important economic and social consequences: Job opportunities are scarce, residents generally have to leave home to acquire secondary and post-secondary education, and physical isolation hinders integration with mainstream society. This last effect is not considered to be a bad thing by many in the Indian community. As Harvey McCue explains:

> To many Indians, reserves represent the last visible evidence that they were the original people of this country. The reserve nurtures a community of 'Indianness' and reinforces spiritual unity among Indians. Despite the manifest poverty, ill health, poor housing and lack of services, the life-style on reserves, traditional values, kinship affiliations and the land itself all contribute to an Indian's identity and psychological well-being. The relative isolation of most reserves enables Indians to socialize their children to values important to their culture: reticence and noninterference, consensus decision-making and nonverbal communication. Reserves, since they are set apart both physically and legally, help Indians to maintain an ethnic identity within Canada.[5]

Sovereignty, Landownership, and the Law

It has always been our belief that when God created this whole world he gave pieces of land to all races of people throughout this world, the Chinese people, Germans and you name them, including Indians. So at one time our land was this whole continent right from the tip of South America to the North Pole. . . . It has always been our belief that God gave us the land . . . and we say that no one can take our title away except He who gave it to us to begin with.[6]

Disputes over land—who owns it, who has the right to live on it, to benefit from it, to make the laws that will apply within the boundaries of a particular territory—are among the most intractable of disputes. Only recently have more than a small minority of non-Aboriginal Canadians come to realize that land is the crux of Aboriginal demands. Phrases like 'self-government for Canada's Aboriginal peoples' have inoffensive and even positive connotations for many Canadians—until the latter realize what they mean in the context of land: namely, exclusive Aboriginal ownership and political sovereignty in territories that the majority of Canadians assume to be part of Canada. The words of James Gosnell, quoted above, have been repeated by many Aboriginal leaders, from Louis Riel to Phil Fontaine, the current National Chief of the Assembly of First Nations (AFN). Their message is simple: The land belonged to us, much of it was never lawfully surrendered by us, and the treaty process through which the rest was surrendered was little more than a swindle. Ownership of and control over lands to which Aboriginal peoples claim a historic right are argued to be necessary for the survival of Aboriginal culture. No discussion of differences between Aboriginal and European-based cultures is complete without a reference to the different ways in which these two cultures think about the land and their relationship to it. Clearly the land was central to the traditional lifestyles of Aboriginal peoples. For this reason Aboriginal hunting and fishing rights were explicitly set out in the treaties. Matters become more complicated when the rights at stake involve mineral or other resources that are important to the lifestyles and economic activities imported into North America by Europeans, but that played little or no role in traditional Aboriginal cultures. This is an issue that Canadian courts have addressed in recent years.

The question of who owns the land and the related issue of whether Aboriginal communities should be considered sovereign are enormously important. At present, literally the entire province of British Columbia is subject to land claims. 'We can claim downtown Vancouver', said an AFN representative in 1994. 'It is ours. There is nothing in anybody's laws saying that it is no longer belonging to Musqueam or Squamish or Capilano or Tsawwassen. Yes, there's a whole province under claim because there's a whole province that hasn't been paid for, hasn't been negotiated.'[7]

Landownership is one thing. Sovereignty is another. The fact that a person (or group) owns a particular parcel of land does not give that person (or group) sovereign authority within its borders—the owner is still obliged to obey the law of the sovereign country within which the land is located. But many leaders within Canada's

Aboriginal communities deny the sovereignty of the Canadian state over them and their land. Former AFN National Chief Ovide Mercredi's position is fairly typical: 'We will not allow some other society to decide what we can do and determine the limits of our authority.'[8] On the other hand, most proposals for Aboriginal self-government seem to envision it as operating within the context of the Canadian state. The issues of sovereignty and landownership are obviously intertwined. There is no question that a sovereign people owns the land over which their sovereignty extends. Sovereignty, by its very nature, is a concept with territorial implications, including the exclusive right to make laws and dispose of property within certain boundaries. The first question that must be addressed, therefore, is whether Aboriginal communities are sovereign nations.

The Legal Case

Those who make the case for Aboriginal sovereignty usually begin with the **Royal Proclamation of 1763** and end with the Supreme Court of Canada's decision in *Calder et al. v. Attorney General of British Columbia* (1973). The Royal Proclamation was issued following the formal surrender of France's North American territories to England under the Treaty of Paris. Setting out the rules that would govern those territories, it included detailed provisions regarding relations between the British and the Aboriginal inhabitants of these territories (see Box 10.1). These provisions, says Donald Purich:

> [suggest] that all lands that had not been surrendered by the Indians to the Crown belonged to the Indians. It reserved all unsettled land for the use of the Indians as their hunting grounds. It provided that lands required for settlement had to be bought from the Indians and could only be bought by the Crown at a public meeting. The Royal Proclamation set the stage for the land surrender treaties signed by the Indians with the Crown in Ontario and on the prairies.[9]

BOX 10.1 Excerpts from the Royal Proclamation of 1763

And whereas it is just and reasonable, and essential to our Interest, and the security of our Colonies, that the several Nations or Tribes of Indians with whom We are connected, and who live under our protection, should not be molested or disturbed in the Possession of such Parts of Our Dominions and Territories as, not having been ceded to or purchased by Us, are reserved to them or any of them, as their Hunting Grounds—We do therefore, with the Advice of our Privy Council, declare it to be our Royal Will and Pleasure, that no Governor or Commander in Chief in any of our Colonies of Quebec, East Florida, or West Florida, do presume, upon any Pretence whatever, to grant Warrants of Survey, or pass any Patents for Lands beyond the Bounds of their respective Governments, as described in their Commissions; as also that no Governor or Commander in Chief in any of our other Colonies or Plantations in America do presume for the present, and until our further Pleasure be Known, to grant Warrants of Survey, or pass Patents for any Lands beyond the Heads or Sources of any of the Rivers which fall into the Atlantic Ocean from the West and North West, or upon any Lands whatever, which, not having been ceded to or purchased by Us as aforesaid, are reserved to the said Indians, or any of them.

And We do further declare it to be Our Royal Will and Pleasure, for the present as aforesaid, to reserve under our Sovereignty, Protection, and Dominion, for the use of the said Indians, all the Lands and Territories not included within the Limits of Our Said Three New Governments, or within the Limits of the Territory granted to the Hudson's Bay Company, as also all the Lands and Territories lying to the Westward of the Sources of the Rivers which fall into the Sea from the West and North West as aforesaid;

And We do hereby strictly forbid, on Pain of our Displeasure, all our loving Subjects from making any Purchases or Settlements whatever, or taking Possession of any of the Lands above reserved, without our especial leave and Licence for the Purpose first obtained.

And, We do further strictly enjoin and require all Persons whatever who have either wilfully or inadvertently seated themselves upon any lands within the Countries above described, or upon any other Lands which, not having been ceded to or purchased by Us, are still reserved to the said Indians as aforesaid, forthwith to remove themselves from such Settlements.

And Whereas Great Frauds and Abuses have been committed in purchasing Lands of the Indians, to the Great Prejudice of our Interests, and to the Great Dissatisfaction of the said Indians; In order, therefore, to prevent such Irregularities for the future, and to the End that the Indians may be convinced of our Justice and determined Resolution to remove all reasonable Cause of Discontent, We do, with the Advice of our Privy Council strictly enjoin and require, that no private Person do presume to make any Purchase from the said Indians of any Lands reserved to the said Indians, within those parts of our Colonies where, We have thought proper to allow Settlement; but that, if at any Time any of the said Indians should be inclined to dispose of the said Lands, the same shall be Purchased only for Us, in our Name, at some public Meeting or Assembly of the said Indians, to be held for the Purpose by the Governor or Commander in Chief of our Colony respectively within which they shall lie; and in case they shall lie within the limits of any Proprietary Government, they shall be purchased only for the Use and in the name of such Proprietaries, conformable to such Directions and Instructions as We or they shall think proper to give for the Purpose. . . .

Aboriginal leaders generally see the Royal Proclamation as an affirmation of their existing right to the lands they occupied. Georges Erasmus, a former National Chief of the Assembly of First Nations, argues that 'by virtue of that Proclamation, it can be said that First Nations became protected states of the British, while being recognized as sovereign nations competent to maintain the relations of peace and war and capable of governing themselves under this protection.'[10] Regarding the agreements that Aboriginal communities subsequently entered into, first with British then with Canadian authorities, Erasmus writes that 'First Nations did not perceive the treaties as being a surrender of authority.'[11]

In fact it is not entirely clear that the Royal Proclamation of 1763—which was formally incorporated into the Canadian Constitution through section 25 of the Charter of Rights and Freedoms—recognizes Aboriginal sovereignty. What is very clear is that the Proclamation speaks of the 'Sovereignty, Protection, and Dominion' of the Crown in relation to the Aboriginal inhabitants who 'live under our protection'. That the Royal Proclamation recognizes Aboriginal rights is indisputable; to maintain that it recognizes Aboriginal sovereignty is quite a stretch, however.

In the case of *St Catherine's Milling and Lumber Company v. The Queen*, decided by the Judicial Committee of the Privy Council in 1888, the Proclamation was interpreted as establishing for Indians 'a personal and usufructuary right, dependent on the good will of the sovereign'. In other words, the Proclamation neither established nor recognized Indian sovereignty over their traditional lands; in fact, it quite clearly refers to the sovereignty of the British Crown over these lands. The legitimacy of this assertion of British sovereignty might well be questioned on various grounds: The point remains that—contrary to the claims made by George Erasmus and other Aboriginal leaders— there is no explicit recognition of Indian sovereignty to be found in the Proclamation.

But perhaps there is an implicit recognition of Aboriginal sovereignty. This seems to be the argument of those who characterize the document as a nation-to-nation agreement because (1) it speaks of 'the several Nations or Tribes of Indians', and (2) it states clearly that certain lands are reserved for the use of Indians and may not be purchased by private individuals or organizations, but only by the Crown. This restriction on the alienation of what the Proclamation refers to as 'Lands of the Indians' might be interpreted as an implicit acknowledgement of Aboriginal sovereignty. At the very least it seems to establish a right to compensation for land transferred by Indians to the Crown. A central question is the nature of Aboriginal land title. In the 1970s Cumming and Mickenberg concluded that 'On both legal and logical grounds, it seems apparent that [with some exceptions] Indian title should be viewed as having all the incidents of a fee simple estate.'[12] In other words, they own the land outright. In the 1990s, however, Melvin Smith, a British Columbian constitutional expert, stated that 'to [his] knowledge no court in Canada has found that aboriginal title includes fee simple ownership'.[13] At issue here is more than who has the right to benefit from and dispose of lands and in what circumstances, for the meaning of Aboriginal title is often linked to the larger question of Aboriginal peoples' status vis-à-vis the Canadian state. This is apparent both in the statements of Aboriginal leaders and in certain court cases, two of which—the *Calder* and *Delgamuukw* decisions—will be discussed in the next pages.

Advocates for Aboriginal sovereignty have often referred approvingly to the 1832 decision of the United States Supreme Court in *Worcester v. Georgia*. Although this case has no official standing in Canadian jurisprudence it nevertheless has been influential in a number of important Canadian decisions on Aboriginal rights.[14] Writing for the majority in *Worcester v. Georgia*, Chief Justice Marshall distinguished between the *right of discovery and possession* that European powers could enforce against one another in the New World, and the *right of historical occupancy* enjoyed by the Aboriginal populations that already inhabited land 'discovered' and claimed by Europeans. The right of discovery and possession, Marshall said,

> gave to the nation making the discovery, as its inevitable consequence, the sole right of acquiring the soil and of making settlements on it. It was an exclusive principle, which shut out the right of competition among those who had agreed to it; not one which could annul the previous rights of those who had not agreed to it. It regulated the right given by discovery among the European discoverers; but could not affect the right of those already in possession, either as aboriginal occupants, or as occupants by virtue of a discovery made before the memory of man. It gave exclusive right to purchase, but did not found that right on a denial of the right of the possessor to sell.[15]

Marshall's argument that the discovery claims of European powers could not impair the prior right of occupancy enjoyed by Aboriginal populations is generally understood as supportive of Aboriginal land claims and even sovereignty. But the Chief Justice also had this to say:

> In the establishment of [relations between whites and Aboriginals] the rights of the original inhabitants were, in no instance, entirely disregarded; but were, necessarily, to a considerable extent, impaired. They were admitted to be the rightful occupants of the soil, with a legal as well as a just claim to retain possession of it, and to use it according to their own discretion; *but their rights to complete sovereignty, as independent nations, were necessarily diminished, and their power to dispose of the soil, at their own will, to whomsoever they pleased, was denied by the original fundamental principle, that discovery gave exclusive title to those who made it.*[16]

This part of *Worcester v. Georgia* is inconvenient for those seeking a legal basis for Aboriginal claims to unrestricted landownership and sovereignty. The legal principles that emerge from this much-cited ruling may be summarized as follows:

- Aboriginal people enjoy a right of occupancy and land use that predates the arrival of Europeans.
- Legal title to New World territory claimed by a European power belongs to the discovering nation.
- Aboriginal rights of occupancy and land use are not unrestricted, but rather are limited by the fact that discovery and possession gave the European authorities legal title to and sovereignty over these lands.

Marshall went on to say that ownership of Indian land could be transferred only to the state, and that Indians' title to lands they claimed by historic right of occupancy and use could be **extinguished** by either conquest or legal purchase. The Chief Justice made specific reference to the Royal Proclamation of 1763, which, as we have seen, set down precisely the same conditions. The nature of Aboriginal people's interest in lands they occupied and used, and which had never been alienated by either military conquest or surrendered under the terms of a treaty, was elaborated further in *St Catherine's Milling and Lumber Company v. The Queen* (1888), in which the Judicial Committee of the Privy Council characterized the Crown's interest in the land under dispute as 'proprietary' and the Aboriginal interest as a 'mere burden' on this legal title.[17]

The land title issue was revisited in a 1973 decision of the Supreme Court of Canada. In *Calder et al. v. Attorney General of British Columbia*, the majority ruled against the Nisga'a people's claim to have unfettered legal title to land they had occupied before the arrival of Europeans. In fact, the case was dismissed on procedural grounds. The court did, however, express itself on the matter of Aboriginal title: One judge denied its existence, three others recognized it but said it had been extinguished, and three others argued that Aboriginal title continued to exist. So while six of the seven judges recognized the concept of Aboriginal title, the majority determined that it did not exist in the case of the Nisga'a.

Because the *Calder* decision is so often cited as the legal basis for a right of Aboriginal landownership, it is worth quoting from the two sets of arguments given in this case: '[W]hatever property right may have existed', said Mr. Justice Judson for the majority, 'it had been extinguished by properly constituted authorities in the exercise of their sovereign powers.' In case there was any doubt regarding the court's meaning, he went on:

> [Crown] Proclamations and Ordinances reveal a unity of intention to exercise, and the legislative exercising of, absolute sovereignty over all the lands of British Columbia and such exercise of sovereignty is inconsistent with any conflicting interests, including one as to 'aboriginal title'.[18]

Why, then, is *Calder* generally viewed as a victory for the advocates of Aboriginal title? In a word, the answer is politics. Since the *Calder* ruling, successive governments in Ottawa and Victoria have preferred to emphasize the arguments of the three judges who maintained that Aboriginal title still existed. In the words of Mr. Justice Emmett Hall:

> This aboriginal title does not depend on treaty, executive order or legislative enactment but flows from the fact that the owners of the interest have from time immemorial occupied the areas in question and have established a preexisting right of possession. In the absence of an [explicit] indication that the sovereign intends to extinguish that right the aboriginal title continues.[19]

Since no treaty or other legal instrument specifically extinguished the Nisga'a title in the land they claimed, it continued to be theirs. The practical ramifications of this legal opinion, though expressed by a minority of the court, were potentially enormous, given that virtually none of British Columbia was covered by treaties between the Crown and Aboriginal communities.

It is simply incorrect to suggest, as many have, that the Supreme Court's *Calder* ruling confirmed the existence of unfettered Aboriginal title in Canadian law. Only three of the seven judges deciding the case took this position, and they recognized that such title could be explicitly terminated by the terms of a formal treaty. At the time of the decision, however, only a few years after the political disaster of the 1969 White Paper on Indian Policy, Ottawa was heading in the direction of a more conciliatory policy on Aboriginal land claims. Consequently, the federal government took the arguments of the dissenters as a framework for future negotiations, rather than those of the technical majority in the *Calder* case. The ruling and its aftermath underline the truth of the adage that today's dissent may become tomorrow's law.

The issue of Aboriginal title has been addressed in a number of cases since *Calder*. In *Hamlet of Baker Lake et al. v. Minister of Indian Affairs* (1980), the Federal Court of Canada appeared to accept the spirit and reasoning of the minority in *Calder*, arguing that 'The law of Canada recognizes the existence of an aboriginal title independent of the Royal Proclamation of 1763 or any other prerogative Act or legislation. It arises at common law.'[20] While acknowledging, as has every other court decision on the issue, that the Crown exercises sovereign authority over Aboriginal lands, the *Baker Lake* ruling repeated the view, expressed by the minority in *Calder*, that Aboriginal title continued to exist until explicitly extinguished by legislation passed by Parliament.

A decade later, in *R. v. Sparrow* (1990), the Supreme Court of Canada again addressed the issue of Aboriginal rights, including property rights. This decision continued the line of reasoning found in the *Calder* dissent and the *Baker Lake* ruling, holding that Aboriginal rights are pre-existing rights that are not created by government legislation and continue to exist until such time as they are explicitly extinguished. 'Historical policy on the part of the Crown', said the court, 'can neither extinguish the existing aboriginal right without clear intention nor, in itself, delineate that right. The nature of government regulations cannot be determinative of the content and scope of an existing aboriginal right. Government policy can, however, regulate the exercise of that right but such regulation must be in keeping with s. 35(1) [of the Charter of Rights and Freedoms].'[21]

The specific issue in *Sparrow* was whether the right to fish was an inherent Aboriginal right. Buried in the Supreme Court's ruling was a warning that common-law notions of property are not always appropriate in cases involving Aboriginal rights: 'Courts must be careful to avoid the application of traditional common law concepts of property as they develop their understanding of the "*sui generis*" nature of aboriginal rights.'[22] What does this mean? It could, one might argue, be interpreted as an argument against an unrestricted right of use and sale of a resource like fish or timber, if that use were to be inconsistent with the traditional practices and values of an Aboriginal community.

In a sense *Calder*, *Baker Lake*, and *Sparrow* were preliminaries to the main event that took place in 1993. In *Delgamuukw v. Attorney General of British Columbia* the issue of Aboriginal title was addressed head-on. A group of Gitksan and Wet'suwet'en chiefs argued that they owned an area in British Columbia roughly the size of the province of New Brunswick. In their statement of claim they asked the court to make three specific findings:

- The Gitksan and Wet'suwet'en owned the territory in question.
- They had the right to establish their own laws for this territory, and these laws would supersede those of the province.
- They were entitled to compensation for all the resources that had been exploited and removed from the territory since 1858.

The stakes could hardly have been greater, nor the issues of Aboriginal title and the inherent right to self-government more squarely framed.

On the first question, whether the Gitksan and Wet'suwet'en owned the land they claimed by historic right of occupancy, British Columbia's Court of Appeals said no. Only existing reserves within the disputed territory were deemed to be owned by the Aboriginal plaintiffs. On the second question, whether the plaintiffs had an inherent right to self-government, the BC court also said no. Finally, on the third question, whether the Aboriginal plaintiffs should be compensated for the resources exploited and removed from the disputed territory, the court also answered no. An appeal to the Supreme Court of Canada, however, eventually produced what may prove to be Canada's most important court ruling on Aboriginal land title.

In a unanimous decision, the Supreme Court ruled that the Gitksan and Wet'suwet'en are the owners of the land to which they claim a historic right of occupancy and use. Where Aboriginal title to land has not been extinguished by the terms of a treaty—and this would include most of the territory of British Columbia as well as parts of Atlantic Canada—Aboriginal communities able to prove that they historically occupied and used the land continue to have property rights.

Does this mean that a non-Aboriginal family living in the Okanagan Valley on a piece of land that they thought they owned are in fact illegal squatters? Will a flurry of eviction notices hit residents of Vancouver? Does a forestry company like Weyerhaeuser now have to renegotiate leases that it signed with the BC government that cover land rightfully owned by its original occupants? In fact, the *Delgamuukw* decision generated more questions than answers. What it did make clear, however, was the Supreme Court's opinion that, at the very least, Aboriginal title means communities like the Gitksan and Wet'suwet'en have a right to compensation for land that is determined to be theirs by historical right. The ruling strengthened the hand of Aboriginal groups in their negotiations with governments, since now they could claim a constitutionally protected right of ownership that can only be extinguished through a treaty with the Crown. Still, the Supreme Court's 1997 decision did not establish a constitutional right to self-government for Aboriginal communities.

There remains the possibility that what Canadian law does not recognize *is* recognized in international law. Those who make this argument point to various United Nations declarations and covenants to which Canada is a signatory, such as the 1960 Declaration on the Granting of Independence to Colonial Countries and Peoples. The Declaration states, among other things, that

1. The subjection of peoples to alien subjugation, domination, and exploitation constitutes a denial of fundamental human rights, is contrary to the Charter of the UN and is an impediment to the promotion of world peace and co-operation.
2. All peoples have the right to self-determination; by virtue of that right they freely determine their political status and freely pursue their economic, social, and cultural development.

However, the Declaration leaves undefined what constitutes a 'people'. Is there a Canadian people? A Québécois people? A Mohawk people? Moreover, the Declaration very clearly refers to colonized peoples and arguably was not meant to apply to indigenous populations in a liberal democratic society like Canada. Finally, in its sixth point the Declaration itself pulls back from the abyss of international disorder and partition that would surely follow from its unqualified application throughout the world. It states that 'Any attempt aimed at the partial or total disruption of the national unity and the territorial integrity of a country is incompatible with the purposes and principles of the Charter of the United Nations.' What the UN giveth, so too it taketh away!

A rather different argument from international law is to maintain that the treaties and other agreements between Aboriginal peoples and the Crown are tantamount to international treaties. If this is so, then it would seem to follow that these Aboriginal peoples have been recognized as sovereign nations that were capable of entering into agreements with other nations on a basis of legal equality. But as Cumming and Mickenberg pointed out in their generally sympathetic treatment of Aboriginal rights, historically and legally there is little basis for interpreting treaties as international treaties. They noted that the Supreme Court of Canada had expressly rejected this view of treaties,[23] and, moreover, that 'the Government did not consider the Indians to be independent nations at the time the treaties were made . . . and both the Government representatives and the Indian negotiators indicate that they considered the Indian peoples to be subjects of the Queen.'[24]

Nevertheless, Aboriginal spokespersons and some governments have insisted that treaties be viewed as international agreements. With regard to the Aboriginal people who agreed to treaties with European powers, Georges Erasmus and Joe Sanders maintain that 'The way [they] dealt with the Europeans is ample proof of their capacity to enter into relations with foreign powers.'[25] In fact, they write,

> Our people understood what the non-native people were after when they came
> amongst our people and wanted to treaty with them, because they had done that
> many times amongst themselves. They recognized that a nation-to-nation agreement, defining the specific terms of peaceful coexistence, was being arranged.[26]

Not only are treaties agreements between sovereign nations, according to this view, but they are emphatically not real estate transactions comparable to, say, the US purchase of Alaska from Russia. This point is crucial, because the courts and most governments in Canada have held that any Aboriginal right to ownership of the land covered by the terms of a treaty is *extinguished* by such an agreement. The nation-to-nation view of treaties denies that any extinguishment occurred, on the grounds that this was not how treaties were understood by the Aboriginal people who agreed to them; that non-Aboriginals understood these agreements differently does not mean that their understanding should be considered the correct one.

On a number of occasions courts have interpreted Indian treaties as contractual agreements. They certainly resemble contracts in that they typically include a detailed enumeration of mutually binding obligations: '[T]hey constitute mutually binding arrangements which have hardened into commitments that neither side can evade unilaterally.'[27] The courts have, however, recognized that Indian treaties constitute an unusual sort of contractual agreement. This may be seen in the courts' tendency, when treaty terms are ambiguous, to give the benefit of the doubt to Aboriginal rights. As the British Columbia Supreme Court said in *R. v. Cooper* (1969), 'The document embodying this larcenous arrangement must have been drawn by or on behalf of the Hudson's Bay Company and so any ambiguity must be construed in favour of the exploited Chiefs.'[28] The Supreme Court of Canada repeated and expanded on this rule of treaty interpretation in a 1983 decision: 'Indian treaties must be construed, not according to the technical meaning of their words, but in a sense in which they would naturally be understood by the Indians.'[29]

However treaties were viewed by the Aboriginal people who agreed to them, there is little doubt as to how the colonial and, after them, Canadian authorities interpreted these agreements. As Cumming and Mickenberg explained:

> The language of real property law as used in the treaties and the reports of the Government negotiators indicate that the purpose of the treaties was to extinguish Indian title in order that lands could be opened to white settlement. The treaties, therefore, can be best understood, from both a legal and historical point of view, when considered as agreements of a very special nature in which the Indians gave up their rights in the land in exchange for certain promises made by the Government.[30]

The question of whether Aboriginal property rights are extinguished by treaties is highly controversial. Morality and justice aside, as a matter of law treaties were clearly intended by the governments involved to put an end to Aboriginal title to land in exchange for specific promises, and this is how they have been interpreted by the courts. Moreover, it is probable that the promises made through treaties (and, for that matter, the Indian Act) did not constitute inalienable rights as we understand them today. To understand this, one must keep in mind that assimilation was an underlying assumption of Indian policy from early times. Moreover, colonial and Canadian authorities very clearly anticipated that the European population of Canada would expand and increasingly occupy lands traditionally occupied by Aboriginal communities. Finally, the Indian Act of 1876 offered the possibility of **enfranchisement**, whereby Aboriginal people could relinquish their Indian status and acquire in exchange the same citizenship and legal rights as non-Aboriginal Canadians. Thus, it seems clear that treaty law saw Aboriginal rights 'more as transitory means of protection . . . than as inalienable rights' as we understand that term today.[31]

In summary, the legal case for Aboriginal sovereignty and landownership is less than compelling. Where treaties exist, the courts have taken the view that any Aboriginal claim to own land outright has been extinguished in exchange for various entitlements. In the case of territory that was never covered by treaties, such as British Columbia and the northern reaches of Canada, the courts have not been sympathetic to the argument that the land belongs outright to the descendants of the Aboriginal peoples who occupied it before European settlement.

There is, however, another argument used to support Aboriginal land claims, even where treaties exist. As Donald Purich observes, 'In Canadian law, contracts can be set aside if it can be proved that one of the parties to a contract was of unsound mind, was pressured to sign the contract, was being unfairly taken advantage of, *or was clearly unaware of the consequences of the contract he was signing*.'[32] It is undoubtedly the case that the Aboriginal leaders who agreed to treaties did not always understand these agreements in the same way that the colonial or Canadian negotiators did. It is also true that the courts have never set aside a treaty on those grounds. Nevertheless, the courts have taken the position that 'treaties and statutes relating to Indians should be liberally construed and uncertainties resolved in favour of the Indians'.[33] Therefore oral testimony and historical evidence relating to the circumstances of a treaty's negotiation may be considered by the court.

Negotiating Aboriginal Claims

Since 1973 federal policy has distinguished between two types of Aboriginal claims: specific and comprehensive. **Specific claims** involve either land or money (as opposed to matters such as hunting, fishing, and trapping rights): more specifically, the alleged non-fulfillment of the terms of a treaty or the misappropriation of money or misuse of land under the Indian Act. Included in the specific claims category is an important subgroup of claims known as **treaty land entitlements**. These involve alleged discrepancies between the amount of land promised as a reserve under a particular treaty and the amount of territory actually provided. **Comprehensive claims**, by contrast, are based on Aboriginal title to land that has not been covered by the terms of a treaty.

Aboriginal leaders themselves have often rejected the 'specific–comprehensive' distinction. Some have rejected the term 'claim' itself because it suggests that Aboriginal people are claiming something that no longer belongs to them. Moreover, because claims negotiations have usually involved the extinguishment of Aboriginal rights—a concept rejected outright by many Aboriginal leaders—the language of claims is viewed with disfavour from the Aboriginal side.

1. Specific Claims

There are currently hundreds of unresolved specific claims. They involve matters ranging from alleged government failures to respect ammunition or livestock allotments for band members, to claims that land has been improperly alienated from a reserve. This last type of claim is the most common one. In the event that the Specific Claims Commission within the Department of Aboriginal Affairs and Northern Development Canada (AANDC) determines that a claim has validity, a cash settlement is paid as compensation for the loss. From 1993 to 2006 there has been a doubling of claims in the federal system.[34] Nonetheless, since 2007 there have been 313 resolved

FIGURE 10.2 Resolving Specific Claims, Results from March 2008 to September 2010

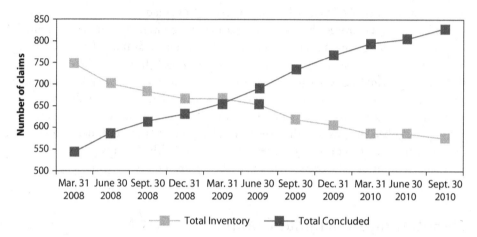

Source: Resolving Specific Claims: Results from March 2008 to September 2010. From Specific Claims—Progress Report April 1, 2010 to September 30, 2010: Indian and Northern Affairs Canada, 2010, http://www.ainc-inac.gc.ca/eng/1100100030541. Reproduced with the permission of the Minister of Public Works and Government Services Canada, 2011.

claims. As can be seen in Figure 10.2 the overall federal inventory is decreasing and the finalized claims are increasing.

The total cost of the 534 specific claim and land treaty entitlements settled by the end of 2010 came to roughly $2.4 billion.[35] Some argue that the cost of settling specific claims is small in comparison with the losses experienced by Aboriginal people. Those who have been the victims of theft or malfeasance, even if it occurred 100 years ago—the normal time limitations on bringing a claim before the courts do not apply to specific claims—deserve to be compensated for their losses. A deal is a deal, after all, and its terms must be respected. Others maintain that it is neither reasonable nor just to expect current Canadians to pay the bill for non-compliance with certain provisions of Indian treaties. Melvin Smith makes this case:

> How is it that when it comes to invoking treaties, the native people demand every jot and tittle of compliance—even to the extent of pressing hundred year old grievances. On the other hand, governments for their part have extended benefits to all Canadians, especially natives, far and beyond anything ever contemplated by the terms of any treaty: medicare, welfare, economic assist- ance, higher education, housing, pensions, tax exemptions, etc. Surely it is not

unreasonable for governments to say that they have more than 'paid in full' any and all obligations arising under these old treaties and, from here on, treaty Indians will be dealt with on the same basis as ordinary Canadians.[36]

Pierre Trudeau took a similar position in 1969 when the White Paper was introduced:

It's inconceivable that in a given society one section of the society have a treaty with the other section of society . . . things that in the past were covered by the treaties like so much twine or so much gun powder and which haven't been paid must be paid. But I don't think that we should encourage the Indians to feel that their treaties should last forever within Canada. . . . They should become Canadians as all other Canadians.[37]

Compare this to Ovide Mercredi's statement that 'We will not allow some other society to decide what we can do and determine the limits of our authority.'[38] The philosophical chasm could hardly be wider.

Trudeau's remarks cut to the crux of the Aboriginal claims dilemma. The case for land claims ultimately rests on a particular vision of Canadian society, one in which Aboriginal peoples are set apart from the rest of Canadian society. It is based on a philosophy of group rights and even group autonomy that sees separate Aboriginal communities and a distinct Aboriginal status (sometimes described as 'Citizens Plus', the title of an Aboriginal response to the 1969 White Paper) as desirable in themselves and certainly necessary for the survival of Aboriginal cultures. It is a vision that is irreconcilably opposed to the universalistic one-Canada vision expressed by Trudeau and Smith.

2. Comprehensive Claims

Nunavut, meaning 'our land' in Inuktitut, is the name of the eastern Arctic region that extends from 60 degrees north to the North Pole and from Great Bear Lake in the west to Baffin Bay and the Davis Strait in the east. It is a territory about twice the size of Ontario, with a population that would about fill the Bell Centre, home of the Montreal Canadiens. Under the terms of a 1993 agreement the new territory, formally established on April 1, 1999, has its own elected legislature whose powers are broadly similar to those of provincial legislatures. The government of Nunavut was to receive approximately $1.17 billion in cash paid out over 14 years, full landownership over some 350,000 square kilometres, exclusive hunting and fishing rights, a share of resource royalties, and participation in all decision making involving land, water, and environmental management. In short, the Nunavut comprehensive claim settlement provides for self-government, financial compensation, and an ongoing voice for the Inuit who make up the vast majority of its population, in exchange for extinguishment of any other Aboriginal claims and interests in the territory covered by the agreement. Under the terms of section 25 of the Constitution Act, 1982, the Nunavut settlement has the status of constitutional law.

The background to Nunavut and other comprehensive claims lies in the 1960s and 1970s. As Murray Angus explains, this period was marked by increasing pressure for exploitation of the mineral resources known to lie buried under the land and seas of Canada's North.[39] The federal government looked favourably on megaprojects such as the proposed Mackenzie Valley natural gas pipeline, particularly after the escalation of world petroleum prices triggered by the 1973 OPEC oil embargo. Development on the scale required to build a pipeline from the Arctic Sea to the markets of the American Midwest clearly had implications for Aboriginal communities and traditional activities. The push for northern resource development sparked increased political mobilization on the part of northern Aboriginals, whose claims were assisted by the anti-development efforts of environmentalists.

A second factor was the *Calder* decision in 1973, after which Ottawa and some provincial governments took the stand that the only way Aboriginal land rights can be extinguished is through a land claims agreement. The nature of Aboriginal title is ambiguous at best, as even some supporters of Aboriginal ownership have acknowledged.[40] Nevertheless, since 1973 successive federal governments have conceded that, at a minimum, the *Calder* ruling imposes on Ottawa an obligation to compensate Aboriginal groups for the 'loss and relinquishment' of 'traditional interest in land'.[41]

A third factor since the 1960s has been elite opinion in Canada's non-Aboriginal population. Since the demise of the 1969 White Paper and its liberal vision of full integration into Canadian society, 'progressive' thinking on Aboriginal issues has been supportive of demands for Aboriginal control and even outright ownership of traditional lands, Aboriginal self-government, and even some form of political sovereignty for Aboriginal communities. Opinion leaders in Canada generally support the continued segregation of Aboriginal communities from the rest of Canadian society, but on much better terms than have existed in the past. Among those better terms are acknowledgement of Aboriginal title to non-treaty land, financial compensation for modern-day uses of that land such as resource extraction, and an Aboriginal role in management of these lands. Progressive opinion accepts the designation of Aboriginal peoples as 'First Nations', a label that carries a whole conceptual framework and set of political claims relating to self-determination and ethnicity-based nationalism—precisely the sorts of ideas and claims pioneered successfully by Quebec nationalists in the 1960s.

It was not always this way. Until the 1969 White Paper was discredited, the vision of liberal integration put forward by Pierre Trudeau had been considered progressive. Indeed, it was widely acknowledged that the reserve system and the fiduciary relationship of the federal government to its Aboriginal wards were, at best, paternalistic sources of shame and, at worst, Canada's particular version of apartheid. Integration of Aboriginal people into the wider Canadian society on the basis of equal and identical rights was the progressive view among non-Aboriginal Canadians. This was the view embodied in the White Paper, and it is clear in retrospect that the Trudeau government seriously misjudged the intensity of Aboriginal opposition to the integrationist reforms it proposed. Within a few years the compass of elite thinking swung around to a collectivist pole, so that opposition to the 1969 White Paper became a litmus test of progressive-mindedness.

The huge scale of comprehensive claims, in both dollars and territory, is reason enough for the attention devoted to them in recent years. As a Bank of Montreal executive put it in the early 1990s, 'by the end of the decade, aboriginal people are going to own or control a third of the Canadian land mass and be the recipient of $5 or $6 billion.'[42] But the other reason why comprehensive claims are so controversial is that they inevitably raise issues of self-government and the relationship of Aboriginal communities to the Canadian political system.

This dimension of Aboriginal land claims was acknowledged in the 1986 federal task force report, *Living Treaties, Lasting Agreements*. The report recommended that comprehensive claims agreements 'should encourage aboriginal communities to become not only economically self-sufficient but also to establish political and social institutions that will allow them to become self-governing.' It called for an end to the extinguishment of Aboriginal rights as a condition for land claims agreements, rejecting what until then had been Ottawa's policy of treating such agreements as final cash-for-land deals. Instead, the report proposed that comprehensive claims agreements be seen as 'living', 'flexible' documents that would facilitate the development of 'self-sufficient aboriginal communities'.[43]

Notwithstanding the enthusiasm of Aboriginal leaders for such an open-ended approach to the land claims process, all 10 comprehensive claims agreements signed by Ottawa between 1975 and 1993, including the massive Nunavut agreement, contained an extinguishment clause. However, it is important to realize that what is extinguished by such clauses is limited to 'native claims, rights, title and interests, whatever they may be, in and to the Territory'.[44] By contrast, rights, benefits, and entitlements enjoyed by virtue of either Indian status under the law or Canadian citizenship are *not* diminished by the extinguishment of Aboriginal property rights. Comprehensive claims settlements do not 'cut the cord' between Ottawa and Aboriginal communities, leading some critics to question the idea that such agreements are justified because they promote self-sufficiency for Aboriginal people.

The Principles Underlying Aboriginal Policy

Although some of the major components of present-day Aboriginal policy have been in place since pre-Confederation, the principles underlying federal policy have undergone important transformations. These transformations began during the 1960s, embodied in the Trudeau government's controversial and ill-fated 1969 White Paper. Since the abandonment of the White Paper, successive federal governments have been groping toward a new set of principles on which to base Aboriginal policy. The most recent formulations appear to involve a new form of segregation based on a collectivist ethos and Ottawa's willingness to recognize an Aboriginal right to self-government.

1. Pre-Confederation to the 1960s: Dependency and Assimilation

Under French colonial rule there was no official recognition of any Aboriginal title to, or other proprietary interest in, the lands that had long been occupied and used by Aboriginals before European settlement. France laid claim to territory in the New World by right of discovery and conquest. As F.G. Stanley writes:

> The French settler occupied his lands in Canada without any thought of compensating the native. There were no formal surrenders from the Indians, no negotiations, and no treaties such as marked the Indian policy of the British period. . . . Whatever rights the Indians acquired flowed not from a theoretical aboriginal title but from clemency of the crown or the charity of individuals.[45]

Conversion of the Aboriginal population to Christianity was a central objective of French colonial policy, implemented by Jesuit and Récollet missionaries. While clearly based on the premise that Indians were uncivilized, economically backward, and morally inferior to Europeans, French policy did not consider the Aboriginal population to be subhuman and beyond redemption. On the contrary, the 1627 Charter of the Company of One Hundred Associates declared that a converted Aboriginal had the same status and rights of a naturalized French citizen. Assimilation and non-recognition of any Aboriginal proprietary interest in the lands claimed by France were, therefore, the two key principles underlying Aboriginal policy in New France.

With the transfer of French territories in Canada to the British, the foundation was laid for Aboriginal policies that would span the next two centuries. The Royal Proclamation of 1763 and the treaties entered into between the colonial authorities and Indian tribes were clearly based on the assumption that Aboriginal people had fallen under the protective stewardship of the British state. It was acknowledged that Aboriginal people had a proprietary interest in the land, but only within the broader context of British sovereignty and the colonial authorities' expectations that European settlement would continue to expand onto land traditionally occupied by Aboriginals. Moreover, as both the Royal Proclamation and early dealings between the British and Indians show, the British believed they were required to compensate the Aboriginal population for land that was formally alienated through treaties and purchase agreements. This was an important departure from colonial policy under the French regime.

Efforts at assimilating the Aboriginal population were much less rigorous under the British than under the French. There is some truth in Francis Parkham's observation that 'Spanish civilization crushed the Indian; English civilization scorned and neglected him; French civilization embraced and cherished him.'[46] The British colonial authorities were much less concerned with the state of Aboriginals' souls than with ensuring that the indigenous population did not impede the growth and development of the colonies they administered. To this end they made it their policy to set aside certain lands for occupation and use by Indians, and this 'reserve' policy was continued after Confederation.

Under the British North America Act (now called the Constitution Act, 1867), Ottawa is assigned exclusive legislative authority for 'Indians, and Lands reserved for Indians' (s. 91[24]). Within a decade the federal government passed the Indian Act, a sweeping piece of legislation that consolidated the dependency relationship that already had been developing between Aboriginals and the state. Under the Act, Indians living on reserves were placed under the almost total control of the Superintendent-General of Indian Affairs, whose god-like powers would be exercised by federal bureaucrats in Ottawa and by officials in the field referred to as Indian agents. Status Indians could do hardly anything of importance without the authorization of the Indian agent. All money paid by the federal government to members of a reserve or generated through economic activities on reserve lands was controlled by the federal authorities. If a company wanted a licence to cut timber on reserve land, for example, that licence had to be granted by Ottawa on the recommendation of the local Indian agent, after which payments from the timber company would be received by the federal authorities in trust for the Indian residents of the reserve. The Indian Act has made it impossible for Indians living on reserves to assume responsibility and control over their social and economic development.

The extremely limited powers of self-government assigned by the Act to reserve bands (powers that were always subject to approval by Ottawa) were to be exercised through band councils and chiefs elected for three-year terms (see s. 61–3 of the Act). This method for selecting chiefs reflects the assimilationist thinking of the time, whereby democratic practices of European origin were expected to replace traditional Aboriginal governance practices based on inherited leadership. The goal of assimilation is even more apparent in those sections of the Indian Act dealing with enfranchisement. The Act laid out a procedure whereby an Indian could request to become a full and equal Canadian citizen. While enfranchisement was automatic for Indians who acquired a certain social rank, including those with university degrees, lawyers, ordained ministers, and physicians, there was no automatic right to Canadian citizenship for status Indians before 1960, when an amendment to the Act extended Canadian citizenship to all Aboriginal people.

The prevailing view until at least the middle of the twentieth century was that Indians would gradually abandon their language, customs, and lifestyles and be absorbed into Euro-Canadian society. Compare, for example, the words of Sir John A. Macdonald in 1880 to those of Minister of Indian Affairs Walter Harris in 1950:

[Our policy is] to wean [Indians] by slow degrees, from their nomadic habits, which have become almost an instinct, and by slow degrees absorb them on the land. Meantime they must be fairly protected (1880).

The ultimate goal of our Indian policy is the integration of the Indians into the general life and economy of the country. It is recognized, however, that during a temporary transition period . . . special treatment and legislation are necessary (1950).

Assimilation progressed slowly, however, despite various prohibitions and inducements intended to eradicate 'backward' practices and reward bands that behaved in what were considered to be suitable ways. The 1884 ban on the potlatch ceremony and Tamanamous religious dances exemplifies the 'stick' approach, while the Indian

Advancement Act of the same year, whereby much more extensive powers could be delegated to a band 'declared by Order of the Governor in Council to be considered fit to have this Act applied to them', was an example of the 'carrots' used to encourage compliance and advance the goal of assimilation.

The 1951 revisions to the Indian Act did not change its paternalistic character and assimilationist logic. The major change in Aboriginal policy during the post-war years was the extension of voting rights to Aboriginals in 1960. But although their political status was thereby brought closer to that of non-Aboriginal Canadians, their legal and social status and their civil rights remained quite distinct. Moreover, instead of disappearing from the scene as the early architects of Canada's Indian policy doubtless hoped and expected, Indian reserves continued to exist as islands of shame within an affluent and democratic society. In 1968, however, with the election of a Liberal government dedicated to building what the new prime minister, Pierre Trudeau, called the 'Just Society', the stage was set for a major change in the direction of Aboriginal policy—the first such change since the passage of the Indian Act nearly a hundred years earlier.

2. The 1969 White Paper: Integration and Equality

The conventional wisdom is that what the 1969 White Paper represented was not a change in direction at all but rather a more focused continuation along the same path: assimilation with a vengeance. The White Paper proposed nothing short of the total dismantling of the Indian Affairs bureaucracy, an end to the reserve system, the abolition of special provisions for Indians under the law (e.g., their exemption from taxation in certain circumstances), and the transfer to the provinces of responsibility for the education, health care, and social needs of Indian citizens (in line with provincial responsibility for all other citizens). The White Paper proposed that most of these reforms be accomplished within five years, although it recognized that some changes, such as the transfer of control over reserve land from the Crown to Aboriginal communities themselves, would probably take more time.

The White Paper was met by a chorus of condemnation from Aboriginal leaders. In one of the best known critiques, Chief Harold Cardinal of the National Indian Brotherhood wrote:

> Now, at a time when our fellow Canadians consider the promise of the Just Society, once more the Indians of Canada are betrayed by a programme which offers nothing better than cultural genocide. . . . [The White Paper] is a thinly disguised programme of extermination through assimilation. For the Indian to survive, says the government in effect, he must become a good little brown white man.[47]

'Betrayed', 'cultural genocide', 'extermination', 'assimilation'—words like these measured the depth of opposition that the Trudeau government's recommendations provoked. Since then, the widely accepted verdict on the White Paper has been that it proposed to replace one bad thing (paternalism) with another (assimilation).

The reforms proposed in that document, however, need to be understood in the context both of the times and of Trudeau's political and social thinking. Moreover, the entirety of the White Paper's analysis and recommendations needs to be examined, not just those bits that critics find convenient to pounce on. What emerges is a vision for Canada's Aboriginal population that is more accurately characterized as *integrationist*, not assimilationist. Those who would argue that the distinction is merely one of semantics do not understand the background against which the White Paper was formulated.

Central to that background was an elevated awareness of social inequality and discrimination during the 1960s. The black civil rights movement in the United States and the student activism that arose during those years took aim at the exclusion of minority groups from the rights and opportunities available to the majority. The remedy that social activists and civil libertarians proposed was integration, whereby barriers to the full economic, social, and political participation of historically disadvantaged minorities would be abolished. Integration was, in fact, the banner under which the civil rights movement marched in the 1950s and 1960s. It was not believed to be synonymous with assimilation, much less the 'cultural genocide' and 'extermination' that some critics have since equated with the liberal integrationist vision. While it is true that many leaders of the black movement in the United States eventually came to reject the integrationist approach (characterized by one prominent leader as 'The movement of all things black toward all things white'), the approach was not intended by its advocates to lay waste to minority ethnic cultures. This certainly was not the intention of either Trudeau or the 1969 White Paper with respect to Aboriginal Canadians.

Proof of this can be found in the White Paper itself, which called for 'positive recognition by everyone of the unique contribution of Indian culture to Canadian society'. This goal would be promoted through the Department of Secretary of State, which was carving out a role for itself as the federal agency responsible for promoting the interests and identities of disadvantaged groups.[48] The White Paper suggested that some of the effort to promote Aboriginal cultures would fall to the provinces because of their responsibility for education. In the context of the time it was entirely reasonable to expect that Ottawa would help finance provincial programs in this area, as it did in so many other areas during the 1960s and 1970s.

The White Paper made clear that an end to 'a policy of treating Indian people as a race apart' did not mean that this profoundly disadvantaged segment of Canadian society would suddenly be cut loose from government support systems and left to fend for itself. 'Equality before the law and in programs and services', the White Paper declared, 'does not necessarily result in equality in social and economic conditions.' Ottawa proposed that programs targeted specially at Aboriginal Canadians would be delivered through agencies like the Department of Manpower and the Department of Regional Economic Expansion. The latter was expected to be particularly important in providing assistance to isolated communities within the context of the federal government's policy of alleviating regional disparities in economic well-being. In line with the Trudeau government's commitment to social justice, the White Paper acknowledged that 'those who are furthest behind must be helped the most.' But at the same time the new approach proposed for Indian policy was based on another idea central to Pierre Trudeau's political thinking, namely that 'Separate but equal services do not provide truly equal treatment.' When the United States Supreme Court said exactly this in the 1954 decision that marked the beginning of the end of legal racial segregation in that country, it was hailed as a great step forward for human equality and freedom. If Ottawa expected a similar reaction to its restatement of this liberal principle it surely was disappointed.

While much in the White Paper proved to be controversial, nothing galvanized Aboriginal opposition more than its proposals concerning treaty obligations and land claims. The White Paper acknowledged that the lawful obligations of the Canadian government must be respected. However, it went on to argue that a 'plain reading of the words used in the treaties reveals the limited and minimal promises which were included in them', and that they should not be expected to define in perpetuity the relationship between Aboriginals and the government of Canada. Here is what the White Paper said on the subject of treaties:

> The significance of treaties in meeting the economic, educational, health and welfare needs of the Indian people has always been limited and will continue to decline. The services that have been provided go far beyond what could have been foreseen by those who signed the treaties. The Government and the Indian people must reach a common understanding of the future role of treaties. Some provisions will be found to have been discharged; others will have continuing importance. Many of the provisions and practices of another century may be considered irrelevant in the light of a rapidly changing society, and still others may be ended by mutual agreement. Finally, once Indian lands are securely within Indian control, the anomaly of treaties between groups within society and the government of that society will require that these treaties be reviewed to see how they can be equitably ended.[49]

Alarm bells went off in the Aboriginal community. The Trudeau government was proposing nothing less than the gradual phasing out of Indian treaties and an end to whatever special rights Aboriginals had under these agreements. This was, of course, entirely consistent with the philosophical and practical thrust of the White Paper, which was to integrate the Aboriginal population into Canadian society on the basis of equal treatment. Obligations regarding 'twine', 'ammunition', and annuities that made sense a century ago had become irrelevant relics in the modern world. Moreover, because reserve land would be transferred into the hands of Indians—thus ending a system as old as the Royal Proclamation of 1763, whereby Indian land was owned and controlled by the Crown for the use and benefit of Aboriginal people—and educational, health, and social services would be provided to Aboriginal people through the same provincial channels used by other citizens, treaties would no longer have practical importance. Finally, the very concept of a treaty between one part of society and the government of all the people was morally and philosophically repugnant to Trudeau and the vision laid out in the White Paper.

Here we arrive at the crux of the White Paper controversy: two competing and irreconcilable visions of the appropriate relationship of Aboriginal Canadians to the rest of Canadian society. For Aboriginal leaders like Georges Erasmus, co-chair of the Royal Commission on Aboriginal Peoples, and Ovide Mercredi, former National Chief of the Assembly of First Nations, Aboriginal peoples stand apart from Canadian society as self-governing nations that should continue to have some relationship to the federal government. The nature of that relationship involves mainly the fulfillment of Ottawa's treaty obligations toward Aboriginal people. The integrationist vision of equal and identical status for Aboriginal and non-Aboriginal Canadians has been rejected outright, from Harold Cardinal's broadside against the 1969 White Paper to the 1996 *Report of the Royal Commission on Aboriginal Peoples*, on the grounds that it is a recipe for what Aboriginal leaders routinely call 'cultural genocide'. The survival of Aboriginal communities and cultures depends on the recognition of the distinct status and rights due to them as the original occupants and owners of the land that is today known as Canada.

The White Paper vision, which flowed directly from Pierre Trudeau's political philosophy, rejects outright the notion that a just solution to the problems that beset Canada's Aboriginal peoples depends on recognition of their sovereignty and distinct status. Critics of the White Paper and Trudeau argue simplistically, and wrongly, that this rejection is due to Trudeau's liberal individualism. In fact, there is a powerful collectivist strand woven through Trudeau's brand of liberalism. As Trudeau wrote, 'It is not the concept of the *nation* that is retrograde; it is the idea that the nation must necessarily be sovereign.'[50] His political philosophy was able to accommodate the existence of national communities within society and even some forms of constitutional recognition for these communities. What he rejected was the concept of the nation-state, the argument that nations have a right to self-determination, and any form of government that rests on the primordial importance of the nation or any other collectivity defined in racial, ethnic, or cultural terms.

Trudeau did not deny the importance of collective identities and group recognition in politics. It was, after all, his government that passed the Official Languages Act, introduced Canada's policy of official multiculturalism, and proposed a Charter of Rights and Freedoms that includes guarantees for members of official-language minorities and Aboriginal Canadians. He was aware that an individual's dignity may be undermined by social practices and government policies that deny recognition to the group that is crucial to one's identity and self-image.

While recognizing that equality and dignity have collective dimensions, however, Trudeau was always firm in maintaining that 'only the individual is the possessor of rights,'[51] and he rejected any concept of human dignity, such as that associated with nationalism, that locates the primary sources of dignity in one's association with a collectivity that is more narrowly drawn than society. Dignity and equality are states that can be achieved only by man in society, he would argue, but they do not require that one's communal identity(ies) be central to personal fulfillment. On the contrary, elevating communal identity to the top rung in politics and all that this may entail (such as granting constitutional recognition of a community's distinct status and rights and guaranteeing these rights to the community as such, rather than to individuals) actually undermines dignity and equality, according to Trudeau.

The liberal–integrationist vision of the 1969 White Paper and the philosophical premises on which it was based survive as a minority point of view among Canada's political and cultural elites. Indeed, it is more than ironic that the sorts of principles espoused by Pierre Trudeau in rejecting the system of segregation in which Canadian Aboriginal policy was based are today most likely to be expressed by members of the Conservative Party of Canada—hardly Trudeau's soulmates in any other respect!

3. The Royal Commission on Aboriginal Peoples: Separate Is Equal

A very different vision is set forth in the 1996 *Report of the Royal Commission on Aboriginal Peoples*. The long-awaited report of the most expensive royal commission in Canadian history started from the premise that Aboriginal Canadians constitute First Nations whose sovereignty should be respected by the government of Canada. In practical terms this would involve providing Aboriginal communities with a sufficiently large land base and either control over or a guaranteed stake in resource development and the revenues generated by such development on Aboriginal land. The *Report* called for the creation of an Aboriginal third order of government whose existence would be based on acknowledgement by Ottawa and the provinces that the inherent right to self-government is a treaty right guaranteed by the Constitution of Canada. A form of dual citizenship for Aboriginal people, who would be both Canadian citizens and citizens of First Nations communities, was proposed by the Commission. The philosophical premises and policy proposals of the Royal Commission could hardly have been further from those of the 1969 White Paper:

- The government should issue a new royal proclamation admitting the wrongs done to Aboriginal people and promising a new relationship between them and governments in Canada.
- The inherent right of Aboriginal self-government should be recognized by all governments as a treaty right that is affirmed by the Constitution.
- An independent lands and treaties tribunal should be established to handle land claims and ensure that the terms and financial arrangements of treaties are fair.
- The Canadian Human Rights Commission should be given responsibility to investigate any complaints relating to the relocation of Aboriginal communities and to recommend appropriate redress.
- Aboriginal people should hold dual citizenship, as Canadians and as citizens of their First Nations communities.
- An Aboriginal parliament, to be known as the House of First Peoples, should be established with an advisory role to advise the government on all legislation affecting Aboriginal Canadians.
- The Department of Indian and Northern Affairs should be replaced by a new bureaucracy that would include an Aboriginal relations department and an Indian and Inuit services department.

- The government should negotiate with Métis representatives on self-government and the allocation to the Métis people of an adequate land base.
- Aboriginal representatives should take part in all future talks on constitutional reform with a veto over any changes that affect Aboriginal rights.
- An additional $30 billion over 15 years should be spent on Aboriginal programs (on top of the estimated $13–$14 billion spent by Ottawa and the provinces on Aboriginal programs in 1996).

Running through the roughly 440 recommendations of the Royal Commission is a simple and fundamental premise: The original sovereignty of Aboriginal peoples and their ownership of the land must be acknowledged, and their continuing right to a land base and self-government must be embedded in the Constitution. Moreover, the survival and development of Aboriginal cultures can be achieved only through policies that recognize Aboriginal people as distinct communities with special rights and powers. The problem with federal policies for over a century is not that they have treated Indians differently from other Canadians; it is that these policies have not provided the Aboriginal population with either the decision-making autonomy or the financial resources required to take control over their lives and escape the cycle of dependency that the Indian Act's paternalism established.

A year before the Commission's final report was issued, former Indian Affairs Minister Ron Irwin stated that the money—more than $50 million—the Commission was expected to cost would have been better spent building houses for Aboriginal people in the North. So it came as no great surprise that the federal government was cool to the Commission's sweeping vision for reform. Ottawa stressed that the dollars needed to implement the Commission's recommendations simply were not available, implicitly rejecting the Commission's rather fuzzily documented claim that sticking with the status quo would be even more expensive. And despite the sympathy expressed by some government spokespersons for the aims of the Commission, it was pretty clear that Ottawa's conception of Aboriginal self-government did not involve the creation of a third order of government, as recommended by the Royal Commission.

Indeed, only weeks before the *Report* was issued the government had released a draft bill proposing extensive revisions to the Indian Act. The affront to the Commission was clear. Not only were Ottawa's proposed reforms far more modest than the grand design that the Commission was bound to produce, but they also included some changes that were entirely out of step with the Commission's philosophy. The most important of these were the proposals involving the legal obligations of Indian bands and the status of reserve land. Bands would, for the first time, be able to hold land in their own right, to sue and be sued, and to borrow money using reserve land as security.

Ovide Mercredi lost no time in denouncing the particular set of proposals as an attempt to impose on his people the 'whiteman's system of private property'. One of the fundamental tenets of Aboriginal culture, he insisted, is the collective ownership of the land. Mercredi argued that to treat land as just another commodity or possession, something to be bought and sold as an individual chooses, is alien to the way Aboriginal people view their relationship to the land. But even if Mercredi was right in his characterization of Aboriginal traditions relating to the land, it was clear that at least some high-profile Aboriginal leaders, including Blaine Favel, the head of the Federation of Saskatchewan Indian Nations, supported Ottawa's proposal.

By issuing its proposed reforms to the Indian Act, Ottawa sent a clear signal that grand schemes of the sort favoured by the Royal Commission on Aboriginal Peoples (RCAP) were not in the cards. Financial costs were not the only reason, although they provided a convenient public justification for not accepting the Commission's recommendations. An additional reason was the nature of Aboriginal self-government as the Commission envisaged it, which went considerably beyond the federal government's notion of what it should mean for Aboriginal communities to be self-governing. Few concepts in public policy debates are as slippery as self-government, but one of the clearest Aboriginal statements of what it should involve was made by Georges Erasmus when he spoke to a national conference on the subject in 1990:

> The kind of powers that would probably be acceptable to us are those that provinces already have in their areas of sovereignty. Canada lends itself very easily to what indigenous people want. We already have a division of sovereignty. We already have a situation where the federal government has clear powers, section 91 powers, and provinces have clear powers, section 92 powers, many in which they are absolutely paramount and sovereign. Not another government anywhere in the world can interfere with their legislation. That model lends itself very nicely to what First Nations always told the people in this country. You already have federal powers, and provincial powers. Let's look at First Nations powers. And we will have three major forms of government. Three different types of sovereignty. Two coming from the Crown, one coming from the indigenous people, all together creating one state.[52]

Erasmus does not address here the controversial question of how the Charter of Rights and Freedoms would apply to an Aboriginal third order of government—would it apply in its entirety and in the same way as it does to Ottawa and the provinces? Nor does he consider other contentious matters, such as the applicability of the Criminal Code to self-governing Aboriginal communities. But while some detail may be lacking, the vision of self-government that Erasmus sets forth is one shared by many Aboriginal leaders.

For its part, however, Ottawa prefers something more modest than self-governing Aboriginal communities with province-like powers. An example of the sort of self-government model that a federal government would be likely to approve can be seen in the Sechelt Indian Band Self-Government Act, 1986, which transferred outright ownership of reserve land to this British Columbia band, relieved it of most provisions of the Indian Act, and assigned the band council a list of powers similar to those exercised by municipal governments across Canada. Since the Sechelt agreement, Ottawa has shown a willingness to concede more ambitious models of self-government, such as those adopted for Nunavut and the Yukon. The legislative powers assigned to the

Legislative Assembly of Nunavut and to several Aboriginal communities in the Yukon are similar to those assigned to provincial legislatures by the Constitution. What Ottawa has not been willing to concede, at least at this writing, is a one-size-fits-all model of Aboriginal self-government, preferring instead to negotiate particular agreements on an individual case basis.

Future Directions in Aboriginal Policy

The year 2000 saw the publication of two major books that offered quite different analyses of what ails Aboriginal policy and what directions it should take in the future. Thomas Flanagan's *First Nations? Second Thoughts* staked out what today would be described as the conservative position on Aboriginal policy, attacking the idea of a distinctive and separate status for Aboriginal Canadians as both unjust and doomed to failure. Instead Flanagan proposed a return to the sort of integrationist philosophy that informed the ill-fated 1969 White Paper. This, as we have seen, was once considered a progressive approach to Aboriginal policy, emphasizing values such as universalism, equality before the law, and the removal of barriers to the movement of marginalized groups into society's mainstream. But as liberalism has morphed into a more group-oriented ideology that sees universalism as an obstacle to the equal participation and status in society of historically disadvantaged minorities, Flanagan's position and those who share it have generally come to be labelled conservative (or something less kind!).

Within months of the publication of Flanagan's broadside against what he called 'The Aboriginal orthodoxy', Alan Cairns weighed in with his book *Citizens Plus*. Cairns puts forward an analysis and proposals for reform that are very much in the spirit of communitarian liberalism that Flanagan rejects. He accepts the argument that Aboriginal Canadians deserve to be treated as First Nations with a sort of dual citizenship status within Canada. At the same time Cairns rejects the view, advanced by some spokespersons for the Aboriginal community, that Aboriginal peoples can or should exist as fully sovereign communities outside the Canadian constitutional and citizenship umbrella. 'Citizens plus' is Cairns's formula for satisfying what he argues are Aboriginal Canadians' just demands for a restoration of dignity through the recognition that they are simultaneously Canadian citizens and rights-bearing members of Aboriginal communities. This is, as Cairns demonstrates, already the situation of many Aboriginal Canadians.

The Flanagan/Cairns debate crystallizes the points of difference that have existed in Canada since the rejection of the 1969 White Paper. Cairns distinguishes between what he calls the *assimilationist integrationist perspective*—he insists that it does not matter whether you call it assimilation or integration: the harm to Aboriginal dignity is the same—and the *institutionalized parallelism approach* embodied in the analysis and recommendations of the RCAP. This second approach is strongly supportive of Aboriginal self-government, a third constitutionally recognized level of Aboriginal government, and, at the extreme, full Aboriginal sovereignty. Cairns describes his own position as a moderate compromise between these two approaches, arguing that a one-size-fits-all citizenship for all Canadians, Aboriginal and non-Aboriginal, will never satisfy the legitimate demands of Aboriginal Canadians, but rejecting the idea that the latter should not share in a common citizenship with other Canadians. On the whole, however, Cairns's position is much closer to what he calls the institutionalized parallelism position than it is to the integrationist model defended by Flanagan.

The case for 'citizens plus' is based on both history and current realities. In terms of history, Cairns argues, the essential fact is that 'the majority built a flourishing, wealthy society on the dispossession of Aboriginal, especially Indian, peoples.'[53] Although many might agree with Pierre Trudeau's sentiment that we are obliged to be just only in our own time, Cairns maintains that in Canada, as elsewhere in the world, there is a real need to come to terms with our past as an imperialist settler society built on the dispossession and marginalization of indigenous peoples.

Cairns notes that Canada's laws and institutions already include numerous instances of what he calls 'the positive recognition of difference'. He lists the following as examples:

- state funding of Aboriginal organizations;
- legal recognition of Aboriginal title to lands that Aboriginal people have traditionally occupied;
- entrenchment of Aboriginal rights in the Constitution through sections 25 and 35 of the Constitution Act, 1982;
- court decisions that have acknowledged a number of Aboriginal rights relating to land use, fishing, hunting, and so on;
- the creation of Nunavut; and
- the use by governments and the wide acceptance in the population of the term 'First Nations' to describe Aboriginal communities.

According to Cairns, Aboriginal Canadians are already 'citizens plus'. The key, he says, is not to lose sight of the 'citizen' component of their status—which they share with all Canadians—while being open to the sorts of policies that will satisfy their legitimate demands for recognition of their difference. He rightly notes that experiments in various forms of self-government are underway in Aboriginal communities across Canada. This, he argues, is the crucible where the concrete meaning of 'citizens plus' is being hammered out.

Flanagan does not disagree that Aboriginal Canadians already enjoy a status different from that of the non-Aboriginal majority. But he argues that this arrangement makes little sense now that Indians, Métis, and Inuit have become more like other Canadians in the way they live. '[T]he plain and simple fact is that aboriginal people now live very much like everyone else.'[54] The fact that Aboriginal demands to be recognized as distinct have received sympathetic responses from policy-makers, courts, and some segment of the general public has far less to do with the inherent distinctiveness of Aboriginal Canadians—distinct subcultures and identities are not uncommon in Canada—and much more to do with the successful politicization of Aboriginal identity.

What Cairns calls the 'positive recognition of difference' Flanagan (borrowing from Thomas Sowell), calls '*government*-mandated preferences for *government*-designated groups'.[55] He agrees with Cairns that such forms of recognition are far-reaching, but disagrees that they are a good thing. Instead of promoting the dignity of Aboriginal Canadians and providing their communities with a basis for economic autonomy and prosperity, Flanagan believes that the more probable consequences of 'citizens plus' include the following:

- An ever-increasing flow of public money will go to the governments of Aboriginal communities.
- More money for reserves will encourage more Aboriginal people to stay or return there, which is fine in the case of the relatively few reserves that are close to centres of employment and economic opportunity, but will serve only to keep the majority of more remote communities on the sort of government life-support system that has been institutionalized in Atlantic Canada and has chiefly perpetuated dependence.
- 'Citizens plus', which in practice means more money and more self-governance, 'will reinforce the already overwhelming presence of government in the lives of reserve residents'.[56]

Not everyone will see these consequences as negative. Aboriginal leaders have often rejected what they characterize as white notions of individual freedom and private property. But for people like Flanagan—those who believe that the individual's freedom to choose is a chief litmus test for determining the goodness of a policy or institution—the notion that Aboriginal communities should become more state-centred is abhorrent. Moreover, predicts Flanagan, 'On each reserve, the aboriginal elite will do well for itself by managing the cash flow of government programs, but most people will remain mired in poverty and misery.'[57]

Cairns and Flanagan offer two very different perspectives on where Aboriginal policy ought to go, based on their contrary readings of the past and current state of the relations of Aboriginal peoples with government and the rest of Canadian society. The only point on which they agree is that any version of Aboriginal sovereignty that excludes or overshadows Canadian citizenship is a disastrously bad idea; rather, Aboriginal policy should be crafted so as to ensure that Aboriginal Canadians are part of the wider Canadian community. Beyond that, their analyses and recommendations are widely divergent. The fact that large numbers of Canadians share one or the other of these two views virtually guarantees that Aboriginal policy will continue to be a political minefield in Canada.

Key Terms

comprehensive claims Claims based on Aboriginal title to land that has not been covered by the terms of a treaty.

enfranchisement The opportunity offered in the Indian Act of 1876 for Indians to relinquish their Indian status and acquire in exchange the same citizenship and legal rights as non-Aboriginal Canadians.

extinguishment (of rights) Nullification of rights; in Canada the courts and most governments have maintained that any Aboriginal right to ownership of the land covered by the terms of a treaty is extinguished by such an agreement.

Inuit The Aboriginal people who make up the vast majority of the population in Nunavut.

Métis The mixed-blood descendants of Indian women and Scots or French-speaking traders and settlers in the Red River region of Manitoba.

reserve system The system devised by the federal government to provide a sort of fixed homeland for Indians; the vast majority of those residing on reserves today are status Indians.

Royal Proclamation of 1763 The document that established the foundations for England's administration of the North American territories acquired from France under the terms of the Treaty of Paris; it included detailed provisions regarding relations between the British and the Aboriginal inhabitants of the territories.

specific claims Claims related to land or money only (not matters such as hunting, fishing, and trapping rights), made by bands that are covered by treaties.

status Indians Aboriginal people who have been or are entitled to be registered under the Indian Act.

treaty land entitlements A subgroup of specific claims involving alleged discrepancies between the amount of land promised under a treaty and the amount actually provided.

BOX 10.2   Native Community Demands Answers on Leaders' Salaries

Residents of a tiny Nova Scotia native reserve delivered a petition to their leaders Monday calling for a meeting to review compensation packages for their chief and councillors.

Cherie Francis, a resident of Glooscap First Nation, said under the bylaws of the reserve near Hantsport, a special community meeting must be held if over 20 people sign a petition calling for the gathering. She says she collected 28 signatures for a petition stating 'it's time that the chief and the councillors be taken to task and be made accountable to the people who voted them into office.'

The salaries of the Mi'kmaq community have not been publicly revealed. However, the Canadian Taxpayers Federation has released figures indicating that one band in Atlantic Canada with 304 members—almost identical to the number of members of Glooscap—provided compensation of $243,000 to its chief in 2008–9. In addition, the group says one unnamed councillor at the band received total compensation of $978,000.

The figures include salaries, honorariums, and travel per diems, and the money is tax-free. The salaries were part of a wider set of figures from across the country—obtained by the federation through federal access to information legislation—showing 82 chiefs and councillors have compensation packages that exceed the prime minister's annual salary of $317,574.

Francis, 47, said the numbers show a forensic audit is needed on her reserve and that nationally, all salaries and other compensation should be disclosed.

'We want to discuss with them (councillors and chief) how we go forward from here and make sure this doesn't happen again, and ensure that these kinds of monies are not being paid to them,' she said. 'We have to be able to set some kind of salary.'

The bylaws of the band require a meeting be held within 30 days.

Brian Smith, another resident seeking a review of the salaries, said that many residents are afraid to speak because they rely on the chief and council for their incomes. However, Smith, an employee of the National Centres for First Nations Governance, said it's important to improve financial accountability.

'I'm embarrassed. I'm embarrassed almost to say I'm a member of this community,' he said.

Karen Dugas, the receptionist at the band office, said the councillors and chief had left her a statement to read to the media. She said they weren't at the office.

'They're working with outside auditors to prepare a fact sheet on the band's financial status,' she said, reading from the statement. 'They will release this later in the week and be available for questions.'

Kevin Lacey, the Atlantic representative for the taxpayers federation, said the larger issue is why the Assembly of First Nations prevents Ottawa from releasing the compensation figures to the public.

'The big problem is that until the assembly supports full transparency of the numbers, you get into these local issues over whether people know what the salaries are,' he said. 'Why doesn't the Assembly of First Nations and the bands just make all of this public so it's out in the open and all of this is public.'

While the federation obtained a list of salaries and compensation, the names of the bands and the public officials are blanked out, with Ottawa citing privacy provisions. A spokeswoman for the Department of Indian Affairs said members from the First Nations reserves can go directly to the department and request the information.

Genevieve Guibert said provisions of funding agreements require the bands to provide audited financial statements that include salaries, honorariums, and travel for all elected and senior band officials. She said when the department is told that a First Nation member isn't able to access information, it first contacts the band to seek co-operation. If the bands won't provide the person with the audited statements, the department will release them directly to the band member.

Source: Michael Tutton, 'Native Community Demands Answers on Leaders' Salaries', Canadian Press, November 29, 2010.

Discussion Questions

1. Box 10.2 shows that 82 chiefs and councillors received salaries and other benefits that exceed the amount paid to the prime minister. Given the extreme poverty on many reservations, what type of institutional arrangement might give reserve Indians more power?
2. Can the collective rights model proposed by some be compatible with Canada's Charter of Rights and Freedoms? How can individuals living on reserves be protected from the majority if collective rights supersede individual rights?
3. The Canadian Constitution implies that Aboriginal people have property rights. Is this guarantee compatible with the understanding of land in Aboriginal cultures?

Websites

The following websites address Aboriginal issues from three distinct perspectives.

Assembly of First Nations (AFN)
www.afn.ca
The AFN is the national representative organization of the First Nations in Canada.

Aboriginal Affairs and Northern Development Canada (AANDC)
www.aandc-aadnc.gc.ca
AANDC is responsible for two separate mandates: Indian and Inuit affairs and Northern affairs. It also provides reports on specific and comprehensive land claims by province and year.

Indian Residential Schools
www.ainc-inac.gc.ca/ai/rqpi/index-eng.asp
Aboriginal Affairs and Northern Development Canada is responsible for addressing and resolving issues arising from the legacy of Indian Residential Schools and works with former students of Indian Residential Schools, Aboriginal organizations, church representatives, and the courts to oversee the timely and effective implementation of the Indian Residential Schools Settlement Agreement.

Frontier Centre for Public Policy
www.fcpp.org
Stating its themes as high-performance government, social policy renewal, and open economy, this think tank dedicated to the development of Western Canada includes Aboriginal issues as part of its focus.

Fisheries and Oceans Canada, Aboriginal Fisheries
www.dfo-mpo.gc.ca/fm-gp/aboriginal-autochtones/index-eng.htm
This government agency shapes Aboriginal fishing policy and programs with an eye to creating thriving Aboriginal communities by supporting stable relationships with government, facilitating Aboriginal participation in fisheries and aquaculture and associated economic opportunities, and managing aquatic resources.

Environmental Policy

Introduction

Governments have long been in the business of defending their territory and making war against their neighbours; building roads, canals, aqueducts, airports, and the other apparatus of ancient and modern commerce; taxing citizens and organizations that fall within their jurisdiction; protecting or suppressing the rights and practices of religious, ethnic, racial, and linguistic groups; and even promoting the arts. They are relative newcomers, however, to matters involving the environment. The very idea that the environment should be the subject of government action is relatively recent. For many people the triggering event was the 1962 publication of Rachel Carson's bestselling book *Silent Spring*.[1] Carson's passionate documentation of the threats posed both to wildlife and to human health by the indiscriminate use of agricultural chemicals—the 'elixirs of death', as she evocatively called them—led directly to the appointment of an American presidential commission to study their use and effects and, eventually, a worldwide ban on the agricultural use of the pesticide DDT. In the process, the biological concept of 'the environment' acquired a significant political dimension.

Since that time public concern and government action regarding environmental matters have ebbed and flowed in response to world events. But even if the attention paid to environmental issues is inconsistent, the clock cannot be turned back to the era of general apathy and ignorance whose illusions of innocence were smashed by *Silent Spring*: The consequences of human activities for the environment today are far too great, and public awareness of environmental issues is too deeply entrenched (if often poorly informed). Moreover, the last couple of decades have seen a proliferation of laws and programs designed to control the effects of human activity on the environment.

Environmental policy-making in Canada, as we will see, is not restricted to a single department or agency. Nor is there a single level of government with primary responsibility for the environment. Some environmental matters are the business of the federal government, but many others come under provincial or municipal jurisdiction. We will examine the current state of environmental policies in Canada in the latter part of this chapter. First, however, we will take a closer look at the concept of the environment itself, how it has evolved, and how it has come to occupy a permanent place on the political agenda, not just in Canada but around the world.

What Is 'the Environment'?

For some people the word 'environment' evokes images of green forests, clear streams, and abundant wildlife—an unspoiled natural world beyond the corrupting influence of humankind. For others the products of that corrupting influence are the first things that come to mind: belching smokestacks, dead fish on a littered beach, cancer-causing chemicals. More broadly, however, the environment may be conceived of as encompassing all the conditions that make human life possible and determine its character. Viewed from this perspective, overcrowded living conditions, excessive noise, choked highways, and the build-up of military weapons would all qualify as environmental issues. 'The environment' in this second sense includes both the natural world and the world created by human activity as they affect the quality and viability of human life. Some, however, criticize this concept of the environment as **anthropocentric**—placing humankind at the centre of existence. Advocates of a more radical perspective, often referred to as '**deep ecology**', make no such distinction between humans and other life forms; for them 'the environment' is the entire interrelated chain of life, and all its parts are of equal value.

The Environmental Conundrum

To say that the modern environmental movement can be traced to *Silent Spring* is not to say that no one thought about the environment before 1962. Until then, however, the primary concern had been the **conservation** of wildlife and wilderness areas. Most developed nations had been setting aside protected lands at least since the early 1900s, and the legislation creating the first national park in the United States was signed in 1872. The Yellowstone Park Act specified that the land was to be set aside for the *benefit* and *enjoyment* of the people. This terminology reflected the prevailing liberal–utilitarian world view, according to which the guiding principle in all things should be the greatest good for the greatest number of people.

The wilderness was put aside above all to preserve it for future human generations; the idea that it might serve as a refuge for bison or wolves was secondary at best. The same world view informed the creation of Banff National Park in 1885, the first park so designated in Canada and the third in the world. The language of the National Parks Act of 1930 was strikingly similar to that of the Yellowstone legislation: 'The national parks of Canada are hereby dedicated to the people of Canada for their benefit, education and enjoyment . . . and [they] shall be maintained and made use of so as to remain unimpaired for future generations.'[2]

Clearly a lot has changed in our understanding of the natural world since the Victorian era. Those changes are reflected in policies that encourage human enjoyment of natural sites, but also recognize that some lands must be set aside for the protection of non-human life.

In earlier editions of this book, Stephen Brooks noted that mainstream economics sees human selfishness (i.e., self-interest) as a positive force leading to desirable outcomes, but that this is rarely the case where the environment is concerned. To explain why normally rational economic behaviour tends to have negative consequences in the case of the environment, environmentalists often point to an essay by Garrett Hardin called 'The Tragedy of the Commons'[3] (1968), in which he asked readers to imagine a pasture or 'commons' on which all the local farmers are free to graze their herds. This system works well for centuries, as long as the numbers of farmers and animals remain well below the carrying capacity of the land. Eventually, however, the forces that kept those numbers in check—war, poaching, disease—are brought under control and the populations in question are able to grow. As each farmer decides that it is in his self-interest to add another animal to his herd, the common pastureland becomes overburdened until it finally collapses. As Brooks pointed out, 'An overstressed commons, incapable of sustaining the demands placed on it, is undesirable from everyone's standpoint. Yet this appears to be the inevitable outcome of a market system that allows individuals to capture all of the benefits of their actions while spreading the costs associated with individual behaviour across the entire community.'[4]

The broader relevance of this parable is clear: Substitute consumers, corporations, car owners, tourists, high-tech farmers, suburbanites with lush lawns, or any other group whose behaviour imposes stress on the environment, and the result is the same. Consumers who enjoy the convenience of using plastic bags to carry home their (already overpackaged) purchases impose a burden on the environment. But most don't recognize the social costs of this behaviour until the regional landfill shuts down or the local council proposes to build a garbage incinerator near their homes. Likewise, a corporation that pollutes the air, water, or soil has no particular incentive to act differently so long as it does not bear the costs associated with this polluting behaviour.

So why does the market, generally effective when it comes to ensuring the most efficient distribution of economic resources and producing the greatest level of material affluence for society, not work so well when it comes to the environment? The answer has to do with how prices are determined, which in turn reflects what can only be described as ideological–ethical presumptions. In a market economy, prices reflect what buyers are willing to pay for a good or service; they represent what economists call the **marginal utility** derived from the use of what is purchased. The fact that poor information on the part of sellers or buyers, or a lack of real competition, may distort price levels is irrelevant. Prices, within these limits, are basically set according to the marginal utility that *individual* buyers *currently* in the market expect to enjoy by purchasing goods and services.

That is one interpretation of Hardin's parable. While mainstream environmentalists might agree that the tragedy of the commons represents a failure of the market system, market-based environmentalists would disagree. For them, the tragedy of the commons is a classic example of the failure of common ownership. In their view, things would work better if each farmer owned his own pastureland, because then he could control the use of it. Market environmentalists would argue that if you eliminate the public lands, you eliminate the temptation to overgraze because individual landowners would recognize the damage that overgrazing would do to their land, and hence its cost to themselves. Similarly in the case of consumer waste, for market environmentalists the problem is the fact that the *disposal* of the waste has been co-opted by the commons. Because most municipalities pool their resources to deal with garbage removal, the incentive for reducing the cost of waste disposal has been removed from the market system. Therefore, market environmentalists argue, it is the state's removing the price mechanism from waste disposal that distorts the market and leads to environmental degradation. It is only when municipalities run out of landfill space that they begin imposing new costs or responsibilities on the public by charging extra to collect household garbage above a certain limit, or introducing recycling programs. Financial penalties, regulations, and moral suasion are all mechanisms that municipalities have used to try to reduce the amount of waste they must somehow dispose of.

'Individual' is one of the key terms here. Prices in a market economy are set impersonally, through the unorchestrated behaviour of buyers and sellers. But as the tragedy of the commons suggests, individual decision makers may have no incentive to consider the collective implications of their individual choices if there are no costs associated with making those choices. The social costs associated with a particular good or service generally are not captured in its price because their impact is not readily apparent—though it may be felt strongly in some other place or at some later time. Economists use the term **externalities** to refer to these costs that are not reflected in the price paid for a good or service. But whatever one calls them, they are costs just the same, and the failure to take them into account means that the goods and services in question are underpriced.

'Currently' is the other key term. Prices reflect the relative value that buyers attach to goods or services in the market at a particular point in time; they seldom take account of how future generations will be affected by current behaviour. And the market does not automatically register the preferences of these later generations. Indeed, it shuts them out and gives them no voice. This would not be the case if individual buyers, whether individuals or organizations, gave thought to those who will succeed them when considering how much something is worth. If, for example, consumers believed that the emissions from gasoline-powered automobiles are leaving future generations a legacy of accumulated carbon dioxide in the atmosphere, which in turn is contributing to global warming, and if—a very big if!—they believed that the current price of gasoline should include the costs that future generations will bear, then the retail price of gasoline would be much higher than it is currently. Terry Tamminen, the environmental advisor to former California governor Arnold Schwarzenegger, has argued that the true price of a gallon of gasoline is somewhere in the neighbourhood of $10 when we factor in the costs associated with gas emissions in terms of birth defects and disorders such as asthma, emphysema, and cancer.[5] Such thinking is uncommon, however. Most people, most of the time, think locally and for the short term. Relatively few reflect regularly on the global impacts of their behaviour or have a time perspective that extends beyond their own and possibly their children's lifetimes.

Nevertheless, some people do think globally and for the long term, and some cultures do show some sensitivity to the interests of future generations as well as the environment as a whole. This brings us back to the claim that prices in a market economy are influenced by ideological–ethical presumptions. It is neither biologically determined nor divinely ordained that the price of a given item must reflect only its **utility** to those currently in the marketplace. If people are aware that certain costs are not captured by conventional pricing practices, and if they believe that these are real costs that should be reflected in the price of fossil fuels, plastic packaging, disposable diapers, industrial emissions, and so on, then this is a starting point for a very different pricing system from the one that currently predominates in market economies. Is there evidence that this is happening? Yes and no. For various reasons, individual buyers and sellers are unlikely to adjust their expectations very much to take into account the long-term and collective consequences of the things they produce and buy. But there is evidence that they are sometimes willing to accept taxation and regulating policies that increase prices when governments justify these higher prices on environmental grounds.

Is the Environment Different from Other Policy Areas?

The matters addressed by environmental policy share many general characteristics with other modern public policy issues. They are often highly technical, requiring an understanding of specialized scientific information and complicated interrelationships. They often have an intergenerational dimension, with the benefits and burdens of current behaviour falling unequally on current and future generations. They also frequently have an interjurisdictional dimension, since ecosystems and the consequences of human actions do not respect political boundaries.

It cannot even be said that the specific matters addressed by environmental policy necessarily form a distinct category. Energy policy—including the choice of energy sources, how they are priced, and the technologies used to exploit and conserve them—covers some of the same turf as environmental policy (although environmentalists have typically had to fight hard to get these matters recognized as environmental issues). Are urban congestion, inner-city decay, and suburban sprawl environmental issues? Certainly, but they are more likely to be recognized by policy-makers as social problems in terms of their connections with housing, for example, or health, transportation, or crime. The 1987 report of the World Commission on Environment and Development (hereafter referred to as the Brundtland Commission) made it clear just how broad the range of 'environmental issues' is when it identified the environmental challenges facing the world's governments:[6]

- global population growth
- food supplies
- preserving species and ecosystems
- energy
- industrial production
- urbanization
- the threat of nuclear and other military conflict

But the very breadth of 'environmental problems' as a category tends to cripple attempts to deal with those issues for two reasons. First, the political constituency that can be called on to support environmental policy is fragmented and is often weak and difficult to mobilize. Citizens who are alarmed at the prospect of a landfill near their homes may care nothing about the impact of carbon dioxide emissions on global climatic change. City dwellers who care passionately about the destruction of the beluga whale's native habitat may give no thought whatever to the way their groceries are packaged, much less where or how they are produced. It is sometimes said that all politics is local. The truth of this adage is brought home by the fact that it is generally much easier to mobilize citizens around an issue like the quality of municipal drinking water than around something like ozone depletion or the pressures that the lifestyles of affluent societies put on the global ecosystem.

A second factor that helps to explain why the sheer scope of environmental problems undermines efforts to deal with them is the nature of existing political institutions. Quite simply, environmental problems tend not to 'fit' the policy-making and representative structures currently in place. The Brundtland Commission referred to this as the problem of institutional gaps.[7] In a world characterized by interdependence, not simply of nations but of human activities and their consequences, it is a stubborn fact that the structures in place for dealing with transnational problems are not up to the job. There are, in fact, two distinct institutional gaps that impede progress on environmental issues:

- *Gap 1: Local and national governance versus transnational problems.* This is the dilemma mentioned above. The chief 'containers' for political decision making are national and subnational governments. Not surprisingly, these governments will be more responsive to the concerns and demands of citizens and interest groups within their own borders than to those of outsiders. This would be fine were it not for the fact that environmental problems often spill over these political boundaries, requiring co-operation to deal with them. Transnational institutions capable of resolving environmental issues in an authoritative way, backed up by sanctions, are rare. Co-operation between jurisdictions is usually not easy to achieve because its benefits and burdens often fall unequally on the co-operating parties. For example, much of the damage inflicted on vegetation, lakes, and buildings by the sulphur dioxide emissions that produce acid rain occurs in jurisdictions outside the major sources of this pollution. Measures to limit these emissions will provide clear benefits for the affected jurisdictions, but the costs will be borne by the polluting jurisdiction(s). Why should they pay? The answer is 'They won't.' Some combination of external threats and/or incentives and domestic pressure is usually needed to persuade the offending jurisdiction to change its ways.
- *Gap 2: New problems and old structures.* All modern state systems are complex organizations comprising dozens or even hundreds of administratively separate units that perform different functions or serve different regions or clienteles. These administrative structures have emerged over time to deal with particular issues and interests. Taken together, they represent a sort of institutional status quo whose

strength is reinforced by the bureaucratic interests tied to existing programs and budgets, and by the societal groups that benefit from this status quo. Environmental policy—a relatively new policy field—does not fit neatly into the existing structures of the modern state. The usual government response has been to create a new agency to deal with environmental matters, such as the federal Department of the Environment, the provincial environment ministries, and the Environmental Protection Agency in the United States. But the mere creation of such an agency does not guarantee that it will have clout. Indeed, it is almost certain to encounter resistance from other departments and agencies representing such traditional policy fields as energy, agriculture, fisheries, industrial development, health, public works, and so on. The bottom line is this: Environmental issues do not fit neatly into the existing institutional machinery of government. Any attempt to create a policy space for these issues is likely to be resisted to the extent that it would encroach on the turf of existing administrative agencies and threaten the interests that depend on their policies.

The Evolution of Environmental Policy in Canada

A brief review of how Canada's environmental policy has evolved over time underscores the relevance of the 'commons' parable. Michael Howlett has identified three distinct periods of Canadian environmental policy:

- pre-regulation private common-law era;
- public-law era; and
- market-based, co-operative, and comprehensive instruments.[8]

1. The Common-Law Period

Canadians have always had some legal recourse against environmental degradation through the property rights provisions of the English **common law** tradition. The property rights provisions that have been used to address environmental pollution fall into three categories. Two of these categories, 'trespass' and 'nuisance', cover offences against the rights of property owners generally; the third covers violations of riparian rights specifically (the special rights enjoyed by those who own or occupy land along the shore of a river or lake).

In the broadest sense, the word 'trespass' may be used for any kind of offence, sin, or violation, but in property law **trespass** refers specifically to intrusion on private property. As one judge explained, 'every invasion of private property, be it ever so minute, is a trespass.'[9] Landowners and even tenants have used trespass law to protect their property against lumber mill sawdust, fluorides from aluminum plants, and pesticide spray.

Less direct invasions of private property, such as smoke, steam, or fumes, are covered by **nuisance law**. A nuisance in legal terms is something that interferes with the use or enjoyment of private property. Property owners have used nuisance law to challenge everything from the use of road salt to leaking oil tanks.

Finally, the common law entitles riparians to, among other things, 'the natural flow of water beside or through their land, without any significant change in the quantity or purity of the water'. Unlike regular property rights, **riparian rights** can be exercised *before* any damage has been done—all that is required is a reasonable expectation of damage. Thus, riparian rights have been used to prevent the pollution of water by coal mine discharges and industrial effluents such as pulp and paper mill wastes. As recently as 1970 a riparian in Sudbury, Ontario, went to court to prevent a speedboat regatta on a small lake on the grounds that 60 racing boats would contaminate the water. The judge issued an order forbidding the race.

Given these powerful tools, one might ask why Canada's lakes and rivers have not been better protected against contamination by industrial effluents, municipal waste, and so on. Are property owners not willing to go to the courts to claim their property rights? No. The truth is that successive governments and various courts have eroded and limited Canadians' environmental property rights and allowed the pollution of Canadian waters.

The riparian, trespass, and nuisance laws available to Canadians had their origins and precedents in British common law. Property rights were protected in medieval times, when one could bring a suit against a neighbour for his barking hounds or for damage resulting from his use of his own land. The law was extended in 1705 when William Aldred brought an action against his neighbour for building a pig sty adjacent to Aldred's house. In English law, the definition of 'property' includes not only physical attributes and productive capacity, but rights and duties, privileges, and obligations— for instance, the obligation not to pollute your neighbour's air or water. The Aldred case illustrated that for a nuisance suit to be successful, the plaintiff must prove that the defendant was under a duty to take care. The case in Canada that provided the most authoritative ruling on this issue was *Groat v. Edmonton* (1928), in which the Groat family objected to the city of Edmonton's practice of discharging sewage into a ravine crossing their land. The court ruled that the quality of water had changed as a result of this practice and that this constituted an infringement on the plaintiff's riparian rights. The ruling made the principle clear: 'Pollution is always unlawful and, in itself, constitutes a nuisance.'[10]

In the absence of zoning regulations, nuisance laws were used to force industries such as soap-making, brewing, and brick-making out of neighbourhoods that were disturbed by their presence. Such industries did not close down, however; they simply moved away to places where the neighbours did not complain. In this way areas were created that tolerated polluting industries. This was fine until the Industrial Revolution sparked dramatic increases in pollution and population alike. In response to industrialization, private property rights were eroded in favour of industry. This was possible, as Joel Brenner explains, because

> the legislature, the courts, and substantial segments of the public . . . were anxious not to burden industry with damage actions. A deterioration of the quality of water and air and higher noise levels were prices they were willing to pay.[11]

Governments encouraged judges to accept what John McClaren, writing in the 1970s, described as 'the facile argument, often used by defendants, that pollution abatement equals economic ruin'.[12] Ontario began eroding riparian property rights in 1885 when the provincial legislature passed a law specifically to limit the courts' ability to protect an individual whose property was being polluted by an upstream sawmill. Citing the public interest, the government ordered that the courts consider the economic importance of the lumber trade before issuing injunctions against a sawmill. In short, the government decided that the public good in terms of economic activity and jobs outweighed a private individual's right to the use of the local river. This was in keeping with British law at the time, which held that one could sue a neighbour for polluting one's property so long as the activity in question was undertaken for private purposes; one could *not* sue, however, if the neighbour's activity provided jobs or services for the town. There evolved a double standard whereby something deemed a nuisance if one person benefited became acceptable if a larger group benefited. As a result, 'strict nuisance liability would apply to John Doe down the street, but Doe Manufacturing Co. Ltd. would be judged by a more lenient rule.'[13] As the judge in the case said:

> where great works have been created and carried on, and are the means of developing the national wealth, you must not stand on extreme rights and allow a person to say, 'I will bring an action against you for this and that, and so on.' Business could not go on if it were so.[14]

Once cases like this one began to set precedents, it became increasingly unlikely that an industrial town would enforce nuisance laws, and as a result fewer and fewer individual property owners bothered taking their grievances to court. One reason was the cost of such action; another was the requirement that the socioeconomic character of the neighbourhood be taken into account when evaluating the nuisance. This double standard was further extended by the 1874 British Alkali Act, according to which any attempt to regulate industrial pollution had to take into account the type of industry involved. If the industry was highly profitable and the cost of preventing pollution relatively low, then the company could be forced to bear that cost. If, on the other hand, the industry's profits were relatively low and the cost of preventing pollution was high, then the damage would be borne by the victims.[15] This perverse incentive system guaranteed the persistence of air and water pollution. It punishes profitable companies who pollute less than losing companies who pollute a lot. Why would any business invest in cleaner technology, even if that would make it more profitable, when it could plod along making small profits and polluting at will?

In Canada, even when a group or individual did succeed in getting the courts to agree that the pollution caused by an industry was injurious, the government would step in and make certain that the industry continued despite the cost to the environment and the violation of individual rights. In 1944, the Kalamazoo Vegetable Parchment Company (KVP) opened a paper mill on the Spanish River in northern Ontario. At the time, the Spanish River was a tourist destination with clean water and enough game fish to support both a sport fishery and commercial fishing interests. Once the mill began production, however, several tonnes of wood fibres and chemicals were released into the Spanish River.

The problem with the wood fibres was not only their volume—up to five tonnes a day—but the fact that they were chemically impregnated. Discharged into the river, they would accumulate in the riverbed where they developed into large spongy masses. Eventually these masses formed gases that forced them to rise to the top and float downstream. When the masses of pulp—some as large as 10 feet across—broke loose, they released a foul odour, similar to that of rotten cabbage, that could be detected all the way into Georgian Bay. Even in winter, when ice was cut near the mouth of the river, the smell would be overwhelming. In the 1940s ice was used for refrigeration, and the ice harvested from the region was filled with black foreign matter. The water was unfit for drinking, cooking, or washing, and when it was heated the vapours were too strong for anyone to remain in the house. Nor were humans the only species affected. Before the pulp mill, wild rice grew near the river's mouth, which was a feeding ground for ducks. That habitat was lost, as was the use of water for farm animals or agricultural purposes.[16]

When a fisherman, a farmer, and several tourist operators sued KVP, claiming that the plant violated their property rights and was destroying their businesses, the judge ruled in their favour, stating that the people who live along rivers have common-law property rights to clean water and that no industry was allowed to alter the water's character in any way. He issued an injunction and warned that unless the company cleaned up its practices it would have to close. The provincial government, however, was determined to save KVP and the jobs it provided. Therefore, it amended the law to require that the courts consider the economic importance of a polluting pulp mill before shutting it down. With this amendment KVP went to the Supreme Court of Canada and asked to have the injunction reconsidered. While the higher court ruled that the injunction should stand, that was not the end of the story.

2. The Public-Law Era

The fight between KVP and the riparians coincided with a change in thinking within governments generally. Now politicians argued that the courts' reluctance to enter into issues of the common good made it necessary for the government to take on a greater regulatory role. In fact, however, the Ontario government's definition of the common good in the case of KVP and the Spanish River was at odds with the courts' definition. After an intense lobbying effort KVP found two prominent politicians—one a Liberal MP, the other the Tory provincial member for the area—to exert their influence on the company's behalf. In addition to this political support, the company had the back-ing not only of local Aboriginal bands, many of whose members worked in its bush camps, but of other corporations in the region, such as Inco and Falconbridge. In the end, the provincial legislature passed a law dissolving the court's injunction. In this case at least, it was not the courts' failure to act that caused the government to enter the regulatory arena, but the government's desire to define the public good in terms of employment rather than the environment. As the attorney general at the time said,

'The development of the North Country depends upon industry, and we cannot allow industry to close down.'[17]

This episode points to the powerful political and economic incentives that can lead governments to favour private interests, even when their activities are harmful to the environment. In many instances, however, government itself is the problem. As John Swaigen argued in 1981:

> We needn't look far to find the reasons our current legislation and policies have failed to solve current problems and anticipate new ones. The legislation is largely symbolic. It says 'Thou shalt not pollute' but fails to back this pronouncement with effective enforcement mechanisms. Governments give themselves sweeping powers to restrict pollution and development, and broad discretion to use those powers. Then they proceed to 'bargain' with polluters over how—if at all —these powers [are] to be exercised.[18]

From a public choice perspective, it is not always in the government's interest to protect the environment. Among the most compelling pressures governments face in any jurisdiction is the demand for jobs. As a consequence, governments are often reluctant to confront industries that are sources of pollution. Faced with a choice between jobs and clean water, for instance, governments have typically protected the jobs in the name of the common good. After all, fish don't vote, and the people who eke out a living fishing or running tourist operations are relatively few compared with the numbers of workers who could benefit from industrial jobs. Since jobs translate into votes, and it is in the interests of governments to attract as many votes as possible, jobs win, even if the jobs that attract those votes are temporary, expensive, or harmful to the environment.

In the case of the Spanish River, what the government did was transfer the costs of industrial pollution to the victims rather than the company that produced it. As long as the negative consequences were apparently limited to a handful of plaintiffs (who received some monetary compensation), the political costs of the government's choice were low. Elizabeth Brubaker summed up the government's failure to protect the common good of the environment as follows:

> Once a government has authorized an activity, those affected by it lose their rights to sue. Parliament, in its wisdom, has overridden the common law. It has replaced legal decisions with political decisions. In other words, it has removed decision-making power from those affected by pollution, and placed that power securely in the hands of politicians and bureaucrats.[19]

At the same time it is important to remember that, regardless of which body (political or judicial) makes the rules, it is up to the society to demand that they be enforced. As Murray Rankin and Peter Finkle point out, there is more to the law than what they call 'black letter' legislation: Public expectation also helps determine which rules will be observed:

Like other areas of law, environmental law might be viewed as a process which is reflected not only in the prescription of the legislation and the decisions of courts, but also in the mutual expectations aroused in the public, the industry and the relevant levels of government by the behaviour which surrounds the law.[20]

Only when the environment becomes so toxic as to pose an immediate threat to the society, or the society becomes affluent enough that it can afford to consider things other than jobs, does the public at large recognize the damage. With public recognition the government will take remedial action (though it tends to choose the least expensive option). In the 1980s the International Joint Commission, established in 1909 to monitor Canada–US boundary waters, identified 43 areas of concern around the Great Lakes, 17 of them in Ontario. The lower Spanish River and its river mouth were one area of concern.[21] As a result, the federal and provincial governments agreed to work together to develop clean-up programs called remedial action plans (RAPs). The RAP team, consisting of water-quality specialists from federal and provincial agencies, identified the extent and causes of pollution within the lower Spanish River and at its entrance into the North Channel of Lake Huron, and proposed a clean-up program. As a result, the Spanish River is once again fit for swimming, fishing, and recreational activities. Due to the improved technology, the Spanish River also remains an important resource for the pulp and paper industry. Domtar's Eddy Specialty Papers is developing a state-of-the-art environmentally responsible pulp and paper mill, and the company supports Friends of the Spanish River projects.[22] As society becomes richer— often as a result of industrialization—public attitudes tend to evolve to a point where pollution is no longer acceptable, even to industry.

Getting and Staying on the Agenda

In 1990 a public opinion poll found that nearly a quarter of Canadians named the environment as the most pressing issue facing the country. This was widely heralded as a breakthrough for environmental awareness. Less than a year later, however, the proportion of respondents naming the environment as their greatest concern had fallen below 5 per cent. Economic recession weighed too heavily on the minds of most Canadians for them to give more than a passing thought to the environment. Pollsters who only a year earlier had made statements like 'The Greening of Canada has almost reached the state of a social movement'[23] were suddenly pontificating on the shallowness of public concern with the environment and Canadians' unwillingness to put the environment before jobs and the state of the economy.

The truth is that public concern over the environment has seldom been very great. Brief bursts of attention triggered by ecological disasters have been separated by long stretches of indifference (see Figure 11.1). The only time the environment has topped the list of priorities since 1990 was in the winter of 2006–7. Indeed, even in the 1960s surveys showed that Canadians seldom identified issues such as conservation or pollution as pressing national concerns.

FIGURE 11.1 Percentage of Canadians Naming the Environment/Pollution as the Most Important Problem Facing the Country, 1978–2010

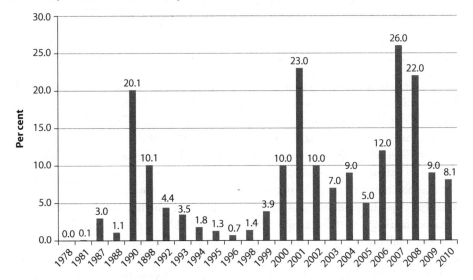

Sources: Based on various surveys from the CORA database, Gallup Report, Ipsos, Nanos, and Strategic Counsel asking Canadians 'What is the most important issue facing the country?' Results indicate the percentage naming 'the environment', 'pollution', 'global warming', or 'Kyoto'.

Moreover, the various groups in favour of 'conservation' were far from united in their goals. As Glen Toner observes, 'Conservationism has been and still is characterized by an internal tension between the wise use or management of resources and the preservation of wilderness areas.'[24] Business-oriented groups like the Canadian Forestry Association understood 'conservation' in terms of responsible harvesting of renewable natural resources (the fact that Canada's forestry industry had a pitiful reforestation record is another matter). For others, however, 'conservation' meant making wilderness areas off-limits to commercial exploitation of any kind.

Where the two factions agreed was in defining the environmental problem in terms of human activity. The preservation of species and their habitats and how best to exploit natural resources were the key issues in this first phase of environmentalism. Most in the conservation movement paid virtually no attention to questions about values, the lifestyles of affluent societies, or the practices of industrial capitalism. Many of the issues that have been at the centre of environmentalism over the last few decades—overpopulation, industrial pollution, toxic chemicals, climate change, modern agricultural practices, to mention only a few—were entirely absent from the earlier phase of the movement.

What happened to transform environmentalism from an issue with very low political visibility into the stuff of headlines and speeches by political leaders? What explains the metamorphosis that took place in the concerns and character of the environmental movement in the 1960s? John Kingdon's model of the agenda-setting process suggests some answers. According to Kingdon, there are three streams that must come together for a given issue to move onto the political agenda: problems, policies, and politics.[25]

1. Problems

A dramatic event or imminent crisis is often the trigger for increased public awareness of some condition. The 1960s brought a cluster of such events and dark forebodings of more to come. A couple of major oil spills (one in the English Channel and the other off the coast at Santa Barbara, California), the spectacle of fire on the oily Cuyahoga River at Cleveland, reports that the lower Great Lakes were 'dead', and evidence of mercury accumulation in the bodies of fish and other animals were among the factors that combined to raise the public's awareness of environmental problems. At the same time, the dire predictions of the British economist Thomas Malthus (1766–1834) about population growth began to be taken seriously. The world's population increased by about 1 billion, or 40 per cent, between 1950 and 1970, and was expected to reach some 7 billion by the year 2000 (it fell a bit short of this predicted level). This spawned fears that the problems of malnutrition and famine in developing countries would be exacerbated and that the world's cities, growing even more rapidly than the global population, would be unable to cope with the strains on their physical infrastructure, economies, and social systems. *The Population Bomb*, the title of a book by biologist Paul Ehrlich,[26] and the Club of Rome's apocalyptic predictions of global collapse in *The Limits to Growth*[27] were among the more prominent alarms that a population crisis was imminent.

These were conditions that could not be ignored. Together, their magnitude and the fact they catapulted to the centre of public attention almost simultaneously in the mid- to late 1960s made it inevitable that the environment would be defined as a problem requiring government action. At the same time the predominant character of environmental concern was transformed as the focus was redirected from conservation to the physical and social costs of industrial society and by Malthusian fears of global scarcity. These concerns reflected a far more sweeping conception of 'the environment', one that called for a much broader range of government action.

2. Policies

Even before the attention of policy-makers and the public was captured by what some interpreted as the portents of eco-catastrophe, a body of specialized knowledge had accumulated on pollution, population growth, industrial chemicals, and the other items on the new environmental agenda. The most prominent example, of course, was Rachel Carson's exposé of the environmental contamination caused by chemicals used in industry and agriculture.

It is important to realize that the data in *Silent Spring* were not new. Carson drew on scientific studies that were already on the public record—in many cases they had been carried out by agencies and departments of government. Her book was instrumental in bringing that research to the attention of the public and policy-makers, but it is unlikely that *Silent Spring, The Population Bomb, The Limits to Growth*, or any of the other specialist-written advocacy books of the era would have pushed environmental issues toward the centre of the political agenda without the cluster of consciousness-raising events discussed previously or without the political changes that were unfolding at the same time.

Environmental issues were kept on the agenda by the public institutions and private organizations spawned during the first wave of environmentalism. In the United States, the National Environmental Protection Act (NEPA) became law in early 1970 and the Environmental Protection Agency (EPA) was created a few months later. The NEPA required all federal agencies to prepare a 'detailed environmental statement to accompany proposals for legislation and other major federal actions significantly affecting the quality of the human environment'.[28] This 'action-forcing' mechanism acquired enormous significance in the hands of environmental groups, providing them with a legally enforceable lever to challenge all sorts of development projects. Other legislative measures spawned by the first wave of environmental concern in the United States included amendments to the Clean Air Act (1970), with timetables for compliance and specifications regarding the pollutants to be reduced and the percentages of the reductions required; the Federal Environment Pesticide Control Act of 1972; and the Federal Water Pollution Control Act Amendments of 1972. All these laws were administered by the newly created EPA, which became a sort of 'super-agency' whose authority cut across more conventional policy fields. Similar institutions were established in many American states, some of which (notably California) imposed far greater restrictions on polluters than did federal regulations.

In Canada the Department of the Environment was created in 1970. It acquired responsibility for those resource management programs previously administered by other departments like energy, mines and resources, fisheries, and transport. But the goals set down in the department's enabling legislation went beyond these traditional conservation functions to include pollution control, assessment of the environmental impacts of development projects, facilitation of federal–provincial co-operation in environmental projects, and public education. A number of environmental laws were passed at the beginning of the 1970s, including the Canada Water Act and Arctic Waters Pollution Act in 1970 and the federal Clean Air Act in 1971.

3. Politics

The new environmentalism that emerged in the 1960s focused on issues and proposed reforms that challenged some values and institutions that previously had been taken for granted by all but a few. Belching smokestacks and the murky lagoons and rivers near factories might not be pretty, but they were seen as signs of economic prosperity. Sprawling highways, dams for hydroelectric power and irrigation, the herbicides and pesticides that made possible enormous increases in agricultural yields, denuded forests, a 'right' to cheap petroleum, and plastics adapted to all sorts of new uses were among the many phenomena that constituted the socially dominant idea of progress in the post–World War II years of steady economic growth.

The unprecedented affluence produced by post-war expansion—in the developed capitalist world, at least—nurtured a generation of people for whom what have been called 'post-materialist' values had political appeal.[29] Accustomed to material affluence, more educated than their fathers and mothers, and the first generation to be raised in the 'global village' created by electronic mass communications, those who entered adulthood during the 1960s tended to espouse less materialistic values than their predecessors had. Ronald Inglehart labelled this the 'silent revolution'. 'The values of Western publics', he argued, 'have been shifting from an overwhelming emphasis on material well-being and physical security toward greater emphasis on the quality of life.'[30] Among those post-materialist values was a concern for environmental beauty. (In Inglehart's survey of Americans, this item read 'Protect nature from pollution', but in the other nine countries where his study was conducted the question referred to 'More beautiful cities and countryside'.)

In fact, Inglehart found only a weak and somewhat ambiguous relationship between attitudes regarding environmental beauty and the other values that made up the post-materialist cluster.[31] Nonetheless, many have argued that the environmental movement of the 1960s and the 'green parties' that arrived on the political scene in Western Europe in the late 1970s have their roots in the post-materialist value system. For example, Glen Toner maintains that 'the first wave of environmentalism was related to the broader counterculture critique of materialist-industrial society of the late 1960s and early 1970s.'[32] Jurg Steiner observes that the 'Greens are united in their emphasis on postmaterial values.'[33] If the post-materialist argument is correct, the emergence of the environment as an important political issue during the 1960s was facilitated by a more receptive climate of public opinion than had existed in the past. Politics—in this case the value shifts occurring in so-called post-industrial societies—helped push this issue onto the agenda.

Even so, public concern over the state of the environment waned somewhat during the mid-1970s. One reason was probably the sense of economic insecurity that was rapidly spreading throughout most industrialized democracies. Indeed, it became common to speak of the 'crisis' of capitalism, the decline of the US-dominated post-war economic order, and the ungovernability of modern democracies. Developments such as the OPEC oil embargo of 1973, rampant inflation and mounting unemployment during the late 1970s, the recession of the early 1980s, and the loss of manufacturing jobs to Japan and the low-wage NICs (newly industrializing countries) conspired to push environmental issues to the margins of public attention and down the scale of government priorities.

Two other factors likely also contributed to the waning of public attention to environmental issues. First, the imminent disaster predicted by Ehrlich and others had not come true—the 'population bomb' had not exploded after all, and fertility rates in both the developed and developing worlds were beginning to decline. (Today, while the global population is still expected to grow, revised estimates suggest that by 2200 it will stabilize at around 10 billion people; see Figure 11.2.) Second, environmentalism actually came under attack in the United States with the election in 1980 of the Reagan administration, which saw environmental regulation as just another instance of excessive government interference in the market.

FIGURE 11.2 World Population Growth, Projected to 2150 (in billions)

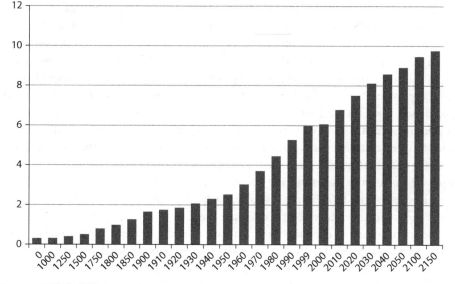

Source: © United Nations.

In any event, environmental issues kept a low profile for about a decade, from the mid-1970s to the mid-1980s, despite a series of ecological disasters and near-disasters. Miscarriages and deformities caused by the toxic waste dump at Love Canal in Niagara Falls, in New York; the accident at the Three Mile Island nuclear generation plant in Pennsylvania; accumulating scientific evidence on atmospheric damage caused by chlorofluorocarbons (CFCs); a number of major oil spills throughout the world; the derailment of tanker cars carrying deadly chlorine and the evacuation of 225,000 people from Mississauga, Ontario; lakes and forests ravaged by acid rain—the list of internationally publicized eco-crises was long. Incidents and developments like these certainly captured the public's attention, but except in a few places like West Germany (where a major recycling effort was launched in 1979 and the Green Party elected members to parliament for the first time in 1983) the concern they generated was well below the levels seen during the previous decade.

Despite the relatively low political profile of environmental issues, however, the environment's place on the policy agendas of industrialized democracies was secure for two reasons. First, environmentalism no longer meant simply nature conservation. Issues such as overpopulation, pollution, industrial and agricultural chemicals, and nuclear power were matters of direct concern to industrial society and the sustainability of human activities in the face of the 'limits to growth'. Conservation was still part of the agenda, but environmentalism had been reconceptualized as something far broader and of greater immediate relevance to the lives and lifestyles of urbanized societies.

Second, the evidence of environmental deterioration had reached a point where it could no longer be ignored. Quite simply, the magnitude of some of the problems on the environmental agenda—air and water pollution, the accumulation of toxic wastes, deforestation, soil erosion, population pressures—had never been greater, and all indications predicted that they would quickly become worse. The Club of Rome's pessimistic bestseller, *The Limits to Growth*, helped to publicize the idea, well known to specialists, that growth is often an *exponential process*. A quantity (accumulated garbage, toxic chemicals, human population, or whatever) that grows exponentially increases by a constant percentage over a given time period. The significance of exponential growth may be seen in Figure 11.2, which shows the increase in the earth's population since the beginning of the Common Era and projects it into the future. A constant rate of growth will, in the early stages, produce small increases in the total size of a given quantity, but eventually a point will be reached where the increase in the absolute size of the quantity becomes much sharper. The curve that plots the increased size of the quantity appears to 'take off', rising steeply. The 'take-off' stage had clearly been reached by the 1960s in the case of many factors believed to threaten the environment and, ultimately, the viability of human life.

The implications of exponential growth were finally brought home to laypersons when overflowing landfills had to be closed and waste disposal became a critical problem for many cities; when several unusually warm years during the 1980s served to popularize the concept of the 'greenhouse effect' (i.e., global warming as a result of accumulating carbon dioxide emissions); and when rapidly accumulating CFCs appeared to be eating holes in the atmosphere's ozone layer, thereby letting in more of the ultraviolet rays that can cause skin cancer and eye cataracts. The gloomy predictions of the Club of Rome once again attracted public attention in the 1980s, and this time they could not be marginalized or dismissed as alarmist because now they were coming true.

As in the United States, the first wave of environmentalism bequeathed to Canada a legacy of new agencies and laws intended to regulate activities affecting the environment. These institutions remained in place after the public concern responsible for their creation had faded. Even when they were not terribly effective in achieving their ostensible goals—which, according to environmental activists, was most of the time—they helped to keep environmental issues on the policy agenda by virtue of their existence and ongoing activities. Environmentalism had become institutionalized in the politics of Canada and other advanced capitalist societies as a result of government responses to the movement's first wave.

While Canadian governments continued to express their support for the goals of environmentalism, their actions spoke louder than their words. The position of Minister of the Environment continued to be a very junior cabinet post, a stepping-stone up or down in one's career, but hardly a power base. Until the appointment of Lucien Bouchard to the portfolio in 1989, no environment minister had ever been a member of the influential Cabinet Committee on Priorities and Planning. As Ottawa's finances worsened, Environment Canada became one of the chief targets for cuts, even though its budget was already comparatively small. The Progressive Conservative government in November 1984 announced a $46 million reduction in spending for Environment Canada, a rollback of about 6 per cent, when its Task Force on Program Review recommended cuts of about $40 million over the years 1985–9.[34] Although cuts were recommended and implemented in other policy fields as well, it was clear that environmental issues did not have the public prominence, nor the political clout, to protect these programs from the Treasury Board's scalpel.

No single development turned things around for environmentalists. Instead, a cluster of eco-events during the latter half of the 1980s refocused world attention on the vulnerability of the environment and humankind to human activities, just as oil spills, toxic chemicals, and fears of overpopulation had a decade and a half earlier. These events included the chemical leak at a Union Carbide plant in Bhopal, India, that killed over 10,000 people and maimed hundreds of thousands more (1984); the discovery of a hole in the ozone layer over Antarctica (1985); the partial meltdown of the nuclear reactor at Chernobyl (1986); a mounting crisis of 'homeless' garbage; unusually warm temperatures, droughts, and other climatic changes that many scientists attributed to the 'greenhouse effect'; the rapid deforestation of the Amazon (and, for that matter, other parts of the world's tropical and temperate forests); and the massive oil spill of the *Exxon Valdez* off the coast of Alaska. By the time the twentieth anniversary of Earth Day arrived in 1990, the environment was once again at the centre of public attention.

By the end of the 1980s environmentalism had acquired what seemed to be an unstoppable momentum. The United Nations World Commission on Environment and Development issued its report, *Our Common Future*, in 1987, and suddenly the term **sustainable development** was heard everywhere. The Montreal Protocol on Substances that Deplete the Ozone Layer, an international agreement to limit and eventually phase out the production of CFCs, was signed in 1987. The following year, in the wake of some of the most blistering summers on record, the Toronto Conference on the Changing Atmosphere called for a 'comprehensive international framework that can address the interrelated problems of the global atmosphere'. International pressure mounted on Brazil and some other tropical states to limit deforestation. 'Green parties' and environmental interest groups enjoyed a resurgence, and the 'greening' of business—businesses tailoring their products, production processes, and marketing to the environmentally conscious consumer—became widespread. The world's nations set their sights on the 1992 Earth Summit, the United Nations Conference on Environment and Development, held in Brazil.

In Canada the signs of environmentalism's ascendance were everywhere. Ontario introduced 'blue box' recycling in 1985. The media were bristling with reports of conflicts between industry and environmentalists over old-growth forests like those of Temagami (Ontario) and South Moresby (BC), pollution by pulp and paper companies, global warming, toxic chemicals, mountains of garbage, and other eco-stories. 'Can we save this planet?' was the headline of a *Globe and Mail* special report that ran to several pages.[35] Southam papers ran a series of articles on the environment in the autumn of 1990, including the results of a specially commissioned Environics poll on the environment. George Hoberg calculates that the number of stories on the environment in Canadian newspapers ranged from 600 to 800 per year between 1983 and 1988, but exploded to about 1300 in 1989.[36] Television documentaries on environmental issues were chock-a-block during 1989–90, when media coverage of these matters peaked.

Governments responded to the undeniable evidence of public concern with policies. Consultations among industry, environmental groups, and the government began in 1986, marking an important shift in policy-making style in this policy sector. Ottawa's 1989 decision to phase out leaded gasoline was a (belated) response to undeniable evidence of lead's toxic effects. Amidst much ballyhoo Ottawa introduced its Green Plan in 1990, earmarking $3 billion over five years to the policies it comprised. Environmental assessments and delays of major development projects became standard, and Ottawa introduced a new environmental assessment law in 1990. Similar developments were unfolding in many of the provinces.

But then the environmental bandwagon stalled, its momentum slowed by the economic recession that deepened in 1990–1. The polls showing enormous public concern over environmental problems looked like a statistical blip by 1991 as the percentage of Canadians naming the environment as the most important issue facing Canada fell back to the very modest levels of the late 1970s and early 1980s. The explanation appeared to be simple enough: Anxiety over the state of the economy had eclipsed the public's fears about the deteriorating environment, the implication being that economic recovery would be accompanied by a recovery of public attention to environmental issues. Perhaps, but the vertiginous rise of public concern over the environment and the even more precipitous fall in the public prominence of this issue certainly said more about the media's influence on the public agenda and the fickleness of public opinion than about the deeply rooted values of Canadians. If environmental issues could be pushed to the margin of public attention so quickly by economic recession, the confident talk about a revolution in public attitudes was certainly premature.

The same trend has occurred more recently. While the environment was at the top of the agenda in 2007, it has fallen in direct proportion to increased concerns over the economic crisis. Not only was Canada in a relatively positive economic position in 2007, but the media, governments, and even Hollywood focused attention on climate change at that time. Al Gore, former US vice-president and presidential candidate, had always been considered a politician who championed the environment, first with his 1992 book *Earth in the Balance* and then with his award-winning documentary *An Inconvenient Truth*. Whether Gore led the parade or got swept up with it is beside the point. The important thing is that at the start of the millennium there was a growing consensus that climate change was happening, that people were the cause of it, and that something had to be done. This consensus could only come to fruition when the media, politicians, and the public are all part of it. Certainly the dramatic events of Hurricane Katrina and media reports suggesting that the 2005 hurricane season was a harbinger of things to come helped to focus government and public attention on the issue. However, that consensus has shifted toward concern over other pressing issues—namely the economy.

Environmental Policies in Canada

When the federal Task Force on Program Review undertook a one-time inventory of government programs in 1985, it identified 34 that fell under the authority of the Minister of the Environment. The range of these programs was broad. They included the heritage and conservation activities of Parks Canada; climatic, meteorological, and air quality monitoring and research; environmental assessment; activities relating to toxic chemicals, commercial and industrial chemicals, and waste management; flood control and water quality programs; wildlife conservation and public education.[37] Together, these activities accounted for $766.5 million in spending, or less than 1 per cent of the federal budget. By 1992 Environment Canada's budget had risen to $1135.5 million, which was still less than 1 per cent of Ottawa's total spending. This, it must be said, was *after* the federal government's much trumpeted Green Plan, which promised to add $3 billion over five years to the environment budget. Since 2000, the environment ministry's budget has averaged about 2.6 per cent of total federal expenditure. While this is not a huge increase, it does represent a doubling of efforts from 1990 to 2000. Total spending on the environment for the federal government in 2010 was 3.4 per cent of total spending. It must be kept in mind, however, that the budget of Environment Canada provides only a partial picture of Ottawa's environmental spending; many environmental programs fall under the authority of other departments. For example, the Department of Fisheries and Oceans administers the Total Allowable Catch program, the Canadian Climate Program, the Canadian Global Change Program, and the Fisheries Resource Conservation Council; the Canadian International Development Agency requires environmental impact assessments for projects that it finances; and the Canadian Forest Service generates numerous programs that are targeted at environmental management, such as reforestation through Tree Plan Canada.

The federal government has maintained that the decentralization of responsibility for environmental policy is a strength. The environment, the 1991 Green Plan argued, 'must be a forethought, not an afterthought, in decision-making throughout the government'[38]—a position that appears to be consistent with the philosophy and recommendations of the Brundtland Commission. On the other hand, some argue that parcelling out authority among numerous departments and agencies—to say nothing of the intergovernmental division of authority regarding environmental matters—means that there is no central agency to deal with environmental issues. In 1990, David Israelson quoted Harold Harvey, a biologist and acid rain activist who had worked for the Department of Fisheries in the 1960s: 'there were three layers of bureaucrats between me and the deputy minister [in the 1960s]. Since that time, they've added another eleven.'[39] Israelson, a one-time environmental writer for the *Toronto Star*, agreed that the bureaucracy of environmental policy-making is a problem, arguing that ministers and senior officials are often more concerned with protecting their turf and taking credit for programs than they are with the problems that these programs are ostensibly intended to address.[40] If the responsibility for environmental policy continues to be dispersed among several departments and agencies, and the Green Plan initiatives and budget are doled out among them, this almost certainly has more to do with jealous bureaucracies and cabinet ministers than it does with a rational strategy for managing environmental issues.

In some circumstances process may be policy. The dispersion of authority for environmental matters across agencies and departments of the federal government may reasonably be interpreted as a major aspect of federal environmental policy. But whereas the government's official explanation is that decentralization ensures that all parts of the administrative machine are sensitive to environmental concerns, there is another possible—perhaps more plausible—interpretation of the policy significance of this process. When the environment is the responsibility of many agencies and departments whose programs and clienteles *do not* have environmental protection as their chief concern, this may be the same as admitting that the environment is a second-rate policy issue. How likely is it that environmental concerns will trump the other interests and objectives of a well-established department like agriculture, energy, mines and resources, or transport? To this one might respond that the idea is not to 'trump' other legitimate policy goals but simply to ensure that environmental concerns are adequately taken into account. Yet, in the absence of either incentives that provide bureaucrats and their political masters with clear pay-offs for doing so or coercive measures requiring them to do so, it seems more reasonable to expect that the environmental implications of policies and programs will usually take a distant back seat to other considerations.

On the other hand, it cannot be assumed that a more centralized system of environmental policy-making automatically shifts the balance of interests in favour of environmental concerns. In the United States, the setting and enforcement of environmental regulations is chiefly in the hands of the EPA. During its first decade of operation it seemed that the EPA was indeed a sort of environmental super-agency whose authority cut across the interests and jurisdictions of other parts of the bureaucracy. This changed, however, with the 1980 election of Ronald Reagan to the White House. It quickly became apparent that the powers of the EPA could be reined in by a determined executive. Budget cuts, the choice of agency director, and changes to the EPA's enforcement policy combined to reduce its stature as environmental watchdog. It is not clear, therefore, that centralizing environmental authority in a single agency necessarily elevates the status of environmental concerns over what it is under a more decentralized system of environmental policy-making.

A fair picture of environmental policies in Canada must cover all three levels of government. Indeed, authority over some of the most important environmental matters, including waste management, conservation and recycling, electrical power, forest management, and industrial pollution, lies chiefly in the hands of provincial and local governments. Although a full account of what governments in Canada do in the name of environmental policy is beyond the scope of this chapter, we will examine some of the major issues of recent years: environmental assessment, pollution, and transboundary environmental problems.

1. Environmental Assessment

The term 'environmental assessment' refers to the effort to identify the consequences that a development is likely to have on the environment. The 'environment' in question is usually understood to be the natural one, but sometimes is defined to include social and cultural effects as well. Environmental assessments are carried out by all levels of government. At the local level, zoning bylaws and other land-use planning regulations constitute a form of environmental assessment. Exemptions from these regulations require special approval by a committee of adjustment, a process that typically involves public hearings and consideration of how an exemption would affect the land-use goals that underlie existing regulations. Any major urban project—a sports complex, a convention centre, waterfront development, a new shopping mall, a highway—is certain to be examined for its effects on things such as local traffic, storm and sanitary sewers, and the character of the surrounding area.

In some provinces, impact studies are required by law for projects and activities that are to be undertaken by departments or agencies of the province or that will take place on land that falls under provincial control. Examples of such projects include dams, pipelines, electricity transmission corridors, landfills, garbage incinerators, or new mining or logging operations on Crown lands. It should be emphasized that provincial laws are very uneven. In some provinces environmental assessment is not required by law and occurs only when political pressures force the government's hand. Ontario's environmental assessment law requires that the social and cultural effects of projects be taken into account, along with the expected impacts on the natural environment. Even in those provinces where environmental impact studies and public hearings are required, environmentalists often charge that their concerns are typically brushed aside by economic and political considerations. For instance, BC's Ministry of Forests Act and Forest Act require that a number of uses and values be considered in managing that province's forests. Critics maintain that the impact assessments and public hearings carried out in compliance with this legislation do more to legitimize timber industry interests than to protect rival claims on the BC wilderness.[41]

Federally, a formal environmental assessment process has been in place since 1973. Following the American lead, Ottawa introduced the Environmental Assessment and Review Process (EARP) as a cabinet directive to departments and agencies. But unlike the NEPA passed in the United States, EARP did not impose non-discretionary duties on the federal government. The fact that EARP was not embodied in law meant that its legal status was questionable. In 1984 the original EARP cabinet directive was replaced by a Guidelines Order issued under the authority of the Government Organization Act. Although this order spelled out quite clearly the scope of its application and the process of environmental assessment, it remained unclear whether the new guidelines were legally binding on the federal government. Critics believed they were not. The issue was resolved, however, by a series of court decisions between 1989 and 1991. Three Federal Court rulings determined that the 1984 EARP Guidelines Order had the status of law and must be complied with in matters coming under Ottawa's jurisdiction.[42] Indeed, a 1991 decision of the Federal Court ruled that the government could not, by Order in Council, exempt a project from environmental assessment required by EARP. Any doubt was removed when a 1992 Supreme Court decision ruled that EARP was legally binding. Under the Canadian Environmental Assessment Act, passed by the Liberal government in 1994 and amended in 2003 to improve the review process, the Canadian Environmental Assessment Agency is assigned responsibility for the assessment function.

The scope and process of federal environmental impact assessment are similar to those at the provincial level. Federal guidelines require that projects be screened for their environmental implications in cases where the federal government

- proposes a project;
- provides financial assistance to a proponent to enable a project to be carried out;
- sells, leases, or otherwise transfers control or administration of federal land to enable a project to be carried out; or
- provides a licence, permit, or an approval that is listed in the *Law List Regulations* that enables a project to be carried out.[43]

This initial screening is done by the department or agency that initiates the review process. In 90 per cent of cases, the process stops here and the project is approved, sometimes with modifications to mitigate damaging effects on the environment. In only 10 per cent of cases is a proposal sent on for further study, and only rarely will a proposal be referred to the Minister of the Environment for review by an independent environmental assessment panel, including public hearings.

According to most environmentalists, environmental assessment is not very effective. There have certainly been some spectacular failures. Foremost among these was the construction of the Rafferty and Alameda dams on the Souris River in Saskatchewan. Ottawa's approval of the project without a federally conducted assessment was successfully challenged in court by the Canadian Wildlife Federation. The federal government responded by carrying out an assessment and again approving the dams' construction. The Canadian Wildlife Federation challenged this re-approval on the grounds that the assessment process set down in EARP was not properly followed. The Federal Court agreed once more, ordering the Minister of the Environment to establish an independent review panel and hold public hearings. Ottawa complied, but in the meantime construction of the Rafferty Dam continued. At this point a major federal–provincial conflict erupted. Ottawa attempted to halt construction pending the results of its review process, while the Saskatchewan government, the province's power corporation, landowners who stood to benefit from the dams, and majority public opinion in Saskatchewan saw this as yet another case of Ottawa meddling in the affairs of the province. While all of this was happening the project was approaching completion. Ultimately, the dams were completed with very little change from the plan proposed in 1986 when the project began. Faced with powerful economic interests and a government committed to a development project, it did not appear that environmental assessment stood much of a chance.

One should not conclude, however, that nothing stands in the way of development projects with the potential to harm the environment. Environmental impact assessments may not derail such projects, but they can certainly add to their costs and lead to long construction delays. Canada is not the only country where this is the case. The head of Hamersley Iron, Australia's largest iron ore producer, recalls that in the 1960s his company was able to put in a mine, a railway, and a port and build two towns around them in western Australia, all within about 18 months. Today, he observes, it would take that long just to get approval for such a project, and then only if the company was extremely lucky![44] Canadian corporate executives tell similar stories.

2. Pollution

The first wave of environmentalism focused mainly on pollution. Oil spills; toxic chemicals in the air, water, and land; hazardous wastes and what to do about them— these were among the lightning rods of the movement. Governments responded by passing a spate of laws whose ostensible goal was the control of these polluting activities. In Canada these laws included the Clean Air Act, the Canada Water Act, the Canada Shipping Act, the Arctic Waters Pollution Prevention Act, the Environmental Contaminants Act, and amendments to the Fisheries Act, among others. The International Boundary Water Treaty Act between Canada and the United States, directed at pollution in the Great Lakes basin, was another important initiative. Provincial governments were also busy passing new pollution laws; in fact, most air and land pollution, and a good deal of water-polluting activities, fell under provincial jurisdiction.

Where Ottawa has sole jurisdiction, as in the case of federally controlled lands, the Great Lakes, or offshore waters, the federal government both establishes pollution standards and is responsible for their enforcement. Divided jurisdiction is more typical, however. Under the Clean Air Act, for example, the federal government would establish national emission standards that were not legally binding on polluters, but that were adopted by most provincial governments in establishing and enforcing air pollution regulations. Provinces rely on a permit system to regulate air and water pollution, requiring companies whose operations will release contaminants into the environment to apply for a pollution permit before starting construction and to conform to provincial guidelines once in operation.

The flexibility of these guidelines has always been notorious. Sudbury's Inco (now Vale) smelting operations, the single largest source of acid rain pollution in North America, was granted lenient extensions of the provincially set targets for reducing its sulphur dioxide emissions after these targets were first set in the 1970s. Throughout the 1980s, the *daily* amount of pollution that Inco's permit allowed was about double the amount released into the atmosphere at the peak of the Mount St. Helens volcano eruption in the state of Washington.[45] Nevertheless, Inco has invested in technology to decrease its emissions and today maintains that its objective is—'if technically and economically feasible'—to reduce its SO_2 emissions by 75 per cent over 2002 regulated levels by 2015 to comply with the Ministry of Environment Control Order.[46] It remains to be seen if Vale will use the phrase 'technically and economically feasible' as a way around compliance, however. Furthermore, even when pollution fines have been levied they have seldom been heavy enough to act as a deterrent to polluters. Dow Chemical, for example, was fined just $16,000 in 1985 after pleading guilty to the accidental release into the St. Clair River of a 'blob' of toxic dry-cleaning fluid that also contained the deadly chemical dioxin. Finally, the claim that a company has practised 'due diligence'—that is, taken reasonable care to avoid causing pollution—is an acceptable defence and makes conviction difficult.

It must also be said that governments are themselves among the worst offenders when it comes to pollution. Sewage from municipalities has long been a major source of water pollution, contributing to the eutrophication of lakes. Many municipalities, particularly in British Columbia, Quebec, and the Atlantic provinces, pour untreated waste into rivers and lakes. In other cases, treatment facilities are often old and inadequate to cope with the volume of sewage they are required to handle. Provincially owned electricity generation plants are important sources of air pollution, many of them relying on carbon dioxide–producing fossil fuels. Nuclear power, which accounts for almost half of all electrical power generated in Ontario, is relatively non-polluting while in operation. But before reaching the operating stage, a nuclear facility produces an enormous amount of carbon dioxide pollution because of all the fossil fuels used in its construction. And then, of course, there is the problem of disposing of the radioactive waste generated by a nuclear power station. Even hydroelectric power generation is not without its pollution downside. The flooding of thousands of square kilometres of land in northern Quebec has produced increased levels of lead in the fish that live in the rivers and streams and has generated greenhouse gases from the decomposition of the forests and other vegetation flooded for hydroelectric dams. One should not imagine, therefore, that private industry is the only culprit when it comes to pollution.

Notwithstanding the aforementioned serious environmental problems, it would be disingenuous to suggest that federal policies have not been effective in reducing pollution. While the federal government may have been a laggard in eliminating lead from gasoline, the effect of the policy has resulted in a 99 per cent decrease in lead in the atmosphere from 1970 to 2008. As a result of policies on sulphur emissions, sulphur dioxide levels have decreased by 96 per cent during the same period. While not as spectacular, both particulate matter and volatile organic compounds have decreased 50 per cent over the past four decades.[47] This is not to say that all our environmental problems have been solved: Ground level ozone has increased by 13 per cent from 1990 to 2007.[48]

3. Transboundary Environmental Problems

One of the distinctive features of the second wave of environmentalism that gained momentum in the 1980s was its concern with global issues. These included acid rain, ozone depletion, global warming, and the growing world trade in garbage and hazardous waste. Problems whose causes and consequences spill across national boundaries require solutions based on international co-operation. But co-operation is usually difficult to achieve, for the reasons illustrated by the parable of the commons. When an individual country receives all the benefits from an activity but bears only a portion of the costs it generates, the incentive to behave differently will probably be weak. The greater the gap between the benefits and the costs, the less likely it is that a country will be prepared to change its behaviour. The jobs and economic benefits associated with, say, clear-cutting rain forests in Malaysia or Brazil, or relatively cheap energy prices in Canada and the United States that encourage consumption, are readily appreciated by policy-makers and those who elect them. On the other hand, the cost effects of the greenhouse gases produced by these activities, which are not limited to their producers' backyards, may seem less tangible to most people.

Unless a country experiences more of the costs than the benefits associated with some environmentally damaging activity, what incentives exist for its policy-makers to control that activity? If altruism was the only answer, the world would certainly be in serious trouble. Self-interest is usually a more reliable basis for action. Unfortunately, experience has shown that transboundary environmental problems must usually have achieved crisis dimensions before the countries that are the net beneficiaries of the damaging activity can be persuaded to take serious measures to control it.

Acid rain is a classic illustration. People have known about acid rain for over a century.[49] Its potentially adverse effects on human health were first identified several decades ago.[50] By the 1970s the environmental costs of acid rain, if not its consequences for human health (still a controversial issue), were becoming undeniable. Despite a sharp jump in the Canadian public's awareness of acid rain as a problem, virtually nothing was done even to limit increases in emissions of sulphur dioxide (produced through the burning of fossil fuels) and nitrogen oxides (generated by vehicles, electricity generation, and other combustion processes), let alone to reduce existing levels of these pollutants. Sulphur dioxide emissions did decline marginally during the 1980s, but most of this reduction was attributable to rising energy costs, which encouraged the use of more fuel-efficient and therefore less-polluting vehicles. Emissions actually increased slightly around 1991,[51] at a time when the Canadian government was taking credit for being a world leader in the fight to control acid rain.

Even slower to act, however, was the United States. Before passage of the Clean Air Act in 1990, the American government's policy was essentially to deny that the scientific data established a conclusive link between activities like mineral smelting and coal-fired electricity generation, on the one hand, and dying forests and lakes, on the other. This reluctance to act had important consequences for Canada, given that an estimated 50 per cent of sulphur dioxide deposition in Canada came from American sources.[52] Without American action to restrict sulphur dioxide emissions at their source, Canadian efforts to deal with the problem could never achieve more than limited success. Likewise, international efforts to control the problem require the co-operation of many governments. This co-operation is made difficult by the fact that some of the worst offenders—notably countries in Eastern Europe, where coal accounts for a large proportion of electricity generation—are less able to afford the costs of conversion and abatement than some other countries, and because some of the main victims of acid rain—such as the Scandinavian countries, whose forest industries are important sources of national income—generate comparatively little in the way of acid-forming emissions.

Just as it has become commonplace to remark that national economies are more interdependent today than at any time in the past, the same is true of 'national' environments (the very concept of a 'national' environment is somewhat absurd). While it is true that some environmental problems involve strictly local effects, many have transboundary and even global dimensions. Is there reason to believe that these transboundary problems can be managed? There are both positive and negative signs.

On the positive side, the governments of Canada and many other countries have entered into agreements on a number of transboundary issues:

- *Ozone depletion.* The Montreal Protocol on Substances that Deplete the Ozone Layer (1987) committed signatories to a 50 per cent reduction in CFC use by 1998 and limits on halon use to 1986 levels by 1992. The Protocol also restricted trade in ozone-depleting chemicals.
- *Global warming.* The World Conference on the Changing Atmosphere, held in Toronto in 1988, recommended that developed countries cut their emissions of greenhouse gases by 20 per cent from 1988 levels by the year 2005. This was followed by the Kyoto conference in 1997, which produced an agreement committing 38 developed countries to reductions in their greenhouse gas emissions from 6 to 8 per cent below 1990 levels by the year 2012. Despite these agreements, CO_2 emissions continue to rise.
- *Acid rain.* In 1985, Canada and several European governments signed the Helsinki Protocol, committing them to a 30 per cent cut in sulphur dioxide emissions by 1994.
- *Species and habitat preservation.* Many of the world's animal populations have been endangered by commercial exploitation, hunting, and habitat destruction. International agreements to ban commercial whaling, drift-net fishing, and the importation of ivory have provided some protection for endangered species. The Convention Concerning the Protection of the World Cultural and Natural Heritage (UNESCO, 1972) and the Convention on Wetlands of International Importance (1971) are two of the main international agreements aimed at habitat preservation. Since 2002 Canada has developed its Species at Risk Public Registry and continues to list new species as threatened or endangered.
- *Water pollution.* The international Law of the Seas, the London Dumping Convention, and the UN Environment Programme Montreal Guidelines respecting land-based sources of marine pollution are examples of international co-operation to deal with transboundary water pollution. In the Great Lakes basin, the Canada–US International Joint Commission monitors water pollution, identifies areas of concern, and commits Ontario and the eight states bordering the lakes to the development of remedial action plans.

This is only a partial list of the international initiatives that have been taken to deal with transboundary environmental issues. Before we conclude that governments are willing and able to co-operate on these issues, however, we must examine the limits of their co-operation. These limits are largely attributable to three factors: conflicting interests, inadequate decision making and enforcement machinery, and the nature of the policy instruments used.

One factor that impedes international co-operation on environmental issues is the fact that the many transnational institutions in place—including bilateral and regional organizations established expressly to deal with transboundary environmental issues, and a clutch of United Nations agencies concerned with environment protection—are inadequate for the task. The basic problem is, of course, that participating countries are generally unwilling to give up any part of their political sovereignty to an international agency. This obstacle can be overcome to some extent on matters regarding international security and economics. On economic matters, the World Trade Organization sometimes is able to impose sanctions on members who violate its restrictions on protectionist policies. Regional free trade agreements like the European Union, the Canada–United States Free Trade Agreement, and NAFTA impose certain restrictions on national sovereignty in matters of trade and investment. But when it comes to environmental matters, international agencies still have not progressed very far beyond their research, monitoring, and 'talking shop' functions. Part of the reason is that international environmental issues still are not considered to be as vital to national interests as economic and security matters.

Given the realities of national sovereignty, governments' natural tendency toward short-termism, and their preoccupation with domestic affairs, can this institutional gap be bridged? This brings us to the third limit on international action, the problem of enforcement. International agreements on transboundary environmental issues typically set targets and then rely on voluntary compliance by member states. The 1997 Kyoto Protocol on greenhouse gases is typical in this respect. The Protocol failed to include enforcement mechanisms, stating simply that 'appropriate and effective' ways of dealing with non-compliance would be determined at a later meeting. Predictably, targets have not been met, or not met on time; some countries have balked at being asked to comply with the same guidelines that apply to less-efficient or more-polluting countries; and some countries just do not want to co-operate at all. Canada, for instance, has no intention even of trying to meet the targets that it agreed to. Ironically, although Canadians criticize the United States for remaining outside the Kyoto agreement, American carbon emissions actually decreased between 1993 and 2003 while Canada's increased at a higher rate than those of either the EU-15 or the United States. Canada's CO_2 emissions rose 27 per cent compared to the G7 average of 12.1 per cent and 13.7 per cent for the United States (see Box 11.1).

BOX 11.1 Billions for Green Energy: Is It Worth It?

Here are the costs of going green:

Ontario's long-term energy plan calls for $4 billion in spending on energy generated from biomass—i.e., composted organics, or methane from garbage dumps.

What will the province get for the $4 billion investment? It will boost the share of power generated by biomass 0.3 per cent, from 1 per cent of the province's supply today, to 1.3 per cent by 2030.

Solar spending will total $9 billion, and boost solar power's share to 1.5 per cent, from near-zero.

Wind investment will be $14 billion, boosting wind energy's share to 10 per cent of the province's share from 2 per cent.

All in all, those three green power technologies will soak up more than 30 per cent of the Liberals' planned investment of $87 billion, while generating 13 per cent of overall power by 2030.

Much of the money will come from the private sector, but the return they earn will be built into the electricity prices paid by Ontario residents and businesses.

Is it worth it?

Energy Minister Brad Duguid pitches the investment in moral terms, arguing it will clean the air and make children healthier.

'There's a cost to that,' he said Tuesday. 'Together we're building cleaner air, together we're building an economy with thousands of clean energy jobs, and together we're building a healthier future for our kids and grandkids. That's something worth fighting for.'

Keith Stewart of Greenpeace says the costs of renewable power are visible, while full social costs of burning fossil and nuclear fuels are not.

'If factored into today's bills, the cost of smog and climate change, and the cost of dealing with radioactive waste, your bill today would be a lot higher than it is because we're not paying those costs,' he said in an interview.

Stewart also predicted there will be 'huge drops' in the cost of developing solar power as the industry matures, and Ontario can be at the forefront of technological developments in solar if it nurtures the sector at home.

Ian Howcroft, vice-president of Canadian Manufacturers and Exporters (CME), said developing a made-in-Ontario renewable energy sector will benefit the province.

But his group is uneasy about the plan's cost estimates of speedy renewable development.

'We have to do it in a businesslike fashion,' he said. 'We have to look at the return on investment, and we have to look at what the ultimate costs are.

'We're supportive of the direction, but we do have concerns about how much we should pay to develop wind, to develop solar, given what the ultimate cost is going to be.'

The CME will participate when the plan is subjected to scrutiny by the Ontario Energy Board, he said.

Jack Gibbons, chair of the Ontario Clean Air Alliance, says that biomass and wind power are still likely to be less expensive than rebuilding nuclear facilities, although conservation and efficiency are the best ways to solve energy issues.

But he said in an interview that Quebec produces huge amounts of renewable power from its hydroelectric plants: 'In terms of new renewable, water power imports from Quebec are lower cost than any of the made-in-Ontario options.'

That would have to be negotiated with Quebec, but Gibbons says Ontario should take the initiative.

'It's low-cost, it's very reliable, it's a base load supply of power, it's not intermittent,' he said.

Source: John Spears, 'Billions for Green Energy: Is It Worth It?' *Toronto Star*, 24 November 2010. Reprinted with permission by Torstar Syndication Services.

Sanctions and inducements are needed to achieve what goodwill cannot. These already exist to some degree. For example, the International Monetary Fund and its lending arm, the World Bank, the Inter-American Development Bank, and other development agencies consider the environmental impacts of the development projects they are asked to finance. One consequence has been a significant reduction in the numbers of dams built in developing countries. India and China, where production of ozone-destroying chemicals is increasing more rapidly than in the developed countries, refused to agree to the Montreal Protocol on CFCs unless developing countries were given longer to restrict their production and developed countries agreed to contribute to the costs of replacing CFCs with ozone-friendly substitutes. At the 1997 Kyoto conference on global warming the gap between developed and developing countries proved unbridgeable. Countries like China—quite understandably, from their point of view— refused to be bound by the limits on greenhouse gas emissions accepted by developed countries. The possibility that rich countries might pay poorer countries to pollute less was raised, as it often is, but the scale of the payments required to buy an appreciable change in the behaviour of developing countries is too high to be politically saleable in most developed countries. It is certainly beyond the political pale in the United States. With roughly 4 per cent of the world's population, the United States generates about one-fifth of global greenhouse gases and would be expected to meet a large part of the bill for any such scheme; furthermore, it has refused to be part of any agreement that would entail buying credits from countries such as China or Russia.

It is worth noting that virtually all the sanctions and inducements currently in place run in one direction: from developed to developing countries. In the case of wealthy industrialized countries, compliance still depends on goodwill and a sense of responsibility to their own future generations and the global community. At the second Earth Summit, in 1997, prime minister Chrétien acknowledged that the target Canada agreed to at Rio de Janeiro in 1992 would not be met. Ottawa blamed the provinces for this failure, provincial co-operation being necessary to regulate the sources of carbon dioxide emissions. While it is certainly true that the federal division of powers complicates environmental policy-making and may prevent Ottawa from being able to follow through on international commitments, federalism may also serve as a convenient excuse for Ottawa to pass the buck for environmental matters to the provinces.[53]

This is particularly true since the Supreme Court's 1997 ruling in *R. v. Hydro-Québec*. This case involved the alleged dumping of PCBs by Hydro-Québec into a river. Hydro-Québec was charged pursuant to the Canadian Environmental Protection Act. The constitutionality of those parts of the Act under which it was charged was challenged by Hydro-Québec and the Quebec government on the grounds that they did not fall within the scope of any federal power set out in section 91 of the Constitution Act, 1867. Relying on a generous and flexible interpretation of Ottawa's constitutional authority to make criminal law, five of the court's nine judges upheld the validity of regulations made under the Canadian Environmental Protection Act. In so doing, the court appeared to extend significantly the scope of Ottawa's authority over the environment. Nevertheless, although the feds may have the Constitution on their side, the hard realities of politics, including the political costs associated with appearing to meddle in a province's affairs to the detriment of its economy, make passing the buck a tempting option.

A Non-Malthusian Case for Environmentally Friendly Policies

As Mark Sagoff has observed, the problem of environmental deterioration is often framed as a problem of overconsumption.[54] Roughly one-fifth of the world's people—those living in the economically developed countries—account for four-fifths of global consumption. Given Earth's finite resources and its limited capacity to tolerate the increasing amounts of waste and pollution that accompany ever higher levels of production and consumption, the overconsuming lifestyles of the world's wealthier countries cannot be sustained indefinitely. The idea that the global economic pie can continue to expand so as to pull the developing world up to the consumption standards considered normal in the developed world is, in Paul Ehrlich's words, 'basically a humane idea made insane by the constraints nature places on human activity'.[55]

Books like Ehrlich's *The End of Affluence* and the Club of Rome's *The Limits to Growth* popularized the idea that scarcity would eventually send the prices of crucial natural resources skyrocketing and that these shortages would bring to a halt the era of constant growth in production and consumption. In fact, however, the exploitable stocks of most of these raw materials have increased and their real prices have fallen. This is the point that political scientist and statistician Bjørn Lomborg[56] makes when he criticizes the Malthusian principle that Earth has natural limits. He and others argue that things are getting better rather than worse. As evidence he points to statistics showing that fewer people are starving, life expectancy is increasing, and pollution has been reduced as a result in part of human ingenuity and in part of economic growth.

Lomborg, Sagoff, and others argue that technology has enabled us to avoid critical shortages despite what neo-Malthusians claim is human overconsumption, especially in the wealthy parts of the world. They examine energy resources, food, and timber, and conclude that in each case supplies are abundant. As Sagoff says of energy, 'The global energy problem has less to do with depleting resources than with controlling pollutants.'[57] But even this potential limit to growth is one that Sagoff believes can be managed through new energy technologies and resource substitution.

'Can' and 'should' have very different meanings. Sagoff and Lomborg say that neo-Malthusians like Ehrlich have been proven wrong in their predictions of global scarcity as a result of overconsumption. They claim that the world can continue to consume at increasingly high rates and that economic arguments for reducing consumption of the world's resources are not justified, since history shows that technology is generally successful in overcoming scarcity.

That consumption can continue to grow does not mean, however, that it should do so. 'The question before us', Sagoff writes, 'is not whether we are going to run out of resources. It is whether economics is the appropriate context for thinking about environmental policy.'[58] Sagoff suggests that it is not. Arguments that the extinction of a particular species of plant or animal life, or the deterioration of some specific habitat, will have calamitous results for the ecosystems on which humankind depends are, he notes, seldom even remotely credible. Very few species are, in biologist David Ehrenfeld's words, 'vital cogs in the ecological machine'.[59] But if arguments rooted in economics and the sustainability of human life fail to convince, why should anyone care about the effects of consumption on the environment?

The answer, according to Sagoff, has to do with our sense of moral purpose. 'In defending old-growth forests, wetlands, or species,' he says, 'we make our best arguments when we think of nature chiefly in aesthetic and moral terms.'[60] The quality of life rather than the standard of living must become the compass that guides our thinking about the environment.

There is, of course, abundant evidence of precisely this sort of moral challenge to the high-consumption society. The David and Goliath court battle between the fast-food chain McDonald's and two British environmental activists during the mid-1990s raised ethical and lifestyle issues. The now commonplace confrontations between North American and European activists, on the one side, and forestry companies and public authorities, on the other, over the fate of old-growth forests in British Columbia represent another such challenge. But so far the general public seems largely unmoved by arguments about the putative sacredness of forests or the great chain of being (although there are significant cross-national variations in popular beliefs). Until there are more votes in conservation than consumption, it is unrealistic to expect policy-makers—most of them, anyway—to use the language of morality in making the case for the environment.

Key Terms

anthropocentric Human-centred; the world view that sees 'the environment', including all other life forms, primarily in relation to humans.

common law The legal system, developed in England, based not on codified written laws but on court decisions, the doctrines implicit in those decisions, and customs and usages.

conservation Preservation of the environment primarily for the sake of humankind, to ensure that natural resources will be available for future human use.

deep ecology The more radical environmental philosophy that makes no distinction between humankind and other life forms, emphasizing the interrelatedness of all the elements that make up the chain of life.

externalities Costs that are not reflected in the price paid for a good or service.

marginal utility The additional satisfaction, or amount of utility, gained from each additional unit of consumption.

nuisance law Law used to regulate or control activity that interferes with the use or enjoyment of private property.

riparian rights The common-law rights of people who own or occupy land beside lakes and rivers; unlike other property rights, riparian rights can be used to prevent damage before it occurs.

sustainable development The idea that humans have the ability to ensure that development meets the needs of the present without compromising the ability of future generations to meet their own needs.

trespass law Law used to regulate or control direct intrusion on private property without the owner's permission.

utility The abstract concept denoting relative value.

Discussion Questions

1. How can the government say that it acts for the public good when it allows industries to pollute the environment? Who can best articulate the public good? Is there a single public good when it comes to environmental protection?
2. As the public's attention becomes more focused on environmental problems such as climate change, do you think that people will come to accept additional taxes (e.g., carbon taxes) to combat those problems? Or will the public instead want those costs to be reflected in their energy prices, as is predicted in Box 11.1?

Websites

The following websites provide information on environmental issues.

Environment Canada

www.ec.gc.ca

The Environment Canada website provides information on the state of the environment and regulations and acts with respect to the environment.

Ecojustice

www.ecojustice.ca

Ecojustice (formally the Sierra Legal Defense Fund) is a national non-profit organization dedicated to enforcing and strengthening the laws that safeguard the environment, wildlife, and public health.

CO_2Now.org

http://co2now.org

CO_2Now posts the latest CO_2 data. The core aim is to continue making atmospheric CO_2 levels visible and recognized far and wide. The site also promotes carbon literacy to help non-scientists understand the different ways that CO_2 is measured, how targets are set, and the pathways that can best address the problems of global heating, climate destabilization, and ocean acidification.

Species at Risk Public Registry

www.sararegistry.gc.ca

This website has been designed to help people better understand Canada's approach to protecting and recovering species at risk, learn about species at risk and what's being done to help them, and get involved in decision making and recovery activities.

The Pembina Institute
www.pembina.org
In its mission to advance sustainable energy solutions, the Pembina Institute includes research, education, consulting, and advocacy on policy amongst its courses of action.

David Suzuki Foundation
www.davidsuzuki.org
Founded by Dr David Suzuki, well-known as the host of the CBC documentary series *The Nature of Things*, the David Suzuki Foundation works with governments, businesses, and individuals to conserve the environment by providing science-based education, advocacy, and policy work, and acting as a catalyst for social change.

Notes

Chapter 1 Basic Concepts in the Study of Public Policy

1. Tavia Grant, 'Recession "Relatively Mild" in Canada', *The Globe and Mail*, March 2, 2010, B7.
2. 'Economy: Income per Capita', Conference Board of Canada, July 2009, www.conferenceboard.ca/hcp/details/economy/income-per-capita.aspx
3. Programme for International Student Assessment (PISA), *Learning for Tomorrow's World: First Results from PISA 2003* (OECD, 2004, 2009), www.oecd.org/dataoecd/1/60/34002216.pdf.
4. Thomas R. Dye, *Understanding Public Policy*, 3rd ed. (Englewood Cliffs, NJ: Prentice-Hall, 1978), 3.
5. 39th Parliament, 1st Session, edited Hansard No. 084, November 22, 2006.
6. 39th Parliament, 1st Session, edited Hansard No. 084, November 23, 2006.
7. Murray Edelman, *Constructing the Political Spectacle* (Chicago, IL: University of Chicago Press, 1988), 12.
8. Statistics Canada, Catalogue no. 13-888.
9. Canada Public Service Agency, Population Affiliation Report, 'Federal Public Administration', www.tbs-sct.gc.ca/pas-srp/report-rapport_e.asp?cat=a.
10. Statistics Canada, 'Government transfer payments to persons', www40.statcan.ca/l01/cst01/govt05a-eng.htm.
11. Richard M. Bird, *The Growth of Government Spending in Canada* (Toronto, ON: Canadian Tax Foundation, 1970), 288, table 43.
12. Based on estimates in Economic Council of Canada, *Responsible Regulation* (Ottawa, ON: Supply and Services, 1979), and the Task Force on Program Review, *Regulatory Programs* (Ottawa, ON: Supply and Services, 1986).
13. Economic Council of Canada, *Minding the Public's Business* (Ottawa, ON: Supply and Services, 1986), 11.
14. Marc Frenette, David Green, and Kevin Milligan, 'Revisiting Recent Trends in Canadian After-Tax Income Inequality Using Census Data', Analytical Studies Branch Research Paper Series, Statistics Canada Catalogue no. 11F0019MIE – No. 274 (2006).
15. Constitution Act, 1982, section 36(2).
16. Department of Finance, 'Transfer Payments to Provinces, Equalization', www.fin.gc.ca/fedprov/eqp-eng.aspl.
17. Kenneth Boessenkool, 'Taxing Incentives: How Equalization Distorts Tax Policy in Recipient Provinces'. The AIMS Equalization Papers (Paper #3), June 2002.
18. Thomas J. Courchene, 'Towards a Protected Society: The Politicization of Economic Life', *Canadian Journal of Economics* 13 (November 1980).
19. Task Force on Program Review, *Economic Growth: Services and Subsidies to Business*, 15.
20. Raymond Breton, 'Multiculturalism and Canadian Nation-Building', in Alan Cairns and Cynthia Williams, eds., *Politics of Gender, Ethnicity and Language* (Toronto, ON: University of Toronto Press, 1986), 30; Charles E. Lindblom, *Politics and Markets* (New York, NY: Basic Books, 1977), ch. 13.
21. 'The Myth of the Powerless State', *The Economist*, October 7, 1995, 15.
22. Neil Nevitte, *The Decline of Deference: Canadian Value Change in Cross-National Perspective* (Peterborough, ON: Broadview Press, 1996).
23. See 'Scénarios de la mondialisation', *Le Monde diplomatique*, November 1996, 6.
24. For a discussion of this possible linkage, see Nevitte, *The Decline of Deference*, 28–41.
25. OECD, 'Tackling the Crisis—A Strategic Response', www.oecd.org/document/27/0,3343,en_2649_201185_41973851_1_1_1_1,00.html
26. Office of the Prime Minister, 'Statement by the Prime Minister of Canada at the Close of the G20 Conference', June 27, 2010.
27. Office of the Prime Minister, 'Notes for Remarks by the Prime Minister at the Harrison Liberal Conference', Harrison Hot Springs, BC, November 21, 1969, 7.

Chapter 2 Theories of Public Policy

1. Mark Sproule-Jones, *Governments at Work: Canadian Parliamentary Federalism and Its Public Policy Effects* (Toronto, ON: University of Toronto Press, 1992), 3.
2. Randall G. Holcombe, *Economic Foundations of Government* (New York, NY: New York University Press, 1994), 3–5.

3. Thomas R. Dye, *Understanding Public Policy*, 2nd ed. (Englewood Cliffs, NJ: Prentice-Hall, 1975), 17.

4. Richard Simeon, 'Studying Public Policy', *Canadian Journal of Political Science* (hereafter CJPS) 9, 4 (December 1976), 566.

5. Michael Atkinson and Marsha Chandler, eds., *The Politics of Canadian Public Policy* (Toronto, ON: University of Toronto Press, 1983), 3–5.

6. See G. Bruce Doern and Richard W. Phidd, *Canadian Public Policy* (Toronto, ON: Methuen, 1983), chs. 1, 6.

7. See Robert I. Jackson and Doreen Jackson, *Politics in Canada* (Toronto, ON: Prentice-Hall, 1990), 585–602.

8. See Fred Block, 'The Ruling Class Does Not Rule: Notes on the Marxist Theory of the State', in Thomas Ferguson and Joel Rogers, eds., *The Political Economy* (Armonk, NY: M.E. Sharpe, 1984), 32–46.

9. Charles E. Lindblom, 'The Market as Prison', *Journal of Politics* 44, 2 (May 1982), 324.

10. These categories were introduced in James O'Connor, *The Fiscal Crisis of the State* (New York, NY: St Martin's Press, 1973), 6.

11. This argument is associated with the French Marxist Nicos Poulantzas. See Poulantzas, *Classes in Contemporary Capitalism* (London, UK: New Left Books, 1975).

12. Block, 'The Ruling Class Does Not Rule', 40.

13. Ralph Miliband, 'State Power and Capitalist Democracy', a paper delivered at Carleton University, Ottawa, July 1984, 6.

14. Stephen Gill, ed., *Globalization, Democratization and Multilateralism* (New York, NY: St Martin's Press, 1999). See also Susan Strange, *The Retreat of the State: The Diffusion of Power in the World Economy* (Cambridge, UK: Cambridge University Press, 1996).

15. Michael M. Atkinson, *Governing Canada: Institutions and Public Policy* (Toronto, ON: Harcourt Brace Jovanovich Canada, 1993), 2–3.

16. Keith Banting, *The Welfare State and Canadian Federalism* (Kingston, ON: Queen's University Press-Institute of Intergovernmental Relations, 1992).

17. For another view of institutionalism that overlaps with Marxism, see Peter Evans, D. Rueschemeyer, and Theda Skocpol, eds., *Bringing the State Back In* (Cambridge, UK: Cambridge University Press, 1985).

18. Charles E. Lindblom, 'The Science of Muddling Through', *Public Administration Review* 19 (Spring 1959), 79–88.

19. David Easton, 'An Approach to the Analysis of Political Systems', *World Politics* 9 (1957), 383–400.

20. Ibid., 386–7.

21. Richard J. Van Loon and Michael S. Whittington, *The Canadian Political System*, 4th ed. (Toronto, ON: McGraw-Hill Ryerson, 1987), 13.

22. Joseph A. Schumpeter, *Capitalism, Socialism and Democracy* (New York, NY: Harper & Brothers, 1943).

23. Robert Dahl, *A Preface to Democratic Theory* (Chicago, IL: University of Chicago Press, 1956).

24. See Anthony King, 'Ideas, Institutions and the Policies of Governments: A Comparative Analysis', *British Journal of Political Science* 3, 3 (July 1973), 291–313, and 3, 4 (October 1973), 409–23; H. Heclo, 'Toward a New Welfare State', in Peter Flora and Arnold Heidenheimer, eds., *The Development of Welfare States in Europe and America* (New York, NY: Transaction Books, 1981), 383–406; Ira Sharkansky, *Whither the State* (New York, NY: Chatham House, 1979).

25. Robert L. Heilbroner, 'The View from the Top: Reflections on a Changing Business Ideology', in Earl F. Cheit, ed., *The Business Establishment* (New York, NY: Wiley, 1964), 12.

26. Charles Lindblom, *Politics and Markets* (New York, NY: Basic Books, 1977), esp. chs. 13–16.

27. Theodore Lowi, *The End of Liberalism* (New York, NY: W.W. Norton, 1979), 280.

28. Lindblom, 'The Market as Prison'.

29. Ibid., 329.

30. William D. Coleman and Grace Skogstad, *Policy Communities and Public Policy in Canada: A Structural Approach* (Toronto, ON: Copp Clark Pitman, 1990).

31. John Peterson, 'Policy Networks', Institute for Advanced Studies, Vienna, July 23, 2003. www.ihs.ac.at/publications/pol/pw_90.pdf.

32. Dennis C. Mueller, ed., *Perspectives on Public Choice: A Handbook* (Cambridge, UK: Cambridge University Press, 1997).

33. Michael J. Trebilcock et al., *The Choice of Governing Instrument* (Ottawa, ON: Supply and Services, 1982), 21.

34. James Buchanan and Gordon Tulluck, *The Calculus of Consent* (Ann Arbor, MI: University of Michigan Press, 1965).

35. Ibid., vi.

36. In Hobbes's words, 'during the time men live without a common power to keep them all in awe, they are in that condition which is called war, and such a war is of every man against every man.' See Hobbes, *Leviathan* (New York, NY: Bobbs-Merrill, 1958), 106.

37. Trebilcock et al., *The Choice of Governing Instrument*, 27–9.

38. Thomas Flanagan, *Game Theory and Canadian Politics* (Toronto: University of Toronto Press, 1998), 20.

39. Mark Sproule-Jones, 'Institutions, Constitutions, and Public Policies: A Public-Choice Overview', in Atkinson and Chandler, eds., *The Politics of Canadian Public Policy*, 127.

40. Ibid., 144.

41. Kenneth Arrow, *Social Choice and Individual Values* (New York, NY: John Wiley and Sons, 1951).

42. Mancur Olson, *The Logic of Collective Action: Public Goods and the Theory of Groups* (Cambridge, MA: Harvard University Press, 1965).

43. Donald Green and Ian Shapiro, *Pathologies of Rational Choice* (New Haven, CT: Yale University Press, 1994).

Chapter 3 The Context of Policy-Making in Canada

1. G. Bruce Doern, Leslie A. Pal, and Brian W. Tomlin, eds., *Border Crossings: The Internationalization of Canadian Public Policy* (Toronto, ON: Oxford University Press, 1996), 5.

2. Ibid.

3. For a good summary of the approach, see Seymour Martin Lipset, *Continental Divide: Values and Institutions of the United States and Canada* (New York, NY: Routledge, 1990).

4. Kenneth McRae, 'The Structure of Canadian History', in Louis Hartz, ed., *The Founding of New Societies* (New York, NY: Harcourt, Brace and World, 1964), 219–74; Gad Horowitz, 'Conservatism, Liberalism, and Socialism in Canada: An Interpretation', CJPS 32 (1966), 143–71.

5. See George Woodcock, *Confederation Betrayed* (Madeira Park, BC: Harbour Publishing, 1981).

6. Philip Resnick, *Parliament vs. People* (Vancouver, BC: New Star Books, 1984).

7. Ibid., 25.

8. Ibid., 38.

9. See Barry Cooper and Mebs Kanji, *Governing in Post-Deficit Times: Alberta in the Klein Years* (Toronto, ON: Centre for Public Management, University of Toronto, 2000), who argue that Ralph Klein's success came from his appeal to voters' self-reliance. According to Cooper and Kanji, these values are closely identified with the Albertan frontier spirit.

10. Royal Commission on Bilingualism and Biculturalism, *The Cultural Contribution of the Other Ethnic Groups*, Book IV of the Final Report (Ottawa, ON: Queen's Printer, 1970).

11. The Honourable Thomas R. Berger, 'Towards the Regime of Tolerance', in Stephen Brooks, ed., *Political Thought in Canada* (Toronto, ON: Irwin, 1984), 84.

12. Nathan Glazer and Daniel P. Moynihan, eds., *Ethnicity* (Cambridge, MA: Harvard University Press, 1975), 30.

13. This function of culture is described in Harold R. Isaacs, *Idols of the Tribe: Group Identity and Political Change* (New York, NY: Harper and Row, 1975).

14. Raymond Breton, 'Multiculturalism and Canadian Nation-Building', in Alan C. Cairns and Cynthia Williams, eds., *The Politics of Gender, Ethnicity and Language in Canada*, vol. 34 of the research studies for the Royal Commission on the Economic Union and Development Prospects for Canada (Toronto, ON: University of Toronto Press, 1985), 30.

15. Ibid., 30–1.

16. Ibid., 49.

17. John Jaworsky, 'A Case Study of the Canadian Federal Government's Multiculturalism Policy', MA thesis (Carleton University, 1979), 59.

18. The studies are cited in Breton, 'Multiculturalism and Canadian Nation-Building', 45–6.

19. 2010-11 Main Estimates, General Summary. www.tbs-sct.gc.ca/est-pre/20102011/me-bpd/sum-som-eng.asp#bm07.

20. Statistics Canada. 'Immigration in Canada: A Portrait of the Foreign-Born Population, 2006 Census: Immigrants Came from Many Countries.' www12.statcan.ca/census-recensement/2006/as-sa/97-557/p4-eng.cfm.

21. Alain Bélanger (Editor-in-Chief), *Report on the Demographic Situation in Canada 2003 and 2004* (Statistics Canada, 2006), Catalogue no. 91-209-XIE, 3.

22. Alan C. Cairns, 'The Governments and Societies of Canadian Federalism', CJPS 10, 4 (1977), 699.

23. With the passage of the Constitution Act, 1982, the BNA Act of 1867 and all of its amendments have been renamed the Constitution Act, 1867.
24. We assume that the readers of this text are familiar with the basic features of Canada's Constitution. Those who are not should consult the appropriate chapter of any introductory text on Canadian government.
25. Cairns, 'The Governments and Societies of Canadian Federalism', 699.
26. Ibid., 706.
27. F.R. Scott, *Essays on the Constitution* (Toronto, ON: University of Toronto Press, 1977).
28. For rather different interpretations of the influence that the JCPC has had on Canadian federalism, see Alan C. Cairns, 'The Judicial Committee and Its Critics', CJPS 4, 3 (September 1971), 301–45.
29. This principle was established by the Judicial Committee of the Privy Council in the *Labour Conventions Case*, 1937. See Peter H. Russell, *Leading Constitutional Decisions*, 3rd ed. (Ottawa, ON: Carleton University Press, 1982), 122–30.
30. See Richard Simeon, *Federal-Provincial Diplomacy: The Making of Recent Policy in Canada* (Toronto, ON: University of Toronto Press, 1972).
31. Alan C. Cairns, 'Citizens (Outsiders) and Government (Insiders) in Constitution-Making: The Case of Meech Lake', in Cairns, *Disruptions: Constitutional Struggles, from the Charter to Meech Lake* (Toronto, ON: McClelland & Stewart, 1991), 136.
32. F.L. Morton and Rainer Knopff, *The Charter Revolution and the Court Party* (Peterborough, ON: Broadview Press, 2000).
33. F.L. Morton, 'The Charter Revolution and the Court Party', *Osgoode Hall Law Journal* 30, 3 (Fall 1992), 649.
34. Statistics Canada, Table A-5, Population of French Mother Tongue, Canada, Provinces, Territories and Canada Less Quebec, 1996–2006. www12.statcan.ca/census-recensement/2006/as-sa/97-555/table/A5-eng.cfm.
35. Donald Smiley, 'Federal–Provincial Conflict in Canada', *Publius* 4, 3 (1974), 7–24.
36. Eric Waddell, 'State, Language and Society: The Vicissitudes of French in Quebec and Canada', in Cairns and Williams, eds., *The Politics of Gender, Ethnicity and Language*, 97.
37. Raymond Breton, 'The Production and Allocation of Symbolic Resources: An Analysis of the Linguistic and Ethnocultural Fields in Canada', *Canadian Review of Sociology and Anthropology* 21 (May 1984), 129.
38. Public Service Commission of Canada, 'Why Are There Positions Designated as Bilingual?' www.psc-cfp.gc.ca.
39. Commissioner of Official Languages, *Annual Report 1985* (Ottawa: Supply and Services, 1986), 50, emphasis added. The most recent study found that 63 per cent of the employees in the National Capital Region have English as their first language; ibid., p. 58.
40. Office of the Commissioner of Official Languages, 'Making it Real: Promoting Respectful Coexistence of the Two Official Languages at Work' (Ottawa, ON: Minister of Public Works and Government Services Canada, 2005), 59.
41. *Attorney General of Manitoba v. Forest* (1979), 2 S.C.R. 1032; Reference on the Constitution Act, 1867, and the Manitoba Act, 1870, June 13, 1985, decision of the Supreme Court.
42. *Attorney General of Quebec v. Quebec Association of Protestant School Boards* (1984), 10 D.L.R. (4th) 321, judgment rendered on July 26, 1984; January 1985 decision of the Quebec Superior Court.
43. In 1985 the Conservative government broadened the scope of this program to include more of the areas covered by the Charter of Rights and Freedoms, with an emphasis on the equality rights section.
44. Canadian Heritage, Financial and Statistical Data, 'Enrolments in Minority Language Education Programs'. www.pch.gc.ca/progs/lo-ol/pubs/2002-2003/ra-ar/23_e.cfm.
45. Patric Blouin, 'Summary of Public School Indicators for the Provinces and Territories 1999/2000 to 2005/2006', Culture, Tourism and the Centre for Education Statistics, 2008, Catalogue no 81-595-M – No. 067. http://dsp-psd.pwgsc.gc.ca/collection_2008/statcan/81-595-M/81-595-MIE2008067.pdf
46. Commissioner of Official Languages, *Annual Report 2004–5* (Ottawa, ON: Supply and Services, 2005), 15.
47. Statistics Canada, 2006 Census, Nation table.
48. John R. Baldwin and Guy Gellatly, *Global Links: Long Term Trends in Foreign Investment and Foreign Control in Canada, 1960–2000* (Ottawa, ON: Statistics Canada, Ministry of Industry, 2005), 18.
49. Statistics Canada, 'Canada's International Investment Position: First Quarter 2010', *The Daily*, June 17, 2010. www40.statcan.gc.ca/l01/cst01/econ08-eng.htm.

50. Elizabeth Smythe, 'Investment Policy', in Doern et al., eds., *Border Crossings*, 192.

51. Claude Morin, *Quebec versus Ottawa: The Struggle for Self-Government 1960–1972* (Toronto, ON: University of Toronto Press, 1976).

52. See the argument set out in Cairns, 'The Governments and Societies of Canadian Federalism', 695–725.

53. Ibid., 708.

54. See Roger Gibbins, *Regionalism: Territorial Politics in Canada and the United States* (Toronto, ON: Butterworths, 1982), ch. 7.

55. See J.C. Morrison, 'Oliver Mowat and the Development of Provincial Rights in Ontario: A Study in Dominion-Provincial Relations, 1867–1896', in *Three History Theses* (Toronto, ON: Ontario Archives, 1961).

56. Constitutional amendments in 1951 and 1964 assigned legislative authority over old age pensions to Ottawa, but with the proviso that provincial authority remained paramount.

57. This interpretation of why Canadian federalism is characterized by a comparatively high degree of decentralization follows Cairns's argument in 'The Governments and Societies of Canadian Federalism'.

58. Calculated from statistics collected by the US Energy Information Agency. www.eia. doe. gov/neic/quickfacts/quickoil.html.

59. Jeffrey Simpson, *Star-Spangled Canadians: Canadians Living the American Dream* (Toronto, ON: HarperCollins, 2000).

60. Ipsos Reid, on behalf of the Canada Institute of the Woodrow Wilson International Center for Scholars and the Canada Institute on North American Issues (CINAI), *A Public Opinion Survey of Canadians and Americans* (May 2005). www.ipsosna.com/news/client/act_dsp_internal_pdf. cfm?pdf=mr050509-1rr.pdf.

61. See Neil Nevitte, *The Decline of Deference* (Peterborough, ON: Broadview Press, 1996).

62. David Brooks, *Bobos in Paradise: The New Upper Class and How They Got There* (New York, NY: Simon & Schuster, 2000).

63. Doern et al., eds., *Border Crossings*, 19–24.

64. Mark Pickup, 'Globalization, Politics and Provincial Government Spending in Canada', CJPS 39, 4 (December 2006), 884.

65. Andrew Cooper and Leslie Pal, 'Human Rights and Security Policy', ibid., 227. The three groups were the Charter Committee on Poverty Issues, the National Anti-Poverty Organization, and the National Action Committee on the Status of Women.

66. Doern et al., eds., *Border Crossings*, 23.

67. G. Bruce Doern and John Kirton, 'Foreign Policy', ibid., 263.

68. Ibid.

69. Leslie A. Pal, *Beyond Policy Analysis* (Toronto, ON: Nelson, 1997).

Chapter 4 Policy Implementation

1. See the seminal article by Woodrow Wilson, 'The Study of Administration', *Political Science Quarterly* 2 (June 1887).

2. Sebastien Lavoie, 'Living Standards Grow Faster in the West', TD *Economics, Special Report* (April 27, 2006), 2; this trend has continued, with Newfoundland surpassing not only the other Atlantic provinces but Quebec as well. See Statistics Canada, *Income Trends in Canada 1976 to 2007.*

3. *The Oxford Universal Dictionary* (Oxford, UK: Oxford University Press, 1955).

4. Martin Albrow, *Bureaucracy* (London, UK: Macmillan, 1979), ch. 1.

5. Robert T. Nakamura and Frank Smallwood, *The Politics of Implementation* (New York, NY: St Martin's Press, 1980), 9.

6. Bank of Canada Act.

7. James Q. Wilson, *Bureaucracy: What Government Agencies Do and Why They Do It* (New York, NY: Basic Books, 1989), 34.

8. Broadcasting Act, 1991.

9. Leslie A. Pal, *State, Class and Bureaucracy: Canadian Unemployment Insurance and Public Policy* (Montreal and Kingston: McGill-Queen's University Press, 1988), 103–18.

10. Jeffrey Pressman and Aaron Wildavsky, *Implementation* (Berkeley, CA: University of California Press, 1984).

11. Ibid., 93.

12. Ibid., 134.

13. Richard E. Neustadt, *Presidential Power: The Politics of Leadership* (New York, NY: Wiley, 1960).

14. This section relies heavily on Pressman and Wildavsky, *Implementation*, and Wilson, *Bureaucracy.*

15. Wilson, *Bureaucracy*, 5.

16. K. Meier and Lloyd D. Nigro, 'Representational Bureaucracy and Policy Preferences: A Study in the Attitudes of Federal Executives', *Public Administration Review* 36 (1976), 406–67.

17. Robert K. Merton, 'Bureaucratic Structure and Personality', *Social Forces* 17 (1940), 560–8.

18. Marc Tipermas, 'Jurisdictionalism: The Politics of Executive Reorganization', Ph.D. thesis (Harvard University, 1976), 35, 76–81, as quoted in Wilson, *Bureaucracy*, 180.
19. Philip Selznick, *Leadership in Administration* (Evanston, IL: Row, Peterson and Co., 1957), 121.
20. Robert Merton, *Social Theory and Social Structure*, rev. ed. (Glencoe, IL: The Free Press, 1957), 199–202.
21. Philip Selznick, *TVA and the Grass Root: A Study of Politics and Organization* (Berkley, CA: University of California Press, 1980).
22. Marver Bernstein, *Regulating Business by Independent Commission* (Princeton, NJ: Princeton University Press, 1955).

23. Wilson, *Bureaucracy*.
24. Ibid., 91.
25. Selznick, *Leadership*, ch. 2.
26. Leslie A. Pal, *Interests of State* (Montreal and Kingston: McGill–Queen's University Press, 1993).
27. Sandra Gwyn, 'The Great Ottawa Grant Boom (And How It Grew)', *Saturday Night* 87 (October 1972), 22.
28. Stewart Goodings, quoted in Pal, *Interests of State*, 161.
29. Ibid., 154.
30. Alan Freeman, 'The Department That Counts', *The Globe and Mail*, June 1, 1992, A5.
31. Ibid.
32. Ibid.

Chapter 5 Policy Evaluation

1. Iris Geva-May and Leslie A. Pal, 'Good Fences Make Good Neighbours: Policy Evaluation and Policy Analysis—Exploring the Differences", *Evaluation* 5, 3 (1999), 259–77.
2. See Government of Canada, Treasury Board Secretariat, *Policy on Evaluation*, www.tbs-sct.gc.ca/pol/doc-eng.aspx?id=15024&section=HTML.
3. Morton and Knopff call these groups the 'Court Party', while Alan Cairns uses the term 'Charter Canadians'. See F.L. Morton and Rainer Knopff, *The Charter Revolution and the Court Party* (Peterborough, ON: Broadview Press, 2000); Alan C. Cairns, 'The Charter, Interest Groups, Executive Federalism and Constitutional Reform', in David E. Smith, Peter MacKinnon, and John C. Courtney, eds., *After Meech Lake: Lessons for the Future* (Saskatoon, SK: Fifth House Publishers, 1991), 13–31.
4. *Policy on Evaluation*, section 6.1.7.1.
5. See Office of the Auditor General of Canada, 'About Us', www.oag-bvg.gc.ca/internet/English/admin_e_41.html.
6. Ibid.
7. Ibid.
8. Norma Greenaway, 'Auditor General Wants Spot Checks of MPs Expenses; Public Was Misinformed, Says Fraser', *Calgary Herald*, May 26, 2010.
9. Office of the Auditor General of Canada, 'Chapter 1: Aging Information Technology Systems', *Report of the Auditor General of Canada to the House of Commons* (Spring 2010).
10. Office of the Auditor General of Canada, 'Chapter 6: Acquisition of Military Helicop-

ters', *Report of the Auditor General of Canada to the House of Commons* (Fall 2010), 18.
11. Ibid., 29
12. See, for example, Office of the Auditor General of Canada, *Canada Deposit Insurance Corporation, Special Examination Report—2010*. www.cdic.ca/multimedia/Website/Documents/pdf/en/14994_SE-R_CDIC.pdf.
13. Treasury Board of Canada Secretariat, *Evaluation Function in the Government of Canada*, DRAFT, Prepared by the Centre of Excellence for Evaluation, (July 2004), 2.
14. Ibid., 6.
15. F.A. Hayek, *Prices and Production*, 2nd ed. (New York, NY: Augustus M. Kelly, Publishers New York, 1935).
16. Geva-May and Pal, 261.
17. F.A. Hayek, 'Nobel Prize Speech', in Asar Lindbeck, ed., *Nobel Lectures, Economics 1969–1980* (Singapore: World Scientific Publishing Co., 1992).
18. Walter Block, 'Realism: Austrian vs. Neoclassical Economics', *Quarterly Journal of Austrian Economics* 6, 2 (2002), 73–6.
19. Ibid.
20. Arnold Harberger, 'Three Theorems of Applied Welfare Economics', *Journal of Economic Literature* 9, 3 (1971).
21. Ibid.
22. Dominique Armentano, *Antitrust: Anatomy of a Policy Failure* (New York, NY: John Wiley & Sons Inc., 1982), 233–4.
23. Ibid.
24. Ibid.
25. Ibid.

26. Hayek, 1992.

27. Ministerial Task Force on Program Review, *Regulatory Programs* (Ottawa, ON: Department of Supply and Services, May 1985).

28. The classic work in this area is A. Downs, *Inside Bureaucracy* (Boston, MA: Little, Brown, 1967). See also J.M. Blumenthal, 'Candid Reflections of a Businessman in Washington', in J.L. Perry & K.L. Kraemer, eds., *Public Management: Public and Private Perspectives* (Palo Alto, CA: Mayfield, 1983), 22–33; R.E. Boyatzis, *The Competent Manager* (New York, NY: Wiley, 1982); B. Buchanan, 'Government Managers, Business Executives, and Organizational Commitment', *Public Administration Review* 35 (1974), 339–47; B. Buchanan, 'Red Tape and the Service Ethic: Some Unexpected Differences between Public and Private Managers', *Administration and Society* 6 (1975), 423–38.

29. James Wilson, *Bureaucracy: What Government Agencies Do and Why They Do It* (New York, NY: Basic Books, 1989).

30. Erasumus U. Morah, UBC Planning Papers, Discussion Paper #21 (Vancouver, BC: School of Community and Regional Planning, 1990), 2.

31. T.K. Gussman, 'Improving the Professionalism of Evaluation, Final Report (2)', for Centre of Excellence for Evaluation, Treasury Board of Canada Secretariat, May 31, 2005, 8.

32. Treasury Board of Canada Secretariat, *Professional Ethics and Standards for the Evaluation Community in the Government of Canada* (2006), 17.

33. Treasury Board of Canada Secretariat, 'Review of the Quality of Evaluations across Departments and Agencies' (October 2004).

34. Ibid.

35. *Canada's Economic Action Plan—Budget 2009*, tabled in the House of Commons by the Honourable James M. Flaherty, Minister of Finance, January 27, 2009.

36. *Canada's Economic Action Plan—Budget 2010*, tabled in the House of Commons by the Honourable James M. Flaherty, Minister of Finance, March 4, 2010, 12.

37. 'Canada's Economic Action Plan Continues to Create Jobs and Economic Growth', Press Release, Vaughan, Ontario, January 31, 2011. www.fin.gc.ca/n11/11-010-eng.asp.

38. Niels Veldhuis and Charles Lammam, 'The Stimulus Didn't Work: Government Stimulus Spending Had Virtually No Effect on Canada's Economic Recovery', *Fraser Forum* (May 2010), 18–19.

39. 'Harper Should Take His Own Advice on Stimulus Spending: Study', CCPA, April 6, 2009. www.policyalternatives.ca/newsroom/news-releases/harper-should-take-his-own-advice-stimulus-spending-study

Chapter 6 Macroeconomic Policy

1. These proposals are not explicitly advocated in John Maynard Keynes, *The General Theory of Employment, Interest and Money* (London, UK: Macmillan, 1936), but are spelled out in other writings of Keynes both before and after the publication of that book.

2. See the discussion in Doug Owram, *The Government Generation: Canadian Intellectuals and the State 1900–1945* (Toronto, ON: University of Toronto Press, 1986), 307–14.

3. Quoted in Maurice Lamontagne, *Business Cycles in Canada* (Ottawa, ON: Canadian Institute for Economic Policy, 1984), xxiv.

4. Figures from *The Economist*, September 22, 1984, 48.

5. Quoted ibid., 49.

6. The following discussion of monetarism draws heavily on Rudiger Dornbusch and Stanley Fischer, *Macroeconomics* (New York, NY: McGraw-Hill, 1978), and the interview with Karl Brunner in Arjo Klamer,

Conversations with Economists (Totowa, NJ: Rowman & Allanheld, 1984), 179–99.

7. Quoted in Dornbusch and Fischer, *Macroeconomics*, 546.

8. Read the interviews with Robert Solow, Alan Blinder, Karl Brunner, and James Tobin in Klamer, *Conversations*.

9. Robert Lucas, quoted ibid.

10. Karl Brunner, quoted ibid., 194.

11. Alan Blinder makes this argument in *Economic Policy and the Great Stagflation* (New York, NY: Academic Press, 1979).

12. Klamer, *Conversations*, 101.

13. See Lamontagne, *Business Cycles in Canada*; Paul Anthony Samuelson, *Economics* (Toronto, ON: McGraw-Hill Ryerson, 1984), ch. 14.

14. Milton Friedman and Anna Schwartz, *Monetary History of the United States 1867–1960* (Princeton, NJ: Princeton University Press, 1963).

15. Samuelson, *Economics*, 255.

16. Joseph Schumpeter, *Business Cycles* (New York, NY: McGraw-Hill, 1939).

17. Alvin Hansen, *Fiscal Policy and Business Cycles* (New York, NY: W.W. Norton, 1941). While Hansen's focus was on cycles of shorter duration, he did provide dates for periods conforming to Kondratieff's theory of long-term movements.

18. Quoted in Lamontagne, *Business Cycles in Canada*, 131.

19. Ibid., 125–6.

20. Bruno S. Frey, *Modern Political Economy* (New York, NY: John Wiley & Sons, 1978), ch. 11.

21. Samuelson, *Economics*, 836.

22. Quoted in J.L. Granatstein, *The Ottawa Men* (Toronto, ON: Oxford University Press, 1982), 167.

23. Quoted in Robert Lekachman, 'The Radical Keynes', in Harold Wattel, ed., *The Policy Consequences of John Maynard Keynes* (Armonk, NY: M.E. Sharpe, 1985), 36.

24. Quoted in Robert L. Ascah, 'The Deficit Debate: A Survey and Assessment', paper presented to the Canadian Political Science Association annual meeting, Winnipeg, June 8, 1986, 1.

25. *Report of the Royal Commission on Banking and Finance* (Ottawa, ON: Queen's Printer, 1964), 398.

26. Economic Council of Canada, *First Annual Review* (Ottawa, ON: Queen's Printer, 1964).

27. Liberal Party of Canada, *Creating Opportunity: The Liberal Plan for Canada* (Ottawa, ON: Liberal Party of Canada, 1993), 15.

28. Jim Stanford, 'The Economics of Debt and the Remaking of Canada', *Studies in Political Economy* 48 (Autumn 1995), 132.

29. Consumer Price Index, 1995–present, Bank of Canada, 2007. www.bankofcanada.ca/en/cpi.htm. Accessed February 6, 2007.

30. Statistics Canada, *Labour Force Information*, September 10, 2010, Catalogue no. 71-001-X.

31. James M. Flaherty, 'Canada's Economic Action Plan: Budget 2009.' Department of Finance Canada.

32. Data obtained from the International Monetary Fund, Historical Public Debt Dataset, www.imf.org, accessed November 5, 2010.

33. Statistics Canada, www.statcan.gc.ca, accessed November 5, 2010; U.S. Bureau of Labor Statistics, www.bls.gov, accessed November 5, 2010.

34. IMF World Economic Outlook Database, October 2010.

35. Jean-Philippe Cotis, 'Benchmarking Canada's Economic Performance', *International Productivity Monitor* 13 (Fall 2006), 6.

36. Mancur Olson, 'How Ideas Affect Societies: Is Britain the Wave of the Future?' in Institute of Economic Affairs, *Ideas, Interests and Consequences* (London, UK: Institute of Economic Affairs, 1989), 39.

37. Andrea Boltho, ed., *The European Economy* (Oxford, UK: Oxford University Press, 1982), ch. 1.

38. Quoted in Lamontagne, *Business Cycles in Canada*, xxii.

39. This interpretation is David Gordon's, in Klamer, *Conversations*, 208.

40. Ernest Mandel, *Long Waves of Capitalist Development* (Cambridge, UK: Cambridge University Press, 1980), 100.

41. Figures cited in John Sargent, ed., *Post-War Macroeconomic Developments*, vol. 20 of the research studies for the Royal Commission on the Economic Union and Development Prospects for Canada (Toronto, ON: University of Toronto Press, 1985), 61.

42. Quoted ibid., 60.

43. Bank of Canada, *Annual Report 1973* (Ottawa, ON: Queen's Printer, 1974), 7.

44. See the brief survey in Craig Riddell, ed., *Dealing with Inflation and Unemployment in Canada*, vol. 25 of the research studies for the Royal Commission on the Economic Union and Development Prospects for Canada (Toronto, ON: University of Toronto Press, 1985), 52.

45. Quoted in John Sargent, ed., *Fiscal and Monetary Policy*, vol. 21 of the research studies for the Royal Commission on the Economic Union and Development Prospects for Canada (Toronto, ON: University of Toronto Press, 1985), 232.

46. Bank of Canada, 'Inflation'. www.bankofcanada.ca/en/inflation/index.htm, accessed October 18, 2002.

47. Gordon Thiessen, 'Uncertainty and the Transmission of Monetary Policy in Canada', lecture delivered at York University, March 30, 1995, 17.

48. Bank of Canada, 'Bank of Canada Keeps Target for the Overnight Rate at 2–3 Per cent'. www.bankofcanada.ca/fixed-dates/rate_161002.htm, accessed October 18, 2002.

49. *Canada's Economic Action Plan Year 2, Budget 2010: Leading the Way on Jobs and Growth.* (Ottawa, ON: Department of Finance, 2010), 175

50. The meaning of 'excessive' in this context is described by John Bossons as a perception 'that a seemingly chronic government deficit may indicate that the current set of government tax, transfer, and expenditure

programs is not sustainable over the long run'. In Sargent, ed., *Fiscal and Monetary Policy*, 92.

51. Paul Boothe and Derek Hermanutz, 'Simply Sharing: An Interprovincial Equalization Scheme for Canada', *Equalization Papers* (Toronto, ON: C.D. Howe Institute, 1999), 16.

52. *Budget 2006*, Annex 2, 'Recent Evolution of Fiscal Balance in Canada'.

53. *Canada's Economic Action Plan Year 2*, 153.

54. Maureen Appel Molot and Glen Williams, 'The Political Economy of Continentalism', in Michael Whittington and Glen Williams, eds., *Canadian Politics in the 1980s*, 2nd ed. (Toronto, ON: Methuen, 1984), 94.

55. This fourth economic stance is relevant to understanding the colonial activities of France and Britain in pre-Confederation Canada and to understanding some of the nineteenth-century tensions in the relationship between the United States and British North America.

56. Richard Pomfret, *The Economic Development of Canada* (Toronto, ON: Methuen, 1981), 69.

57. Arthur Lower has described the 1879 tariff as 'a frank creation of vested manufacturing interests living on the bounty of government'. See ibid., 91–4, for his quotation and a survey of interpretations of the 1879 tariff.

58. J.L. Granatstein, 'Free Trade: The History of an Issue', in Michael D. Henderson, ed., *The Future on the Table: Canada and the Free Trade Issue* (Downsview, ON: York University, 1987), 5.

59. Economic Research and Analysis Division, Department of Finance, *The Economy* (Newfoundland: Queen's Printer, 2010), 16. www.economics.gov.nl.ca, accessed November 5, 2010.

60. See the discussion in Richard Harris, *Trade, Industrial Policy and International Competition*, vol. 13 of the research studies for the Royal Commission on the Economic Union and Development Prospects for Canada (Toronto, ON: University of Toronto Press, 1985), 39–40.

61. Foreign Affairs and International Trade Canada, 'Overview of NAFTA: A Foundation for Canada's Future Prosperity', December 13, 2006. www.dfait-maeci.gc.ca/nafta-alena/over-en.asp.

62. Keith Banting, 'Social Policy', in G. Bruce Doern et al., eds., *Border Crossings: The Internationalization of Canadian Public Policy* (Toronto, ON: Oxford University Press, 1996), 52.

63. See ibid., 38–9, for an analysis of surveys demonstrating the gap between the values of elites and those of the general public.

64. Cotis, 'Benchmarking Canada's Economic Performance', 5.

65. Hugh G. Thorburn, *Planning and the Economy* (Ottawa, ON: Canadian Institute for Economic Policy, 1984), 245.

66. Banting, 'Social Policy', 38.

Chapter 7 Social Policy

1. This is the title of the report prepared by the federal New Democratic Party Policy Review Committee, Halifax, June 1991.

2. Social Expenditure: Aggregated Data, OECD Social Expenditure Statistics (database) doi: 10.1787/20743904-2009-table1.

3. OECD. *Extending Opportunities: How Active Social Policy Can Benefit Us All*, 2005, Table 8.1, 148.

4. United Nations, '2010 Human Development Report: 40-Year Trends Analysis Shows Poor Countries Making Faster Development Gains', November 4, 2010. http://hdr.undp.org/en/mediacentre, accessed November 9, 2010.

5. Statistics Canada, *Income in Canada, 2008* (Ottawa, ON: Statistics Canada, 2010), Series 400, Total Income.

6. An absolute measure of poverty, defined as the income needed to pay for the basic needs of a household of a given size, is used by some organizations, such as the Social Planning Council of Metropolitan Toronto.

7. E. Sabatini, *Welfare—No Fair: A Critical Analysis of Ontario's Welfare System (1985–1994)* (Vancouver, BC: Fraser Institute, 1996), 197.

8. René Morissette and Marie Drolet, 'To What Extent Are Canadians Exposed to Low-Income?' Business and Labour Market Analysis, Statistics Canada, April 2000, 6.

9. National Council of Welfare, *Poverty Profile 2008* (Ottawa, ON: Summer 2010).

10. Sabatini, *Welfare—No Fair*, 197.

11. Statistics Canada, 'Income of Canadians,' *The Daily*, March 30, 2006.

12. Statistics Canada, *Income in Canada, 2007*, 14.

13. Ibid.
14. John Richards, 'Reducing Poverty: What Has Worked and What Should Come Next', C.D. Howe Institute Commentary, no. 255, October 2007, 2.
15. Statistics Canada, 'Canada's Population Estimates: Age and Sex', *The Daily,* July 1, 2009.
16. Richards, 'Reducing Poverty'.
17. René Morissette and Anick Johnson, 'Are Good Jobs Disappearing in Canada?' Business and Labour Market Analysis Division, Statistics Canada, 2005, 6.
18. Department of Finance Canada, Fiscal Reference Tables October 2010, Table 9, 'Expenses (per cent of total)'. www.fin.gc.ca/frt-trf/2010/frt-trf-1002-eng.asp#tbl10, accessed November 9, 2010.
19. Thomas Courchene, *Social Policy in the 1990s* (Toronto, ON: C.D. Howe Institute, 1987).
20. National Council of Welfare, *Pension Reform* (Ottawa, ON: Supply and Services, February 1990), 52.
21. Department of Finance, *The Canada Pension Plan: Keeping It Financially Healthy* (Ottawa, ON: Supply and Services, 1985), 4.
22. Department of Finance, *Ensuring the Ongoing Strength of Canada's Retirement Income System,* March 24, 2010. www.fin.gc.ca/activty/consult/retirement-eng.asp, accessed November 9, 2010.
23. *Report of the Royal Commission on the Economic Union and Development Prospects for Canada,* vol. 2, 611–19.
24. *Report of the Royal Commission on Unemployment Insurance,* 115–19.
25. Paul Martin, *Budget Speech 1995* (Ottawa, ON: Department of Finance, 1995), 16.
26. Marc Frenette, David Green, and Kevin Milligan, 'Taxes, Transfers and Canadian Income Inequality', *Canadian Public Policy* 35, 4 (2009), 403.
27. Budget 2010.
28. National Council of Welfare, *Poverty Profile,* 1999.
29. National Council of Welfare, 'Poverty Facts 2003', July 2006.
30. Human Resources and Skills Development Canada, Financial Security—Low Income Incidence. www.hrsdc.gc.ca.
31. See the summary of these studies in Sabatini, *Welfare—No Fair,* 182–4.
32. See the survey in B.G. Dahlby, 'The Incidence of Government Expenditures and Taxes in Canada: A Survey', in François Vaillancourt,
Income Distribution and Economic Security in Canada, vol. 1 of the research studies for the Royal Commission on the Economic Union and Development Prospects for Canada (Toronto, ON: University of Toronto Press, 1985), 129–35.
33. Jens Arnold, 'Do Tax Structures Affect Aggregate Economic Growth? Empirical Evidence from a Panel of OECD Countries', Economic Department, OECD Working papers No. 643, 2008.
34. W. Irwin Gillespie, *The Redistribution of Income in Canada* (Ottawa, ON: Carleton University Press, 1980), 160. The same conclusion is arrived at by D. Dodge, 'Impact of Tax, Transfer and Expenditure Policies of Government on the Distribution of Personal Incomes in Canada', *Review of Income and Wealth* 21 (1975), 1–52, Table 9.
35. Frenette et al., 408.
36. Milagros Palacios and Niels Veldhuis, 'The Canadian Consumer Tax Index, 2010', *Fraser Alert,* April 2010.
37. Simeon Djankov, Tim Ganser, Caralee McLiesh, Rita Ramalho, and Andrei Shleifer, 'The Effect of Corporate Taxes on Investment and Entrepreneurship', National Bureau of Economic Research Working Paper Series, January 2008.
38. Constitution Act, 1982, section 36(2).
39. Robin Boadway and Frank Flatters, *Equalization in a Federal State: An Economic Analysis* (Ottawa, ON: Economic Council of Canada, 1982).
40. Bob Rae, 'Mexican Trade Deal Only Adds Insult to Ontario's Injuries', *Toronto Star,* April 27, 1993.
41. Maude Barlow, 'The Free Trade Area of the Americas and the Threat to Social Programs, Environmental Sustainability and Social Justice in Canada and the Americas'. www.canadians.org/campaigns/campaigns-ftaa-threat-MBarlow.PDF, accessed December 18, 2002.
42. Parbudyal Singh, 'NAFTA and Labor: A Canadian Perspective', *Journal of Labor Research* 23, 3 (Summer 2002), 434.
43. Ibid., 444.
44. Melvyn Krauss, 'Free Trade Helps, Not Hurts, Social Programs', *Hoover Digest* 2 (1998).
45. Ibid.
46. Willem Thorbeck and Christian Eigen-Zucchi, 'Did NAFTA Cause a "Giant Sucking Sound"?' *Journal of Labor Research* 23, 4 (Fall 2002), 656.

Chapter 8 Health Policy

1. For example, the 2010 Commonwealth Fund International Health Policy Survey in Eleven Countries found that 51 per cent of Canadians thought the health-care system needed fundamental change and an additional 10 per cent thought that it should be rebuilt completely.

2. The Canadian Community Health Survey has consistently found that a substantial proportion of Canadians rate both the satisfaction with their health and the quality of care as very high. For example, in 2007 90 per cent of Canadians rated the quality of physician care in the past 12 months as excellent. Further, 90.5 per cent were very satisfied or somewhat satisfied with physician care. Source: Canadian Community Health Survey. Statistics Canada CANSIM table 105-4082.

3. See 'Federal Support for Health Care: The Facts'. www.fin.gc.ca/facts/fshc7_e.html#return2.

4. Stanley H. Hartt and Patrick J. Monahan, *The Charter and Health Care* (Montreal, QC: Institute for Research on Public Policy, 2002).

5. Stanley H. Hartt and Patrick J. Monahan, 'Waiting Lists Are Unconstitutional', *National Post*, May 15, 2002, A18.

6. Nadeem Esmail, 'Waiting Your Turn: Hospital Waiting Lists in Canada 2009 Report 19th ed.', *Studies in Health Care Policy* (Vancouver, BC: Fraser Institute, October 2009), 5.

7. *National Health Expenditure Trends, 1975–2010*. Canadian Institute for Health Information, October 2010, 8.

8. Ibid., 33

9. Commission on the Future of Health Care in Canada, *Shape the Future of Health Care*, *Interim Report*, February 2002, 25.

10. Public Accounts of Canada, 2010, Volume 1, 1.8: Financial Statements Discussion and Analysis.

11. Ibid., Table 1.1: Detailed Statement of Operations and Accumulated Deficit.

12. Lynda Buske, 'Does Canada Really Rank 30th in World in Terms of Health Care?' *Canadian Medical Association Journal* 164, 1 (January 9, 2001), 84.

13. 'Is There a Cost Crisis in Health Care?' Atkinson Letter, Health Series, '#1: Interview with Robert Evans and Greg Stoddart', November 29, 1996. http://atkinsonfdn.on.ca/publications/atkinson_letter/ health1.html.

14. Ibid.

15. Ibid.

16. Brenda Hemmelgarn, William Ghali, and Hude Quan, 'A Case Study of Hospital Closure and Centralization of Coronary Revascularization Procedures', *Canadian Medical Association Journal* 164, 10 (2001), 1431–5.

17. 'Is There a Problem with Access?' Atkinson Letter, Health Series, '#2: Interview with Vivek Goel and Dr Noralou Roos', December 13, 1996. http://atkinsonfdn.on.ca/publications/atkinson_letter/health 2.html.

18. 'Rate of Hospitalizations Continues to Decline', Canadian Institute for Health Information, http://secure.cihi.ca/cihiweb/dispPage.jsp?cw_page=media_26jun2002_e], accessed September 3, 2007.

19. 'Is There a Problem with Access?'

20. Commission on the Future of Health Care in Canada, *Interim Report*, 31.

21. 'Canada's New Government Announces Patient Wait Times Guarantees'. Government of Canada press release, April 4, 2007.

22. 'How Do We Turn a Non-System for the Treatment of Illness into a Health System?' Atkinson Letter, Health Series, '#4: Interview with Michael Decter', January 10, 1997. http://atkinsonfdn.on.ca/publications/atkinson_letter/health4.html.

23. Ibid.

Chapter 9 Family Policy

1. *The Economist*, 'The Family: Home Sweet Home', September 9, 1995, 25.

2. Margrit Eichler, *Family Shifts: Families, Policies, and Gender Equality* (Toronto, ON: Oxford University Press, 1997), 6.

3. Ibid., 159.

4. Statistics Canada, *Canada Year Book 2010*, 177.

5. OECD, *Babies and Bosses: Reconciling Work and Family Life: Canada, Finland, Sweden and the United Kingdom*, vol. 4, 2005, 57.

6. Janine Stafford, 'A Profile of the Childcare Services Industry', Services Indicators, 4th Quarter 2001, 18.

7. Tracey Bushnik, 'Child Care in Canada', Children and YOUTH Research Paper Series, No. 003, Statistics Canada, 2006.

8. Stafford, 21.

9. National Council of Welfare, *Child Benefits: A Small Step Forward* (Ottawa, ON: Supply and Services Canada, 1997), 2.

10. Hillary Rodham Clinton, *It Takes a Village, and Other Lessons Children Teach Us* (New York, NY: Simon and Schuster, 1996).

11. Ibid., 13.

12. June Callwood, 'Citizens' Shame', *Homemaker's*, May 1997, 92.

13. Clinton, *It Takes a Village*, 76.

14. Ibid., 99.

15. Ibid., 107.

16. Ibid., 39.

17. Jean Bethke Elshtain, 'Suffer the Little Children', *The New Republic*, March 4, 1996, 33–4.

18. Richard Weissbourd, *The Vulnerable Child: What Really Hurts America's Children and What We Can Do about It* (New York, NY: Addison Wesley, 1996), 97.

19. Ibid., 104.

20. Clinton, *It Takes a Village*, 41.

21. Eichler, *Family Shifts*.

22. Ibid., 148–9.

23. Ibid., 164.

24. Ibid., 159.

25. Ibid., 95.

26. Ibid., 74–5.

27. This is the title of Elizabeth Fox-Genovese's review of Richard Weissbourd's book, *The Vulnerable Child*, which appeared in *The New Republic*, June 3, 1996, 41–4.

28. David Popenoe, 'The Family Condition of America: Cultural Change and Public Policy', in Henry Aaron, Thomas Mann, and Timothy Taylor, eds., *Values and Public Policy* (Washington, DC: Brookings Institution, 1994), 96.

29. Barbara Dafoe Whitehead, 'Dan Quayle Was Right', *Atlantic Monthly* (April 1993), 47.

30. John Myles, Feng Hou, Garnett Picot, and Karen Myers, 'Why Did Employment and Earnings Rise among Lone Mothers during the 1980s and 1990s?' *Analytical Branch Research Paper Series*, Statistics Canada Catalogue no. 11F00919MIE – No. 282 (June 2006), 23.

31. Dafoe Whitehead, 'Dan Quayle Was Right', 62.

32. Sara McLanahan and Gary Sandefur, *Family Background, Race and Ethnicity, and Early Family Formation* (Madison, WI: University of Wisconsin, Institute for Research on Poverty, 1990), 51.

33. D.J. Eggebeen and D.T. Lichter, 'Race, Family Structure, and Changing Poverty Among American Children', *American Sociological Review*, 56, 6 (1991), 801–17.

34. Dafoe Whitehead, 'Dan Quayle Was Right', 74.

35. Judith Wallerstein and Sandra Blakeslee, *Second Chances: Men, Women, and Children a Decade after Divorce* (New York, NY: Ticknor & Fields, 1989).

36. Deborah A. Dawson, 'Family Structure and Children's Health: United States, 1988', National Center for Health Statistics, *Vital and Health Statistics*, series 10, no. 178 (Hyattsville, MD: Department of Health and Human Services, June 1991).

37. James Wilson, 'Culture, Incentives, and the Underclass', in Henry Aaron and Thomas Mann, eds., *Values and Public Policy* (Washington, DC: Brookings Institution, 1994), 63.

38. Sara McLanahan and Gary Sandefur, *Uncertain Childhood, Uncertain Future* (Cambridge, MA: Harvard University Press, 1996).

39. Nicolas Zill and Charlotte Schoenborn, 'Developmental, Learning, and Emotional Problems: Health of Our Nation's Children, United States, 1988', in National Center for Health Statistics, *Advance Data*, no. 190, November 16, 1990.

40. See the summary of these studies in Dafoe Whitehead, 'Dan Quayle Was Right', 66–7.

41. Amitai Etzioni, *The Spirit of Community: Rights, Responsibilities, and the Communitarian Agenda* (New York, NY: Crown Publishers, 1993).

42. Quoted in 'The Family', *The Economist*, September 9, 1995, 29.

43. Eichler, *Family Shifts*, 74–5.

44. 'The Family', *The Economist*, 29.

45. Quoted in Dafoe Whitehead, 'Dan Quayle Was Right', 77.

46. Ibid., 71.

47. Popenoe, 'The Family Condition of America', 96.

48. McLanahan and Sandefur, *Uncertain Childhood, Uncertain Future*.

49. Dafoe Whitehead, 'Dan Quayle Was Right', 72.

50. Cited ibid.

51. Cited ibid.

52. William Mattox Jr., 'Running on Empty: America's Time-Starved Families with Children', Working Paper 5 (New York, NY: Council on Families in America, Institute for American Values, 1991).

53. Popenoe, 'The Family Condition of America', 100–1.

54. McLanahan's arguments are summarized in Dafoe Whitehead, 'Dan Quayle Was Right', 82.

55. Ibid., 84.
56. See Cindy Silver, 'Family Autonomy and the Charter of Rights: Protecting Parental Liberty in a Child-Centred Legal System', Discussion Paper 3 (Gloucester, ON: Centre for Renewal in Public Policy, 1995).
57. *Egan v. Canada*, Supreme Court of Canada, 1995.
58. Clinton, *It Takes a Village*, 223.
59. Danielle Crittenden, 'The Mother of All Problems', *Saturday Night* (April 1995): 44–54.
60. Tracey Bushnik, 'Child Care in Canada', Research Paper, Children & Youth Research Paper Series, Statistics Canada Catalogue No. 89-599-mie, No. 3, 14
61. House of Commons, *Hansard*, May 29, 1996, Motion 30, 3155–8.
62. Clinton, *It Takes a Village*, 221.
63. France is not the only European country to have such a system. Belgium and Italy are among the other countries that operate publicly funded preschools.
64. Clinton, *It Takes a Village*, 228.

65. Popenoe, 'The Family Condition of America', 102.
66. Mary Ann Glendon, *The Transformation of Family Law* (Chicago, IL: University of Chicago Press, 1989).
67. Popenoe, 'The Family Condition of America', 102.
68. Linda J. Waite, Don Browning, William J. Doherty, Maggie Gallagher, Ye Luo, and Scott M. Stanley, 'Does Divorce Make People Happy? Findings from a Study of Unhappy Marriages', Institute for American Values, 2002.
69. Details and a critical analysis can be found in Canada, National Council of Welfare, *Child Benefits: A Small Step Forward* (Ottawa, ON: Supply and Services, 1997).
70. Frances Woolley, Judith Madill, and Arndt Vermaeten, 'Credits in Crisis: Evaluating Child Benefit Reform in Canada', in Meg Luxton, ed., *Feminism and Families* (Halifax, NS: Fernwood, 1997), 74.
71. Canada, Department of Finance, *Budget Plan, 1997* (Ottawa, ON: Supply and Services, February 1997), 107–8.

Chapter 10 Aboriginal Policy

1. *Regina v. Howson* (1894), 1 Terr. L.R. 492 (S.C.N.W.T), 494.
2. Peter A. Cumming and Neil H. Mickenberg, eds., *Native Rights in Canada* (Toronto, ON: General Publishing, 1972), 9.
3. *Reference Re: Whether Eskimo Are Indians*, C.L.R. (1939): 104.
4. Olive Patricia Dickason, *Canada's First Nations: A History of Founding Peoples from Earliest Times*, 3rd ed. (Toronto, ON: Oxford University Press, 2002), 485, n. 27.
5. Harvey McCue, 'Indian Reserve', *The Canadian Encyclopedia*, vol. 2 (Edmonton, AB: Hurtig, 1988), 1056.
6. Indian leader James Gosnell, quoted in Michael Asch, *Home and Native Land: Aboriginal Rights and the Canadian Constitution* (Vancouver, BC: University of British Columbia Press, 1993), 29.
7. Quoted in Melvin H. Smith, *Our Home or Native Land?* (Toronto, ON: Stoddart, 1995), 97.
8. Ibid., 143.
9. Donald Purich, *Our Land: Native Rights in Canada* (Toronto, ON: James Lorimer, 1986), 46.
10. Georges Erasmus and Joe Sanders, 'Canadian History: An Aboriginal Perspective',

in Diane Engelstad and John Bird, eds., *Nation to Nation: Aboriginal Sovereignty and the Future of Canada* (Concord, ON: House of Anansi Press, 1992), 6.
11. Ibid., 8.
12. Cumming and Mickenberg, eds., *Native Rights in Canada*, 41.
13. Smith, *Our Home or Native Land?* 47.
14. For example, *St Catherine's Milling and Lumber Company v. The Queen* (1888), 14 A.C. 46 (JCPC); *Regina v. White and Bob* (1965), 50 D.L.R. (2d) 613; *Calder et al. v. Attorney General of British Columbia* (1973), S.C.R. 313, 4 W.W.R. 1.
15. Quoted in Cumming and Mickenberg, eds., *Native Rights in Canada*, 17.
16. Ibid., 18. Emphasis added.
17. See excerpts from this ruling in David De Brou and Bill Waiser, eds., *Documenting Canada: A History of Modern Canada in Documents* (Saskatoon, SK: Fifth House Publishers, 1992), 158.
18. Quoted ibid., 572.
19. Ibid.
20. Ibid., 595.
21. Ibid., 665. Section 35(1) of the Constitution Act, 1982, recognizes and affirms Aboriginal and treaty rights existing as of 1982.

22. Ibid., 666.
23. Cumming and Mickenberg, eds., *Native Rights in Canada*, 55.
24. Ibid.
25. Erasmus and Sanders, 'Canadian History', 3.
26. Ibid., 4.
27. Cumming and Mickenberg, eds., *Native Rights in Canada*, 58.
28. Quoted ibid., 61–2.
29. Quoted in Purich, *Our Land*, 110.
30. Cumming and Mickenberg, eds., *Native Rights in Canada*, 53.
31. Roger Gibbins and J. Rick Ponting, 'Historical Overview and Background', in J. Rick Ponting, ed., *Arduous Journey: Canadian Indians and Decolonization* (Toronto, ON: McClelland & Stewart, 1988), 30.
32. Purich, *Our Land*, 109. Emphasis added.
33. *R. v. Sioui*, [1990] 1 S.C.R. 1025 (1990).
34. 'Specific Claims: Justice at Last', Aboriginal and Northern Affairs, Minister of Public Works and Government Services Canada, 2007, 4
35. Aboriginal Affairs and Northern Development Canada, *Settlement Report on Specific Claims*.
36. Smith, *Our Home or Native Land?* 122.
37. Quoted in Peter A. Cumming and Neil H. Mickenberg (Toronto, ON: Indian-Eskimo Association of Canada in association with General Publishing, 1972), Appendix 6, 331.
38. Quoted in Smith, *Our Home or Native Land?* 143.
39. Murray Angus, *And the Last Shall Be First: Native Policy in an Era of Cutbacks* (Toronto, ON: NC Press, 1991).
40. See, for example, ibid.
41. Canada, Department of Aboriginal Affairs and Northern Development, 'Statement on Claims of Indian and Inuit People', press release, August 1973.
42. Quoted in John Greenwood, 'This Land', *Financial Post Magazine* (March 1993), 17.
43. The recommendations of this task force are summarized in Angus, *And the Last Shall Be First*.
44. These are the words used in the James Bay and Northern Quebec Native Claim Settlement Act, 1977.
45. F.G. Stanley, 'The First Indian "Reserves" in Canada', *Revue d'histoire de l'Amérique française* (1950), 168, 209–10.
46. Francis Parkham, *Jesuits in North America* (Toronto, ON: George N. Morang, 1906), 131.
47. Harold Cardinal, *The Unjust Society* (Edmonton, AB: Hurtig, 1969), 1.
48. See Leslie A. Pal, *Interests of State* (Montreal and Kingston: McGill-Queen's University Press, 1993).
49. See De Brou and Waiser, *Documenting Canada*, 540.
50. Pierre Trudeau, *Federalism and the French Canadians* (Toronto, ON: McClelland & Stewart, 1969), 151.
51. Pierre Trudeau and Thomas Axworthy, *Towards the Just Society: The Trudeau Years* (Toronto, ON: Viking, 1990), 364.
52. In Frank Cassidy, ed., *Aboriginal Self-Determination* (Halifax, NS: Institute of Research on Public Policy, 1991).
53. Alan Cairns and Tom Flanagan, 'An Exchange', *Inroads: A Journal of Opinion* 10 (2001), 112.
54. Ibid., 117.
55. Ibid., 104.
56. Ibid., 107.
57. Ibid.

Chapter 11 Environmental Policy

1. Rachel Carson, *Silent Spring* (Boston, MA: Houghton Mifflin, 1962).
2. National Parks Act, 1930.
3. Garrett Hardin, 'The Tragedy of the Commons', *Science* 162 (1968), 1243.
4. Stephen Brooks, *Public Policy in Canada: An Introduction*, 3rd ed. (Toronto, ON: Oxford University Press, 1998), 241.
5. Terry Tamminen, *Lives per Gallon: The True Cost of Our Oil Addiction* (Washington DC: Island Press, 2006).
6. World Commission on Environment and Development, *Our Common Future* (Oxford, UK: Oxford University Press, 1987).
7. Ibid., 9–10.
8. Michael Howlett, 'Policy Instruments and Implementation Styles: The Evolution of Instrument Choice in Canadian Environmental Policy', in Debora VanNijnatten and Robert Boardman, eds., *Canadian Environmental Policy: Context and Cases* (Toronto, ON: Oxford University Press, 2002).
9. Rachel Szymanski, 'Protecting the Environment with Property Rights: The KVP Story' (August 1992). www.environmentprobe.org/enviroprobe/pubs/ev525.htm.
10. *Groat v. Edmonton (City)* (1928), [1928] S.C.R. 522, [1928] 3 D.L.R. 725, (S.C.C.).

11. Joel Franklin Brenner, 'Nuisance Law and the Industrial Revolution', *Journal of Legal Studies* 3, 2 (June 1974), 408.

12. John McLaren, 'The Common Law Nuisance Actions and the Environmental Battle—Well-Tempered Swords or Broken Reeds?' *Osgoode Hall Law Journal* 10 (1972), 508.

13. Ibid., 415.

14. *St. Helen's v. Tipping*, 11 Eng. Rep. 1483, 11 H.L. Case. 642, at 653 (1865).

15. Brenner, 'Nuisance Law', 428.

16. Friends of the Spanish River, 'Who Are the Friends of the Spanish River?' www.etown.net/spanishriver, accessed May 3, 2002.

17. Ibid.

18. John Swaigen, *Environmental Rights in Canada* (Toronto, ON: Butterworths, 1981), 2.

19. Elizabeth Brubaker, 'The Role of Property Rights in Protecting Water', *Journal des Economistes et des Études Humaines* 7, 2–3 (June–September 1996), 413.

20. Murray Rankin and Peter Finkle, 'The Enforcement of Environmental Law: Taking the Environment Seriously', *UBC Law Review* 17, 1 (1983), 36.

21. Friends of the Spanish River, 'Who Are the Friends of the Spanish River?'

22. Ibid.

23. Angus Reid, commenting on the results of the poll done for the Southam Environment Project, autumn 1990.

24. Glen Toner, 'The Canadian Environmental Movement: A Conceptual Map', Carleton University, unpublished paper, 1991, 4.

25. John Kingdon, *Agendas, Alternatives, and Public Policies* (Boston, MA: Little, Brown, 1984).

26. Paul R. Ehrlich, *The Population Bomb* (New York, NY: Ballantine Books, 1969).

27. Dennis L. Meadows et al., *The Limits to Growth* (New York, NY: New American Library, 1972).

28. Richard Liroff, *A National Policy for the Environment* (Bloomington, IN: Indiana University Press, 1976), 12.

29. The post-materialist hypothesis was first laid out in Ronald Inglehart, *The Silent Revolution* (Princeton, NJ: Princeton University Press, 1977).

30. Ibid., 3.

31. Ibid., 43–50.

32. Glen Toner, 'Whence and Whither: ENGOs, Business and the Environment', unpublished paper, October 1990, 3.

33. Jurg Steiner, *European Democracies* (New York, NY: Longman, 1986), 40.

34. Task Force on Program Review, Environment (Ottawa, ON: Supply and Services, 1985), 27.

35. *The Globe and Mail*, April 15, 1989, section D.

36. George Hoberg, 'Representation and Governance in Canadian Environmental Policy', paper presented at McMaster University, October 26, 1991, 5.

37. Task Force on Program Review, Environment.

38. Environment Canada, *Canada's Green Plan: The First Year* (Ottawa, ON: Supply and Services, 1991), 1.

39. Quoted in David Israelson, *Silent Earth: The Politics of Our Survival* (Toronto, ON: Viking, 1990), 212.

40. Ibid. Israelson provides examples of this throughout his book.

41. Jeremy Wilson, 'Wilderness Politics in BC: the Business-Dominated State and the Containment of Environmentalism', in William D. Coleman and Grace Skogstad, eds., *Policy Communities and Public Policy in Canada* (Toronto, ON: Copp Clark Pitman, 1990), 154–62.

42. *Canadian Wildlife Federation v. Canada (Minister of the Environment)* 4 C.E.L.R. (NS) I; *Friends of the Oldman River Society v. Canada (Minister of Transport)*, Federal Court of Appeal, March 13, 1991; *Canadian Wildlife Federation et al. v. Minister of the Environment*, 4 C.E.L.R. (NS).

43. Canadian Environmental Assessment Agency, Basics of Environmental Assessment. www.ceaa.gc.ca/default.asp?lang=En&n=B053F859-1#screening, accessed December 2, 2010.

44. 'Survey of Australia', *The Economist*, April 4, 1992, 10.

45. Israelson, *Silent Earth*, 169.

46. Inco, 'Performance Scorecard'. www.inco.com/development/reports/ehs/2004/summaries/environment/air/sulphur, accessed September 19, 2007.

47. Environment Canada, 'The National Air Pollution Surveillance Program: Forty Years of Air Quality Monitoring and Assessment'. www.ec.gc.ca/air-sc-r/default.asp?lang=En&xml=D3E7EE2D-D712-44DA-8717-44C301188BCA, accessed December 2, 2010.

48. Environment Canada, 'Air Quality'. www.ec.gc.ca/indicateurs-indicators/default.asp?lang=En&n=4B5631F9-1, accessed December 2, 2010.

49. The phenomenon was first labelled by a British chemist, Robert Angus, who published a voluminous study of the effects of industrial pollution in Manchester, England, on precipitation in that area.

50. M. Firket, 'The Causes of Accidents which Occurred in the Meuse Valley During the Fogs of December 1930', cited in Jon R. Luoma, 'The Human Cost of Acid Rain', *Audubon* (July 1988), 17.

51. Environment Canada, *The State of Canada's Environment—1991* (Ottawa, ON: Supply and Services, 1991), 24–8, Figure 24.4.

52. This estimate is cited in ibid., 24–7.

53. See Kathryn Harrison, *Passing the Buck: Federalism and Canadian Environmental Policy* (Vancouver, BC: University of British Columbia Press, 1997).

54. Mark Sagoff, 'Do We Consume Too Much?' *Atlantic Monthly* (June 1997), 80–96.

55. Quoted ibid., 92.

56. Bjørn Lomborg. *The Skeptical Environmentalist: Measuring the Real State of the World* (London, UK: Cambridge University Press, 2001). See also Bjørn Lomborg, *Cool It: The Skeptical Environmentalist's Guide to Global Warming* (New York, NY: Alfred A. Knopf, 2008).

57. Sagoff, 'Do We Consume Too Much?' 90.

58. Ibid., 96.

59. Quoted ibid.

60. Ibid.

Index

About Oxford University Press

Oxford University Press (often referred to as 'OUP') is one of the oldest publishing companies in the world, as well as one of the largest. It is a department of the University of Oxford, and, like the University as a whole, OUP is devoted to the spread of knowledge: any surplus generated through its activities is directed toward the publication of works which further scholarship and education, or to encouraging and sustaining research on which these books may be based.

The Press dates its origins back to the fifteenth century. The first book to be printed in Oxford—the *Commentary on the Apostles' Creed*, attributed to St Jerome, by Theodoric Rood—was issued in 1478, barely a quarter-century after Gutenberg's invention of the printing press. Over the following century, a number of short-lived private businesses, some patronized by Oxford University, took the field, but in 1586 the University itself obtained a decree from the Star Chamber confirming its privilege to print books. That same year, Oxford University lent £100—a small fortune at that time—to a local bookseller, Joseph Barnes, to set up a press. Barnes produced many books now prized by collectors, including the first books printed at Oxford in Greek (1586) and Hebrew (1596), and Captain John Smith's *Map of Virginia* (1612). The Great Charter, secured by Archbishop Laud from King Charles I in 1632, increased the independence of the Press, entitling the University to print 'all manner of books', and approximately 300 books were printed before Barnes retired in 1617.

In 1633, the University first appointed 'delegates' to oversee printing and publishing. Records of their deliberations date back to 1668, and to this day, OUP's editorial work is overseen by delegates appointed from the University's faculty. The operations of the Press as a whole are directed by a board that includes the vice chancellor of the University and other University administrators, as well as a number of delegates and officers of the Press.

The University established its right to print the King James Authorized Version of the Bible in the seventeenth century. This 'Bible Privilege' formed the basis of a successful publishing business throughout the next two centuries and was the spur for OUP's expansion. In London, the Press established a Bible warehouse, which later grew into a major publisher of books with educational and cultural content aimed at the general reader. OUP then began to expand internationally, starting with the opening of an American office in 1896 and the Canadian branch in 1904.

Today, OUP is the world's largest university press, publishing more than 6,000 new titles a year and employing approximately 5,000 people in 50 countries. Few if any organizations publish a more diverse range of titles than Oxford, including scholarly works in all academic disciplines; Bibles; music reference works as well as sheet music; textbooks; children's books; materials for teaching English as an additional language; dictionaries and reference books; professional books in fields such as law, brain science, and medicine; academic journals; and a burgeoning online publishing program of electronic resources and publications. Oxford and New York are the two largest publishing centres within the Press, but publishing programs of significant size and scope exist the world over, in such countries as Australia, China, India, Kenya, Malaysia, Mexico, Pakistan, South Africa, and Spain, as well as in Canada.

About Oxford University Press Canada

Established in 1904, OUP's Canadian branch was the only the second overseas office to be set up (following New York in 1896). Before the twentieth century, the main suppliers of books in Canada were the Copp Clark Company, the W.J. Gage Company, and the Methodist Bookroom (eventually renamed The Ryerson Press after its founder, Egerton Ryerson). These three firms represented other lines that were later distributed directly by branches of their parent houses or by exclusive Canadian agents. Prior to 1904, Oxford books had been sold in Canada by S.G. Wilkinson, who, based in London, England, travelled across Canada as far west as Winnipeg. Wilkinson did a large trade with S.B. (Sam) Gundy, the wholesale and trade manager of the Methodist Bookroom. When OUP opened its own branch in Toronto, Gundy, already familiar with Oxford books, was invited to become its manager. The premises were at 25 Richmond Street West and, lacking an elevator of any kind, were perhaps not ideal for a publishing house!

In 1929, the branch moved to Amen House, named after Oxford's global headquarters in England and located at 480 University Avenue. After Gundy's death, the branch became closely allied with Clarke, Irwin and Company, an association that continued until 1949 when that firm moved to its own offices. In 1963, the Press moved to a new building at 70 Wynford Drive in Don Mills, a site which served it well for the next 46 years. By 2009, however, the branch had outgrown 70 Wynford. An extensive search process culminated in the move that November to a split-site configuration. The offices relocated to new premises at the Shops at Don Mills, an innovative retail/office/residential development, while the warehouse moved to a site in Brampton that not only offered more affordable rent and carrying charges but also provided a modern high-bay space much closer to major customers and Pearson International Airport.

Today OUP Canada is a major publisher of higher education, school, and English-as-a-second-language textbooks, as well as a significant trade and reference publisher. The Higher Education Division publishes both introductory and upper-level texts in such disciplines as sociology, anthropology, social work, English literature and composition, geography, history, political science, religious studies, and engineering. Its authors include many of Canada's most accomplished scholars and educators. Each year, the division publishes more than 60 new Canadian texts and 150 student and instructor supplements deriving two-thirds of its total sales from books and other learning materials written, edited, and published in Canada.

OUP Canada's first home, at 25 Richmond Street West in Toronto.